Ius Gentium: Comparative Perspectives on Law and Justice

Volume 92

Ius Gentium is a book series which discusses the central questions of law and justice from a comparative perspective. The books in this series collect the contrasting and overlapping perspectives of lawyers, judges, philosophers and scholars of law from the world's many different jurisdictions for the purposes of comparison, harmonisation, and the progressive development of law and legal institutions. Each volume makes a new comparative study of an important area of law. This book series continues the work of the well-known journal of the same name and provides the basis for a better understanding of all areas of legal science.

The *Ius Gentium* series provides a valuable resource for lawyers, judges, legislators, scholars, and both graduate students and researchers in globalisation, comparative law, legal theory and legal practice. The series has a special focus on the development of international legal standards and transnational legal cooperation.

More information about this series at http://www.springer.com/series/7888

Lucia Busatta • Carlo Casonato
Editors

Axiological Pluralism

Jurisdiction, Law-Making and Pluralisms

Springer

Editors
Lucia Busatta
Faculty of Law
University of Trento
Trento, Italy

Carlo Casonato
Faculty of Law
University of Trento
Trento, Italy

ISSN 1534-6781 ISSN 2214-9902 (electronic)
Ius Gentium: Comparative Perspectives on Law and Justice
ISBN 978-3-030-78474-4 ISBN 978-3-030-78475-1 (eBook)
https://doi.org/10.1007/978-3-030-78475-1

This Springer imprint is published by the registered company Springer Nature Switzerland AG.
The registered company address is: Gewerbestrasse 11, 6330 Cham, Switzerland

Contents

Part III Case Studies

Introduction

Carlo Casonato and Lucia Busatta

1 Axiological Pluralism and Biolaw

In recent years, we have witnessed an increasing trend in ideological conflicts on a variety of issues. Contemporary societies have developed such a profound internal pluralism as to undermine, in some cases, the possibility of holding common basic values, and of reaching a widely recognized and therefore effective regulation. Within this broader framework, life sciences related issues are a strong catalyst for very harsh disagreements. Their inherent ethical sensitivity is more and more capable of activating very distant and sometimes even opposite value systems. Moreover, the possibilities offered by the technological development daily pose new issues and challenges. Parliaments should intervene to accommodate this pluralism, but they are often late in providing rules, and courts have to stand in for them.

Alongside the traditional pro-life and pro-choice approaches to abortion, for instance, conflicting factions have emerged on assisted reproduction techniques, end-of-life issues, vaccination, limits to genetic engineering, use of neuroscience and artificial intelligence.

The magnitude and rapidity of the developments in life sciences and their respective technological applications, combined with the ethically delicate nature of the assets involved, configure biolaw (i.e. the legal phenomenon dealing with life sciences) as one of the typical grounds for this axiological pluralism, calling into play all the figures of the legal system. Accordingly, legal scholars are often split into very nuanced and different positions. Parliaments are struggling to enact laws that have to be, at the same time, shared, effective and up-to-date. Furthermore, in the delay of legislative intervention, courts, together with quasi-jurisdictional or

C. Casonato · L. Busatta (✉)
Faculty of Law, University of Trento, Trento, Italy
e-mail: carlo.casonato@unitn.it; lucia.busatta@unitn.it

L. Busatta, C. Casonato (eds.), *Axiological Pluralism*, Ius Gentium: Comparative Perspectives on Law and Justice 92, https://doi.org/10.1007/978-3-030-78475-1_1

consultative bodies, are at the forefront in trying to deal with the disagreements and set the limits of sustainable axiological pluralism.

A certain amount of pluralism, in fact, is an inherent and essential part of the structure of the constitutional state. In this framework, Constitutions do not usually establish precise and specific solutions, but they set rules and principles from the outside—so to speak—delimiting a space of the 'constitutionally-possible' which can also be broad. The principles of equality and proportionality, due process, right to privacy or to the full development of the person, and concepts such as dignity, for instance, can be read differently and are compatible with different normative choices and judicial decisions which are all lawful. Faced with the technical difficulties and the moral sensitivity that feature as the objects of biolaw, Parliaments are often late in providing rules, and courts have to stand in for them.

2 The Role of the Courts: Lords of Law?

Axiological pluralism, in the first place, has fully involved the judiciary, asking courts to play a much more intense role, in terms of discretion and creativity, than the one traditionally, and in some ways rhetorically, recognized in terms of *bouche de la loi* (in civil law) or, in any case, of finder of the law of the land (in common law).

The various courts, just to give a few examples, have found themselves facing issues related to: the definition of a human embryo (see the Court of Justice of the European Union in C-34/10, Brüstle in 2011 or in C-364/13, International Stem Cell in 2014); the role and limits of doctors in the face of patients' self-determination (see the case-law reported by Roger Brownsword or, in Italy, the Decision no. 282 of 2002 of the Constitutional Court); compliance with the Constitution (if present) on the part of the law on assisted reproduction techniques or end-of-life issues (Canada, the United Kingdom, Italy or France); compliance with the national rules of the ECHR on access to healthcare, mandatory health treatments, assisted reproduction techniques, assisted suicide, interruption of life-saving and life-sustaining treatments and so on. All of this taking place in legal systems that risk reaching a very high level of inconsistency, so much so that in some cases they end up appearing as a 'legal dis-order' instead of a legal order.

In facing this task, courts adopt very different attitudes, depending on a series of variables that cannot be easily singled out and codified. In some cases, they strongly limit the recognition of pluralism, confirming or imposing the prevalence of a single value on others. Other times, they promote axiological pluralism, recognizing equal status to interests and instances different from the dominant ones. In doing so, they sometimes show a self-restraining approach, recognizing a broad margin of discretion to the lawmaker. On other occasions, they widen instead the margins of their own intervention, making decisions oriented towards a strong judicial activism. In any case, whether there is judicial review of legislation or not, whether there is a clear set of rules or whether said rules are uncertain or absent, judges are often asked to perform a function integrating that of the legislator, and to become the real protagonists of the legal discourse, so much so that they can be described as the 'lords of biolaw'.

On this basis, this book brings together a series of papers aimed at achieving different purposes.

In his essay, Roger Brownsword gives a definition of axiological pluralism and traces the possible scenarios opened by it, focusing on both the physiological and pathological expressions of the phenomenon. Within a range of possible reactions on the part of the law, the author analyses the directions taken by the most recent British case-law, providing a conceptual scheme which is very useful also in a comparative perspective.

Comparison is at the centre of the methodology adopted in the essays of Lucia Busatta and Simone Penasa which, the former focusing on the overall role of the different actors, and the latter on the courts, build a partially convergent model. The division into 'preclusive, inactive and integrative' approaches leads Lucia Busatta to systematize a series of experiences in which the law has to consider the scientific factor. Simone Penasa compares the case-law of the ECHR with the national ones, highlighting the importance of the combination of scientific reasonableness and the constitutional dimension in managing the growing axiological pluralism. From this point of view, the 'rights oriented' approach of the courts must find a reconciliation in the division of powers that leads to limit judicial activism (in the 'institutional based' perspective). In a similar viewpoint on a specific issue, Ricardo Chueca detects in the Courts dealing with end-of-life decisions a preclusive approach, an inactive one and a promotional one.

3 The Role of Other Institutions (Quasi-Jurisdictional or Consultative) and Other Tools

Besides courts, other institutions have made their own headway in the task of accommodating axiological pluralism.

In the first place, there are ethical committees or Institutional Review Boards which, exercising their power both upstream and downstream of important decisions such as placing drugs on the market or deciding on the best interests of children or incapable persons, play an important role in orienting and sometimes in making crucial decisions. Thus, starting from the declaration of Helsinki, clinical trial regulations provide for independent committees with the role of controlling both scientific validity and respect of ethical principles and the rights of participants. Extending attention beyond clinical trials, the role of ethical committees, or equivalent bodies, has grown a great deal, so much so that it has been decisive and sometimes exclusive in certain areas. This expansion has taken place both nationally and internationally, although, as highlighted by the essay by Itziar de Lecuona, the growth of ethics committees has not led to the resolution of all problems. In retracing the history of the ethical and legal evaluation of clinical research, the author focuses on some risks related to inactivity or to the insufficient effectiveness of the control system aimed at protecting the rights of participants.

In the same light, Carlos Maria Romeo Casabona extends the focus to the international dimension, dealing with the Universal Declaration on Bioethics and Human Rights adopted by the UNESCO General Conference (2005). At this level, international ethics committees are able to expand their range of action beyond state boundaries, losing—which is not necessarily a bad thing—the binding character of their opinions. Bodies such as the Bioethics Committee of UNESCO or the European Group on Ethics in Science and New Technologies (EGE) have been designed to address the axiological pluralism that typically characterizes the different reactions present at international level towards biomedical innovations. In this way, their activity is characterized by specialization, multidisciplinarity, and independence.

The purpose of accommodating axiological pluralism present at a social level is typically pursued also through different strategies and tools.

Conscientious objection allows for not following a law which conflicts with the dictates of personal conscience or religion. In the face of the current extensive increase of requests for this instrument, however, it is necessary to identify some criteria that can establish appropriate exercise of said right and to unmask attempts to take advantage of this tool for purely instrumental reasons or to calculated effect. According to Davide Paris, respect for individual conscience cannot lead to a nullification or a sabotage of the law: as "the conscience must be protected by the law, so must the law be protected from the conscience". One way to make conscientious objection sustainable, maintaining it in terms of exemption, is to respect two things. Objection "can only be exceptionally introduced when a moral conflict is as deep as it implies on the human being's dignity" and when the infringement of the personal conscientious obligation is direct. In this way, conscientious objection is an irreplaceable but at the same time workable tool in contemporary societies in order to achieve sustainable pluralism.

The discussion on professional ethics and deontology in general is linked to these dynamics. It clearly represents and exemplifies the plurality of systems that allows, once again under certain conditions, that axiological pluralism be maintained within reasonable limits. In this case too, as written by Elisabetta Pulice, it is necessary that the exercise of deontological autonomy respects some supreme or constitutional principles, outside of which, axiological pluralism returns to be a matter for judicial intervention, becoming the object of the courts.

4 Case-Studies for a Sustainable Pluralism

The third part of the book aims at verifying all the principles and reflections set out in more general terms in the first two parts, in the light of some of the most significant and up-to-date case studies. In this section of the book, themes have been chosen in order to paradigmatically represent the most current challenges of axiological pluralism. Roger Brownsword deals with the specific conflicts in the area of health and the division of tasks between the different institutions involved. In this context, as mentioned earlier, the author identifies and validates a model which turns out to be very useful also in general terms.

Marta Tomasi deals with two very controversial topics at an international level: non-validated therapies and vaccinations. This area constitutes a new arena of confrontation between freedom and power, between health and free choice (even that based on irrational motivations). The author identifies how a concrete action inspired by individual ideas cannot be tolerated when it leads to damage to third party interests and fundamental rights. She also reflects on how science cannot be constructed in a pluralistic sense, having to be evidence-based. At the same time, law that deals with science must be an evidence-based law.

The relationship between science and law is also the subject of Andrea Perin's essay, which deals with a particular pluralism linked to HIV infection. The author writes about the difficult relationship between criminal law, which needs to be based on facts which are as certain as possible, and science, which proceeds by way of hypotheses which are always open to a process of confirmation or disconfirmation. In this sense, there could be a clash between a desired certainty (on the legal side) and a physiological uncertainty and mutability (on the scientific side).

The third part of the book continues with two traditional topics of biolaw: beginning of life and end of life issues.

Elena Falletti writes about a traditional issue in biolaw: reproductive rights. In this area also, there is a traditional conflict between self-determination and protection of the health or wellbeing of the person (the same person who determines for him or herself or, in the case of abortion, the foetus).

Ricardo Chueca deals with the end of life, an area in which, in paradigmatic terms, increased technical progress implies more room for different decisions and pluralism. Under a comparative perspective, the Author provides an overview of a number of legal systems in which the contrast between respect for axiological pluralism and the state's interest in protecting life is differently approached. Erick Valdes and Juan Alberto Lecaros bring the same theme up to date in the light of the Chilean legal debate. The authors write of the inadequacy of state law in respecting personal values and legal and constitutional rights claimed by people when entering the final phase of their life. Lastly, the authors propose some broader considerations in order to specify the main points of a sustainable legal framework of end-of-life issues.

Sustainability in this context means the possibility to find a point of balance among these tensions: the legal framework proves to be capable of integrating different axiological positions with the scientific datum. Thus, sustainable pluralism in biolaw depicts a legal framework in which different individual moral positions find equal protection, provided that they are not in conflict with scientific certainty or that they do not endanger health and safety of the others.

Contributions in this volume clearly show that it is extremely difficult for a contemporary constitutional state to find the correct point of balance among different positions and that, in any case, when such equilibrium has been found, it could never be considered immutable. The basic and inherent feature of the law trying to reconcile axiological pluralism in the field of biolaw, which is characterised by a rapid scientific development, is that it has to be frequently updated to the changing social sensitivity and to the evolution of science and technology.

Through the lenses provided by the combination of the general reflections of the first and second parts of the book with the case studies analysed in the third part, it is possible to understand how, on the one hand, pluralism is an element of the constitutional state's inner core, but on the other, it must be limited within sustainable boundaries. In this sense, the book addresses and revitalizes, in the light of some of the most recent innovations in life sciences, one of the traditional issues of the law as a whole: identifying how much is enough and how much is too much.

5 A Last Disclaimer: Biolaw and the Pandemic

This book has been designed and planned within the framework of a research project on Jurisdictions and Pluralisms funded by the Italian Ministry of University (PRIN 2010-11: Jurisdiction and Pluralisms, coordinated by Prof. Roberto Toniatti), which involved both national and international legal scholars for a few years. The research kept going even after the formal end of the project, as a proof of its high profile and scientific value. This edited book is aimed at collecting the contributions of distinguished colleagues from different legal systems. We would also like to thank Prof. Roberto Toniatti for the design of the project on Judicial Pluralisms and for his scientific support and encouragement; our gratitude to all authors for their rich and inspiring contributions.

The world is continuously evolving and after the first version of this manuscript has been send to the publisher, the pandemic outbreak dramatically changed our lives and the world. Of course, what happened had a significant and relevant impact also on the field of law.

The complexity of the phenomenon, together with the need to metabolize the shock in order to appropriately systematize what happened, convinced us that many months would have been necessary to integrate the pandemic emergency into our book's design. This is due not only to the need to systematize the various events, the different national approaches, and the countless issues that the pandemic emergency has brought to light. It is redundant to notice that health rights and healthcare organization have been deeply changed by the pandemic for the present and the future. We are well aware of the difficult questions concerning pluralism, biolaw, axiological values and science that the pandemic raised and that would be interesting to further develop. The hope is that this project could continue in further publications on pluralism and the pandemic.

Therefore, it is a risky but aware choice of editors not to include a chapter on the pandemic emergency into the book, nor to ask authors to change their contributions in light of what happened. Nevertheless, all chapters are updated to March 2021 as to the most relevant legislative and jurisdictional changes concerning their field of interest.

Part I
Adjudication and Regulation Facing Pluralisms: Models and Trends

BioLaw Facing Pluralisms: Three Simple Models for Complex Issues

Lucia Busatta

Abstract The aim of the paper is to shape models to describe the different legal approaches towards the regulation of biolaw issues, characterised by tension between different axiological orientations. These models highlight the various interactions between the legislature and the judiciary at the crossroads between the legal recognition of different moral values and the regulation of scientific development in medical sciences. The three models could be described as follows. The preclusive model is characterized by the rigidity of the legislative datum, which requires the intervention of the jurisdiction. In the inactive model, the abstentionist behaviour of the lawmaker does not thwart individual demands and needs. Finally, the integrative legislative approach, while trying to reconcile different positions, may also require judicial intervention. Conclusions show that in this field any decision is never permanent and has always to be open to review.

1 Introduction

Any legal discipline has a morally and ethically sensitive nature because it implies choices. Any decision, from this perspective, entails the election of criteria, the exclusion of some subjects from those benefits provided by law or the inclusion of others into the legal provision. Therefore, by definition, legal choices have an ethical dimension which is related to the way criteria are set, exceptions are made, individuals are granted protection or not.

In the specific field of biolaw, this moral and ethical dimension is particularly emphasized. This is due to the intersection between the need for a uniform legal regulation of highly complex matters and the different individual demands which legal intervention in the field of life sciences aims at satisfying.

Regulation of life sciences, which is the main object of biolaw, requires policymakers and lawmakers to take complex decisions. On the one hand, they

L. Busatta (✉)
Faculty of Law, University of Trento, Trento, Italy
e-mail: lucia.busatta@unitn.it

L. Busatta, C. Casonato (eds.), *Axiological Pluralism*, Ius Gentium: Comparative Perspectives on Law and Justice 92, https://doi.org/10.1007/978-3-030-78475-1_2

hold a duty to envelop scientific progress into legal norms, to grant society access to advanced treatments and to keep pace with the development of medicine. This allows for the acknowledgement of several fundamental rights and contributes to the general development and wellbeing of society. On the other hand, though, those in charge of the adoption of choices connected to the legal regulation of biolaw issues have to face complex dilemmas: the legal discipline of new medical technologies entails not only the evaluation of its scientific implications, but it also requires lawmakers to appraise its ethical and moral connotations. Societies are growing in complexity: the multi-layered composition of contemporary societies continuously poses new challenges for policymakers. Inclusive contemporary societies are thus facing complex issues related to the difficult composition of different individual and collective needs vis-à-vis scientific and technological progress. Moreover, sometimes the potential regulation of a new medical technique or product might clash with those moral or ethical values on which the legal order relies.

Nowadays, pluralism of values is the key feature of contemporary societies, especially in countries belonging to the Western legal tradition.[1] From a legal viewpoint, this trait significantly influences the relationship between state powers (especially the legislature and the judiciary) and the guarantee of individual fundamental rights.

More precisely, pluralism of values constitutes a key element in the regulation of biolaw issues, where the axiological dimension of individual morals, needs and beliefs intersects the legal recognition of scientific development. Legal regulation of biotechnologies and human health often has to cope not only with the possibility of ensuring equality of access to scientific development, but also (and maybe more importantly) with the need to incorporate different moral values and sometimes divergent individual needs into a uniform legal text.[2]

This paper suggests shaping models to describe the different legal approach towards the regulation of biolaw issues characterised by tension between different axiological orientations. These models allow the highlighting of the various interactions between the legislature and the judiciary at the crossroads between the legal recognition of different moral values and the regulation of scientific development in medical sciences.

2 The Added Value of Models

When dealing with legal comparison, the use of a modelled schematization can help unravel a complex amount of data and describe the object of the research in a rational way. An abstract model through which to read concrete phenomena allows, through

[1]For a wide description of legal traditions see Glenn (2010), in particular 273 ff.

[2]On this aspect see *inter multis*, Bin et al. (2012).

a work of subsumption, for classification and therefore for the creation of a synthesis of complexity through logical categories.[3]

In this perspective, we can theorize a first pattern which describes the legal order's attitude towards the constitutional protection of minority rights. This model was originally theorised with reference to linguistic, ethnic and religious minorities within multicultural contemporary societies. The same model seems, for several reasons, to be effective also when dealing with the constitutional recognition of axiological pluralism.

Firstly, individual values and morals are often connected to religious beliefs or to cultural identity. In this sense, the axiological dimension appears to be one of the possible features of the identity of a minority, be it a group or an individual.

Secondly, the elaboration of this model departs from the observation that contemporary societies are characterised by diversity, differences and distinctions. Pluralism of values, under this perspective, is just one of the possible facets of our composite societies.

Thirdly, the concept of minority brings us to reflect upon the relationship between a majority (i.e., a prevalent group) and minorities. While the majority group could be considered as a whole, because it entails the prevalent orientation of the social group, minorities should be considered as pluralities. They could be several or a few; they could also be organised in different groups or be made up of individuals. Regardless of the entity, in terms of number, or extent of these groups or individuals, minorities still deserve due consideration within contemporary societies; in a democratic legal order, their position is granted not only legal recognition but also protection, provided that claiming rights is not in contrast with the rights of others or with the general fundamental principles upon which the state is founded. Therefore, in a democratic society, the legal order has to ensure the same level of constitutional protection and rights protection to all individuals, regardless of the "group" or "individuality" they belong to.[4]

Therefore, the approach that divides the levels of recognition and protection of minority groups into four main models seems to be applicable also to the description of the constitutional protection of individual rights regarding cultural, axiological and moral pluralism *vis à vis* scientific and medical progress.

This model is therefore characterised by four categories which describe the different degree of recognition and integration of pluralism at a constitutional level. We can count (i) a "repressive model", characterized by the express negation of any pluralism;[5] (ii) an "agnostic liberal model", the essence of which is identifiable in the guarantee of merely formal equality;[6] (iii) a "pluralist promotional

[3]On legal comparison see Eberle (2009), Husa (2006) and Monateri (2012).

[4]On this aspect, see for example the interesting reasoning developed in Tie (1999), p. 161 ff.

[5]Toniatti (1995), p. 206 defines this model as "The uniform national identity of the population is ideologically over-inflated."

[6]Ibidem: "This envisages the coincidence between the nationality ... and the citizenship of the population."

model", in which the main purpose of the State is achieved through the differentiation guaranteed by the application of the principle of substantial equality;[7] (iv) finally, a "pluralist equal model",[8] within which the exception is the rule and any differentiation is dissolved in the equal degree of recognition that it obtains from the legal system.

This classification appears to be apt in order to describe the degree of pluralism recognised at a constitutional level. Based on the intersection between the principle of equality and the recognition of other fundamental rights, such as freedom of expression, freedom of thought, conscience and religion, the recognition of the right to use minority languages in specific circumstances, and so on, this model is useful to address the issue of legal acknowledgement of pluralism within the constitution.

Nevertheless, when dealing with more specific and detailed issues, such as the regulation of medical technologies and the integration of axiological pluralism in the field of biolaw, a further specification is needed. In the complex relationship between law and life sciences, the axiological dimension is represented by different moral or ethical needs that could either derive from a majority understanding of the values involved or from individual requests. In this sense, science makes a difference, as it could highlight the existence of new minority groups[9] or the need to grant protection to specific individual needs or to a particular category of subjects.[10]

The presence or absence of a legal discipline might also make a difference. In this sense, the regulation of a specific area of life sciences unveils a political choice. On the contrary, the absence of a legal discipline in a given bio-medical area might either be the sign of the political decision not to intervene or the marker of a (physiological or pathological) delay of the lawmaker in addressing a given matter.[11]

Moreover, when existing, the legal discipline of a specific field of biolaw could also be considered as inclusive and permissive (when it allows access to a given medical technique to a wide number of individuals or groups) or preclusive and rigid (when it provides for several restrictions or bans in access to scientific innovations in the medical field).

Abstractly, none of these legal approaches could be evaluated in absolutely positive or negative terms, unless the specific regulation (or lack of regulation) is compared to the level of protection or recognition of the fundamental rights of the

[7]This model is "typified by the predominance of a national group and the presence of one or several minority groups. . .", Ibidem.

[8]The "paritarian multinational state", in which the constitutional order is framed in order to incorporate and reflect the multinationality of its permanent social pattern on a paritarian basis", Ibidem.

[9]For example, from a medical viewpoint, those affected by a rare disease could be qualified as a minority group. Parallelly, from an axiological perspective, those who refuse blood transfusions (be it for moral, religious or other reasons) can be considered as a minority group as well.

[10]Such as in the case of specific disabilities or in the occurrence of a severe degenerative illness.

[11]Casonato (2017), p. 86.

individuals or groups involved.[12] Therefore, the theoretical elaboration of this categorisation departs from the observation of the legislative scenario, applied to a concrete object of regulation: the preclusive, inactive or inclusive approach of the legislature needs to be measured against the judicial attitude towards the recognition of individual needs and positions. The object of the regulation (i.e. access to a drug; availability of a medical procedure; regulation of abortion, assisted suicide, conscientious objection in the medical field; assisted reproduction; right to refuse medical treatments; etc.) is central for the identification of those relevant legal positions and fundamental rights involved.

In this perspective, we can therefore distinguish three basic categories which correspond to the level of integration of axiological pluralism at a legislative level and which could be listed as (i) a preclusive model; (ii) an inactive model; (iii) an integrative model. In this scale, the distinction between models refers to the level of recognition of axiological pluralism in the legal regulation of life sciences.

Given this context, we offer an analysis of the relationship between legislation and jurisdiction organised into these three main categories, in which the legislative approach is the starting point. Depending on the level of "rigidity" or "flexibility" of the legislation with respect to the acknowledgement of individual moral values and to the integration of the scientific dimension at a normative level, the role of the judiciary may vary significantly.

In a framework in which the lawmaker tends to deny or refuse pluralism (preclusive model), jurisdiction is called to guarantee the necessary balance between the different components of society. As we will see, this does not necessarily correspond to the recognition of the individual jurisdictional request, as the judiciary may consider that—given the circumstances of the specific case—the legislative approach respects the legal order's general principles (this could be the case in which proportionality, precaution or public policy prevail over the individual position).

Differently, in the case of an "inactive" lawmaker (second category), judicial interventions prove to be crucial in answering needs and issues arising at a scientific and social level in the absence of a specific regulation. This approach is even more evident when the judiciary faces a "pathological" silence of the legislature.

Finally, with regard to the third category (integrative), even if the different levels of pluralisms find legislative protection, courts might open the way to new rights or new individual positions that deserve protection on the part of the legal order.

The aim of this schema is to rationalise the relationship between lawmaker and jurisdiction in biolaw issues, when science and pluralism of values significantly impact on the ethical direction of legal regulation. As we will see, these models are

---

[12]On this aspect, it has to be remarked that any categorisation—especially when dealing with moral or cultural individual feelings and values—must not be taken as absolutely objective nor rebuttable. The aim of models, in this field, is to offer a description of a phenomenon and the possible institutional reactions it generates. Any of the models proposed hereinafter is therefore to be intended as plastic and possibly adaptable to different issues or contexts. On this aspect see also Tie (1999), p. 50.

based on the object of legislation. Therefore, they can describe the nature of different legislative or jurisdictional choices adopted within the same legal system.

After having presented the three models and their main features, in the concluding paragraph we will try to identify the reasons for this apparently multi-layered legal approach to scientific issues with high ethical implications.

3 The "Preclusive" Model

The tendentially preclusive model is characterized by a certain degree of rigidity of the legislative datum. The lawmaker (consciously or not) decides to give priority to a certain moral or ethical orientation within the regulation of a specific field of biolaw. Consequently, those axiological tendencies which are different from the prevailing one and which are naturally present within society are neither recognized nor protected.

Sometimes this legislative choice could even be in contrast with the scientific datum: medical sciences might offer a new technique which shows great promise or which satisfies an individual need, desire or aspiration, but the lawmaker decides to prohibit or severely restrict access to it.

Therefore, the basic features of this first model consist in the presence of regulatory bans enforced by severe sanctions (often of a criminal nature) or in the provision of rigid subjective or organisational limitations, with the effect of substantially restricting individual access to a medical technique. The eventual breach of individual legal positions which, under constitutional data, deserve due protection, could cause the intervention of the judiciary. Supreme Courts and constitutional Tribunals may be called to find the point of balance between the political choice that led to a preclusive regulation and the spectrum of fundamental rights the challenged limitations involve.

A few examples may help. The criminal prohibition of assisted suicide, which is still in force in many states, clearly demonstrates the tensions that can arise when a given behaviour or technique is concretely and effectively possible at a medical level and when its scientific accessibility can satisfy a specific individual need.[13] In this sense, the ban is felt to be in contrast with the constitutional guarantee of fundamental rights by those who, by virtue of their specific clinical situation, wish to be left free to decide on the end of their lives.

[13]The example of assisted suicide serves as a case to discuss legal pluralism also in Scheffer (2018).

3.1 *The Many Shades of Constitutional Adjudication Regarding Assisted Suicide*

In recent years, some national provisions on the criminalisation of assisted suicide have been challenged before constitutional judges, to ascertain whether such a discipline is compliant with the guarantee of fundamental rights, with the principle of equality or with human dignity.[14] Decisions on these cases vary substantially from one legal order to another, depending on the features of the concrete case presented before the Court, on the interpretation of national constitutional rights and principles and, finally, on the judicial approach towards such sensitive issues. As to the latter, in fact, a comparative analysis of constitutional decisions on this topic shows that the spectrum of judicial intervention can vary from the recognition of wide political discretion on the part of the lawmaker (substantial deference) to the declaration of unconstitutionality and the judicial creation of a new right (judicial activism).

From a medical and technical viewpoint, the administration of lethal drugs provided by a physician for the purpose of ending the suffering of a patient affected by a terminal illness or an incurable condition is a concrete possibility.

From a moral and ethical perspective, however, the nature of assisted suicide and mercy killing are highly controversial as they involve the definition of human dignity, sanctity of life and the extent of individuals' power to decide upon the end of life.[15]

Some states, such as Belgium and the Netherlands,[16] have decided to regulate the circumstances under which a patient with a terminal illness or in an incurable condition can have access to assisted suicide. Some other states still maintain a criminal provision that bans this conduct and provides for severe sanctions for physicians or other people who find themselves involved in such requests. This is one of the most controversial dilemmas in biolaw.[17]

In recent years, judges worldwide have been involved in legal challenges against the prohibition of assisted suicide. The frequency of these issues demonstrates the existence of a social need (which probably does not affect the majority of people, but is nonetheless relevant) to address these problems and their inherent controversial nature. Within a repressive model, legal prohibition has the effect of preventing

---

[14]Among others, the most recent and significant cases are: Supreme Court of Canada, *Carter v. Canada*, 2015 SCC 5, Supreme Court of the United Kingdom, *R (Nicklinson) v Ministry of Justice*, [2014] UKSC 38, Court of Appeal, Civil Division, *R (on the application of Conway) v Secretary of State for Justice*, [2018] EWCA Civ 1431, Italian Constitutional Court on the Cappato Case, court order no. 207 of 2018 and decision no. 242 of 2019.

[15]Holm (2015), pp. 40–43.

[16]Moreover, in the USA this is a matter of state competence. Therefore, each State decided either to regulate assisted suicide or not. Among the first ones that provided for a comprehensive discipline on physician assisted dying is the Oregon Death with Dignity Act 1997. More recently, as is well-known, the case of Brittany Maynard, who moved from California to Oregon for assisted dying, urged the Californian Assembly to approve the End of Life Option Act in 2015.

[17]McMorrow (2019), p. 267.

those in need from having access to a dignified (from their personal perspective) way to end their lives, with a general justification based on the prevailing public interest in protecting the weakest persons from harm.[18]

The various judges involved in such claims have adopted different approaches and solutions which clearly exemplify the diverse reactions of judiciary systems towards a repressive lawmaker.

A first step is represented by a general acceptance of the legislative choice and the confirmation that, given the circumstances of the specific case, the law strikes a fair balance between the interests involved. This approach can be seen in the UK Court of Appeal's decision in the case of Mr Conway, an English man suffering from a neuro-degenerative illness, who claimed that section 2 of the Suicide Act is in contrast with Article 8 of the ECHR. In deciding on his case, the Court stated that the contested law "achieves a fair balance between the interests of the wider community and the interests of people in the position of Mr Conway" (par. 206), and that Parliament is in a better position than the Court to assess the likely impact of such a discipline. This deferent approach of the English Court is also informed by the unsuccessful attempt to reform the relevant legislation by means of the Assisted Dying Bill in 2015 (which would have allowed terminally ill patients with less than six months to live to have access to assisted dying), which did not obtain parliamentary approval. As a consequence of the lack of political consensus on changing laws, the jurisdiction chose to confirm the legitimacy of the existing (preclusive) legislation, thereby excluding a breach of the ECHR.[19]

A second degree of judicial intervention consists in the confirmation of the legitimacy of the contested legislation, accompanied by a warning or an admonishment towards the lawmaker. In these cases, the judges respect the political discretion of the legislature but recommend a political assessment of new social needs or a change in the existing rules. Here, the judicial recommendation might be softer or weaker, depending on the case and on the constitutional rights involved.

For example, in *Nicklinson*, in 2014, the UK Supreme Court rejected a declaration of incompatibility of Section 2 of the Suicide Act, stating that "Parliament is certainly the preferable forum in which any decision should be made, after full investigation and consideration, in a manner which will command popular acceptance."[20] Nevertheless, the Supreme Court suggested that, in the absence of due consideration of the matter by Parliament or in the light of changed circumstances and social needs, the Court might change approach (par. 191, quoting a precedent). In other words, at the point at which *Nicklinson* was decided, Parliament was

[18]Of great significance in this perspective is the recent decision of the UK court of Appeal in *R. (on the application of Conway) v Secretary of State for Justice* [2018] EWCA Civ 1431, in which the Court highlighted the reasons that stand behind such a legislative choice: "[...] to protect the weak and vulnerable, [...] to give proper weight to the moral significance of the sanctity of life and [...] to undermine relations of trust and confidence between doctors and their patients." (par. 204).

[19]Hobson (2018), p. 256.

[20]*R (on the application of Nicklinson and another) v Ministry of Justice* [2014] UKSC 38, paragraph 190.

working on a new Bill on Assisted Dying. Therefore, a judicial declaration of incompatibility regarding the prohibition of assisted suicide would have been inappropriate, even though the Court hinted at the need for a reform.[21] As the bill's approval was unsuccessful in Parliament, subsequent case law has taken the view that at the moment there is no political consensus around the changing of the law. Differently, if parliamentary debate had remained silent, the courts could have chosen to adopt a different and more interventionist approach.

A similar attitude was also adopted by the Irish Supreme Court in 2013, when the judges excluded that the prohibition of assisted suicide breached the Constitution, but also stated that it is up to the democratic assembly to properly balance these complex issues and that, once a new legislative solution is adopted, it is the duty of the Court to determine whether the new balance is respectful of constitutional principles and fundamental rights.[22]

Therefore, the two supreme courts do recognise the complexity of the legal problems involved in the decision concerning assisted suicide. This is the reason underpinning the need that such a decision be taken by the democratically elected body and not by judges. Nevertheless, the Courts do not expressly exclude that, in the absence of a due consideration by Parliament with regard to such important issues, judicial scrutiny might become more intense.

A further nuance of judicial scrutiny in matters where the lawmaker adopted a preclusive solution can be seen in constitutionally oriented interpretation. Here, the constitutional judge does not declare the challenged provision void, but the court indicates the "correct" interpretation of the legal rule, in order to make it compliant with constitutional protection of fundamental rights. Once again, the prohibition of mercy killing serves as the scope. In 1997, the Constitutional Court of Colombia stated that the article of the criminal code punishing mercy killing should be read taking into account that the physician acting in compliance with the will of a terminally ill patient cannot be considered guilty of such offence.[23] In these cases, the normative datum is not invalidated by the judiciary; rather, it is given a new interpretation (which, in fact, deeply changes its meaning and implications), which is more compliant with the living constitutional interpretation of fundamental rights. In such circumstances, judicial activism has an intrinsically temporary nature, as a change in the laws would indeed be necessary in order to grant legal certainty for subjects involved especially (i.e. physicians, who need to exactly know what behaviour could amount to a criminal offence and what, on the contrary, might be justifiable). Lack of legislative intervention could lead to further litigation, to a likely subsequent declaration of unconstitutionality and to a fracture breaching the legitimacy of the preclusive solution.

[21] Davis and Finlay (2015) and Dyer (2015).

[22] Irish Supreme Court, *Fleming v. Ireland & Ors.* [2013] IESC 19, par. 108. For a commentary on the case see Mitchell (2014).

[23] Colombia Constitutional Court, decision no. C-239/97. Casonato (2011), p. 252.

Lastly, the most intense degree of judicial scrutiny within a repressive model is represented by the declaration of unconstitutionality.

The rules governing constitutional adjudication at a national level could impose a variability on the effects of the judgement. Here, with reference to assisted suicide, the decision by the Canadian Supreme Court proves particularly useful in clarifying the implications of such a decision. In *Carter v. Canada*, the Supreme Court found the prohibition of assisted suicide provided by the criminal code to be in breach of the Charter of Rights and Freedoms, thereby recognising for mentally competent adults with an intolerable and enduring terminal illness the right to have a physician's assistance in dying. The ruling was suspended for 12 months: in this way, the Supreme Court gave adequate time to the Parliament to enact a new legislation on the matter. This intermediate solution (i.e. a "suspended" declaration of unconstitutionality) is functional in demonstrating that judicial activism could *per se* be useful in recognising individual fundamental rights and legitimate positions. Nevertheless, in order to grant legal certainty and to avoid the risk of undue prosecution for those involved in such a procedure, the intervention of the legislature is still necessary.

It is worth pointing out that in this case, the degree of judicial scrutiny is not overly intense. A complete declaration of unconstitutionality might also be possible.

The most recent Italian case serves as a further example. By means of ordinance no. 207 of 2018, the Constitutional Court decided to schedule its decision on the matter of assisted suicide for September 2019, therefore giving Parliament the opportunity to legislate on the matter. It is worth highlighting that, among the reasons that pushed the Italian constitutional judge to do so, the very complex issues deriving from a pure declaration of unconstitutionality have quite a driving role. In other words, as a consequence of a decision of unconstitutionality, a normative vacuum would have been created. The Court rejected the idea of leaving a regulatory gap between its decision and the time when the legislator could adopt new legislation and therefore postponed its decision on the matter to a subsequent time, thereby giving Parliament clear procedural and substantial directions.

In the meantime, Parliament did not work on new legislation. Therefore, during the hearing held on September 24th, 2019, the Constitutional Court decided the matter and declared Article 580 partially void. Decision no. 242 of 2019 was published on November 22nd, 2019, and explains the very narrow limits of the application of the exception to the criminalisation of assisted suicide and how healthcare structures and professionals should behave until the lawmaker will provide for specific rules on the matter.[24]

[24]The case of assisted suicide in Italy is currently widely debated both for the substantial implications of the decision of the Court and for the peculiar typology of decision. In fact, the Court first postponed its decision, giving some substantial suggestions for the legislative intervention. Secondly, in the absence of a new legislation on the matter, the Constitutional Court decided to declare the prohibition of assisted suicide partially void, but it narrowed the application of the discipline to a given set of very specific requirements. These are that the person shall be "(a) affected by an illness that is incurable and (b) causes physical or psychological suffering, which they find absolutely intolerable, and who are (c) kept alive by means of life support treatments, but remain (d) capable of

The range of judiciary reactions towards the prohibition of assisted suicide is quite indicative of the variety of approaches that case law can adopt in the regulation of ethics, medicine and the law. To a certain extent, this unpredictability reflects the relevance of different starting points: both the constitutional tradition as well as the recurrence of a given issue might influence the concrete judicial decision.

From another perspective, the degree of variation might be read as randomness in judicial decisions, especially when dealing with the same legal system or with very similar ones, and might give rise to some perplexities with regard to the effectiveness of the principle of equality.[25]

In these terms, a preclusive approach of the lawmaker never stands as a good starting point when fundamental rights are at stake, and the need to file a petition or to claim the unconstitutionality of the applicable law implies that only a minority can strive for the recognition of these rights, turning out to be economically and morally onerous and time-consuming.

4 The Inactive Model: Basic Features

The inactive model is characterised by an abstentionist behaviour on the part of the lawmaker, who tends not to intervene in ethically sensitive decisions. In the face of normative silence, which might depend on different factors, jurisdiction is called upon to respond to individual requests, in order to re-establish a sustainable level of legal certainty and to ensure due protection of the fundamental rights at stake.

In the absence of a clear normative framework, the role of judges is particularly complicated given the often divisive and challenging nature of concrete cases. Therefore, the variability of the individual situation brought before courts proves to be a determining factor for the judicial decision.

---

making free and informed decisions." (Court ordinance no. 207 of 2018). In these cases, the person can obtain withdrawal of life-sustaining treatments and, therefore, there is no reason to criminally persecute those who help the person to find a dignified way of dying.

[25]In this sense, a seminal example of this kind of contradiction is shown in the Constitutional Court's decision on the matter of donation of gametes in artificial reproduction (Italian Constitutional Court, decision no. 162 of 2014). In this case, the total ban on the donation of gametes was challenged before the Court. The Court decided for a declaration of unconstitutionality, saying that the ban infringed the principle of equality, because the law itself was devoted to offering reproduction opportunities to those with problems of sterility or infertility (article 1 of law no. 40 of 2004 on medically assisted reproduction). The Court found a clash between this general objective of the law and the ban on the donation of gametes and declared such a provision void. Differently from the case on assisted suicide, the Court gave some directions concerning the subsequent application of the law, especially with reference to the vacuum concerning provisions on donation. It is worth pointing out that, five years after the Constitutional Court's decision, legislative provisions on the donation of gametes have not yet been enacted and the matter still suffers from a lack of adequate regulation. See Cecchi et al. (2017).

When considering the lack of a legislative solution to a legal problem at the crossroad between medicine and ethical values involving the granting of fundamental rights,[26] we can identify three different levels of intensity of judicial scrutiny.

Firstly, judges can state that judicial intervention cannot change the *status quo* deriving from the lack of legislation. Therefore, the object of the regulation is a matter of political discretion. Courts might add a recommendation for the legislature if they observe that there is a relevant social need that deserves due legislative consideration. This approach can be viewed as similar to a mild reaction on the part of the judiciary facing a repressive normative framework.

A second level of intensity of judicial scrutiny consists in the elaboration of a specific answer to a concrete case (which might eventually find an application in similar future cases), using the tools available at that moment in the legal system. Here, the degree of intensity of judicial scrutiny may vary, depending on the scientific and axiological implications of the issue at stake. The decision can offer a new (updated or innovative) interpretation of general principles (such as community interest, public policy, social justice, . . .) brought up by the legal problem they are required to provide an answer for.

A few examples can clarify the different jurisdictional reactions to an inactive lawmaker.

One of the most challenging issues of contemporary biolaw concerns the legal discipline of surrogacy.[27] The possibility of being recognised as parent(s) of a newborn when the pregnancy has been carried out by another woman following an arrangement is one of the most controversial legal topics of our times. From a medical viewpoint, thanks to assisted reproduction techniques, surrogacy does not involve significant complexities. The difficult task for the lawmaker is to regulate the legal relationships between the subjects involved and the recognition of parenthood, because surrogacy is a concrete possibility that raises complicated ethical issues. Heterosexual couples in which the female partner is unable to carry a child or male same-sex couples (or even single men) are subjects that might be interested in a surrogacy agreement leading to a pregnancy.

Within European and North-American countries, some have decided to adopt a restrictive approach towards surrogacy,[28] whereas others, on the contrary, have adopted a very detailed regulation with a considerable degree of differentiation between one state and another regarding accessibility criteria, limitations, economic compensation for the surrogate mother and so on.[29]

---

[26] On these complexities see also Lecaros (2019).

[27] Stefanelli (2019).

[28] Meaning a legal prohibition, accompanied by severe criminal sanctions, such as in Italy (law no. 40/2004, article 12).

[29] For example, in the UK the Human Fertilisation and Embryology Act 2008, which changed the 1985 Surrogacy Arrangements Regulation. The updated discipline on surrogacy in the UK and the most relevant case law is collected in the dossier *L'evoluzione normativa e giurisprudenziale della gestazione per altri nel Regno Unito*, at the following link https://www.biodiritto.org/Dossier/L-evoluzione-normativa-e-giurisprudenziale-della-gestazione-per-altri-nel-Regno-Unito. Another

A very interesting case is that of Ireland where the strong religious orientation of the constitution has often led to repressive normative solutions.[30] Interestingly enough, this constitutional approach has not influenced the legal regulation of assisted reproduction techniques and surrogacy. On the contrary, Ireland has not enacted any legislation on the matter and throughout the years quite a permissive regime has prevailed.[31]

In the lack of a legal discipline on surrogacy, in 2014 the Irish Supreme Court was involved in a case concerning the legal recognition of motherhood for two twins born from a surrogate mother. Amongst the adults involved in the procedure there was no dispute on the desire to register the genetic mother as the legal mother of the twins. In the absence of a legal framework governing such situations, the Supreme Court stated that the general legal principle underpinning the recognition of motherhood is the legal presumption that the woman who gives birth is the mother of the child (*mater semper certa est*): "Under the current legislative framework it is not possible to address issues arising on surrogacy, including the issue of who is the mother for the purpose of the registration of the birth." (par. 119). Nevertheless, in addressing the issue, the Court underlined that there is a lacuna in the law "as to certain rights, especially those of the children born in such circumstances. Such lacuna should be addressed in legislation and not by this Court" and that "The issues raised in this case are important, complex and social, which are matters of public policy for the [Parliament]." (paras 116 and 118).

It is worth pointing out, as a matter of comparative law, that a similar approach was adopted by the Italian Constitutional Court in the previously mentioned ordinance concerning the prohibition of assisted suicide. The Constitutional Judge in 2018 stated that the prohibition *per se* is not in breach of the constitution, as the criminal provision is intended to protect the lives of the weakest and most fragile. Yet, the Court found a *lacuna* in the law, because it stated that the lawmaker should take into consideration "situations that were unimaginable at the time when the challenged law was introduced, but which have been brought within its scope of application by medical and technological advancements, which are often able to save

example could be Greece, where surrogacy is regulated by law 4272/2014. See Maria C. Vastaroucha, Surrogacy Proceedings in Greece after the implementation of law 4272/2014, available at the following link http://www.greeklawdigest.gr/topics/aspects-of-greek-civil-law/item/217-surrogacy-proceedings-in-greece-after-the-implementation-of-law-4272-2014; Chortara et al. (2016).

[30]That had been the case for abortion, until the constitutional amendment in 2018. See Busatta and Reale (2018).

[31]A bill regulating assisted reproduction techniques is currently under debate before the Irish Parliament. The Assisted Human Reproduction Bill 2017 was drafted by the Irish Government in October 2017. The Bill provides a detailed discipline on assisted reproduction and regulates surrogacy, which will be permitted under certain circumstances. For an overview see McDonnell and Allison (2006).

the lives of patients in extremely dire conditions, but not able to restore a sufficient level of vital functions."[32]

The Irish decision cited shows one of the possible jurisdictional approaches towards the silence of the lawmaker: the judge simply registers the existence of a normative vacuum, stating that in the absence of a legal discipline it is not possible for a Court to recognise new rights. Nevertheless, judges recall the necessity and the social, moral and legal importance of a legislative intervention, in order to provide legal certainty and to give an answer to a (new and) existing social and scientific phenomenon.

A different and rather opposite jurisdictional reaction to a silent lawmaker consists in the decision to intervene. Here, two examples may serve to illustrate: one regards the dense judicial adjudication concerning the right to refuse medical treatments, on which English courts are working widely, whereas the second consists in Italian case law regarding advance decisions before law no. 219 of 2017 was enacted.

With regard to the first issue, in English law there is no legal rule concerning the individual right to refuse medical treatment, which is to be seen as an implication of the principle of informed consent. Nevertheless, for years,[33] Courts have widely recognised this right for individuals who claimed an unlawful interference on the part of the healthcare structure unwilling to withdraw a life sustaining treatment. Very recently, for example, while drawing up the distinction between a (denied) right to assisted suicide and the right to refuse, the Court of Appeal noted that "In withdrawal of treatment cases, such as Bland and Briggs, where the court is dealing with common law rights, that is the absolute right to refuse or terminate medical treatment even if it is necessary to keep a person alive, and Parliament has not intervened and is not proposing to intervene in relation to them, the court has had no option but to tackle difficult moral, ethical and social considerations in order to reach a decision."[34]

In other words, in such cases, the court recognises that an answer to the concrete case is required on the part of the judge. Therefore, either recognising or denying the existence of the right is part of the duty of the Court, especially when there is a lacuna in statutory sources.

---

[32]Italian Constitutional Court, ord. no. 207 of 2018, par. 8. The English translation is available on the dedicated section of the Constitutional Court's website: https://www.cortecostituzionale.it/documenti/download/doc/recent_judgments/S_207_2018_EN.pdf.

[33]See, for example, *re MB (Medical Treatment)* [1997] 2 FLR 426, at 432: "A mentally competent patient has an absolute right to refuse to consent to medical treatment for any reason, rational or irrational, or for no reason at all, even where that decision may lead to his or her own death", or the well-known case of Ms B, in which the trial judge stated that "I am therefore entirely satisfied that Ms B is competent to make all relevant decisions about her medical treatment including the decision whether to seek to withdraw from artificial ventilation.", *Ms B v An NHS Hospital Trust* [2002] EWHC 429 (Fam) (22nd March, 2002), at 95.

[34]*Conway, R (on the application of) v The Secretary of State for Justice & Ors* [2018] EWCA Civ 1431 (27 June 2018), paragraph 180.

The difference between this approach and the previous one resides in the legal implications of the concrete object of regulation. From a scientific viewpoint, surrogacy represents just one of the possible applications of assisted reproduction techniques, whereas from a legal and ethical perspective it requires a complex balancing of several legal positions and subjects (the intended parents, the surrogate, the newborn) and requires that the legal order tackle difficult issues that also involve an evolution in the definition of public policy.[35]

Differently, when dealing with the right to refuse medical treatment, the medical/technical element is more uncertain, because it strongly depends on the variability of the concrete case. In other words, the intrinsic variability of concrete cases in end of life issues does not offer one solid and definite solution at the medical and scientific level, thereby leading also to legal uncertainty. Hence, the pluralistic nature of the issue basically concerns the recognition of different desires and orientations among individuals in the same clinical situation. As a consequence, a uniform rule does not serve the purpose of recognising a pluralism of values, unless it recommends taking into account different moral values. An appropriate legal approach, in this particular field, leaves the decision open to the individuals involved, following due information on the clinical situation.

In short, when dealing with surrogacy the lawmaker has to balance several public and private interests (in particular, the certainty of family relationships and legal statuses) and a plurality of subjects (the intended parents, the donators, the newborn). On the contrary, with regard to the right to refuse medical treatment, the focus of the legal issue concerns the realisation of the patient's best interest and self-determination.

Extremely interestingly, in a recent decision, the UK Supreme Court stated that for the withdrawal of clinically assisted nutrition and hydration (CAHN), which are keeping a patient with a "prolonged disorder of consciousness" alive, judicial intervention is not required if clinicians and family members agree that this would be towards the patient's best interest.[36] This is a key point when tackling the nature of judicial reactions towards a "silent" legislature. In the specific case, there was no legal provision addressing the matter,[37] and UK courts have been widely involved in cases concerning the withdrawal of CAHN in such clinical circumstances.[38] The added value of this recent judgement concerns the recognition that courts are not necessarily the best subjects to decide upon an individual clinical situation, especially when there is no contrast between next of kin and clinicians. In this perspective, the silence of the lawmaker allows a balanced solution to be found which could

---

[35]Tomasi (2016), p. 83.

[36]An *NHS Trust and others (Respondents) v Y (by his litigation friend, the Official Solicitor) and another (Appellants)* [2018] UKSC 46.

[37]The Mental capacity Act 2005 did not provide for a clear rule in cases involving an unconscious patient with no outlook of improvement who had not expressed any advance decision concerning the withdrawal of CAHN.

[38]Wicks (2019) and Halliday et al. (2015).

better reconcile the clinical-scientific datum (no outlook of improvement, and appropriateness of medical treatment) with the axiological one (due consideration of the patient's previously expressed wishes and those of the people close to him or her).

The Court's approach in *Y* is very realistic as it recognises that judicial intervention necessarily implies time (par. 119) and other resources (par. 120) that it is not appropriate to spend when there is no disagreement on the decision to be taken and when the last moments of an individual existence are to be dealt with: "In a case where all the proper procedures have been observed and there is no doubt about what is in the best interests of the patient, there is much to be said for enabling the family and the patient to spend their last days together without the burden and distraction, and possibly expense, of court proceedings." (par. 121).

In other words, this approach shows that the silence of the lawmaker is not always problematic: in some circumstances and against a background of solid and shared general principles, it could serve the aim of realising moral pluralism in the wide variability of clinical concrete situations better than a detailed and up-to-date legislation. Facing this intended and pluralistic silence, Courts as well should refrain from adding unnecessary complexity: the *Y* decision serves as a good example of a judicial check on the adequacy of a normative discipline that does not trap individuals and institutions into schemes which are too rigid and allows them to act in compliance with their values. In these circumstances a normative silence is rather more similar to an integrative approach than to a guilty or unconscious abstention.

5 The Integrative Model

These considerations bring us at last to tackle the integrative legislative approach towards an ethically controversial matter. In this model, the legal framework allows for the reconciliation, in the same legal discipline, of the pluralism of values that naturally characterises contemporary societies with the medico-scientific datum. This is not an easy task if we consider that, when dealing with biolaw issues, the variability of moral values and the natural evolution of social needs is boosted by the rapid progress of the medical sciences.

To this regard, it has been pointed out that, in order to be properly integrative, biolaw should be "open to both science and ethics, updated and attentive".[39] This means that the lawmaker should adequately address all emerging social and ethical needs and correctly merge them with the possibilities offered by the medical sciences.[40] Moreover, to properly keep pace with scientific development and social changes, legislature should be up-to-date, which means that, hopefully or probably,

[39]Casonato (2017), p. 86.

[40]Among other definitions of pluralism, there is one that particularly fits the purposes of this integrative model, that is: "Pluralism is thus a normative framework for an ordered plurality,

the legal regulation of medical sciences and access to new biotechnological treatments should undergo periodic revisions and amendments.[41] Lastly, an attentive biolaw has been defined as a legislative datum paying "particular attention to the specific characteristics of individual cases".[42] The inherent variability of concrete cases, in other words, must be given due consideration and should have its place within the abstract and general rule.

Even in those (rare) cases in which all these features are satisfied, the integrative approach adopted by the lawmaker could be challenged in court.

Even if different moral values do obtain (at least formally) legislative recognition and although the law appears to be in line with scientific development, the judiciary might be called to respond to new social needs or to the request to give recognition to new rights or new individual positions. In this regard, we can discern different reactions of the jurisdiction to those claims, depending on the kind of axiological position requiring acknowledgement and on the certainty of the scientific datum in question.

5.1 An Integrative Approach Lacking Effectiveness

It could happen that the courts are called to intervene in order to ascertain that the conceptual recognition of axiological pluralism is applied effectively. In this hypothesis, the problem does not directly concern the legislative datum considered *per se*, but rather its interpretation or implementation.

A clear example of this model and of the possible reactions of the judiciary can be seen in the Italian discipline on abortion. Law no. 194 of 1978 was approved after several years of intense debate in a context in which guaranteeing reproductive rights was at the centre of the political agenda in many western states.[43] The compromising approach chosen by the Italian lawmaker, over forty years of law enforcement, attempted to integrate the different ethical feelings of Italian society. Under the law, abortion is accessible as a medical treatment in public healthcare structures within the first 90 days of pregnancy for a wide range of reasons; after that moment, interruption of pregnancy is possible only under limited circumstances related to a serious threat to the health of the mother, which might also be linked to foetal suffering or malformities. First trimester abortion is accessible only in public healthcare institutions following a specific procedure that includes a first meeting

which stands for the right to be different and to do things one's own way in recognition of equal human dignity". Avbelj (2018), p. 107.

[41] For example, the Canadian Assisted Human Reproduction Act 2004, which has to be reviewed by Parliament every three years, or the French Lois de Bioéthique, which have to be reviewed every seven years, by means of participative and deliberative democracy.

[42] Casonato (2017), p. 93.

[43] For an overview on the legal recognition of reproductive rights see Cook et al. (2003).

between the woman and a gynaecologist, a period of seven days in which the woman is required to duly consider her choice after having received all the information, and the medical procedure itself. The law also provides for the possibility of a conscientious objection to be raised on the part of physicians.

This general framework seems to be able to accommodate all different axiological perspectives: that of the woman who wants to interrupt her pregnancy, and the conflicting moral values of the physician. Across the four decades of legislative implementation, the legitimacy of some provisions of the law has been challenged before the Constitutional Court, which always rejected the claims, thereby confirming the constitutional legitimacy of the law.[44]

Nevertheless, a deeper look at the implementation of the law reveals some discrepancies between an apparently pluralistic normative datum and the effective recognition of moral values and individual rights. In particular, across the years, the percentage of conscientious objection among physicians has significantly increased (70% in 2017, with a maximum of 80% in some regions) and this phenomenon has been indicated as a possible risk of an inappropriate implementation of the law. In particular, it has been argued that the lack of adequate intervention by the health administration in order to make the service effectively available in all healthcare structures places an undue burden both on women seeking a safe and timely abortion and on non-objecting gynaecologists.[45]

This example shows that, in some cases, a law which is widely considered as integrative, open to different axiological positions and appropriate from a medico-scientific viewpoint might nevertheless be lacking in effectiveness. This means that when applied, it presents some difficulties in granting the level of protection it promises to all subjects involved. In the particular case of the Italian law on abortion, the problem is caused by inadequate management of two conflicting positions which are difficult to balance.

5.2 *If It Is Scientifically Possible, Then Do It!*

Another possibility is the increasing legal relevance of new axiological perspectives, which is connected to the claim for recognition of new rights or legal positions.

A significant example of this interaction between individual claims, science and the legal approach is shown by recent jurisdictional developments concerning national laws on transsexualism. In the long-awaited decision on the case of *A.P., Garçon and Nicot v. France* (6th April 2017), the European Court of Human Rights

[44]For example, Italian Constitutional Court, decisions no. 35/1997, nos. 109/1981, 162/1981.

[45]See also the decision by the European Committee of Social Rights, complaint no. 91/2013, published on 11th April 2016, in which the Committee found Italy in violation of the European Social Charter with regard to the lack of effectiveness in the application of the law on abortion. The high percentage of conscientious objection among health personnel should be properly addressed by the Italian health administration, locally and at a national level.

ruled that the requirement of compulsory sterilizing surgery or treatment for legal gender recognition provided for by French law violated Article 8 of the Convention.[46]

Referring to the previous case law on sterilisation, the Court observed that "since sterilisation concerns an essential human bodily function, it has implications for multiple aspects of individuals' integrity, including their physical and mental well-being and their emotional, spiritual and family life. [...] while it may be performed legitimately at the request of the person concerned [...] the situation is different where it is imposed on a mentally competent adult patient without his or her consent" (par 128).

Interestingly enough, the Court did not rely excessively on the scientific datum, highlighting the lack of a wide consensus within the member States of the Council of Europe on the necessity of irreversible reassignment surgery. The possibility of obtaining a change in appearance through hormone therapy is indirectly considered to be a sufficient result to permit reassignment of civil status without obliging a competent adult to undergo a medical treatment that would definitely cause a physical impairment without his or her consent. A similar approach was recently also undertaken by the Italian Constitutional Court in a decision concerning the same issue: with regard to the Italian legal framework, though, the Court acknowledged that the legislative text was broad enough to also include the position of those who require civil status reassignment without surgery.[47]

This way, these legal positions (i.e. the acknowledgement of the legal relevance of gender reassignment without irreversible surgery) find a place in the legal order, thanks to the combination between axiological pluralism and the new chances offered by technological development. Here, the medico-scientific datum is important both for the lawmaker and the judge because it represents the factual basis on which to allow the inclusion of the new moral position within the legal order. In other words, as from a scientific viewpoint the position claimed is not only medically possible but also scientifically appropriate and feasible, then an integrative legal framework should give it due consideration.

---

[46]Case of *A.P., Garçon and Nicot v. France*, appl. nos. 79885/12, 52471/13 and 52596/13, 6th April 2017, paragraph 132: "The Court fully accepts that safeguarding the principle of the inalienability of civil status, ensuring the reliability and consistency of civil-status records and, more generally, ensuring legal certainty, are in the general interest. However, it notes that, on the basis of this interpretation of the general interest, French positive law as it stood at the material time presented transgender persons not wishing to undergo full gender reassignment with an impossible dilemma. Either they underwent sterilisation surgery or treatment – or surgery or treatment very likely to result in sterilisation – against their wishes, thereby relinquishing full exercise of their right to respect for their physical integrity, which forms part of the right to respect for private life under Article 8 of the Convention; or they waived recognition of their gender identity and hence full exercise of that same right. In the Court's view, this amounted to disrupting the fair balance which the Contracting Parties are required to maintain between the general interest and the interests of the persons concerned."

[47]Italian Const. Ct., Decisions nos. 221/2015 and 180/2017.

5.3 A Scientific Evolution That Brings More Inclusion

A third hypothesis consists in scientific evolution *vis-à-vis* integrative regulation. In this case, the progress of medical sciences suggests new possibilities or obtains the necessary level of certainty that allows for the inclusion of individual pleas which could not find recognition before, due to the uncertainty of the scientific datum.

A good example of this mechanism and reaction is given by the significant evolution that medical research on AIDS and the HIV virus has gone through in the last decades and in the greater awareness that the scientific community has of this illness and the mechanisms to control its spreading.

Within this context, the CJEU was called to take into consideration the permanent ban on blood donation for men who had had sexual intercourse with other men. This prohibition was originally widely enforced by national legislations in order to prevent the spread of the HIV virus. On this subject, the CJEU had to verify whether such prohibition was compatible with the EU Directive on the safety of blood and whether such a decision respected the principle of proportionality. After an in-depth analysis of the scientific prerequisite to the legislative decision, the Court concluded that it is a matter for the national judge to ascertain whether such prohibition is compliant with the current level of scientific development in this area, or if a temporary suspension from blood donation (i.e. for a 'window period' after the risky behaviour) should be more proportionate. The permanent prohibition shall be considered lawful only if "there are no less onerous methods of ensuring a high level of health protection for recipients", in the event that "with the current state of scientific knowledge" there is no technique for detecting HIV in order to avoid transmission to recipients.[48]

This example shows that scientific progress could help to find a legal solution which incorporates in a better way the interests of all subjects involved (here: blood donors and recipients).

5.4 Against a Falsely Integrative Model

A fourth hypothesis, which deserves due consideration, given its importance in current biolaw, highlights the risks created by a falsely integrative model.

Contemporary societies are more and more pluralistic, from a cultural, religious and behavioural viewpoint. This means that the legal order should integrate differences, should guarantee due protection to minorities (especially against the dangers of a 'tyranny of the majority'), and should try to identify a way to accommodate differences within a sustainable equilibrium between different needs, duties and rights.

[48] C-528/13, *Léger*, 29 April 2015, ECLI:EU:C:2015:288, paras. 63–65.

As we have already seen, this is not an easy task and is even more complicated when axiological pluralisms intersect biolaw, a field in which the lawmaker has to reconcile moral positions with due consideration for the scientific datum.

In this sense, integrative pluralism does not mean that *any* moral position shall find legal recognition: the lawmaker, as well as the judge, has to evaluate and balance individual needs with the general interests and principles upon which the legal order is founded. In the specific field of biolaw, this balance is even more complicated, as the extra-juridical element represented by the medico-scientific datum plays a key role in legal decisions. In other words, as we have seen, if a specific treatment or action is *scientifically* possible, then the lawmaker can evaluate whether it could be integrated within the legal order. This is a matter of legislative discretion that has some limits (as noted with reference to the repressive model) but that is also itself limited by the scientific affordability and sustainability of a given choice.

The problematic case of vaccinations and the freedom of choice demanded (that is, freedom not to vaccinate) serves as a good example of the risks connected to a falsely integrative model.[49] The claim for the freedom to choose whether to vaccinate or not has proven to be medically dangerous, as it brought to a sharp decrease in the level of protection of the population, with the danger of losing 'herd immunity', the threshold required to grant immunity also to those who cannot be vaccinated for medical reasons.

This example clearly shows that, even within a democratic, plural and integrative society, not every individual position can impose itself upon the others, by claiming recognition. This would lead to the unsustainability of the general order and the oppression of other legally relevant individual positions.[50]

6 Conclusions: In Search of Sustainable Pluralism

The proposed categorisation has highlighted how, in the specific field of biolaw, the accommodation of axiological pluralisms with respect for the scientific datum is not an easy task both for the lawmaker and the judge. The three models proposed have also shown that no decision is ever definitive: even the best one could always be subject to revision or to updating, in the first place due to the continuous development of life sciences.[51]

In particular, a central element that, in the field of biolaw, emerges from the proposed categorisation concerns the object of the study: when law crosses life sciences and ethically controversial issues (i.e. beginning or end-of-life issues,

[49]On this subject see *infra* the contribution by Tomasi in this volume.

[50]To this regard: "[. . .] excessive plurality or radical pluralism can pose a threat to the stability of a society [. . .]", Reber (2017), XXVII.

[51]Casonato (2017), p. 90.

healthcare protection and promotion, etc.), legal problems overcome their strictly state dimension. The concrete object of the legal dispute, in these cases, opens the field to particularly effective comparison, even between apparently distant legal systems. Therefore, it may happen that the comparison can show unexpected similarities between civil law and common law systems; on the contrary, the comparison could underline a significant difference in the solutions adopted by states that have for a long time shared the same legal tradition. Moreover, as shown by the examples offered in this contribution, a given legal system can, at the same time, present the characteristics of different models, depending on the subject of regulation.

This variability may depend on numerous factors, such as, for example, the historical moment in which a certain discipline was adopted, the level of social conflict existing within the legal system at a given time, the current political scenario, the impact of the debate on public opinion or the coincidental occurrence of a particular episode that urged the legislative or jurisdictional intervention.

In this complex context, the lawmaker definitely has a difficult task: accommodating axiological diversities must necessarily be done, inter alia, respecting the scientific sustainability of the normative choice. In this sense, the level of legislative discretion (and, therefore, of the democratic exercise of legislative power) is highly influenced by a non-legal element, which consists in the progress of the medical sciences.

At the same time, the jurisdiction too must exercise its delicate role by carefully balancing all interests involved. The fact that the jurisdiction is *per se* called to give an answer to individual claims presents an intrinsic risk which consists in giving a response to the concrete case and opening up, at the same time, to new similar pleas or creating new rights. This could lead to an increase in the fragility of the difficult equilibrium that characterises the crossroads between law, life sciences and moral values.

On these premises, extra-juridical platforms for deliberation or information (such as technical bodies, independent authorities, ethics committees or even expert auditions before parliaments and courts) acquire a very important role, capable of guiding the decision-making process at a legislative level and also the jurisdictional decision.[52]

The models proposed present a margin of approximation, as they are basically aimed at offering an orientation on the type of legislative regulation of life sciences and on the corresponding reaction of the jurisdiction faced with individual claims in opposition to these normative solutions. Nevertheless, the categorisation shows and confirms the intrinsic nature of the legal order, which is called both to accommodate diversities and to shape the basic aims and the extent of state powers, pointing out the direction that the order as a whole shall pursue.

[52]On this matter see also the contribution by Penasa in this volume.

References

Avbelj M (2018) Human dignity and EU legal pluralism. In: Davies G, Avbelj M (eds) Legal pluralism and EU law. Elgar, Glos, pp 95–110
Bin R, Lorenzon S, Lucchi N (eds) (2012) Biotech innovations and fundamental rights. Springer, Milan
Busatta L, Reale CM (2018) The Celtic Tiger al referendum: l'Irlanda verso una nuova stagione di tutela costituzionale dei diritti? Diritto pubblico comparato ed europeo 4:1223–1242
Casonato C (2011) Informed consent and end-of-life decisions: notes of comparative law. Maastricht J Eur Comp Law 18(3):225–256
Casonato C (2017) 21st century biolaw: a proposal. BioLaw J 1:81–95
Cecchi R, Masotti V, Meo AU, Rinaldi R (2017) The law on artificial insemination: an Italian anomaly. Acta Biomed 88(4):403–408
Chortara T, Penasa S, Busatta L (2016) The best interests of the child born via cross-border surrogacy. A comparison between Greece and Italy. BioLaw J 1:189–210
Cook RJ, Dickens BM, Fathalla MF (2003) Reproductive health and human rights: integrating medicine, ethics, and law. Clarendon Press, Oxford
Davis J, Finlay I (2015) Would judicial consent for assisted dying protect vulnerable people? BMJ 351:h4437
Dyer C (2015) MPs will debate assisted dying bill in September. BMJ 350:h3187
Eberle EJ (2009) The method and role of comparative law. Wash Univ Global Stud Law Rev 8:451
Glenn HP (2010) Legal traditions of the world, IVth edn. Oxford University Press, Oxford
Halliday S, Formby A, Cookson R (2015) An assessment of the Court's role in the withdrawal of clinically assisted nutrition and hydration from patients in the permanent vegetative state. Med Law Rev 23(4):556–587
Hobson CA (2018) Assisted dying challenges: dynamic and stasis in the UK courts: Conway v. Secretary of State for Justice. Med Law Int 18(4):256 270
Holm S (2015) The debate about physician assistance in dying: 40 years of unrivalled progress in medical ethics? JME 41(1):40–43
Husa J (2006) Methodology of comparative law today: from paradoxes to flexibility? Revue internationale de droit comparé 58(4):1095
Lecaros JA (2019) Biolaw and bioethics: convergences and divergences. In: Valdés E, Lecaros J (eds) Biolaw and policy in the twenty-first century. International library of ethics, law, and the new medicine. Springer, Cham, pp 93–118
McDonnell O, Allison J (2006) From biopolitics to bioethics: church, state, medicine and assisted reproductive technology in Ireland. Sociol Health Illness 28(6):817–837
McMorrow T (2019) Voluntary Euthanasia, assisted suicide & law reform: a sketch of the Canadian experience. BioLaw J 1:267–282
Mitchell B (2014) Constitutional equality law after Fleming v Ireland. Dublin Univ Law J 37:252
Monateri PG (ed) (2012) Methods of comparative law. Elgar, Cheltenham
Reber B (2017) Precautionary principle, pluralism and deliberation: science and ethics. Wiley-ISTE
Scheffer T (2018) Commentary: toward a trans-sequential analysis of plural legal orders: some thoughts on "states of uncertainty". J Leg Pluralism Unofficial Law 50(3):330–335
Stefanelli S (2019) Biological mother. In: Bartolini A, Cippitani R, Colcelli V (eds) Dictionary of statuses within EU law. Springer, Cham, pp 65–70

Tie W (1999) Legal pluralism. Ashgate, Aldershot

Tomasi M (2016) Towards an emerging notion of European ordre public: a comment on the case-law about international surrogacy in Europe. In: Toniatti R, Strazzari D (eds) Legal pluralism in Europe and the ordre public exception: normative and judicial perspectives. Università degli Studi di Trento, Trento, pp 83–105

Toniatti R (1995) Minorities and protected minorities: constitutional models compared. In: Dunne M, Bonazzi T (eds) Citizenship and rights in multicultural societies. Keele University Press, Keele, p 195

Wicks E (2019) An NHS Trust and others v Y and another [2018] UKSC 46: reducing the role of the courts in treatment withdrawal. Med Law Rev 27(2):330–338

Some Patterns for "Scientific Adjudication": The Role of Courts in Reconciling Axiological Pluralism and Scientific Complexity

Simone Penasa

Abstract The aim of the article is to provide a rationalisation of different approaches that courts, especially those possessing constitutional review functions, commonly develop when facing scientifically complex issues. In the light of this, the impact of scientific complexity will be particularly weighted, particularly focussing on how the latter can influence the axiological assessment made by courts and how it shapes the entire attitude of courts, especially in the light of guaranteeing the margin of appreciation of legislatures. In the light of this, the analysis will start by focusing on the approach taken by the European Court of Human Rights (ECtHR); subsequently it will shift to the national level by analysing cases resulting from three contexts where scientific complexity and axiological pluralism achieve the highest level of relevance and interconnection: assisted reproductive technologies (ARTs), surrogacy and end of life decisions.

1 "Scientific Adjudication": Courts as 'Mediator' Between Scientific Complexity and Ethical Sensitiveness as a Coherent Expression of Constitutional Pluralism

Together with political decision-makers, courts also are increasingly facing questions arising from the intertwining of scientific and technological evolution of healthcare and the new social demands which it stimulates and augments. Courts are always more implicated in the confrontation between science, society and law.[1] The paper aims at understanding and systematising the different approaches that courts may undertake when are called upon to assess political choices made by legislatures in the biomedical field. The general starting point is twofold: on the one hand, from a 'rights-oriented' perspective, it recognises the role of courts in the

[1]Montgomery et al. (2014), pp. 343–378.

S. Penasa (✉)
University of Trento, Trento, Italy
e-mail: simone.penasa@unitn.it

L. Busatta, C. Casonato (eds.), *Axiological Pluralism*, Ius Gentium: Comparative Perspectives on Law and Justice 92, https://doi.org/10.1007/978-3-030-78475-1_3

biomedical field, as one of the legal tools which can contribute to define the balance of rights; on the other hand, from an 'institutionally-based' perspective, the relationship between political decision-makers and courts is meant to be viewed from the perspective of cooperation rather than antagonism between legal actors.

Therefore, courts must be considered an essential co-author within the regulatory enterprise[2] in the field of biomedicine. Additionally, courts seem to be suitable sites for avoiding, or at least reducing, what has been defined the "regulatory disconnection"[3] between regulatory tools and regulatory target. Recently, "connection" has been defined as "both maintaining a fit between the content of the regulatory standards and the evolving form and function of a technology, and the appropriate adaptation of existing doctrines or institutions, particularly where technologies might be deployed in ways that enhance existing legal or regulatory capacities".[4]

According to Brownsword, "where the law is no longer fully connected to the technology, judicial interpreters, too, face a choice: either, they can interpret and apply the law as declared on the face of the legislation; or, they can seek to reconnect the law to the technology by adopting a creative approach".[5] This enterprise, according to Brownsword, is not "unproblematic", as both choices—to stay tuned to the letter of the law or to retuning the law through a purposive interpretation—risk affecting core legal values, such as the principles of equality, coherence and certainty of the law.[6]

In order to reduce the risks highlighted above and assuming that the proactive role of courts is in line with the essential goal of ensuring coherence between regulatory tools and regulatory targets, the centrality of the constitutional dimension will be strengthened. By directly linking the role of courts with the constitutional context, an "intelligent purposive interpretation" will be more easily achievable.[7]

It is therefore not only a matter of outdated or incomplete laws, but also illegitimate political choices, when evaluated from the perspective of their congruence with the scientific context on which they are intended to bear. Evidently, the role of courts, which is strictly linked with implemented methods and arguments, is not boundless. As a matter of fact, it is necessary to keep together the 'rights-oriented' and the 'institutional-based' perspectives: the exercise of judicial functions—from granting a remedy to assessing political choices in the light of constitutional principles—must also be sustainable in the light of the principle of separation of powers. It is proposed here that by referring the functions of courts and legislatures to constitutional principles, the risk of conflict will be reduced. The role of courts must be

[2]Bennet Moses (2017), p. 575, stating that "the increased popularity of the term 'regulation' compared to 'law' reflects an enhanced awareness of the variety of sources and forms of powers in modern society".

[3]See Brownsword and Goodwin (2012), p. 63.

[4]Brownsword et al. (2017), p. 11.

[5]Brownsword (2008), p. 160.

[6]Ib.

[7]Ivi, 183–184.

weighed in the light of their commitment to constitutional goals, from the perspective of a theory of powers according to which parliaments are no longer the exclusive "owners" of law; by assuming the centrality of the Constitution, both actors become co-producers of rules, in the light of the common objective of the most effective achievement of constitutional goals.

A distinctive element of the regulation of biomedicine is represented by the twofold nature of scientific and technological data: they can be considered both as a regulatory target and a regulatory tool.[8] From the perspective of the role of courts, scientific data can act as the subject-matter of the case to be decided, but also—especially in the context of constitutional adjudication—as a parameter which courts may take into account. The role specifically played by the scientific dimension within the judicial momentum will constitute an essential variable which will guide the following comparative analysis. One of the hypotheses of the paper is that the approach to scientific data taken by courts when dealing with cases which feature a high level of scientific complexity becomes decisive in determining their attitude to assessing political choices towards a more deferential or proactive approach. In the following sections, a comparative survey of some courts' attitude to 'scientific adjudication' will be conducted. The essential objective is to provide a rationalisation of different approaches that courts, especially those possessing constitutional review functions, commonly develop when facing scientifically complex issues. In the light of this, the impact of scientific complexity will be particularly weighted: how the latter influences the axiological assessment made by courts and how it shapes the entire attitude of courts, especially in the light of guaranteeing an appropriate space for the margin of appreciation of legislatures.

Thus, the analysis will start by focussing on the approach taken by the European Court of Human Rights (ECtHR); subsequently it will shift to the national level by analysing cases resulting from three contexts where scientific complexity and axiological pluralism achieve the highest level of relevance and interconnection: assisted reproductive technologies (ARTs), surrogacy and end of life decisions.

2 ECtHR Case-Law: Axiological Prevalence vis à vis States' Margin of Appreciation

In the ECHR context, scientific complexity and the ethical sensitivity of issues at stake represent often key variables within the case-law of the ECtHR.[9] Once the Court considers that the case involves "choices of social strategy" or the need to determine the "exact content of the requirements of morals in their countries", it thus

[8]See Brownsword and Goodwin (2012), cit.; Rodotà (2006), p. 140, that considers facts not only as something to control, but which can also become a means for the decision-making process.

[9]See Murphy and Ó Cuinn (2010), p. 601 ff.; Ashcroft (2013), p. 310.

acknowledges that national authorities have a broad margin of appreciation, as "the authorities' direct knowledge of their society and its needs means that they are in principle better placed than the international judge to appreciate what is in the public interest".[10] The scientific nature of the issues at stake emphasises the Court's approach: accordingly, when cases are characterised by "sensitive moral and ethical issues against a background of fast-moving medical and scientific developments", the margin of appreciation is usually wider.[11] Thus, scientific and axiological complexity induces an attitude of self-restraint, which finds its rationale in the fact that—according to the Court—confronting issues which raise sensitive moral and ethical questions in an area that is constantly evolving in scientific and social terms, it is not Court's task "to substitute its own judgment for that of the national authorities in choosing the most appropriate regulations".[12]

It does not mean that the assessment of the balance struck by national decision-makers is completely excluded. However, it will be determined by a strong presumption of compatibility, even if the Court affirms the expediency of carrying out a careful examination of the arguments taken into consideration during the legislative process.[13]This trend is clearly detectable with regard to both beginning of life and end of life issues. In *Lambert*, the Grand Chamber stated that "in this sphere concerning the end of life, as in that concerning the beginning of life, States must be afforded a margin of appreciation (...)", even if this margin is not "unlimited".[14] Accordingly, in *Lambert*, the Court's scrutiny was limited exclusively to the assessment of procedural guarantees afforded by French law and Court abstained from pronouncing on the balance of interests at stake.[15]

Accordingly, the Court will affirm incompatibility only when national legislation is evidently disproportionate or incoherent, such as happened—in the context of ARTs—in *Dickson* and *Costa and Pavan*. In both cases, although it recognises the existence of a wide margin of appreciation for national authorities, as the issues at stake involve "choice of social strategy",[16] the Court makes a thorough assessment. On the one hand—in *Dickson*—by assuming that the regulation which limits the access to ARTs for detained individuals did not allow a balancing of the competing individual and public interests,[17] due to the lack of any evaluation within the

[10]Among other judgments, see A., B. and C. v Ireland, GC, 16 December 2010, § 223. Recently on ECtHR's case-law on ARTs, Murphy (2017), p. 964 ff.

[11]Evans v UK, GC, 10 April 2007, § 62.

[12]Parrillo v Italy, GC, 27 August 2015, § 173; see also Hristoz and Others v Bulgaria, 2012, § 125; Durisotto v Italy, 2014, § 40. On the ECtHR's case-law on ARTs, see Poli (2017), pp. 1–18.

[13]S. H. and Others v Austria, GC, 3 November 2011, § 97.

[14]Lambert and Others v France, GC, 5 June 2015, § 148–149.

[15]Sartori (2018), pp. 23–43.

[16]Dickson v UK, GC, 4 December 2007, where "the Court would generally respect the legislatures policy choices unless it is manifestly without reasonable foundation", § 78; Costa and Pavan v Italy, 28 August 2012, "While acknowledging that the question of access to PGD raises sensitive moral and ethical questions", § 68.

[17]Dickson v UK, § 82.

decision-making process aiming to "assess the proportionality of the restriction";[18] on the other hand—*Costa and Pavan*—by declaring the incoherence of the ban on the access to PGD when compared to the regulated access to a similar diagnostic tool (prenatal diagnosis in the context of abortion).[19]

The Court can also assess the compatibility of national legislation on the ground of the characteristics of the law-making process.[20] The Court seems to require that the wide margin of appreciation afforded to States be exercised through decision-making procedures able to guarantee the adequate representation and inclusion of both social and ethical pluralism and scientific and technological development. Therefore, if it is indisputable that national authorities—and within them, the legislature[21]—are in principle better placed to appreciate what is in the public interest, national decision-makers must give evidence that political choices in scientifically relevant and ethically sensitive fields have been taken through a reliable and inclusive decision-making process.

Since *Evans*, the Court has become accustomed to carrying out an in-depth assessment of the national law-making process: the fulfilment of procedural requirements goes to strengthen the presumption of compatibility of national laws (*S.H.*, *Parrillo*). It occurred in *Evans*, where the Court stated that the legislation (in the specific case, the UK 1990 HFE Act) was "the culmination of an exceptionally detailed examination of the social, ethical and legal implications of developments in the field of human fertilisation and embryology";[22] and in *Parrillo*, where the Court declared the compatibility with art. 8 ECHR of the absolute ban on donating surplus embryos for research purposes in Italian legislation including on the ground that "the drafting of the Law had given rise to discussions that had taken account of the different scientific and ethical opinions and questions on the subjects".[23]

Therefore, as also underlined in an obiter dictum of the Grand chamber's *S.H. v Austria* judgment, national authorities must perform a "thorough assessment" of rules governing medical or technological issues at stake, taking into account the dynamic developments in science and society.[24] Accordingly, those areas, "(...) in which the law appears to be continuously evolving and which is subject to a particularly dynamic development in science and law, need to be kept under review by the Contracting States".[25]Thus, according to the Court, procedural variables must

[18]Ivi, § 83.

[19]Costa and Pavan v Italy.

[20]Hatton and Others v UK, GC, 8 July 2003. On procedural review made by the ECtHR, see Popelier (2013a), pp. 230–262, in particular 253; Id. (2012), p. 275 ff.; Saul (2015), pp. 745–774.

[21]See Nicklinson and Lamb v UK, 23 June 2015, § 84.

[22]Saul (2015), p. 763.

[23]§ 184; "during the drafting process of the Law in question the legislature had already taken account of the different interests at stake, particularly the State's interest in protecting the embryo and that of persons concerned in exercising their right to individual self-determination in the form of donating their embryos to research", § 188.

[24]Parrillo v Italy, § 170.

[25]S.H. v Austria, GC, § 118.

be taken into account as well, when assessing how national authorities have balanced competing interests, in contexts characterised by axiological pluralism and scientific complexity. In the light of the general goal to guarantee the connection between regulatory tools and regulatory target, the fulfilment of procedural requirements can also contribute to increasing the level of responsiveness and flexibility of laws.[26] Nonetheless, it must be underlined that the Court has never declared the incompatibility with ECHR on this ground, even when it expressly states the Parliaments' failure to satisfy procedural requirements (*S.H. and Others v Austria*, GC); on the contrary, this parameter, when implemented, generally reinforces the Court's tendency to declare the compatibility (*Evans, Parrillo*).

3 National Courts Assessing Political Choices: Constitutional Principles as the Golden Thread Running Through Scientific Adjudication

The scientific nature of the issues tackled represents a variable which may influence the traditional methods and reasoning implemented by courts, especially when the latter are endowed with a constitutional adjudication function. Scientific knowledge and technological advancement are, in this context, to be taken as meaning not only a 'target' of laws subject to constitutional adjudication, but also as a 'tool' for courts. This trend is clearly detectable from the analysis of comparative constitutional adjudication, which will be the subject of the following sections.

The theoretical grounds on which the analysis will be based must be clarified: the compatibility between science and technology, on the one hand, and law, on the other. Their relationship cannot be understood in terms of dominance but more properly in terms of co-existence, where constitutional principles, by expressing a high level of axiological pluralism, act as legitimising factor. Science can thus act as triggering factor for regulatory innovation. From the latter perspective, science can be considered a constitutional tool: it becomes a decisive factor for legal renewal[27] and it has been significantly defined as the "driving force" for constitutional interpretation.[28] Within Italian legal scholarship, the constitution is also interpreted as the result of scientific innovation.[29] Constitutional and scientific factors are linked together and they influence each other reciprocally: in order for scientific knowledge to be functional with regard to constitutional innovation, it must be coherent and

[26] According to Murphy and Ó Cuinn (2013), p. 305, "good law is also regularly reviewed law; it is a law that is subject to 'thorough assessment', 'taking into account the dynamic developments in science and society'". The Authors expressly refer to the ECtHR case-law.

[27] D'Amico (2005), p. 261.

[28] Veronesi (2011), p. 138.

[29] D'Amico (2005), p. 262.

consistent with constitutional values, which can find at the same time concrete and dynamic implementation also through the "scientific channel".

It perfectly fits the idea of bioconstitutionalism, according to which "periods of significant change in the life sciences and technologies should be seen as constitutional or, more precisely, bioconstitutional in their consequences".[30] Jasanoff refers to the concept of interoperability of biological knowledge and constitutional norms,[31] where their dynamic interaction allows "a fine-tuned specification of existing principles to deal with new contingencies".[32] If we accept this approach, we must reject the separatist tendency which tends to characterise the traditional understanding of law-science relationship,[33] while acknowledging the idea of "interactional coproduction" between law and life sciences.[34] In legal terms, coproduction means the awareness of regulatory context is necessary for the understanding of science and science becomes source of many normative changes.[35]

Courts also take part in this co-productive enterprise. As a matter of fact, courts are always more on the front-line in setting the pace of the regulatory commitment to the biomedical field. The function of the courts is amplified within the biomedical context, where the conjunction between ethical sensitiveness and scientific complexity seems to reduce statutory law, especially when inadequately designed, to an auxiliary source. Technological advancement (in terms of innovations available for medical purposes) and social evolution (in terms of new demands in the field of procreation, family, autonomy) require the capacity of regulatory tools to constantly, promptly and efficiently adapt themselves and be responsive:[36] courts, due to their functions, are becoming the privileged interlocutor of individuals who ask the law to metabolise technological innovation acting as a renewed context of the exercise of individual rights.

Therefore, courts may be viewed as a normative transformer between axiological pluralism arising from the societal and scientific complexity which derive from technological advancement in the field of biomedicine. Thus, courts can be defined "sub-political sites",[37] as under the concomitant pressure of individuals and interest groups they are "increasingly called upon not only to uphold citizens' basic rights, but also to 'flesh out' the meaning of the fundamental freedoms they are designed to protect":[38] it has been said that "courts are sites of a political process that exists independently of parliament".[39]

---

[30] Jasanoff (2011), p. 3.

[31] Ivi, 4.

[32] Ivi, 9.

[33] Ivi, 13.

[34] Ivi, 15.

[35] Rodotà and Tallacchini (2010), LI.

[36] Casonato (2017), pp. 81–95.

[37] Veitch (2007), p. 49, that refers to U. Beck.

[38] Ivi, 48.

[39] Ib.

As anticipated, the role of courts as regulatory actors can be regarded as physiological as far as it remains within the exercise of judicial power consistent with constitutional principles: the legislature and courts share the common function to implement effectively constitutional values in times of biomedical change. They both take part in the progressive and dynamic definition of "bioconstitutional settlements", which "(...) cannot be fixed once and for all in the form of rigid principles of decision rules".[40]

Inevitably, the co-productive role of courts may raise concerns with regard to the identification of more legitimated institutional subjects to strike a balance and the intense scrutiny of specific cases which courts are allowed to perform in assessing Parliament's political choices. In the following sections, a systematisation of different approaches that courts endowed with a judicial review function can enact will be proposed: in line with the theoretical grounds defined above, the *fil rouge* is to understand how science interacts with the axiological dimension within the constitutional adjudication, in the view of testing the role of courts in guaranteeing the sustainability of the normative co-productive process between law and science.

4 Science Integrates the Axiological Dimension: Tool for Managing Axiological Pluralism

The analysis will now follow a path led by the idea of a connection between scientific, axiological and constitutional dimensions: thus, whether the scientific nature of the issues at stake plays a role within the judicial review performed by competent constitutional courts, in terms of their attitude towards political choices made by legislatures—self-restraint *vis à vis* activism—and the intensity and scope of scrutiny will be evaluated. Some main categories have been identified in those cases where the scientific dimension helps to integrate the axiological one and can accordingly become an independent parameter for assessing political choices, on the one hand; and in those cases in which science represents the context where axiological pluralism finds expression, but it does not directly play an active role within judicial review, on the other.

[40]The concept is proposed by Jasanoff and Meltzer (2018), p. 5. It seems to recall the concept of "incompletely theorized agreements" in Sunstein (2001).

4.1 *Science as a Tool for Constitutional Interpretation: The Case of the "Unborn Child" and the Supreme Court of Ireland*

Scientific evidence can have direct access to judicial review when courts decide to refer to scientific criteria or standards in their reasoning. It may happen when courts make use of it in order to clarify the actual scope of application of a constitutional provision which expressly refer to non-legal concepts. The Supreme Court of Ireland in *Roche v Roche*,[41] asked to assess whether the protection of the "right to life of the unborn" guaranteed by section 40.3.3 of the Irish Constitution was applicable also to in vitro embryos, took this approach. The Supreme Court recalls the absence of a consensus within the scientific community on when life begins. On the one hand, the Supreme Court adheres to an approach which is shared among other jurisdictions (ECtHR), according to which "absent a broad consensus or understanding on that truth, it is for legislatures in the exercise of their dispositive powers to resolve such issues on the basis of policy choices".[42] On the other hand, the Court traces a distinction between the legislature's exclusively reserved political choices, and the Court's function "to interpret the Constitution and to make a legal decision on interpretation of an article of the Constitution".[43] After having limited the scope of its intervention to constitutional interpretation, while acknowledging the legislature's competence to resolve the issues on the basis of political choices, Irish judges founded their assessment of the actual scope of sec. 40.3.3. of the Constitution on the selection of a biological parameter. According to a purposive interpretation of the constitutional provision, the protection afforded to the "unborn" is conditional upon the implantation of embryo in the uterus, as it is only after this stage that a special relationship between the embryo and the mother is established. Thus, basing on what can be defined a science-based purposive interpretation, the Supreme Court excludes from the scope of application the "pre-implantation embryo", as the "capacity to be born", which arises after implantation, defining the right protected.[44]

In this case, the Irish Court recognises the legislature's reserved power to make a political assessment, but at the same time it firmly declares its own function of constitutional interpretation:[45] therefore, the legislature's discretionary power in striking a balance is broadened due to the lack of scientific consensus and the ethical sensitivity of the issues at stake; at the same time, the interpretation provided by the Court finds explicit grounds in scientific notions, such as the use made by the Court

[41] Irish Supreme Court, Roche v. Roche [2009] IESC 82, 15 December 2009. See Gough (2010), pp. 239–247; McGuinness and Ui' Chonnachtaugh (2011), pp. 396–408.

[42] Ivi, J Murray C.J.

[43] Ivi, J Denham, § 46.

[44] J Denham, §§ 64–65.

[45] Cahill and Ó Conaill (2017), p. 260 ff., subsume Roche in the category "inchoate activism" (260 and 263).

of a biological parameter representing a key element in orienting the judges' reasoning.

4.2 Science as a Tool for Assessing Political Choices: From Self-Restraint to Scientific Reasonableness

A further dimension where the scientific dimension may interfere with judicial review is constitutional reasoning. Better said, whether the judicial review of political choices is influenced by the specificity of the legislature's target must be checked: technological advancement applied to biomedicine. Is it possible to detect a direct influence on the courts' approach, able to direct the scrutiny towards a more restrained or active reasoning? In the following sub-sections, a set of different approaches will be provided.

4.2.1 Judicial Self-Restraint Reinforced by the Scientific Nature of Issues at Stake: France

As outlined in Sect. 2, the ECtHR generally acknowledges to national authorities a broad margin of appreciation, which is strengthened by the scientific complexity and ethical sensitivity of the issues at stake. This approach is emerging also at the national level, when courts with judicial review functions declare a lack of legitimacy to substitute their own assessment for the one settled by the legislature. The example of the French Constitutional Council is especially relevant.[46] Self-restraint which traditionally characterises its case-law becomes stronger in the biomedical field. The Council systematically refers to the principle which establishes that it is not the function of the Council to substitute its own evaluation for that provided by the legislature, as it does not rely on a general power of assessment comparable with the parliamentary one.[47] Therefore, the Council is not allowed to question the balancing set out by the legislature, basing its reasoning on a different evaluation of the state of scientific knowledge, except when legislative choices are manifestly unreasonable or arbitrary. The Council took a similar stance in assessing law no. 2016-87 of 2 February 2016, which has introduced a procedure for authorising the suspension of life-saving treatments in end of life decisions (the so-called *Loi Leonetti*).The Council plainly quashed the appeal against the law, by affirming that is not the responsibility of the Constitutional Council, which does not have general powers of assessment and decision-making with the same scope as those of the Parliament, to substitute its assessment for that of the legislature with regard to the conditions in which, in the absence of the known wishes of the patient, the physician

[46]Bergougnous (2013), p. 294 ff.

[47]Chenede and Deumier (2013), p. 354 ff.

may take a decision to halt or continue treatment, in the context of unreasonable therapeutic obstinacy. After having proclaimed this general principle, it considers the legislative framework adequate to protect the dignity and freedom of persons involved.[48] It is worth noting that the Council gives particular weight to the situation where the legislature bases political choices on the assessment of current state of scientific knowledge[49] or when the law provides mechanisms capable of adapting it contents and aims to the changing scientific or medical situation.[50] The Council seems to consider the latter as normative elements which can guarantee the scientific legitimacy of political choices, together with the scientific soundness of legislative features, which can constantly adapt and re-connect the law with the regulatory target.

An even more restrained approach occurs when courts abstain from assessing the merit of the appeal by referring to an absolute lack of legitimacy to enter in ethically sensitive issues, as the evaluation belongs exclusively to the legislature. This is the case of the Irish Supreme Court in the context of surrogacy agreements. Hearing an appeal aimed at having the legitimacy of a surrogacy agreement recognised, the Supreme Court stated that it is thus "quintessentially" a matter for the Parliament.[51] Therefore, even if affirming that nothing at the constitutional level precludes the enactment of appropriate laws on surrogacy,[52] the Court recognises that the balancing of competing interests at stake belongs exclusively to the legislature: according to the Court, "such lacuna should be addressed in legislation and not by this Court"[53] as "the issues raised are important, complex and social, which are matters of public policy for the Oireachtas".[54] Therefore, so long as the Parliament does not take position on the issue, the Court must abstain from striking a balance between affected rights which goes beyond existing rules at the legislative level.

4.2.2 Judicial Review Based on Scientific Reasonableness of the Law: Italy

The case-law of the Italian Constitutional Court shows that a restrained approach when coming to assessing legislative choices does not automatically stem from the acknowledgment of a reserved space for discretionary evaluation of political and technical bodies. The Italian Constitutional Court has progressively defined and

[48]Judgment no. 2017-632 QPC, 2 June 2017.

[49]See the case of the Law on cord blood donation, judgment 2012-249 QPC, 16 May 2012.

[50]In case of a law introducing mandatory vaccination, judgment 2015-458 QPC.

[51]M.R. and D.R. (suing by their father and next friend O.R.) &ors -v- An t-Ard-Chláraitheoir&ors, [2014] IESC 60, 7 November 2014; Denham C.J., §113.

[52]"(...) Nor is there anything in the Constitution which would inhibit the development of appropriate laws on surrogacy", § 114.

[53]§ 116.

[54]§ 118.

enforced a standard of review for laws in the biomedical field, aiming at assessing the way in which the legislature exercises its discretionary power when confronted with scientific or medical issues. It has been defined as the "scientific reasonableness"[55] of laws, essentially structured on two principles, which represent the golden rule for legislation in the field.

On the one hand, the Court stated that, when other constitutional rights or duties are excluded, the legislature is not the body tasked with determining which healthcare practices are more adequate and what the limits and conditions they must comply with are. Since medical practice is based on scientific and experimental knowledge which is continuously developing, the golden rule is the autonomy and accountability of physician who, with the patients' consent, makes professional choices on the grounds of the existing state of that knowledge.

On the other hand, the Constitutional Court does not prevent the legislature from exercising its own regulatory power in absolute terms. However, the Court sets conditions and limits to such an intervention. According to the Court's case-law, a legislative intervention related to the substance of appropriateness of healthcare choices should not be founded only on the assessment deriving from the legislature's discretionary power. Rather, it should provide for guidelines (advices) grounded on the corroboration of the existing state of scientific knowledge by means of technical institutions and bodies—national and international—which play a prominent role in the field. In any case, the approved rules should result from and be based on such verification.[56]

This is the idea of scientific reasonableness: law must be scientifically consistent and feasible, as well as coherent with the nature of medical and scientific phenomenon; and the law-making process must be structured in order to guarantee an assessment of current scientific knowledge and to provide mechanisms capable of adapting normative contents to scientific development.[57]

The law on assisted reproductive techniques (Law n. 40/2004) has been one of the main targets of scientific reasonableness. By implementing the latter principle, the Court has stated that limits imposed by the law unreasonably constrains the autonomy of healthcare professionals and the woman's right to health. It thus falls to the expertise of physicians to determine the most appropriate treatment based on established medical and scientific knowledge and the specificity of each case. The Court recalls—in line with its own settled case law—"the limits that scientific and experimental knowledge, which are constantly evolving and upon which the art of medicine is founded, place on the legislature's discretionary power".[58] Law 40 did

[55]Penasa (2009), p. 81 ff.; see also Id. (2012), p. 371 ff.

[56]Italian Constitutional Court, judgment n. 282/2002.

[57]Non directly referring to the biomedical field, Popelier (2013b), p. 267, refers to "rational law" as the "product of complex intellectual process which makes use of tools to seek and analyse information with certain boundaries and to draw decision from this assessment which is justifiable on the basis of present information and context and adaptable to changes in insights or techniques".

[58]Italian Constitutional Court, judgment n. 151/2009.

not comply with this principle, as the legislative provision does not afford a doctor the possibility to adequately assess the specific case being treated based on state-of-the-art and accredited technical and scientific knowledge. Moreover, the Law does not permit health professionals to identify, on a case by case basis, the suitable number of embryos to be transferred which is likely to ensure a serious attempt at assisted reproduction, while at the same time minimizing the health risks for the woman and the foetus.

It must be emphasized that the significance attributed to medical autonomy and scientific expertise, which significantly binds the legislature's discretion, refers to the constitutional dimension, as it aims at guaranteeing the effective protection of constitutional rights (the woman's right to health, interests of the embryo and reproductive needs). When the level of ethical sensitivity reaches a particularly high degree, the Court normally concedes a broader margin of appreciation to the legislature, in a way similar to the approach usually implemented by the ECtHR, thus abstaining from triggering the scientific reasonableness standard of review.[59] This was the case of the decision on the absolute ban on embryo research introduced by Law 40, where the Court considered that the "tragic choice" between the protection of the principle of life expressed by embryos and scientific research belongs to the legislature, which acting as the interpreter of the collective will (morals) is called to translate, at the normative level, the balancing between values, taking into consideration the more deep-rooted tendencies of society.[60] It goes to narrowing the scope and intensity of Court's scrutiny over the law, which cannot be subject to review, due to the axiological nature of political choices implicated, which are—according to the Court—inevitably reserved to the legislature.

4.2.3 'Science-Based' Judicial Review: Portugal (ARTs)

References to a scientific or biological concept can also be important when they enter judicial reasoning, developing a key function in directing the courts' scrutiny. In other terms, the courts' assessment depends on the way in which scientific concepts referred to by law are interpreted, more than on axiological evaluations. A paradigmatic case is the concept of 'embryo', which can have very divergent meanings from a biological perspective and thus can be subject to a plurality of different normative interpretations. Courts usually abstain from providing a definition of embryo, as they reserve this evaluation to democratically legitimated bodies, such as parliament. This cautious approach is typical of ECtHR case-law and many national constitutional courts, such as the Italian Constitutional Court. Notwithstanding, courts may decide to confront the issue, when they consider the interpretation which is decisive to

---

[59] See Morvillo (2016), pp. 475–484.

[60] Italian Constitutional Court, judgment n. 84/2016.

carrying out the scrutiny. This was the case of judgment n. 101/2009 of Portuguese Constitutional Tribunal, which concerned the Law on ARTs (Law n. 32/2006).[61]

With specific regard to embryo research, the Portuguese Tribunal bases its decision on the distinction between 'true' embryo and the product of non-reproductive cloning, on which scientific community is—according to the Tribunal—debating in order to understand if it can be defined as 'embryo' and thus being deemed equivalent to the latter for all ethical and legal purposes. In the face of the absence of a broad scientific consensus as to the nature of the product of a somatic cell nuclear transfer, the Tribunal opts for distinguishing the two entities in order to secure internal coherence of law, which prohibits the production of embryos via ARTs for research purposes (art. 9.1), while allowing the use of embryos obtained in absence of the fertilisation of ova for the same purpose. This case is especially relevant, as the definition of a biological entity as a "mere laboratory artefact without the capacity to turn into a human being" instead of 'embryo' seems to be based on biological parameters, which is the absence of fertilisation and thus the capacity to develop into a human being. In this case, the level of constitutional protection afforded depends essentially on the "scientific-based" assessment made by the Tribunal. It is worth noting that a similar approach has been taken by the CJEU in the *Brustle* saga,[62] where the specific scope of the concept of "embryo" provided by Directive 98/44 of 6 July 1998 on the protection of biomedical inventions was determined by applying the standard of the embryo's "capability to commencing the process of development of a human being", understood in a narrow sense as "inherent capacity".[63] It is noteworthy that in both cases—the Portuguese Constitutional Tribunal and CJEU—the choice to provide a legal definition of embryo has been based on the necessity to guarantee both legal coherence and certainty. With specific regard to the Portuguese case, the legislature's competence to take a position is not questioned, as the Tribunal's goal is precisely to restore legal coherence of political choices and it is achieved by referring to scientifically disputed standards.

In conclusion of this Section, the *fil rouge* is represented by the role acknowledged by courts as belonging to legislature in assessing scientifically complex and ethically sensitive issues in the biomedical field. Parliaments' role is always considered the essential tool for balancing competing interests at stake, although the scope of political margin of appreciation can be very divergent, moving from exercising a reserved power (France) to a stricter scrutiny also based on scientific standards (Italy). A common feature is that science becomes a tool for assessing political choices, even assuming different judicial approaches, in the sense of more restrained or proactive attitudes.

[61] Raposo and Vale e Reis (2009), pp. 125–158.

[62] Inaugurated since Oliver Brüstle v. Greenpeace e.V., C-34/10, 2011.

[63] International Stem Cell Corporation v Comptroller General of Patents, Designs and Trade Marks, C-364/13, 18 October 2014. See Vauchez (2017), p. 67 ff., that tackles the issue of whether the CJEU is "science 'objective'".

5 Science Is Absorbed by Axiological Dimension: Context of Expression for Axiological Pluralism

Science can also act as context in which axiological pluralism finds expression in contemporary societies. In this case, the scientific dimension becomes a factor of expansion for the axiological one, as scientific advances applied to biomedicine offer new tools for social demands, especially in the reproductive field. Therefore, such as in the case of surrogacy, science does not usually play a direct role within either the law-making or the judicial review process, as happens when science integrates axiological dimensions and acts as tool for managing the latter (Sect. 4). When the scientific dimension is absorbed by the axiological one, the latter becomes essential within the judicial review process, while the relevance of the former tends to decrease.

5.1 Legislature's Supremacy and Axiological Complexity: End of Life Issues (UK)

The trend described can affect the relationship between legislatures and courts in all those cases in which ethical sensitivity is not characterised also by an uncertain and complex scientific background, open to different interpretations, such as in cases analysed in Sect. 3. When complexity characterises only the axiological dimension, courts may act as 'passive detectors':[64] they identify the necessity to adjust legal tools to social changes produced also by technological advancement, but merely bring it to the attention of democratically legitimated bodies without interfering in the axiological assessment.

End of life issues paradigmatically express this tendency, as they are not characterised by a special scientific complexity but achieve the highest level of axiological density. In such a context, a relevant example of a court acting as 'passive detector', where new social claims are detected but not directly guaranteed at the judicial level, can be found in common law systems. The UK Supreme Court in *Nicklinson*[65] has been called upon to assess the compatibility of the crime of assisted suicide with art. 8 ECHR in the context of end of life issues.[66]

In a controversial judgment, the Court declined to declare the incompatibility with the ECHR, even though five judges agreed that incompatibility should "in principle" have been declared and two of them were of the opinion that it ought to

---

[64]See Casonato and Penasa (2018), pp. 879–888.

[65]R (on the application of Nicklinson and another) (Appellants) v Ministry of Justice (Respondent) [2014] UKSC 38.

[66]See Wicks (2014), pp. 144–156, especially 152 ff.

have been declared in the specific case.[67] Notwithstanding, according to Lord Neuberger's reasoning, "it would not be appropriate to grant a declaration of incompatibility at this time", as it would be advisable to accord Parliament the opportunity of considering whether to amend the law so as to enable individuals facing a similar situation to the applicants to be assisted in ending their lives.[68] Therefore, due also to the difficult, controversial and sensitive issue raised by the case which justifies a cautious approach by court, it would be "institutionally inappropriate" to declare the incompatibility,[69] while it would have been more suitable to enact mechanism of collaboration—or dialogue—between courts and Parliament, in order to give room for the latter to reconsider within the law-making process the more adequate and reasonable balancing.[70]

The Court reserved to itself and other courts the power to eventually declare an incompatibility in the future, whether or not Parliament has resolved to specifically and effectively reassess the issue. Arguments provided by the UK Supreme Court clearly explain why this approach has been labelled 'passive detector' and why it is not automatically ascribable to a mere deferential approach: it should be defined as active deference, as it strongly calls upon the legislature to activate its procedural means in order to handle the issue.

The approach taken by UK courts (see also *Conway*) eventually found support in ECtHR case-law. In *Nicklinson and Lamb v UK* the European Court stated that "it would be odd to deny domestic courts charged with examining the compatibility of primary legislation with the Convention the possibility of concluding, like this Court, that Parliament is best placed to take a decision on the issue in question in light of the sensitive issues, notably ethical, philosophical and social, which arise".[71]

5.2 Legislature's Primacy and Axiological Assessment: Surrogacy in Portugal and Assisted Suicide in Canada

It is worth noting that the UK Supreme Court's ruling is not a case of judicial review of legislation, thus judicial powers involved are quite specific and limited as to justify a deferential attitude in the actual case under scrutiny. When coming to courts with judicial review functions, the approach implemented can be different. Even

---

[67] § 111–112: "where the court has jurisdiction on an issue falling within the margin of appreciation, I think it would be wrong in principle to rule out exercising that jurisdiction if Parliament addresses the issue: it could be said with force that such an approach would be an abdication of judicial responsibility".

[68] R (on the application of Nicklinson and another) (Appellants) v Ministry of Justice (Respondent), cit., § 113.

[69] § 116.

[70] § 117.

[71] Nicklinson and Lamb v UK, 16 July 2015, § 84. See Wicks (2016), pp. 633–640.

when courts acknowledge that legislatures take priority in determining what the most appropriate balance is, it does not prevent them from verifying whether the legislative scheme is adequate to guarantee the effective protection of all constitutional rights affected. Therefore, under this judicial approach, legislative primacy does not amount to a legislature's supremacy: political choices are not covered by a strong presumption of legitimacy but they can be subject to strict scrutiny based on traditional parameters such as proportionality, reasonableness and adequateness.

In a case of assisted suicide, the Supreme Court of Canada[72] granted a "high degree of deference (...) to Parliament's decision to impose an absolute prohibition on assisted death" as it involves "complex issues of social policy and a number of competing societal values";[73] at the same time, it declared disproportionate the absolute prohibition of this practice based on the "minimal impairment" standard. According to the Supreme Court, the goal of protecting vulnerable individuals may also have been achieved through a "carefully designed and managed system" which is able to verify the specific will and physical and mental condition of the individual, without unreasonably limiting the right to life, freedom and security of person.[74] Consequently, the Supreme Court declares void the prohibition of physician-assisted death for a competent adult person who clearly consents and has a "grievous and irremediable medical condition (...) that causes enduring suffering that is intolerable to the individual in the circumstances of his or her condition".[75] At the same time, the Court rules the suspension of the declaration of invalidity, in order to give Parliament the opportunity to enact legislation consistent with the constitutional parameters set out in its reasoning,[76] as happened with the entry into force of Bill C-14 (An Act to amend the Criminal Code and to make related amendments to other Acts (medical assistance in dying)) on June 2016.[77] Therefore, the acknowledgment of the legislature's power to set out a comprehensive regulation does not prevent Court from preliminarily assessing the actual constitutional compatibility of political choices: differently from the previous case, here the court acts as 'active detector' which develops its functions in a constructive way and in dialogue with the legislature.[78]

In assessing the constitutionality of a law allowing gestational surrogacy,[79] the Portuguese Constitutional Court adopted a similar approach.[80] The Portuguese Tribunal stated that surrogacy, due to the uncertainty relating to its long-term effects, cannot be considered as a constitutionally necessary legal institution, thus the

---

[72]Carter v Canada (Attorney General), 2015 SCC 5, 6 February 2015.

[73]§ 98.

[74]Sec. 7 Canadian Charter of Rights and Freedoms.

[75]Carter v Canada (Attorney General), § 127.

[76]§ 126.

[77]See McMorrow (2019), pp. 267–282.

[78]Hogg and Amarnath (2017), pp. 1053 and 1067–1068.

[79]Only for altruistic purposes and under strict conditions, see Law n. 25/2016.

[80]Portuguese Constitutional Court, judgment n. 225/2018.

decision to introduce a controlled regime for this practice is the legislature's preferred choice functional to fostering constitutional rights, such as the right to found a family and to procreate.[81] Therefore, the legislature is endowed with a broad margin of appreciation when arriving at a decision whether to regulate the practice; notwithstanding, the Constitutional Tribunal must assess if the actual legislative means provide concrete protection of all rights involved. In the specific case, the scrutiny led to the declaration of unconstitutionality of the legislative regime as a whole, as it resulted in an unsatisfactory and disproportionate protection of the gestational mother's rights (right to personal and procreative autonomy) and legal certainty (lack of an adequate regime of authorisation). What has been challenged by the Tribunal is not the legislature's choice to introduce an authorisation regime for surrogacy agreements, as it represents an option which entirely belong to Parliament: it does not require a change of paradigm—from a permissive to a prohibitionist approach—but rather a more effective and fair definition of legislative structure, whose re-configuration is expressly reserved to the legislature.[82]

Significantly enough, this decision has been interpreted as an example of "dialogic mechanism" between the Tribunal and Parliament, in which the former gives detailed advice acting as constitutional interpreter to the latter, to which belong the power and the responsibility to design a constitutionally consistent regulatory regime.[83]

5.3 *Legislature's Choices and Axiological Interpretation: Surrogacy Agreements in Argentina*

Within the category of judicial approaches which stem from a process of absorption of scientific dimension into the axiological one, courts can also take a very proactive attitude, once they have recognised the need for legal protection for a social demand which is not covered by legislation. In these cases, courts may act as 'diligent agents', as they do not simply detect an unprotected social need but they directly provide an effective remedy in order to fill the existent regulatory gap. In so doing, they differ from 'active detector' courts because 'diligent agent' courts do not refer to legislature once having identifying a system failure, particularly when constitutional rights remain unprotected: by making dynamic use of interpretative tools and in the light of the principle of the separation of powers, courts do not prevent the legislature from introducing ad hoc legislation, while guaranteeing a transparent and comprehensive regulatory framework while ever the legislature does not take action.

The Argentinian approach to the regulation of surrogacy agreements is especially relevant. Faced with a lack of legislation, Argentinian ordinary courts have designed

[81] § 27.

[82] § 53.

[83] Violante (2018).

a regulatory framework by offering an interpretation consistent with constitutional principles of existing rules on reproductive issues (the 2015 Civil Code's provisions on parenthood and the Law on ARTs).[84] They base this attitude on two assumptions: the definition of surrogacy as a form of assisted reproductive technique which is allowed by the law, from both a medical and legal perspective; the applicability to surrogacy of the "procreative will" criteria, set out by the civil code as the standard for attributing parenthood in the context of ARTs as an alternative to birth (sec. 558–562). On these grounds, courts, practically unanimously, agree in allowing a model of parenthood based on consent and reproductive will, under specific and strict conditions both settled and verified by themselves in each specific case.[85]

Faced with the legislature's immobility, judges consider it appropriate to take a stand and enforce, in the field of surrogacy agreements, a model of parenthood based on individuals' consent and reproductive will, once the *ex-ante* judicial authorisation has been obtained. Significantly, courts decide to act as 'diligent agent', once they have identified the constitutional need to provide a regulatory framework for a practice which can be—when adequately regulated—functional to the effective enforcement of individuals' rights in the reproductive field. Accordingly, the courts' reasoning is based on an axiological interpretation of the existing legislation, aimed at recoupling regulatory tools and constitutional goals.

6 Scientific Enhancement of Law as Prerequisite for a Sustainable Scientific Adjudication: The Essential Integration Between Axiological and Scientific Pluralism

Judicial comparative analysis has confirmed courts as being regulatory actors integrating the role performed by legislature. When they possess a constitutional judicial review function, the scientific nature of the issues at stake can influence approaches that traditionally characterised the scrutiny of the legislature's political choices: the spectrum is always broad, as to include self-restrained or proactive judicial reasoning; notwithstanding, within this spectrum the relationship existing between scientific and axiological dimension can decisively influence the way in which courts concretely implement their function. We qualify this dynamic in terms of integration or absorption: in both cases, reference to the constitutional dimension allows courts to act in a more proactive way (Ireland, Italy, Argentina), in light of the common goal to interpreting or enforcing constitutional principles or rights.

In case of 'integration' between the scientific and axiological dimensions, the use of scientific facts decisively guides the courts' approach (Portugal, Ireland, Italy),

[84] Among others, see judgments R., L. S. y Otros s/ Solicita Homologación, 22 November 2017, Juzgado de Familia 2da Nominaciòn, Cordoba (SAIJ: FA17160037); and H., M.E. y Otros S/Venias y Dispensas, Tribunal Colegiado de Familia N° 7, Rosario, 5 December 2017.

[85] Quaini (2016), pp. 99–105; Lamm (2013).

also when the latter coincides with an attitude of self-restraint (France): in the latter case, scientific uncertainty goes to strengthen the deferential approach of courts (see also ECtHR). A rights-oriented approach seems to be prevalent, since courts understand science as an essential tool for constitutional interpretation and scrutiny: by referring to scientific expertise or knowledge, courts orient their reasoning in terms of both interpretation (Ireland) and scrutiny (Italy and Portugal).

In case of 'absorption', science becomes a triggering factor for axiological complexity, more than an ad hoc/auxiliary parameter within the constitutional scrutiny. Thus, the institutional-based approach becomes central—in terms of balance between powers—and accordingly the way in which courts understand their relationship with legislative power is the golden thread which links the different attitudes that constitutional scrutiny may assume: also when courts detect (potentially, UK, or concretely) the illegitimacy of law, they carefully recall the role of the legislature in balancing affected rights (UK), by acknowledging alternatively its supremacy (UK) or at least its priority (Portugal and Canada) in managing axiological pluralism.

Comparative analysis has shown that if the regulatory role of the courts in managing axiological complexity in a scientific context cannot be doubted, as long as their role in enforcing constitutional principles is established, the scope and intensity of their co-productive function belongs essentially to the legislature, to which courts are normally accord a wide margin of appreciation, as comparative analysis has clearly revealed. The more legislature exercises its power in a science-friendly way (open-to-science method), in the light of a more adequate, balanced and effective achievement of constitutional goals, the more courts will usually endorse legislative choices, especially when the issues at stake are characterised by a high level of axiological sensitivity and scientific complexity. This goal can also be achieved through the "scientific enhancement" of law, by adapting both methods and contents of legislation to the characteristics of the regulatory target, in order to "to improve the capacity of the legal system to adapt to rapidly evolving technologies (. . .)".[86]

References

Ashcroft R (2013) Novel rights-based approaches to health technologies. In: Flear ML, Farrell AM, Hervey TK, Murphy T (eds) European law and health technologies. Oxford University Press, p 310

Bennet Moses L (2017) Regulating in the face of sociotechnical change, p 575. See R. Brownsword, M. Goodwin, Law and technologies of the twenty-first century. Text and materials. Cambridge University Press, 2012, p 63

Bergougnous G (2013) Le Conseil constitutionnel et le législateur, in Les Noveaux Cahiers du Conseil Constitutionnel, 1, 294 ff

[86]Marchant (2011), p. 20.

Brownsword R (2008) Rights, regulation, and the technological revolution. Oxford University Press, p 160
Brownsword R, Goodwin M (2012) Law and the technologies of the twenty-first century: text and materials
Brownsword R, Scotford E, Yeung K (2017) Introduction. In: Bronwsword R, Scotford E, Yeung K (eds) The Oxford handbook on the law and regulation of technology. OUP
Cahill M, Ó Conaill S (2017) Judicial restraint can also undermine constitutional principles: an Irish caution. Univ Queensland J 36(2):260 ff
Casonato C (2017) 21st century BioLaw: a proposal. BioLaw J-Rivista di BioDiritto 1:81–95
Casonato C, Penasa S (2018) Dinamiche costituzionali e biodiritto. Il ruolo del giudice tra inerzia e solerzia. In: Mezzetti L, Ferioli E (eds) Giustizia e Costituzione agli albori del XXI secolo. Bonomo Editore, pp 879–888
Chenede F, Deumier P (2013) L'œuvre du Parlement, la part du Conseil constitutionnel en droit des personnes et de la famille. Les Noveaux Cahiers du Conseil Constitutionnel 2:354 ff
D'Amico G (2005) I dubbi della scienza al vaglio della Corte costituzionale: dalle incertezze della scienza alle certezze del diritto (materiali giurisprudenziali). In: D'Aloia A (a cura di) Bio-tecnologie e valori costituzionali, p 261
Gough F (2010) Ireland and the frozen embryo: a slight thawing. Med Law Rev 18:239–247
Hogg, Amarnath (2017) Understanding dialogue theory. In: Oliver, Macklem, Der Rosiers (eds) The Oxford handbook of Canadian constitution, p 1053
Jasanoff S (2011) Introduction: rewriting life, reframing rights. In: Jasanoff S (ed) Reframing rights: bioconstitutionalism in the genetic age. MIT
Jasanoff S, Meltzer I (2018) Borderlands of life: IVF embryos and the law in the United States, United Kingdom, and Germany. Sci Technol Hum Values, 29 January 2018
Lamm E (2013) Argentina. In: Trimmings K, Beaumont P (eds) International surrogacy arrangements: legal regulation at the international level. Hart
Marchant GE (2011) The growing gap between emerging technologies and the law. In: Marchant GE, Allenby BR, Herkert JR (eds) The growing gap between emerging technologies and legal-ethical oversight: the pacing problem. Springer, p 20
McGuinness S, Ui' Chonnachtaugh S (2011) Implications of recent developments in Ireland for the status of the embryo. Camb Q Healthcare Ethics 3:396–408
McMorrow T (2019) Voluntary Euthanasia, assisted suicide & law reform: a sketch of the Canadian experience. BioLaw J-Rivista di BioDiritto 1:267–282
Montgomery J, Jones C, Biggs H (2014) Hidden lawmaking in the province of medical jurisprudence. Med Law Rev 3:343–378
Morvillo M (2016) Between politics and expertise. An Italian perspective on constitutional law and scientific legitimacy. Eur J Risk Regul 3:475–484
Murphy T (2017) Human rights in technological times. In: Bronwsword R, Scotford E, Yeung K (eds) The Oxford handbook on the law and regulation of technology. Oxford University Press, Oxford, p 964 ff
Murphy T, Ó Cuinn G (2010) Works in progress: new technologies and the European Court of Human Rights. Hum Rights Law Rev 4(10):601 ff
Murphy T, Ó Cuinn G (2013) Taking technology seriously: STS as a human rights method. In: Flear ML, Farrell A-M, Hervey TK, Murphy T (eds) European law and health technologies
Penasa S (2009) La 'ragionevolezza scientifica' delle leggi nella giurisprudenza costituzionale. Quaderni costituzionali 4:81 ff
Penasa S (2012) Converging by procedures: assisted reproductive technology regulation within the European Union. Med Law Int 3–4:371 ff
Poli L (2017) Bioethics, human rights and their interplay in the legal reasoning of ECtHR's case law on artificial reproductive technologies, in federalism.it. Focus Hum Rights 1:1–18
Popelier P (2012) Preliminary comments on the role of courts as regulatory watchdogs. Legisprudence 6(3):275 ff
Popelier P (2013a) Procedural rationality: giving teeth to the proportionality analysis. Eur Constit Law Rev 9(2):230–262

Popelier P (2013b) The courts as regulatory watchdog. The procedural approach in the case law of the European Court of Human Rights. In: Popelier P, Mazmanyan A, Vandenbruwaene W (eds) The role of constitutional courts in multilevel governance. Intersentia, p 267
Quaini FM (2016) Gestational surrogacy in Argentina. In: Scott Sills E (ed) Handbook of gestational surrogacy: international clinical practice and policy issues. Cambridge University Press, pp 99–105
Raposo VL, Vale e Reis R (2009) Assisted reproductive technologies in Portuguese Law – Commentary to the Judgment n. 101/2009, of march the 3rd of the Portuguese Constitutional Court. Revista de Derecho y Genoma Humano 31:125–158
Rodotà S (2006) La vita e le regole. Tra diritto e non diritto, Feltrinelli
Rodotà S, Tallacchini M (2010) Introduzione. In: Rodotà S, Tallacchini M (a cura di) Ambito e fonti del biodiritto, Giuffrè, LI
Sartori D (2018) End-of-life issues and the European Court of Human Rights. The value of personal autonomy within a 'proceduralized' review. Quest Int Law 52:23–43
Saul M (2015) The European Court of Human Rights' margin of appreciation and the processes of national parliaments. Hum Rights Law Rev 15:745–774
Sunstein C (2001) Design democracy: what constitutions do. OUP
Vauchez SH (2017) EU law and bioethics. In: Cremona M (ed) New technologies and EU law. OUP, p 67 ff
Veitch K (2007) The jurisdiction of medical law. Ashgate
Veronesi P (2011) Uno statuto costituzionale del corpo. In: Canestrari S, Ferrando G, Mazzoni CM, Rodotà S, Zatti P (a cura di) Il governo del corpo, I vol., Trattato di biodiritto, Giuffrè, p 138
Violante T (2018) (Not) striking down surrogate motherhood in Portugal. VerfBlog, 2018/4/28. https://verfassungsblog.de/not-striking-down-surrogatemotherhood-in-portugal/
Wicks E (2014) The Supreme Court Judgment in Nicklinson: one step forward on assisted dying; two steps back on human rights. A commentary on the Supreme Court judgment in R (Nicklinson) v Ministry of Justice; R (AM) v Director of Public Prosecutions [20014] UKSC 38. Med Law Rev 23(1):144–156
Wicks E (2016) Nicklinson and Lamb v United Kingdom: Strasbourg fails to assist on assisted dying in the UK. Med Law Rev 24(4):633–640

Part II
Accommodating Pluralisms Beyond Courts: Institutions and Tools

Research Ethics Committees

Itziar de Lecuona

Abstract Ethics committees represent a "way of doing bioethics" that is useful in plural and democratic societies. Although there are different types of ethics committees, clinical ethics committees, national ethics committees or ad hoc committees, I will focus my analysis on research ethics committees in biomedicine. I will examine their international legal framework in order to define them, identify their functions and analyse their possible instrumentalisation. Lastly, I will provide some practical information as a member of two research ethics committees in Spain, the Bioethics Committee at the University of Barcelona and the Research Ethics Committee at Hospital Clínic de Barcelona, to draw some conclusions and make proposals.

1 Introduction

States must articulate legal regulations to define the conditions for exercising freedom of research such that other recognised rights are not undermined, and to protect human beings when participating as subjects of research. Likewise, coordinated action is necessary to develop international legal regulations based on principles, rights and guarantees. A framework to guide the development of regulations to allow the same level of protection for individuals involved in research, regardless of the places where research is carried out. In societies in which pluralism is a legally recognised value[1] there can be different, equally valid, ways of dealing with the same situation. The law cannot respond to rapidly changing research and innovation.[2] Advances in scientific knowledge and its applications persistently question the limits established by legal regulations and ethical guidelines. Therefore, the role of

[1]Article 12. Universal Declaration on Bioethics and Human Rights, UNESCO (2005).
[2]Rodotà (2009).

I. de Lecuona (✉)
Department of Medicine and Bioethics and Law Observatory—UNESCO Chair in Bioethics, University of Barcelona, Barcelona, Spain

L. Busatta, C. Casonato (eds.), *Axiological Pluralism*, Ius Gentium: Comparative Perspectives on Law and Justice 92, https://doi.org/10.1007/978-3-030-78475-1_4

multidisciplinary research ethics committees must be explored in order to solve these problems, and to make decisions of profound importance for individuals and groups in societies potentially in conflict. This is the reason why these research bodies have become a significant part of the research system; without their review, the development of biomedical research is inconceivable. Research ethics committees are considered the most appropriate mechanism to ensure the protection of the rights of the people involved.

2 Bioethics and Research Ethics Committees in Biomedicine

The origin of bioethics is linked to the creation of multidisciplinary and independent research ethics committees, to respond to the need to review and monitor research projects that involve human participation. Consider, for example, clinical trials for the development of medicinal products for human use, genetic or observational studies. These committees must weigh up the research freedom of the researcher, the main impetus for the advancement of knowledge with other implied rights, such as autonomy, physical or mental integrity, the free development of personality and the privacy of patients and healthy volunteers who participate. It is well-known that the first research ethics committees were established to avoid abuses on participants, for instance, not asking for their consent, not providing them with adequate information and placing them in situations of disproportionate risk in relation to potential benefits.[3]

Ethics committees in biomedical research are, in my opinion, "a way of doing bioethics". They make a move from theory to action in research where bioethics has been and is the main protagonist,[4] largely due to the spread of the principles in bioethics of autonomy, beneficence, and justice, imported from the US research and health-care setting.[5] Thus, international regulations establish that research ethics committees must analyse, along with methodological aspects, the ethical, legal and societal issues involved in the research projects.[6]

We start here from a conception of bioethics that takes the legal and ethical minimum represented in internationally recognised human rights as reference, in order to reflect on scientific and technological progress.[7] This ethical reflection has

[3]Beecher (1966).

[4]De Lecuona (2011).

[5]"The Belmont Report" Office of the Secretary Ethical Principles and Guidelines for the Protection of Human Subjects of Research The National Commission for the Protection of Human Subjects of Biomedical and Behavioral Research U.S.A, April 18, 1979.

[6]The Convention for the Protection of Human Rights and Dignity of the Human Being with regard to the Application of Biology and Medicine: Convention on Human Rights and Biomedicine, Council of Europe (1997a).

[7]Casado and López Baroni (2018).

legal-political consequences and must also consider cultural and local issues.[8] Thus, the challenge for research ethics committees in biomedical research is to be able to integrate these different perspectives.

The creation of research ethics committees has accompanied bioethics since its beginnings, with the goal of guaranteeing that the interests of science and society do not prevail over those of the individual.[9] Annas notes that ethics committees were first created in part from fear of the legal responsibility of medical institutions and from societal rejection of certain abusive situations, which necessarily led to regulations that have fostered the development of bioethics since the 1970s.[10] The Declarations and Reports considered milestones in bioethics, such as the World Medical Association's Declaration of Helsinki[11] and the Belmont Report, are about ethics in biomedical research. Their purpose is to establish ethical guidelines for proper conduct in research that does not undermine the rights of the subjects involved and does not impede the advancement of knowledge. It is in these documents that we find the first references to the need to establish research ethics committees that review specific requirements before, during and after research conducted with human beings. The history of biomedical research has been written through the public disclosure of incidents in which human beings, especially those most vulnerable, such as prisoners, the disabled and minors, have been damaged, apparently for the purpose of research.[12] These episodes have acted as a catalyst for the development of ethical guidelines such as the above-mentioned Declaration of Helsinki, which make it possible to carry out biomedical research through the exercise of scientific freedom in a way that is compatible with respect for the individuals involved and their rights. With this purpose, research ethics committees signed on to and were consolidated into the original version and further revisions of the Declaration of Helsinki from 1964 until the last revision carried out in Fortaleza, in 2013 that states the following:[13]

[8]Hottois (1990).

[9]Article 2. Convention on Biomedicine and Human Rights, Council of Europe (1997b).

[10]Annas (1991).

[11]Declaration of Helsinki: Ethical Principles for Medical Research Involving Human Subjects, World Medical Association (1964).

[12]Brody (1998).

[13]Research Ethics Committees: 23 Declaration of Helsinki: Ethical Principles for Medical Research Involving Human Subjects, World Medical Association (WMA) Adopted by the 18th WMA General Assembly, Helsinki, Finland, June 1964 and amended by the: 29th WMA General Assembly, Tokyo, Japan, October 1975 35th WMA General Assembly, Venice, Italy, October 1983 41st WMA General Assembly, Hong Kong, September 1989 48th WMA General Assembly, Somerset West, Republic of South Africa, October 1996 52nd WMA General Assembly, Edinburgh, Scotland, October 2000 53rd WMA General Assembly, Washington DC, USA, October 2002 (Note of Clarification added) 55th WMA General Assembly, Tokyo, Japan, October 2004 (Note of Clarification added) 59th WMA General Assembly, Seoul, Republic of Korea, October 2008 64th WMA General Assembly, Fortaleza, Brazil, October 2013.

> The research protocol must be submitted for consideration, comment, guidance and approval to the concerned research ethics committee before the study begins. This committee must be transparent in its functioning, must be independent of the researcher, the sponsor and any other undue influence and must be duly qualified. It must take into consideration the laws and regulations of the country or countries in which the research is to be performed as well as applicable international norms and standards but these must not be allowed to reduce or eliminate any of the protections for research subjects set forth in this Declaration. The committee must have the right to monitor ongoing studies. The researcher must provide monitoring information to the committee, especially information about any serious adverse events. No amendment to the protocol may be made without consideration and approval by the committee. After the end of the study, the researchers must submit a final report to the committee containing a summary of the study's findings and conclusions.

The creation and implementation of ethics and bioethics committees has been promoted by international governmental organisations, such as UNESCO, the Council of Europe and the European Union, and non-governmental organisations, such as the World Medical Association. Likewise, states have considered it necessary to regulate the conditions for the creation and functioning of these committees. Consequently, research ethics committees have taken a prominent place in biomedical research, such that the mandatory and favourable opinion of a research ethics committee is necessary for the responsible authority to approve research being conducted that involves the participation of human beings, or in which biological samples of human origin or personal data are used. They are agile mechanisms to operate in biomedicine.

3 International Legal Regulation of Research Ethics Committees

Biomedical research aims to develop or contribute to generalizable knowledge, as well as to improve the health, well-being and quality of life of individuals.[14] Biomedical research is necessary to test and verify the effectiveness and safety of new methods of diagnosis, prevention and treatment in humans. Beyond research interests, biomedical research generates knowledge and power, as well as economic profits for public and private initiatives. In a market society[15] there are different

---

[14]The Council for International Organizations of Medical Sciences CIOMS International Ethical Guidelines for Biomedical Research Involving Human Subjects (2016) Preamble "The term "research" refers to a class of activity designed to develop or contribute to generalizable knowledge. Generalizable knowledge consists of theories, principles or relationships, or the accumulation of information on which they are based, that can be corroborated by accepted scientific methods of observation and inference. "Research" includes both medical and behavioural studies pertaining to human health. Usually "research" is modified by the adjective "biomedical" to indicate its relation to health.

[15]Sandel (2013).

interests and there is a trend to commodification in biomedical research. Those involved in research may be unprotected if the necessary precautions are not instituted. In this section we analyse the response provided by the international legal framework considered to be a reference in bioethics for regulating ethics committees in biomedical research with human subjects. The Convention for the Protection of Human Rights and Dignity of the Human Being with regard to the Application of Biology and Medicine of the Council of Europe of 1997 (also known as the Convention on Human Rights and Biomedicine); its Additional Protocol on Biomedical Research of 2005 and the Universal Declaration on Bioethics and Human Rights of UNESCO of 2005.[16]

The Convention on Human Rights and Biomedicine was the first binding international treaty on the protection of human rights with respect to applications of biology and medicine. In relation to scientific research, the Convention establishes that "the research project has been approved by the competent body after independent examination of its scientific merit, including assessment of the importance of the aim of the research, and multidisciplinary review of its ethical acceptability" (article 16. iii). It also establishes that the state authority responsible for authorising research will delegate decision-making to a multidisciplinary group including professionals and lay members. The contributions of the 2005 Additional Protocol to the Convention on Human Rights and Biomedicine, concerning Biomedical Research, which further developed the previsions contained in the cited Convention of the Council of Europe related to biomedical research, should also be considered. The Protocol mandates, first of all, that states must assure conditions that allow real independence, establishing that research ethics committees cannot suffer any type of improper external influence (article 10.1) that could lead to a biased conclusion. Secondly, a mandate is addressed to each of the member of an ethics committee in biomedical research: They must make a declaration of interests, whose purpose is "to declare all those circumstances which could lead to a conflict of interest" (article 10.2). In addition, it establishes that members faced with a conflict of interest related to a research project under evaluation cannot participate in that evaluation.

In relation to multidisciplinarity, the analysis of the ethical acceptability of a research project should be carried out by professionals with different types of experience and knowledge (article 9.2), as well as by individuals who are not experts on the subject. The Protocol does not, however, indicate the number of members or the profile of the individuals that must form part of the committee. It requires that committees include "different types of knowledge and experiences and different points of view", and it emphasises that there should be lay members so that the interests and concerns of the community are represented.

[16]The Convention for the Protection of Human Rights and Dignity of the Human Being with regard to the Application of Biology and Medicine: Convention on Human Rights and Biomedicine and The Additional Protocol to the Convention on Human Rights and Biomedicine, concerning Biomedical Research.

It seems that the presence of lay or community members in ethics committees generates trust in the system established to control biomedical research. In the Explanatory Report to the Additional Protocol[17] the term, "layperson" refers to individuals who have no experience in biomedical research and who are not healthcare professionals. The participation of people who are not experts in research, but who have expertise in other areas, does not disqualify them from issuing valid opinions. It is also considered necessary for committees to have balanced representation in regard to gender and cultural perspective. The Protocol also considers the *ad hoc* participation of experts to issue an opinion on a specific research project under consideration related to their area of knowledge, so that they can contribute to making a proper assessment to protect the rights of individuals, their safety and wellbeing. This temporary participation is necessary given the highly specialised nature of scientific knowledge today. Likewise, research ethics committees should consider the possibility of patients' organisations being consulted on specific issues.

Research ethics committees must issue a reasoned judgment after the multidisciplinary assessment of the methodological and ethical aspects of the research, in which they justify the conclusions they have reached, whether positive or negative (article 9.3) and written in a clear and understandable language. In addition, the Protocol states that the judgment must be made available to potential participants in the research project evaluated.[18]

UNESCO's Universal Declaration on Bioethics and Human Rights, adopted by acclamation by the international community in 2005, and addressing "ethical issues related to medicine, life sciences and associated technologies as applied to human beings, taking into account their social, legal and environmental dimensions" (article 1.1), makes the following sound contributions: (1) it defines ethics committees in general terms as independent, multidisciplinary and pluralist bodies; (2) it places ethics committees in a strategic position in the area of applying the principles it upholds, which, among others, include autonomy and individual responsibility (article 5) and respect for cultural diversity and pluralism (article 12); (3) it establishes a typology of ethics committees, including committees in biomedical research, and assigns them the function of evaluating the ethical, legal and scientific problems of research projects related to human beings. The Declaration states that these committees must also evaluate relevant social factors, which implies that the context in which the research is carried out is also an issue of analysis for ethics committees examining biomedical research projects (article 19 a)); (4) the Declaration indicates that states should encourage the creation of these bodies to address biomedicine either through policies or regulations (article 22.2); (5) the Declaration assigns them the functions of promoting social debate and raising awareness around bioethical issues (article 19 d)) which are considered part of the discipline of bioethics, and allowing ethics committees to move from theory to action; (6) research ethics

[17]Explanatory Report to Additional Protocol on Biomedical Research of 2005 Available. http://www.coe.int/en/web/conventions/full-list/-/conventions/treaty/195.

[18]Casado and López Baroni (2021).

committees should evaluate the integrity, honesty and the professionalism of the researchers that direct and participate in the projects undergoing evaluation (article 18) and apply the principle of transparency in decision-making. In this regard, research ethics committees must analyse projects and monitor them from beginning to end, including possible publication of the results in scientific journals, in order to avoid, for example, scientific fraud as well as to detect research misconduct; (7) the Declaration states that transnational research in health should respond to the needs of the host countries and alleviate urgent health problems worldwide. The principles established should be applied and transnational research, which takes place in different states at the same time, should be ethically reviewed by the research ethics committee in the country where the funding comes from in addition to the country or countries where the research is going to be carried out (article 21). In this transnational framework it is possible that practices can occur related to, for example, trafficking in samples, organs and tissue or to the undesired or illegal use of data and parts of the human body. Research ethics committees must detect these situations, including the possible commodification of the human body and its parts. The exercise of biomedical research, which can cause harm to human subjects, poses an unavoidable challenge: to protect their rights, safety and wellbeing. Thus, the creation of research ethics committees becomes necessary. It acquires a universal dimension, as biomedical research is today transnational.

In sum, research ethics committees must evaluate: the design of the study; the competence and qualifications of the researcher; the procedure foreseen for obtaining informed consent from individuals; and the risk-benefit ratio, crucial for evaluating if the rights of the participants or individuals involved will be disproportionately affected.

4 The Instrumentalisation of Research Ethics Committees

Are ethics committees in biomedical research independent and impartial? Do they have the proper methodologies for reviewing and decision-making?[19] In theory, research ethics committees ensure the protection of participants in research projects thereby guaranteeing the safety of the public. But in practice, they can respond to certain interests, which have nothing to do with that goal.

When bioethics emerged in the 1970s its aim was to strengthen the establishment and development of biomedical research. Its tasks included creating ethics infrastructures, ethics and bioethics committees, as well as obtaining social approval for research. However, bioethics may have already made the subtle move from the rhetoric of defending the freedom and autonomy of the individual to converting the person into a "docile body" in the interest of industry or the state, as a form of control and management of individuals, and especially their bodies, as power is manifested

[19] Baron (2006).

through them. Not only should we speak of "docile bodies", but also of "docile states", as occurs with research in developing or underdeveloped countries.[20] From this perspective, although biomedical research involving the participation of human beings is considered necessary, it must be done through equitable sharing of the costs and benefits among those who will bear the disadvantages and who will presumably enjoy the benefits, and satisfy their needs or expectations of health. It is for this reason that the principle of justice has taken on a major role in biomedical research, especially when it comes to research carried out in developing countries that is sponsored by industrialised countries.

Biomedical research is synonymous with progress and power for certain agents such as the state, industry and institutions, which have diverse scientific, economic and social interests. The development of diagnostic, preventive and therapeutic methods, as well as new types of health interventions that may be beneficial for individuals, is carried out through research protocols that must be reviewed and approved by independent research ethics committees, as established by the legal regulations previously discussed. Bioethical reflection in advance of the development of the necessary legal rules to regulate research can be seen as a bioethics at the service of a politics that strengthens the development of the biomedical industry and research, in contrast to a process of bioethical reflection that leads to genuine social debate. According to Lysaught, it strengthens the interests of private enterprise with state participation, with its resulting economic benefits, and does so under the discourse of the interest and wellbeing of the person and the protection of his/her rights. The result is a strengthening of public and private structures of biomedical research through the establishment of docile subjects, enabling the development of a powerful new economic structure based on biomedical research, of which the pharmaceutical industry lobby is an example. A bioethics that is considered above other humanitarian or social considerations would be at the service of a politics that pursues the development of the biomedical industry and its financial gain.

From this critical perspective, the trend toward the marginalisation of research ethics committees in the area of clinical trials is of concern, as the European Group on Ethics has stated.[21] In the European context, research ethics committees that review clinical trials on medicinal products for human use have experienced major changes due to legislative reforms. The current definition is striking: "'Ethics committee' means an independent body established in a Member State in accordance with the law of that Member State and empowered to give opinions for the purposes of this Regulation, taking into account the views of laypersons, in particular patients or patients' organisations" (article 2.11).[22]

[20]Lysaught (2009).

[21]European Group on Ethics in Science and New Technologies, "Statement on Clinical Trials", 2013.

[22]Regulation (EU) No 536/2014 of the European Parliament and of the Council of 16 April 2014 on clinical trials on medicinal products for human use, and repealing Directive 2001/20/EC.

The repealed 2001 Directive defined research ethics committee as: "an independent body in a Member State, consisting of healthcare professionals and non-medical members, whose responsibility it is to promote and protect the rights, safety and wellbeing of human subjects involved in a trial and to provide public assurance of that protection, by, among other things, expressing an opinion on the trial protocol, the suitability of the investigators, the adequacy of facilities, and on the methods and documents to be used to inform trial subjects and obtain their informed consent" (article 2k).[23]

Definitions are relevant because of the impact they have on discourse and practice in research. My experience as a member of two research ethics committees makes it possible to offer a practical perspective, although not exempt from criticism, with the intention of highlighting that research ethics committees in clinical research are weakly defined in the new European legislation. Probably the main characteristics of these bodies are being diluted. It is of concern if research ethics committees lose, via European legislation, what makes them distinctive, their independence and multidisciplinarity, and instead could come to respond to institutional or commercial pressures rather than the objectives for which they were initially created.

There is a trend to incorporate as members of biomedical research ethics committees, individuals that represent the interests of the community, the public and/or members of associations of patients affected by the specific diseases that are going to be studied. By incorporating such individuals, the aim is to promote multidisciplinarity and plurality, as well as transparency in decision-making and public trust in the research being conducted. However, patients' associations can be created and supported by the pharmaceutical, food and biotechnology industries. Is this the desire of patients or of the industry behind it? Patient's associations represented in research ethics committees may act as lobbies in favour for specific interests and to promote research and marketing of certain drugs or products of interest to the industry.

Authors such as Evans argue that the institutionalisation of bioethics in the US through the establishment of governmental advisory committees avoids democratic control by the public. In his opinion, although bioethics should be a space open to deliberation and public debate, scientists do not support public involvement in their research, arguing that the public is unable to understand it. Bioethics did not arise to increase or promote individual freedom, but rather, to regulate and control the population in order for research to freely follow its course and achieve agreed upon objectives. Those goals are determined in decisions that preceded its approval and development through research ethics committees, whose deliberative and decision-making process is inaccessible to the average citizen.[24]

---

[23]Directive 2001/20/EC of the European Parliament and of the Council of 4 April 2001 on the approximation of the laws, regulations and administrative provisions of the Member States relating to the implementation of good clinical practice in the conduct of clinical trials on medicinal products for human use.

[24]Evans (2002).

In the opinion of Annas, also regarding the US context, the change in name from "committees on human research" to Institutional Review Boards (IRBs) would indicate that the primary role of these committees is to defend the interests of the institutions in which they are embedded. This author notes that the success of these committees lies in the specificity of their mandate, in their decision-making process which is established by federal law, and in the support that they receive from doctors and foundations that finance biomedical research. Identifying with the needs and interests of the institution on which they depend is a disadvantage for IRBs, which in many cases do not have the experience necessary to analyse complex research proposals. Thus, it is not surprising that IRBs have, with the protection of regulations, approved research that otherwise could never have taken place because of its potential harmful effect on human beings.[25] This critique reveals that behind the rhetoric of the principles of autonomy, beneficence and justice, essential to bioethics are the efforts of the biomedical research industry to maintain the support of ethics committees, especially in developing countries, where much transnational research is being conducted and where the research takes precedence over improving health and educational conditions. It appears that what is needed would be to create ethics committees in biomedical research and train their members in the countries where research involving human beings is taking place.

Although the need for training members of ethics committees in biomedical research is not disputed, in my opinion local and cultural issues must be taken into consideration in capacity-building rather than the imposition of a particular model. It is not about exporting ideologies to local governments and researchers. Research ethics committees must avoid a kind of bioethics that serves institutional interests distant from, and even contrary to, their main goal that is to be the guarantors of the rights of individuals in research.

5 Research Ethics Committees from an Institutional Perspective: Unresolved Issues

From the institutional perspective, for ethics committees to function properly, they need institutional support, and must contribute to raising awareness in society of biomedical research. The rights and interests that are at stake justify this: autonomy and freedom to decide, privacy and confidentiality, freedom of research, and non-discrimination. Transparency and accountability are essential principles in the biomedical field. Information and the requirement for informed consent are not sufficient, in my opinion, as a safety valve for the system. On many occasions the informed consent does not operate; it is the case of epidemiological research or the opt-out systems where presumed consent rules operates.

---

[25] Annas (1991).

There are various initiatives that set out to connect research activity in biomedicine with patients, with individuals, and with society. In this regard, the responsible research and innovation (RRI) that Europe promotes has among its goals public engagement in the design of research projects, scientific education, ethics, open access and promoting gender equality.[26] RRI implies that all societal actors, including patients and healthy volunteers work together to align the research process with the values, needs and expectations of society. Thus, RRI raises a question that seems crucial for plural societies: decision-making and control of research by the people who finance it through taxation, by those who provide the material (bodies, human biological samples, personal data), and by those who receive the treatment or intervention.

From the practical point of view, in the Spanish case for example, each centre or institution that carries out research in human beings must either have its own research ethics committee or be registered with that of another centre. The accreditation and control come under the general health authority of each autonomous community. Europe has adopted different models: a state committee, various committees depending on the type of research (clinical trials, other types of biomedical research, etc.). Normally the research ethics committees are organised in a full committee and a standing committee that will later bring to the full committee the most important issues for discussion and for decisions to be made as to whether or not to approve the reviewed projects. National and international lawmakers have resolved to create research ethics committees to tackle highly controversial and changing issues. Scientific research moves rapidly and ethics committees must be prepared to give answers to, for example, gene editing (including the CRISPR/Cas technique), cell therapy, or synthetic biology, even when these possibilities are not regulated at all. In this regard, research ethics committees may have turned into consultants rather than just reviewers. Research can bring with it processes of innovation, of development of business models based on personal human data as happens with *mHealth* (health apps) that raise new scenarios. The innovation areas of public and private research centres and institutions, consult these figures about ethical, legal and societal issues related to innovation. So, research ethics committees have become an ethical guarantee that goes beyond research. It is necessary rethink the function of research ethics committees in the twenty-first century.

It is not common to share protocols and conferences and seminars are not held to share experiences, lessons learned and working procedures that will make it possible to improve deliberations and decision-making and to develop good practices. There is a lack of methodologies and route maps to identify the problems in different areas of biomedical research.[27] One example is the need for research ethics committees on guidance for reviewing research protocols that applied big data analytics. In biomedicine big data analytics is oriented towards developing precision medicine and improving health care systems, making them more effective and efficient. Through

[26]Casado et al. (2016).

[27]*Guide for research ethics committees members* (Council of Europe 2011).

mathematical algorithms it is possible to correlate data sets, including personal information, to predict patterns of behaviour in order to improve decision-making.[28] It has its risks and advantages, but the problem is not in applying it, but in the ability of the members of the ethics committees to understand it, identify the challenges and its impact on the rights that are at stake. With the widespread of big data analytics it is necessary to incorporate as members of research ethics committees profiles such as the data scientists who will contribute to properly review research protocols. This is one of the new trends in research to which the ethics committees must give a response as soon as possible.

Regarding the use of human biological samples and their storage in biobanks, it could be said that in Spain, for example there is no standardisation of decision-making processes. Biobanks are central features of translational biomedicine and they are fed by biological samples from individuals. While there is a legal framework from 2007, there are still many outstanding questions that must be solved by consideration of the rights and interests at stake. The tension between individual freedom and solidarity, and decisions about the benefits and drawbacks of scientific progress must be reviewed by research ethics committees. Questions that are closely related to national Research and Development and Innovation plans, prioritising the resources and research lines and establishing public-private synergies so that therapies, interventions and treatments can be developed and delivered.

The composition and working procedures of the research ethics committees are key for understanding the virtues and defects and identifying the unresolved issues. Regarding these practical questions, which lawmakers have not been able or have not wished to go into too much detail, there are very few published works that allow conclusions to be drawn about the current situation and that go beyond clinical trials with drugs for human use. The trend is to work in isolation, precisely because there are few reference points and because the wide margin of appreciation of the research ethics committees conferred by law leads their members to confuse their competencies. Are they judges? Do they interpret applicable law? Must all members have training in ethics or bioethics? There are many questions that arise from practice. Even neighbouring committees barely communicate, if at all, a very curious situation and even more so when scientific research is the pillar of excellent healthcare. To alleviate disconnection between ethics committees and to share problems and working procedures from the University of Barcelona and the Bioethics and Law Observatory, the network of ethics committees of the public universities and other research bodies was set up.[29] This network has become a European benchmark in the framework of the European Research Universities League (LERU), precisely because it proposes a hybrid model that combines face-to-face meetings dealing with specific, highly controversial situations and with a permanently updated online

[28]Mittelstadt and Floridi (2016).

[29]The Network of ethics committees of the public universities and other research bodies http://www.ub.edu/rceue/ accessed Aug 2019

platform for sharing the know-how generated by each of the universities and public research bodies that it comprises.

"No time, no money, no resources" this is the common response in research when requests are made for improvements in the research ethics committees. It is a fallacy that, in my opinion, persists and lingers precisely in order to favour certain interests that are possibly not those interests that justify the creation of research ethics committees. There seems to be institutional bioethics and a radical bioethics. Only the latter will allow change and adaptation to new times. There is not enough time to assess projects properly: the committees usually meet every fortnight, though meetings now might be weekly for assessing clinical trials and health products (see European rules for clinical trials); the question should be raised of whether it will be necessary to professionalise the research ethics committees that have up to now relied excessively on voluntary contributions from people who are contracted by the institution, as well as by those who are independent members. The complexity of research calls for more hours of dedication from members. Projects are not monitored properly despite the legal requirement to do so. Monitoring is fundamental and is closely connected with the principles of transparency and accountability. Competitiveness and the race for funding are always present and generate tensions that members of research ethics committees have to manage appropriately. Many of them are hired by the research institution and may have conflicts of interest without even being able to detect them. This leads on to the unexplored and highly controversial matter of conflicts of interest and issues related to scientific integrity.[30]

Research ethics committees have to apply the principle of proportionality as a starting point in determining the ratio of risk to benefit for the individuals taking part or affected, above the interests of science and of society itself, which desires to apply experimental treatments and have access to proven therapies. Research ethics committees must avoid making subjective and arbitrary decisions; they must interpret applicable regulations, specify which arguments are used, and justify their decisions after weighing up the rights that are at stake.

With the application of the European Data Protection Regulation since May 2018[31] research ethics committees should adapt their dynamics to the new requirements. Risk analysis in personal data treatments must be one of the issues that these committees will require from researchers and centres where the research is to be carried out. The goal is to make a proper study of the rights and interests at stake according to the information they receive concerning the treatment and use of personal data in each of the projects submitted for review. For this matter Data Protection Officers, new figures in each research institution that should be independent, are crucial and must be consulted by research ethics committees in case there is any doubt on data protection. So, research ethics committees now must identify what

[30]See *The European Code of Conduct for Research Integrity* (ALLEA, 2017).

[31]Regulation (EU) 2016/679 of the European Parliament and of the Council of 27 April 2016 on the protection of natural persons with regard to the processing of personal data and on the free movement of such data, and repealing Directive 95/46/EC (General Data Protection Regulation).

may seem to be research but is not, being pure market niches for marketing goods that should be outside the market because of their impact on people and societies. The protection of dignity through the protection of personal data in research in the digital society has become a priority task for the research ethics committees.

6 Conclusions and Proposals

The protection of the rights and interests of individuals, their safety and their well-being are the reason for the existence of research ethics committees. Thus, these bodies are mechanisms to protect human subjects in biomedical research, as they allow a way of doing bioethics based on respect for internationally recognised human rights and universally accepted bioethical principles.

Research ethics committees represent a practical bioethics that is useful in plural, democratic societies provided that there is adequate training and strengthening of skills in bioethics, and also that procedures are fostered that allow proper decision-making. In this way, the committees will be able to adequately perform the duties assigned to them. It is thus a matter of taking into consideration the contribution they can make based on the expertise and aptitudes of their professional and lay members. The need to establish research ethics committees is justified in particular because of their independent and interdisciplinary character, and the transparency of their work procedures. The deliberative process carried out by ethics committees is an additional value in dealing with bioethical research issues. Because of the profile of their members, research ethics committees contribute to social cohesion on controversial issues that can divide the public and for which there are no unshakable and risk-free answers.

It is necessary to strengthen a line of research in bioethics that analyzes the situation of research ethics committees, that is critical, and that will contribute to revising and improving the conditions for the creation of committees, their composition, functions, working procedures, and the training and capacity-building of their members. These committees have become necessary to address ethical, legal and societal issues in biomedical research. In addition, they have an important role in training and raising awareness about bioethics.

Research ethics committees in the biomedical setting are still today closely linked with clinical trials to develop medicinal products protocols for human use, as are often their members. There has been no in-depth analysis about who should have the competence to make decisions, and what changes are needed to properly review other types of biomedical research, such as big data analytics applied to research in health care or research that involves social interventions. In particular, there has not been enough discussion about the evaluation of research that involves applying gene editing techniques, which is becoming widespread today and lacks adequate regulation.

The implementation of new regulations in the field of research with human beings should be analysed in the face of possible distortions and instrumentalisation of research ethics committees. Research ethics committees should not generate a false sense of security; nor should they carry out a bioethics removed from the ends for which they were established, or to provide support to private, institutional and illegitimate interests.

It is necessary to generate working procedures and spaces for communication between research ethics committees, in order to share positive and negative experiences and generate good practices in research, incorporating the specific characteristics of each type of research, the challenges that are raised and possible solutions. In the digital society research ethics committees must pay special attention to the rights and interests that are at stake. Fairness, non-discrimination, free development of the personality and intimacy without adversely affecting freedom of research must be analysed in depth, ensuring that enthusiasm for technology does not prevent identification of the necessary ratio of risk to benefit or favour market niches, especially of personal data disguised as research. Research ethics committees have the obligation to analyse research taking into consideration its impact on future generations.

References

Annas GJ (1991) At law: ethics committees: from ethical comfort to ethical cover. The Hastings Center Report 21

Baron J (2006) Against bioethics. MIT Press, London

Beecher HK (1966) Ethics and clinical research. N Engl J Med 274:1354–1360

Brody BA (1998) The ethics of biomedical research: an international perspective. Oxford University Press, Oxford

Casado M, López Baroni MJ (coords) (2018) Handbook of Secular Bioethics I. Edicions Universitat de Barcelona, Barcelona

Casado M, López Baroni MJ (coords) (2021) The Oviedo Convention turns 20 years old: proposals for its modification. Edicions Universitat de Barcelona, Barcelona

Casado M, Patrao MDC, De Lecuona I, Carvalho AS, Araujo J (2016) Declaration on scientific integrity in responsible research and innovation. Edicions Universitat de Barcelona, Barcelona

Council of Europe (1997a) The Convention for the Protection of Human Rights and Dignity of the Human Being with regard to the Application of Biology and Medicine: Convention on Human Rights and Biomedicine

Council of Europe (1997b) Convention on Biomedicine and Human Rights, Article 2

Council of Europe (2011) Guide for research ethics committees members

De Lecuona I (2011) Ethics committees: the challenges facing bioethics in the 21st century. ABR 3 (2):164–169

Directive 2001/20/EC of the European Parliament and of the Council of 4 April 2001 on the approximation of the laws, regulations and administrative provisions of the Member States relating to the implementation of good clinical practice in the conduct of clinical trials on medicinal products for human use

European Group on Ethics in Science and New Technologies (2013) Statement on Clinical Trials

Evans JH (2002) Playing God?. Human genetic engineering and the rationalization of public bioethical debate. The University Chicago Press, Chicago

Explanatory Report to Additional Protocol on Biomedical Research of 2005 (http://www.coe.int/en/web/conventions/full-list/-/conventions/treaty/195). Accessed 18 Aug 2019

Hottois G (1990) Le paradigme bioéthique: une éthique pour la technoscience. De Boeck Université, Paris
Lysaught MT (2009) Docile bodies: transnational research ethics as biopolitics. J Med Philos Aug 34(4):384–408
Mittelstadt BD, Floridi L (eds) (2016) The ethics of biomedical big data. Springer, London
Regulation (EU) 2016/679 of the European Parliament and of the Council of 27 April 2016 on the protection of natural persons with regard to the processing of personal data and on the free movement of such data, and repealing Directive 95/46/EC (General Data Protection Regulation)
Regulation (EU) No 536/2014 of the European Parliament and of the Council of 16 April 2014 on clinical trials on medicinal products for human use, and repealing Directive 2001/20/EC
Research Ethics Committees: 23 Declaration of Helsinki: Ethical Principles for Medical Research Involving Human Subjects, World Medical Association (WMA) Adopted by the 18th WMA General Assembly, Helsinki, Finland, June 1964 and amended by the: 29th WMA General Assembly, Tokyo, Japan, October 1975 35th WMA General Assembly, Venice, Italy, October 1983 41st WMA General Assembly, Hong Kong, September 1989 48th WMA General Assembly, Somerset West, Republic of South Africa, October 1996 52nd WMA General Assembly, Edinburgh, Scotland, October 2000 53rd WMA General Assembly, Washington DC, USA, October 2002 (Note of Clarification added) 55th WMA General Assembly, Tokyo, Japan, October 2004 (Note of Clarification added) 59th WMA General Assembly, Seoul, Republic of Korea, October 2008 64th WMA General Assembly, Fortaleza, Brazil, October 2013
Rodotà S (2009) La vita e le regole. Tra diritto e non diritto. Feltrinelli, Rome
Sandel M (2013) What money can't buy. The moral limits of markets. Penguin, London
The Convention for the Protection of Human Rights and Dignity of the Human Being with regard to the Application of Biology and Medicine: Convention on Human Rights and Biomedicine and The Additional Protocol to the Convention on Human Rights and Biomedicine, concerning Biomedical Research
The Council for International Organizations of Medical Sciences CIOMS (2016) International Ethical Guidelines for Biomedical Research Involving Human Subjects
The European Code of Conduct for Research Integrity (2017)
The National Commission for the Protection of Human Subjects of Biomedical and Behavioral Research, USA (1979) The Belmont Report. Office of the Secretary Ethical Principles and Guidelines for the Protection of Human Subjects of Research, April 18
The Network of ethics committees of the public universities and other research bodies http://www.ub.edu/rceue/. Accessed Aug 2019
UNESCO (2005) Universal Declaration on Bioethics and Human Rights. Article 12
World Medical Association (1964) Declaration of Helsinki: Ethical Principles for Medical Research Involving Human Subjects

Consultative Boards at International Level

Carlos Maria Romeo-Casabona

Abstract Biomedical sciences are constantly raising new and very specific questions related with ethics and law. Since these problems often have a universal dimension, international bioethics committees have provided guidance criteria to help focus and reasonably resolve ethical and legal issues beyond the limited scope at the state level, as well as governance related matters. This paper analyses the functions and competences of the most relevant committees currently in place: Committee of Bioethics (DH-BIO) of the Council of Europe, the International Bioethics Committee of UNESCO (IBC) and the European Group on Ethics in Science and New Technologies (EGE), which advises the Chair of the European Commission and the European Commissioners.

As a result, we conclude that International and supranational committees of bioethics should possess namely formative and training qualification, multidisciplinarity, independence, pluralism and transparency. Some criteria are provided in the light to improve their work and the main quoted principles.

1 The Need for Bioethics Committees as Independent Advisory Bodies

For several decades, great attention has been paid to the problems of ethical or legal nature arising during clinical care of patients and attention to their environment. Furthermore, the qualitative leaps that have occurred in the field of biomedical

---

This work is carried out within the framework of the Basque Government funding to Research Groups of the Basque University System (IT 1066-16). When I wrote it, I was a member of the DH BIO (Committee of Bioethics) of the Council of Europe (see below) and when first proof review was carried out, I was a member of the European Group of Ethics in Science and New Technologies (EGE, see below). Currently I remain a member of both bodies.

C. M. Romeo-Casabona (✉)
University of the Basque Country, Bilbao, Spain
e-mail: carlosmaria.romeo@ehu.eus

L. Busatta, C. Casonato (eds.), *Axiological Pluralism*, Ius Gentium: Comparative Perspectives on Law and Justice 92, https://doi.org/10.1007/978-3-030-78475-1_5

research have aroused greater sensitivity in many social sectors, given that a relevant number of the technical-scientific applications in humans cast doubts on their ethical acceptability and their possible effect on the rights of human beings involved in their use.

To deal with them, healthcare and clinical trial ethics committees have been created many years ago. Both seek to be decisive interlocutors in these activities, with the primary role of ensuring the protection of fundamental rights of people involved in these activities, especially patients and individuals participating in clinical research. In fact, clinical trial ethics committees are mandatory and their decisions are binding for researchers and promoters in almost all developed countries.

Notwithstanding the foregoing, we are aware that effective protection of human beings involved in activities related to biomedicine cannot be achieved only through solutions and practical responses deriving from the national laws of states and other non-strictly legal regulatory procedures, since, when human rights are affected in many occasions, universal responses are increasingly required. On the other hand, biomedical sciences are constantly raising new and very specific questions, which limit or hinder the application of more general legal instruments on the protection of human rights that have been adopted within the international community.

Old and new dilemmas posed by healthcare and biomedical research and progress, in short, the protection of the health and autonomy of citizens, demand a special and growing attention from the international community, as a privileged way of promoting certain forms of behaviour and penetrating national laws with the purpose of being respectful towards human rights.

It is true that fundamental rights and civil freedoms of all the inhabitants of the planet, who are their theoretical titleholders, have found acceptance in their prior condition as human beings, in various treaties and declarations, as with the Universal Declaration of Human Rights (1948) and the International Covenant on Civil and Political Rights (1966). Therefore, universal instruments must also be considered as legal references that design an appropriate framework for the current research needs regarding health sciences and the development of related technologies, based on respect for human dignity and other rights that are inherent to it.

In this sense, the ethical discourse has been providing an axiological framework over several decades of reflection, discussion and configuration. The result of this was the Universal Declaration on Bioethics and Human Rights adopted by the UNESCO General Conference.[1]

The singularity of this statement is that of listening to the concerns of the human being emerging with the millennium, as an archetype of the "bioethical man",[2] as it

[1]Adopted by the General Conference on 19 October 2005. See Caporale and Pavone (2018), passim.

[2]I do not want to confuse the reader by making him/her believe that by mentioning (Bio)ethics and (Bio)law he/she is identifying both normative universes, whose differences and relations I have emphasized in other works of mine [namely, Romeo-Casabona (1998), p. 151 ff.], but I just intend

is the awareness of their responsibility not only in relation to other human beings, but also to their surroundings (the environment, the biosphere) and to the human beings who will come after them: namely the future generations. On the other hand, the Declaration has been sensitive to cultural, ideological and political differences,[3] as well as to social and economic inequalities, which are widespread across the planet.[4]

Therefore, it can be said that it has achieved a universal set of principles for the identification of which Bioethics has been instrumental, adding diverse knowledge, including ethical and legal, and that, as explained above, are rooted in human rights, some of them being new. Therefore, rather than *Global* Bioethics, we should speak—like a magma nutrient of the Declaration of UNESCO—of *Universal* Bioethics and Biolaw. This latter satisfies a minimal but sufficient set of principles and values *shared by the whole of humankind* today and which are guaranteed by the human rights recognised by the Declaration and other similar international legal instruments.

This entire legal arsenal does not arise, however, by chance or whim, because there was and still is a social and, especially, scientific and technological context that has become necessarily relevant. Indeed, we are sufficiently aware of the benefits that could be promoted by research in biomedicine and the innovations that this knowledge can generate in the field of biotechnology.

With regard to human biotechnology, its achievements focus on two areas of great importance for humans: health (diagnostic procedures and treatments, including gene editing) and reproduction, whether or not linked to health problems of a partner or future child. The development and use of biotechnological processes and products in humans and research that supports them should be respectful towards human rights and compatible with taking precautions and safety measures in handling living matter, even more so when it has been the subject of genetic interventions, the interference of which in other living beings, including humans, is still unpredictable.

The complexity of the analysis of these kinds of issues, have made national political and institutional authorities and international agencies understand the need for specialised and qualified and independent figures to provide them with criteria in order to advise them before making their decisions. On the one hand, scientific and technological issues, and on the other, ethical and legal questions, are intermingled, as well as various aspects that complete the need for a plural and all-encompassing perspective.

International and supranational bioethics committees emerge to meet the need in this area of clarification by experts. These committees are based on multidisciplinary and transparency and plural and independent members as well, and their main task is

---

to highlight the parallel road they follow, as well as the connections between them, particularly in the international arena.

[3]See Article 12 of the Universal Declaration on Bioethics and Human Rights: "The Importance of cultural diversity and pluralism should be given due regard [...]".

[4]See Articles 14 & 15 of the Universal Declaration on Bioethics and Human Rights.

to fulfil an advisory or consultative non-executive function for public bodies and authorities and serve as guidance for citizens.

It is almost unanimous that the methodology of these committees should be based on a deliberative process, i.e. on the evaluation by all their members of the various arguments in favour of or against one or more possible decisions. Decision-making is the final phase of a deliberative process, unless none is chosen, and provided that this option is within the powers of the relevant body. Transparency and publicity are also often seen as essential requirements; however, it may be problematic to apply these two principles to the deliberative phase.[5]

2 Background

Existing bioethical committees with an international or supranational—European—level have two immediate antecedents: setting up national bioethics advisory committees, and a favourable climate towards taking this step beyond national borders.

Notwithstanding the greater importance which is granted to ethics research committees and healthcare ethics committees, these are very different in nature. They are created with a very limited territorial area (healthcare ethics committees are usually assigned to a single hospital or health centre, as are clinical trial committees, although they can extend their action to several research centres in the same area or territory). Also they can perform executive and not only advisory functions (e.g. ethics research committee decisions can be crucial in the authorisation of a specific clinical trial or other biomedical research project).

These features are not present in international committees. However, international committees have adopted their traits of independence, multi-disciplinarity, specialisation, transparency and their method of working (dialogue, deliberation and decision by consensus). In any case, I will try to clarify below whether the latter are sufficiently independent and ideologically plural.

2.1 A Favourable International Context[6]

Other previous international legal instruments on human rights (the Universal Declaration of Human Rights of 10 December 1948, the European Convention for the Protection of Human Rights and Fundamental Freedoms of 4 November 1950 and the American Convention on Human Rights, 22 November 1969), arose in the context of the dramatic experience of a terrible world war. They found their

[5]In favour of applying transparency and publicity to deliberations see Bellver Capella (2016), p. 141.

[6]I have already dealt with this subject more extensively: Romeo-Casabona (2000), p. 15 ff.

ideological and legal precedents even earlier, in revolutionary times, as a reaction and victory against the dominant political power (such as the Declaration of Rights of the Good People of Virginia, USA, 1776, and the French Declaration of the Rights of Man and of the Citizen, 1789). In contrast, those legal tools relating to Biomedicine have been implemented in a very different atmosphere.

Indeed, the development of this normative activity has taken place in a context in which, fortunately, there is no need to claim that serious abuses have been committed on the part of various levels of power, be they political, economic or social. However, several circumstances have contributed decisively to the culmination of several initiatives related to biomedicine and biotechnologies applied to human beings. Such circumstances I would now like to highlight as follows:

(i) An awareness for the need to promote scientific knowledge and development in this field has arisen, from which many results for the good of humankind are expected. There is also a consciousness that their proper use must be ensured for all human beings, without any geographical, cultural or economic distinction, but at the same time, any danger arising from a deviant use of scientific achievements linked to biomedical sciences and technologies should be prevented, since it could lead to uncontrollable and irreversible catastrophes of an incalculable magnitude.

(ii) These hazards—as well as the benefits—can affect both individuals and all humankind as a species.[7]

(iii) It can be perceived a potential confrontation with freedom of research, if it were subject to prohibitions or important restrictions, as well as with private or sectorial interests of some de facto powers, the latter being linked to some areas of international productive activity. Therefore, we must seek equilibrium and, in any event, ensure protection of the rights of both individuals and human groups.

(iv) This double individual and collective—regarding the species—approach on the one hand, and the involvement of scientific and technological development on the other, have highlighted that previously existing international (and also national) legal instruments, which mainly regard human rights, were not sufficient for the new challenges of protection of the rights, goods and values concerned. There was an agreement on the need to also look for other partly new procedures, while recognising the importance of the rights already enshrined, and of values and legal goods accepted or recognised, such as dignity, life, freedom, equality and privacy, among others.

(v) A rapid legal internationalisation of these matters has taken place. Firstly, due to the very internationalisation of scientific research on biomedical sciences and ethical debates that have promoted the results of such research; and, secondly, because fundamental expressions of the sovereignty of nations were not directly and immediately compromised.

[7] Also in this sense, Bergel (1998), p. 38.

Indeed, the emergence and early development of the law of biomedicine and biotechnology has usually manifested itself as a "soft law" or non-coercive law or not having burdensome legal consequences. Probably, the most evident exception to this trend concerns certain aspects of human biotechnology, in which several offenses generally with very high penalties have been introduced in penal comparative law (e.g. in relation to human reproductive cloning and genetic engineering applied to human beings). This criminalisation approach has given rise to a debate on the purely symbolic effect that Criminal Law could radiate.

(vi) Finally, this normative or pre-normative activity has given rise to the delegation of initial work to non-political instances, such as international bioethics committees, which in principle consist of experts only and not politicians, being the latter excluded as members of these bodies.

2.2 Institutional Antecedents

Firstly, a direct antecedent has been the creation of national ethics committees, particularly those of a permanent nature.[8] One should not forget, however, how important the existence of advisory bodies of bioethics committees *ad hoc*, i.e., to perform a certain temporary task, was for this current creation of international bodies. I would like to highlight The *National Commission for the Protection of Human Subjects of Biomedical and Behavioural Research* (1974–1978), who developed the so-called "Belmont Report" (1978). However, the first national body to be created with a permanent nature and complying with the other abovementioned features was that of France in 1983, whose very name delineated its strictly consultative role.[9]

With regard to joint international bodies, the following may be mentioned:[10] firstly, the Bioethics Committee of the Council of Europe. Shortly after, almost at the same time (1993), the other two instances of international or supranational character that currently exist were created: The International Bioethics Committee of UNESCO (IBC) and the European Group on Ethics, which advises the European College of Commissioners, European Commission.

Attention shall now be focused on these three bodies.

[8]Díez Fernández (2007), p. 9 ff.

[9]*Committee Consultatif National d'Ethique pour les Sciences de la Vie et de la Santé*, created by a Decree of the President of the Republic.

[10]There are some others, most notably: The Committee on Medical Ethics of the World Medical Association, The World Commission on the Ethics of Scientific Knowledge and Technology (COMEST), UNESCO, composed of eighteen experts from all over the world; The Council for International Organisations of Medical Sciences (CIOMS).

2.2.1 The Bioethics Committee (DH-BIO) of the Council of Europe

Council of Europe took the first step in the creation of an advisory committee on International Bioethics in 1985 with the establishment of the *Ad Hoc Committee of Experts on Bioethics* (CAHBI) under the direct authority of the Committee of Ministers. Since then, this committee and its successors (*Steering Committee on Bioethics, CDBI, Committee of Bioethics,* currently named DH-BIO) have performed an immense task, organising international conferences and workshops and elaborating numerous legal tools and documents on the most diverse subjects related to biomedicine and human biotechnology. Most of them got agreement and have been approved by the Committee of Ministers of the Council of Europe (Ministers for Foreign Affairs) in the form of Recommendations and Conventions.

Notwithstanding the great importance of this type of work, the most relevant achievement of this body in the field of Biomedicine was undoubtedly the preparation of an international treaty, which was also approved by the Committee of Ministers and submitted for signing by the nations: The Convention on Human Rights and Biomedicine (Oviedo Convention).[11] This international legal instrument was the first to be approved by the international community and deals with many legal issues related to biomedicine. Furthermore, it has been implemented by means of an already abundant number of additional protocols.[12]

It should be noted that this Committee was not only a pioneer in the international arena and produced numerous drafts of legal instruments, but, above all, it has always held vanguard positions on issues and always with respect for human rights and seeking to reconcile this position as a guarantor with the promotion of science.[13]

The Bioethics Committee (DH-BIO) is composed of the delegates from the forty-seven Member States of the Council of Europe (between one and four per nation, according to the decision of each government, who has only one vote) and observers from other non-member States (Mexico, The Holy See), the EU, various international non-governmental bodies and representatives of other committees or Directions of the Council of Europe, all with a voice but no vote. The governments appoint their representatives according to their own criteria, usually without observing any transparent and objective selection procedure. In addition, at least in theory, representatives may receive instructions on specific issues from their respective governments, although in fact most of them operate with a wide margin of independence.

[11] *Convention for the Protection of Human Rights and Dignity of the Human Being with regard to the Application of Biology and Medicine: Convention on Human Rights and Biomedicine*, submitted for signature in the city of Oviedo on 4 April 1997.

[12] The work of other non-permanent committees consisted in two other Conventions on biomedical issues: Convention on the Counterfeiting of Medical Products and similar crimes involving threats to public health, 2011; Convention against Human Organ Trafficking (Convention of Santiago), 2015.

[13] Romeo-Casabona (2002), p. 45 f.

2.2.2 The International Bioethics Committee (IBC) of UNESCO

This Committee, which is both permanent and multidisciplinary, was created in 1993 and is the only universal forum acting as a think tank, which reflects on bioethics. There is no doubt regarding the influence that the work of this Committee can have on the formal adoption of certain instruments by the UNESCO General Conference, as a Declaration, and due to the universal spatial competence enjoyed by this body, which had created that Committee. As mentioned above, the Committee was responsible for drafting the Universal Declaration on the Human Genome and Human Rights (1997), the International Declaration on Human Genetic Data (2003) and the Universal Declaration on Bioethics and Human Rights (2005).

The abovementioned committee is composed of 36 experts appointed by the Director General of UNESCO for a term of four years, based on equitable geographical representation. However, candidates are usually proposed in one way or another by the Governments of Member States, which is certainly not a guarantee of the independence of those appointed, at least for the political ideology of their governments, who may well seek an affinity of this nature. It is also true that deliberations within the Committee are based on budget independence.

Regarding the effectiveness of this committee,[14] it is important to mention the Intergovernmental Bioethics Committee (IGBC). It was created in 1998 and consists of 36 Member States elected by the General Conference of UNESCO, which meet at least once every two years to review the IBC's advice and recommendations, present their views and submit perspectives and propositions. It in fact constitutes a kind of second instance that filters political interests from the drafts of the Declarations. This second draft's review is carried out almost openly, before approval, to then proceed to the final instance: the General Conference.

2.2.3 The European Group on Ethics in Sciences and New Technologies

The European Group on Ethics in Sciences and New Technologies (EGE)[15] is a permanent and independent advisory body of supranational (European) rank, which advises the President of the European Commission and the College of Commissioners. Since its creation in 1991, the EGE has provided the Commission with high-quality and independent advice on the ethical aspects of science and new technologies in relation to EU legislation or policies.

[14]Some provisions of the Declarations of 1997 and 2003 establish that it is a task of the IBC to control the application of Declarations by nations. It has been considered a very positive new task by Gros Espiell (2006), p. 1412 f.

[15]Its current full name is The European Group on Ethics in Science and New Technologies (EGE).

It has given numerous opinions and statements which are stances adopted on various topics related to biomedicine and technologies in general.[16] They are addressed to EU Authorities (as mentioned above, the President of the EC or the Commissioners) as per an express request on their part or on the Committee's own initiative.

Opinions are not explicitly articulated proposals that serve as the basis for approval by the formal channels of policy development and approval established in the EU, but rather guidelines for those decisions—normative or political—that can be made by the highest EU political decision-making bodies. The EGE tends to take into account the ethical, cultural and ideological pluralism existing in Europe and its proposals are usually the result of a broad consensus, so as a rule they are not too rigid.[17]

EGE members are appointed on the basis of their professional qualifications. Currently they submit their candidature directly to the European Commission without the intermediation of the governments of Member States or other political entities, and are experts in the fields of empirical, nature and social sciences, philosophy, ethics and law, guaranteeing an independent and multidisciplinary perspective on the ethical issues posed by scientific and technological innovation. The candidates' pre-selection is entrusted to a small group of people (three persons), qualified in these matters from different perspectives or with a previous political extent approach, and who currently do not usually assume responsibilities directly linked to the political actions of the EU.

3 Features of International and Supranational Committees

As can be seen from the above considerations, despite the efforts made only in a very broad sense, it can be argued that a definitive standard has been established regarding the most important features of these committees (functions, procedure for designating their members, duration of mandate).[18] It is true, however, that one can point to some of the most relevant features shared by the various systems that have been designed; but, as shown above, they do not always appear with the same intensity.

We should distinguish the traits of members that, on the one hand, must ensure the quality of their work and the effectiveness and fairness of their proposals (specialisation and multidisciplinary nature) and, on the other, those that must ensure pluralism in their decisions (independence and ideological, cultural and political pluralism and transparency as well).

[16]The last Opinions approved by the EGE are: European Group on Ethics in Science and New Technologies (EGE), Artificial Intelligence, Robotics and 'Autonomous' Systems, (2018a); Future of Work? Future of Society? (2018b); Ethics of Genome Editing (2021), among others.

[17]On this opinion see also Bioy (2016), p. 77.

[18]VVAA (2006), p. 18 f.

3.1 Specialisation

It is generally accepted that the specialisation and qualification of members of advisory committees on bioethics must be essential requirements. Fortunately, this is often the case, and one can see that this trend is becoming more marked.

However, it should not be forgotten that, at an international level, the members of some of these committees are appointed by national governments, and sometimes these governments prefer to select a public employee regardless of his or her expertise in the management of medicine, research, technology, ethics or law, but frequently failing of experience in the bioethical discourse or knowledge of issues related to bioethics.

This procedure, which should be avoided in any case, is sometimes adopted for convenience (in order not to have to look for an "expert" to request his or her services pro bono) or due to a preference to rely on the loyalty of the public employee to the position of the government itself. However, in many cases political authorities have not yet taken a stance due to their lack of knowledge of the relevant aspects and the criteria that should be adopted to carry out executive or policy decisions and therefore the expert cannot be provided with instructions or guidelines.

On the other hand, these types of committees have been criticised, both nationally and internationally, for the risk that decisions of great social importance will ultimately be taken by a group of "wise men and women", who are said to have no democratic legitimacy, since they have not undergone a process of participatory election. However, this criticism is not based on reality. As experience shows, the work of the committees is the result of dialogue and agreement (usually by consensus) with which it is intended, at least theoretically, to provide answers that are socially acceptable for most of the population, or which, as far as possible, consider the interests of the minority positions of some groups of citizens.

Final decisions are always taken by public authorities and politicians, without neglecting their obligations to the benefit of what experts have proposed or recommended, as they can decide to adopt or reject their proposals. This is so—and this is how it should be—as the authorities possess the democratic legitimacy to decide what they consider best for the common interest, and this is without prejudice towards being advised by experts, individually or jointly (i.e. by committees) and whether or not they decide to follow their recommendations.

Consequently, criticisms concerning the lack of democratic legitimacy of these committees are also unfounded, since designation is governed by—or should be governed by—the principle of merit and capacity with respect to the specific profile of the expert sought, without prejudice to the fact that authorities prefer putting the political affinity of those against their knowledge and suitability for the position to be filled.

3.2 Multidisciplinarity

It is known that reflection on matters related to biomedical ethics in new technologies generally requires a pluralistic approach or perspective from the point of view of training or specialisation of those somehow involved in it.

The mere participation of people representing a sector of knowledge or professional practice, no matter how qualified they were when elected, would entail the risk of a relativisation of the ethical issues involved, which could thus be unduly put on hold. For example, if bioethical analysis was left only to scientists or clinicians, they could argue that other conflicting interests (e.g., rights of third parties, the value system of society) are subordinate to the "highest" aim of scientific achievement and its alleged benefits for society.[19] Conversely, entrusting the development of proposals exclusively to ethics experts or lawyers could lead to rigid solutions that could block or paralyse scientific research without a clear justification and thus halt the progress of humanity.

This plurality of training and/or "professional mentality" favours, on the contrary, as a first step, debate and confrontation, even in relation to issues that for some may be evident and for others problematic, whether they are closer professionally to scientific research, as they are alien to it and tend, on the contrary, to view it as controversial. At the same time, this educational disparity necessarily leads, as a second step, to seek more balanced and pondered solutions, which is the very spirit that should govern the decisions of the committees.

What the professional profiles or basic training of the committee members should be is a different matter. It seems wise that their profile should not appear too closed and previously assessed, integrating people with clinical and investigative experience, as well as in ethics and legal matters, in the committees, without excluding other profiles.

The former should be part of the committees, as they should not be limited in their analytical function to the "external" issues of the matter on which they must decide. However, sometimes also in order to perceive with precision the importance of the matter assessed from an ethical point of view, the contents and purposes of the projected activity should be assessed in full, and sometimes its methodology as well.

The latter, as a basis in ethical formation, is necessary to make decisions on precisely ethical matters, although it should be assumed that such training can also be possessed—as is increasingly occurring—by people who, in principle, are outside those professions directly related to ethics.

It is also equally essential to include a lawyer among the members, as the conclusions reached by the committee cannot in any way be contrary to human rights, which—e.g., the rights of the subjects of the research to be performed—may be seriously affected by it.

---

[19]The contrary may be derived from the Oviedo Convention: "Primacy of the human being. The interests and welfare of the human being shall prevail over the sole interest of society or science" (Art. 2).

Finally, the presence of members with different training to those mentioned above helps to ensure that intellectual or technical plurality have a marked balance. This does not exclude the temporary assistance *ad hoc* of invited experts to some specific matters.

It is also desirable to ensure the diversity of geographic origin of international committee members, since this will foster the presence of the economic, social and cultural peculiarities and differences of the countries represented in the debates and their deliberations and this should be taken into perspective. And the gender perspective also appears to be necessary.

3.3 Independence

It is a fundamental precondition for committees to be able to carry out their work satisfactorily and ensure that they are effectively fulfilling the objectives assigned to them or on which they have decided to regulate. Without this guarantee, the whole task of the committee will be doomed to failure.

This independence and autonomy of operation is required, firstly, with respect to the subject matter under discussion, so committee members should not be directly or indirectly involved in the matter being evaluated or should abstain from the process of deliberation and decision of the committee (existence of a conflict of interest).[20] This requirement seems easily achievable in committees solely with advisory functions, such as international committees.

Moreover, committee members should not be involved in lobbies or pressure groups when they are making decisions that could directly affect the economic or social interests of companies, financial groups or the like. Something similar should be ensured with regard political and ideological groups or religious affiliation, except in the latter case, when it is formally represented in the committee itself by the ideological or confessional pluralism that is desired to be guaranteed within the same.

It is no less important to safeguard this independence with regard the governments of member states in which committee members are nationals, even if they would have been designated by governments. In this we are faced with a major challenge, namely that it is usual for members of some international committees to formally represent the position of their own governments, as their sovereignty is involved, which implies a clear loss of their independence as experts. In relation with this, we have seen some mixed experiences that exist to separate the expert and the political levels.

Finally, this independence must also be ensured with regard high-level authorities and public employees of the international bodies to which the committees belong; nor should the committee deliberations, decisions and proposals be influenced by

[20]See, more extensively, on the various emerging conflicts, Loris Paul (2011), p. 412 f.

them. Given the increased personal and functional proximity of the Committee secretariats (or similar bodies), senior employees thereof must take special care to constantly keep a neutral and impartial position on the deliberation and decision processes of the committees. They should also facilitate consultations with highly qualified external experts, approved by the committee, when dealing with particularly complex or new or innovative matters, also verifying their expert qualifications and independence.

3.4 Pluralism

This requirement, particularly relevant in the perspective of this book, is very important in any national or international advisory body. The independence of the committee, the credibility of its proposals and therefore its acceptability and, ultimately, its prestige, are at stake. At national level, we provide examples of how pluralism is ensured among members of committees by various means, often by establishing election procedures that are totally or partially unrelated to political power. Regrettably, we also have many examples of practices to the contrary.

The election system can lead political power to control the ideological or political profile of members, also when the designation corresponds to individual organs. In these cases, policy makers often prefer to ensure political affinity rather than professional or training qualification, plurality or independence of those appointed, anticipating that proposals (in the form of reports, opinions, positions) will be those most convenient to the political circumstances and interests of the moment.

Although this risk is real, one should not conclude that ideological and political pluralism is not sufficiently guaranteed. Indeed, in the case of international committees, each nation unilaterally designates or proposes members according to their own criteria and interests (apart from the fact that normally the most highly qualified are chosen, according to an exclusive or priority criterion), without having to negotiate with other member states. In the same way that states are plural, so will be also the members of committees, since their designation does not correspond to a single body, which could monopolise the governments' preferences from the point of view they intended to prioritise, not only politically or ideologically (e.g., preferring scientists or clinicians, or philosophers or lawyers, etc., thereby ruining multidisciplinarity and the advantages implied), or if it were so—the choice by a single body—, there have previously been diverse proposals of candidates from different instances that the electoral body has to take into account.

On the other hand, the sum of many experts dilutes the risk of an objectionable ideological or political bias of the international committee, since the randomness of its profile increases proportionally to the number of members. It may seem paradoxical that the assurance of the pluralism of international committees is ultimately left to chance, but there is no doubt that this factor is safer and more effective than others that could be established, which might have the disadvantage of being rejected by Member States that consider them an intrusion of their sovereignty.

Furthermore, these bodies do not have the necessary requirements to adopt a path of self-nomination as is the case in the European Group of Ethics, which in this way ensures greater independence than pluralism, as this group is not at the service of an international body made up of sovereign states, but of a European supranational body, in which sovereignty, at least in this matter, has been left in the background (without being naïve about the indirect influences that can also be had with this procedure of choice).

3.5 Transparency

In order to ensure pluralism and independence when taking decisions, international and supranational committees need to operate under the principle of transparency, i.e. with clarity of objectives, procedures, deliberations and conclusions, both within their membership and from the officers and staff assisting them.

All committee members have the right to know the information that is relevant to the body's decision-making, without it being withheld from them for any reason whatsoever.

For their part, the officials who assist these committees are compelled to provide all relevant information so that the members can deliberate and decide with sufficient knowledge and freely. This includes providing information related to the body to which they are attached, unless such information is classified as secret and without prejudice to the members' obligation to undertake to comply with duties of confidentiality. The obligation of transparency also entails avoiding any form of discrimination against committee members in terms of limiting the access of any of them to certain information, objectives or procedures.

The principle of transparency also applies to the general public, without prejudice to any restrictions on access to or communication about the deliberative processes of individual committee members, that should be kept confidential.

4 Conclusions

We have seen that the briefly mentioned features that international and supranational committees of bioethics should possess. These are namely formative and training qualification, multidisciplinarity, independence, pluralism and transparency, among others, in one way or another do meet in the main existing committees, at least in those that enjoy greater recognition and prestige, as seems to be the case of the three bodies described above. In particular, ideological and political pluralism clearly seems to comply with minimum acceptable levels in order to be able to trust the credibility of the proposals and opinions of committees.

On the other hand, there are certain working procedures that could contribute to reinforcing the five characteristics of the international committees discussed above:

(i) Ensuring broad (but not endless, sterile and boring) deliberative processes, so that they can express all axiological, scientific and technical perspectives.
(ii) Preferring the agreements reached by consensus which are not the result of a vote, but without excluding the legitimacy of the latter, when reaching consensus is not possible. As a measure of last resort, when a topic of discussion has been adopted by the committee itself, it may be more prudent and pragmatic to "park" or postpone the continuation of its debate if the difficulty of reaching an agreement is perceived as being widely supported.[21]
(iii) Admitting the possibility of collecting dissenting opinions from the document approved by the majority, in the form of a single vote or by a similar procedure, would also strengthen pluralism[22] and provoke to take care of opinions of minority members in the final approved document. However, it is also true that this procedure is not very feasible or practical when it comes to a committee made up of a large number of members.
(iv) Finally, being constantly aware that the impassable barrier for all committees is respect for human dignity and human rights. This respect not only concerns those rights enshrined in general or specific terms in relation to biomedicine and technologies in the various legal instruments, but also those that are the result of reflection, debate and report by bodies such as bioethics committees.

This also means that the appointment procedures should be greatly improved, even when kept under the responsibility of member states who appoint their own representatives, by establishing a common procedure for all of them, as far as possible objective, participatory and transparent.

States or other bodies or persons entrusted with appointing members of committees should be aware that the credibility and prestige they may deserve is largely based on the fact that their independence in the deliberation and decision-making process, as well as their ideological pluralism, is sufficiently guaranteed.

Nor should be it forgotten that, subsequent to the decisions that may have been taken by the committees, political bodies and institutional authorities have adequate forums and other procedures that allow their criteria to prevail.

Nonetheless, it is right to recognise that, on some occasions, State-related decisions will be less comfortable if they run counter to the conclusions and proposals made publicly by the committees.

[21]This was the case, e.g. with a document of the Bioethics Committee (CDBI) Council of Europe on the status of the human embryo, in the preliminary draft stage, as it was soon apparent that it would not be easy to reach an agreement and that perhaps Member States should maintain their own normative divergences. What in other times can be criticised, as a way of circumventing the problematic and therefore uncomfortable areas, and doing so might be a sign of prudence and expression of the existing pluralism.

[22]This way has been previewed at the EGE.

References

Bellver Capella V (2016) International bioethics committees: conditions for a good deliberation. In: Serna P, Seoane JA (eds) Bioethical decision making and argumentation. Springer International Publishing, Switzerland

Bergel SD (1998) Human Rights and Genetics: los principios fundamentales de la Declaración Universal sobre el Genoma y los Derechos Humanos. RevDerGenH 9:17–58

Bioy X (2016) Biodroit. De la biopolitique au droit de la bioétihique. LGDJ, Issy-les-Molineaux

Caporale C, Pavone IR (2018) International biolaw and shared ethical principles: the Universal Declaration on Bioethics and Human Rights. Routledge, London

Díez Fernández JA (2007) Los comités nacionales de bioética. Ed. Comares, Granada

European Group on Ethics in Science and New Technologies (2018a) Artificial intelligence, robotics and 'autonomous' systems. European Commission, Brussels

European Group on Ethics in Science and New Technologies (2018b) Future of work? Future of society? European Commission, Brussels

European Group on Ethics in Science and New Technologies (2021) Ethics of genome editing. European Commission, Brussels

Gros Espiell H (2006) Las declaraciones de la UNESCO en materia de bioética, genética y generaciones futuras. Su importancia y su incidencia en el desarrollo del derecho internacional. Anuario de Derecho Constitucional Latinoamericano, 1405–1416

Loris Paul C (2011) Comité de ética de la investigación (CEI). In: Romeo Casabona CM (Dir.) Enciclopedia de Bioderecho y Bioética, Granada, Cátedra Interuniversitaria de Derecho y Genoma Humano y Editorial Comares I:407–413

Romeo-Casabona CM (1998) La relación entre la Bioética y el Derecho. In: Romeo-Casabona CM (coord) Comares & Ministerio de Sanidad y Consumo, Granada- Madrid

Romeo-Casabona CM (2000) The human genome, object of international law. Revista de la Sociedad Internacional de Bioética 3:105–126

Romeo-Casabona CM (2002) Los genes y sus leyes. El derecho ante el genoma humano. Cátedra Interuniversitaria de Derecho y Genoma Humano - Ed. Comares, Bilbao-Granada

VVAA (2006) Operation of bioethics committees: procedures and policies Guide No. 2. UNESCO, Paris

Reckoning with Growing Pluralism. Potentials and Limits of Conscientious Objection: Conscience Clauses in Abortion Laws in Europe

Davide Paris

Abstract In recent years, conscientious objection has been confronted with growing hostility among the public as well as in scholarly debate. With regard to termination of pregnancy, the right to conscientious objection has frequently been depicted as an unjust and antidemocratic privilege for religious minorities or as part of an illiberal attack to women's rights. This paper argues that, if properly regulated, conscientious objection is not only compatible with the liberal principles western democracies rest on but is also an essential tool of democratic societies committed to pluralism. It discusses the case-law on conscience clauses in abortion laws of supreme and constitutional courts of several European legal orders to show that conscientious objection can significantly contribute to protect pluralism in democratic societies, provided that two criteria are met. First, the right to conscientious objection should be granted only exceptionally, when a moral conflict is as deep as to impinge on the human being's dignity. Second, it should not be granted without providing for adequate mechanisms to ensure the law's effectiveness notwithstanding conscientious objection.

1 Conscientious Objection: A Technique for the Protection of Pluralism

Liberal democratic societies are increasingly confronted with the challenge of axiological pluralism, *i.e.*, the need to ensure that a growing number of different cultures and religions can live together in a context of equal freedom. This puts to the test the endurance of the law as a general and abstract rule. General rules can hardly obtain widespread acceptance in societies characterised by the coexistence of strongly discordant value systems.

This is particularly apparent in the field of bio-law, where the democratic legislature has to reckon with opposing and irreconcilable views on basic concepts

D. Paris (✉)
University of Foggia, Foggia, Italy
e-mail: davide.paris@unifg.it

L. Busatta, C. Casonato (eds.), *Axiological Pluralism*, Ius Gentium: Comparative Perspectives on Law and Justice 92, https://doi.org/10.1007/978-3-030-78475-1_6

like "life", "health", or "dignity". Abortion laws are a case in point. There is no way the legislature can find a satisfactory compromise between those who consider human life untouchable since its conception and those who consider it expendable for the protection of a woman's health. Making the voluntary termination of pregnancy legal necessarily clashes with values a part of the society considers most fundamental.

Conscientious objection then emerges as a technique to ensure a minimum protection of pluralism when the legislature, squeezed between opposing and irreconcilable value systems, cannot strike a fair balance that can be accepted by the whole society. By exempting the minorities from the duty to cooperate in the enforcement of laws they oppose as unjust, conscientious objection makes the law more acceptable to the entire society. Here, conscientious objection shows its potential as a tool to enable the minorities' integration by reconciling their conscience with the law's obligations. Conscience clauses in abortion laws allow anti-abortion physicians to carry on their job within the public health service, without being required to act against their most profound beliefs. Otherwise, they would be forced to choose between complying with the law by disregarding their conscience and complying with their conscience by waiving their job.

However, if not properly regulated, conscientious objection may turn from a liberal into an antidemocratic institution. Nothing prevents a small number of medical practitioners (basically gynecologists and anesthetists) to jeopardise women's access to lawful termination of pregnancy if the law does not provide for adequate mechanisms to avoid this. A well-organised minority can then in practice nullify a law, escaping all democratic procedures. In the law's application, minorities take revenge for their defeat in the law's making. Under this perspective, conscientious objection does not serve minorities' protection but rather their unjust predominance. Should conscientious objection therefore be completely rejected as an improper way to sabotage a law? The answer is in the negative, as long as it is possible to establish some criteria that allow to exploit conscientious objection's potentials to protect pluralism without paving the way for the sabotage of the democratic process' outcomes.

This paper aims at exploring two of these criteria, focusing on the case of conscientious objection to abortion.[1] Firstly, it stresses that the right to conscientious objection introduces an exception to the basic principle that laws are to be complied with regardless of one's consideration of their justice. It is therefore argued that the right to conscientious objection does not concern all cases of disagreement between the law and one's conscience, but can only be exceptionally introduced when a moral conflict is as deep as to impinge on the human being's dignity. Secondly, this paper claims that as the conscience must be protected from the law, so must the law

[1]This contribution builds on my previous work Paris (2011). In this book I discuss several criteria the legislature and the judge should consider when confronted with a request of conscientious objection. Here I confine myself to discussing two of these criteria focusing on a specific issue, namely conscientious objection to abortion.

be protected from the conscience. This means that the right to conscientious objection cannot be granted without providing for adequate mechanisms to ensure the law's effectiveness notwithstanding conscientious objection. For both criteria, examples are given and discussed from the case-law of supreme and constitutional courts of several European legal orders as well as of the European Court of Human Rights.

2 Protecting Conscience: Direct and Indirect Involvement in the Law's Application

Obedience to law does not depend on one's sharing of the law's values. As far as they do not infringe constitutional rules and principles, laws are to be obeyed no matter whether the affected person considers them fair and just or not. In principle, the individual is required to accept that the society's values do not necessarily coincide with her owns. Whereas she remains free to internally disagree with what the law prescribes and to manifest her disagreement publicly, she cannot escape the obligation to comply with the law by alleging her simple moral disagreement. After all, no legal order can make its rules' cogency conditional to their compatibility with every single individual's conscience.[2]

In some exceptional cases, however, the collision between the obligations the law imposes and one's personal belief is so strong that the introduction of the right to conscientious objection appears to be justified by the need to protect one's freedom of conscience.[3] Since it introduces an exception to the principle of laws' cogency—a most essential principle for the very existence of whatever legal order—, conscientious objection should however be limited to those cases in which the moral conflict is so deep as to affect the dignity of the concerned person.[4] It is no surprise that the

[2]This argument has been developed mainly in the Spanish case-law on conscientious objection. *See* in particular *Tribunal Constitucional*, STC 161/1987, FJ 3, concerning conscientious objection to military service, and *Tribunal Supremo*, STS 342/2009, FD 8, concerning conscientious objection to the teaching of "Education for Citizenship and Human Rights." Since *Arrowsmith v UK* App no 7050/75 (ECommHR, 12 October 1978) the European Court of Human Rights has stressed several times that the freedom of conscience enshrined in Art. 9 ECHR "does not protect every act motivated or inspired by a religion or belief and does not always guarantee the right to behave in the public sphere in a way which is dictated by one's personal beliefs." More recently *see*, for example, *S.A.S. v France* App no 43835/11 (ECtHR, Grand Chamber, 1 July 2014), at para. 125.

[3]Here I follow Böckenförde's suggestion to avoid both the risk of confining freedom of conscience to the mere internal forum (a freedom "all dictators that are not interested in Orwellian methods would easily accept") and the risk of defining it as an unconditional right to always act according to one's conscience, which is obviously incompatible with the legal order's normativity: Böckenförde (1970), p. 51.

[4]In the same sense *see* de Sousa e Brito (2002), p. 158. Under this perspective is Art. 12 of the Portuguese Law of Religious Freedom No 16/2001 (21 June 2001) extremely interesting: "1. Freedom of conscience includes the right to object to the compliance with laws that contradict

most well-known forms of conscientious objection, namely to military service and to abortion, somehow involve the moral obligation not to kill anyone.

However, assessing when a moral conflict is deep enough to justify the right to conscientious objection is extremely difficult. On the one hand, there is no relying simply on the individual's allegation and considering intolerable everything that it is subjectively claimed to be so. On the other hand, a person's conscience fails to be protected when the law passed by the majority simply does not see its troubles. An interesting, although not recent, decision of the then European Commission for Human Rights clearly shows this dilemma.[5] An English citizen of the Quaker denomination claimed that the obligation to pay taxes infringed her personal pacifist belief, protected by Art. 9 of the Convention, insofar as she could not prevent that forty percent of her taxes would be used for weapon procurement, weapon development and other defence-related expenditure. In the applicant's view, this obligation was unacceptable to her conscience and "the diversion of forty per cent of [her] taxes to peaceful purposes [was] not merely consistent with her beliefs, but necessary for the manifestation of them." Notwithstanding, in its decision of inadmissibility, the Commission denied the moral implications of paying taxes by stating that "the obligation to pay taxes is a general one which has no specific conscientious implications in itself." Whereas the applicant alleged the moral implications of paying taxes from a subjective point of view, the Commission denied them from an objective point of view. This is a good example for a "dialogue of the deaf."

Although difficult, it is nevertheless not impossible to establish some objective criteria to distinguish cases where the conflict of conscience is sufficiently deep to require conscientious objection from those where the individual can legitimately be required to act against her conscience. The most reliable criterion consists in assessing whether the required act infringes conscientious obligations directly or only indirectly. Whereas a moral obligation is by its nature subjective, the link between a moral prohibition and a legal obligation can be measured objectively. As far as military service is concerned, European legal orders widely acknowledge the right to refuse to be a soldier, but at the same time deny the right to be exempted from the duty to pay taxes for the purpose to finance others being soldiers. The difference can be explained by the distinction that in the former case, a direct link exists between the moral obligation not to kill and the act required by the law, whereas the link is only indirect in the latter case.

---

the imperative doctrines of one's conscience, within the limits of the rights and duties imposed by the Constitution and under the terms of laws that may govern the exercise of conscientious objection. 2. The doctrines of conscience that are considered as imperative are *those whose infringement involves a serious offense to one's moral integrity and, consequently make it inappropriate to require any other behaviour*" (quoted by de Sousa e Brito 2004, p. 277, emphasis supplied). Similarly, the European Court of Human Rights holds that "the right to freedom of thought, conscience and religion denotes views that attain *a certain level of cogency, seriousness, cohesion and importance*": *see* for example *Eweida and others v UK* Apps nos 48420/10, 59842/10, 51671/10 and 36516/10 (ECtHR, 15 January 2013), para. 81, emphasis supplied.

[5]*C. v UK* App no 10358/83 (ECommHR, 15 December 1983).

As for abortion laws, they are often unclear in delimiting the precise scope of the right to conscientious objection to abortion, *i.e.*, in defining who can legitimately claim to be exempted from which activities. The UK Abortion Act 1967, for example, confines itself to stating that "no person shall be under a duty [...] to participate in any treatment authorized by this Act to which he has a conscientious objection."[6] French and German legislation on the issue provide for similar general clauses.[7] Art. 9 of the Italian abortion law provides for a complex distinction that increases uncertainty rather than reduce it: a physician can refuse the "procedures and activities specifically and necessarily designed to bring about the termination of pregnancy", but not the care before and after the termination of pregnancy.[8] A similar provision was introduced by the 2010 reform of abortion law in Spain.[9]

In these legal orders, the issue concerning the scope of the right to conscientious objection has been sometimes dealt with by the highest judicial authorities. This case-law, in general terms, tends to confine the right to conscientious objection within the limits of direct involvement in terminating the pregnancy.

In the UK, the House of Lords held in *Janaway*, that the conscience clause of the Abortion Act did not allow a secretary to refuse to type a letter which referred a pregnant patient to an appointment with a consultant for the latter to form an opinion as to whether the pregnancy should be terminated.[10] In its view, the words "participate in any treatment authorized by this Act" refer to "actually taking part in treatment administered in a hospital [...] for the purpose of terminating a pregnancy." More recently, in *Doogan*, the UK Supreme Court rejected the view of the appellate court, according to which the right to conscientious objection should extend to "any involvement in the process of treatment, the object of which is to terminate a pregnancy."[11] The Supreme Court held that the narrow meaning of the conscience clause "is more likely to have been in the contemplation of Parliament when the Act was passed." Accordingly, the right to conscientious objection only encompasses participating in a treatment bringing about the termination of pregnancy "in a hands-on capacity", but not the ancillary, administrative and managerial tasks that may be associated with the termination of pregnancy. The Court then considered that most of the tasks of the two labour-ward coordinators, petitioners in the case, fell outside the scope of the right to conscientious objection.

---

[6]Abortion Act 1967, s 4(1).

[7]*Schwangerschaftskonfliktgesetz*, § 12(1) and *Code de la santé publique*, Art. L2212-8(1) and (2).

[8]*Legge 22 maggio 1978, n. 194, Norme per la tutela sociale della maternità e sull'interruzione volontaria della gravidanza*, Art. 9, (1) and (4).

[9]*Ley Orgánica 2/2010, de 3 de marzo, de salud sexual y reproductiva y de la interrupción voluntaria del embarazo*, Art. 19(2). Previously there was no legislative provision on conscientious objection, that had been nevertheless exercised on the basis of a judgment of the Constitutional Tribunal (*see* STC 53/1985, FJ 14). See Capodiferro Cubero (2015).

[10]*Regina v Salford Area Health Authority ex p Janaway* [1988] UKHL 17.

[11]*Greater Glasgow Health Board v Doogan and another* [2014] UKSC 68, §28. Following quotations are taken from para. 38.

In a decision of 2001, the *Conseil constitutionnel* did not hold unconstitutional a reform of the French abortion law that eliminated the possibility for a public hospital's head of department to oppose abortions in his department.[12] In the court's words, "even though the head of a department in a public health establishment cannot, pursuant to the disputed provision, oppose pregnancies being terminated in his department, he retains the right [...] to refrain from terminating them himself; this safeguards his freedom of personal conscience, which cannot be exerted at the expense of that of other doctors and medical staff working in his service." The *Conseil* thus seems to consider necessary the right to conscientious objection when a physician is directly involved in a termination of pregnancy, but not when this direct link is absent.

The Italian Constitutional Court, in a judgment of 1987, refused to extend the right to conscientious objection to the judge that has to authorize the termination of pregnancy of a minor if the consent of one or both parents is missing.[13] The court excluded both a violation of the principle of equality, given that the role of the judge in the procedure is different from that of the physicians, and a violation of the judge's freedom of conscience, since her duty to render a decision prevails over her freedom of conscience.

An issue that has frequently been debated in some legal orders and is still not settled for good concerns the possibility to invoke the conscience clause to refuse the signature of the certificates necessary to terminate pregnancy. In Italy, although the law's text seems to include them in the activities that can be lawfully refused, administrative courts consider that Art. 9 of the abortion law only concerns the treatment to terminate pregnancy and not the certificates' signature.[14] In an *obiter dictum* to the already mentioned *Doogan* case the UK Supreme Court considered that these certificates are not covered by the conscience clause in section 4(1) of the Abortion Act since they are not part of the treatment but rather constitute precondition. Nevertheless, the Supreme Court acknowledged that "the contractual arrangements made by the National Health Service with general practitioners, and the employment contracts made with hospital doctors, do in practice contain such

---

[12] *Conseil constitutionnel*, decision no 2001-446 DC (27 June 2001), at para. 15.

[13] *Corte costituzionale*, judgment no 196/1987 (25 May 1987).

[14] *See* the judgment of the Administrative Court of Apulia annulling an administrative act that reserved for non-objecting candidates a certain number of vacancies in Family Counselling Services (*Tribunale Amministrativo Regionale per la Puglia*, judgment no 3477 of 14 September 2010). In the court's view, the activities offered within these services, including the certificates' signature, are outside the conscience clause's scope of application. Therefore, objecting doctors working in Family Counselling Services are obliged to perform the same activities as non-objecting doctors. Conscientious objection being irrelevant, the Region cannot exclude objecting doctors from the selection. The Regional Administrative Court of Lazio upheld a decree of the President of the Region Lazio, which prevents doctors working within the Family Counselling Services from refusing to sign the certificates (*Tribunale Amministrativo Regionale per il Lazio*, judgment no 8990 of 2 August 2016). The court maintained that this activity is not covered by the conscience clause. An appeal against this judgment is currently pending before the Council of State.

clauses."[15] In France, the abortion law of 1975 initially provided for the right to object not only the treatment but also previous activities necessary to make it lawful, like the delivery of a dossier and the acceptance of the woman's written consent. In 1979, however, the law was amended and, among others, the right to conscientious objection restricted to the sole treatment.[16]

Therefore, the mentioned case-law tends to interpret narrowly the conscience clauses provided for in abortion laws and to refuse to extend the right to conscientious objection to those who are not directly involved in the treatment that leads to the termination of pregnancy. Judgment 145/2015 of the Spanish Constitutional Tribunal represents an exception to this judicial trend. In its decision, it upheld the constitutional complaint of a pharmacist who had been fined for not having at disposal in his pharmacy the so called "morning-after pill."[17] The reasoning of the Constitutional Tribunal is not as such worthy of criticism. The judges correctly review, first, whether the moral conflict is serious enough to deserve protection through the right to conscientious objection, and, second, how this right would affect the rights of others. In applying these reasonable criteria, however, the Tribunal briskly makes the position of the pharmacist who refuses to sell the morning-after pill equal to that of the physician who has to perform an abortion. Even assuming an abortion effect of the mentioned drug, the difference in the involvement's degree between a physician performing an abortion herself and a pharmacist selling a potential abortive drug cannot be overlooked. In the former case, the physician herself directly infringes her conscientious obligation not to kill the conceived. In the latter case, it is not the pharmacist that performs the abortion: she cooperates in the taking of a drug, the responsibility of which rests entirely with the woman.[18] This is not to deny that even for a pharmacist it may be hard to sell a drug with potentially abortive effects; rather, it should be emphasized that in the pharmacist's case, the connection between the moral obligation and the legal duty is not as direct as to justify the right to conscientious objection to be recognized in the absence of a specific legislative provision. Admittedly, the Constitutional Tribunal acknowledges that there exist differences, both in quantitative and in qualitative terms, between the two positions.[19] In practice, however, it refuses to take them into account.

---

[15] *Doogan*, supra n. 11, at para. 36.

[16] *Loi n° 17-75 du 15 janvier 1975 relative à l'interruption volontaire de la grossesse* (so called *loi Veil*) and *Loi n° 79-1204 du 31 décembre 1979 relative à l'interruption volontaire de la grossesse.*

[17] STC 145/2015 (25 June 2015). In *Pichon and Sajous v France* App no 49853/99 (ECtHR, 2 October 2001) the European Court of Human Rights held that the refuse to sell contraceptives pills is not protected under Art. 9 of the Convention.

[18] Del Bò (2012), p. 139, argues that the main argument against pharmacists' conscientious objection to the sale of the emergency contraception pill is that "the responsibility of the effect of taking a pill lies entirely with those who actually take it, and not with those who dispense it" (142).

[19] STC 145/2015, supra n. 17, FJ 4.

3 Protecting the Law from Conscientious Objection

As mentioned, conscientious objection is a technique for the protection of pluralism and not a lawful means to sabotage the application of democratically approved laws. Under this perspective, the right to conscientious objection should not be confused with civil disobedience.[20]

Civil disobedience aims at challenging an alleged unjust law by intentionally infringing it with a view to the law being repealed or amended. Its purpose is to publicly show the law's injustice by accepting the punishment for its violation. When it is exercised, civil disobedience is not considered a due opposition to an unjust imposition but rather a mere unlawful breach of the legal order. Therefore, there can be no previous legal protection for civil disobedience. After all, if the legislature considers a law unjust it should repeal it rather than protecting those who violate it. Only if civil disobedience succeeds and the law is repealed are those who breached it usually considered *ex post* to have acted correctly; they do not undergo any punishment.

The opposite is true for the right to conscientious objection. This is not meant to allow dissenters to legally sabotage a law by disapplying it. The fact that the legislature allows conscientious objection does not imply that it considers the law unjust, quite the opposite. It is exactly because it does not consider it unjust and therefore does not want to repeal it that the legislature allows those who oppose it for reasons of conscience to refrain from complying with it. Conscience clauses then aim at stabilizing a law, not at challenging it. Unlike those who exercise civil disobedience, conscientious objectors do not violate a legal obligation when they exercise their right to conscientious objection.[21] So they know in advance that they will not face any harm for their non-compliance. In sum, while resistance entails a relationship of mutual exclusion between the law and the dissenters—*either* the law endures and the dissenters are punished *or* the law is repealed and the dissenters succeed—, the right to conscientious objection rather aims at conciliating law and the dissent: *both* the law *and* the dissenters' conscience remain binding.

If conscientious objection is not a legalized form of civil disobedience, the law must then provide for appropriate mechanisms to avoid it becoming what it should not be, *i.e.*, for adequate mechanisms that prevent the right to conscientious objection to negatively affect the law's application and to jeopardize the rights it guarantees. That is the reason why a legislative intervention is generally necessary for

[20]Literature on the distinction between civil disobedience and conscientious objection: for a first account and further references *see* Brownlee (2012), p. 527. Here I follow the distinction drawn by Galeotti (2011), p. 17, who stresses that whereas civil disobedience deals essentially with the (un)justice of the law—civil disobedience aims at repealing an allegedly unjust law—, conscientious objection rather poses the question of tolerance, for conscientious objection aims at preserving one's conscience's integrity.

[21]*See* Brownlee (2012), p. 532: "Whereas civil disobedience is paradigmatically a breach of law, conscientious objection is not."

conscientious objection to be exercised.[22] If the law itself does not provide for limits to conscientious objection and for mechanisms to neutralize its negative effect on the law, conscientious objection is likely to adversely affect the law's correct implementation.

As far as conscience clauses in abortion laws are concerned, this point has been correctly emphasized by the European Court of Human Rights in its judgment *R.R. v Poland*. For the Court, "States are obliged to organise the health services system in such a way as to ensure that an effective exercise of the freedom of conscience of health professionals in the professional context does not prevent patients from obtaining access to services to which they are entitled under the applicable legislation."[23]

National legislation and case-law reflect the need to protect the law from conscientious objection's impact. This entails, first, limitations to the exercise of conscientious objection. Conscientious objection, in particular, is generally excluded when the physician's intervention is required to save the life of a pregnant woman or to prevent grave permanent injury to her health.[24] This means that when the coexistence of law and conscientious objection is not possible, the former enjoys priority.

Second, the restrictive judicial trend mentioned in the previous paragraph can also be explained under this perspective. The broader conscientious objection, the more difficult the guarantee of the law. Abortion laws' application becomes impossible if every moral conflict, even if not directly related to the treatment, allows the concerned person to refuse a legally prescribed act.[25]

Furthermore, either the legislation or the case-law frequently impose on those who avail themselves of the conscience clause the duty to refer the pregnant woman

---

[22]The question whether a specific intervention by the legislature (the so called *interpositio legislatoris*) is necessary for conscientious objection being lawfully exercised has been particularly discussed in Spain, both in legal scholarship and in the jurisprudence of the Spanish Constitutional Tribunal. For the former *see* the detailed and comprehensive analysis by Gómez Abeja (2016), p. 201 ff.; for the latter *see* the dissenting opinion to STC 145/2015, supra n. 17, by judge Adela Asua Batarrita, who maintains that the Constitutional Tribunal's previous jurisprudence makes the exercise of conscientious objection conditional upon its legislative recognition (§4). I consider that a specific legislative provision is generally required for conscientious objection being exercised. This does not exclude, however, that in the absence of such a provision, in exceptional cases, also the judge can recognize conscientious objection by way of interpretation, provided that strict conditions are met: *see* Paris (2011), p. 263 ff.

[23]*R.R. v Poland* App no 27617/04 (ECtHR, 26 May 2011), at para. 206. *See* also *P. and S. v Poland* App no 57375/08 (ECtHR, 30 October 2012), at paras. 106–107.

[24]*See* Abortion Act 1967, s 4(2) and *Schwangerschaftskonfliktgesetz*, § 12(2). Improperly, the Italian abortion law mentions as ground to limit conscientious objection only the need to save the life of a pregnant woman and not also the need to avoid a grave injury to her health: *see* Art. 9(5). Art. 19(2) of the Spanish *Ley Orgánica 2/2010* (supra n. 9) does not mention this limit: for criticisms *see* Capodiferro Cubero (2015), pp. 189 and 211.

[25]Also under this perspective STC 145/2015, supra n. 17, is to criticize because it simply stated that, being the pharmacy of the conscientious objector located in the city centre of Sevilla—a town of roughly 700,000 inhabitants—the concerned drug could have been easily obtained from another pharmacy.

to another professional who is not a conscientious objector.[26] The professional can refuse herself to participate in what clashes against her conscience but may neither stop the course of the abortion procedure nor abandon the pregnant woman in such a difficult situation.

Finally, it remains to be investigated which means the law provides to redress situations in which the number of those who avail themselves of the right to conscientious objection is so high as to potentially jeopardize women's access to lawful abortion. This problem arose in Italy in particular, where the rate of conscientious objection among gynecologists, anesthetists, and other health professionals has historically been extremely high and has further increased in recent years.[27] In *International Planned Parenthood Federation – European Network (IPPF EN) v Italy*, as well as in *Confederazione Generale Italiana del Lavoro (CGIL) v Italy*, the European Committee of Social Rights found the respondent State in breach of Art. 11§1 of the European Social Charter (right to protection of health), alone as well as read in conjunction with art. E (non-discrimination), due to the inadequate application of the legislative provision on conscientious objection.[28] In the Committee's view, Italian authorities did not take all measures necessary to ensure that "abortions requested in accordance with the applicable rules are performed in all cases, even when the number of objecting medical practitioners and other health personnel is high."[29]

Whereas the principle underlying both decisions—conscientious objection should not affect the law's correct implementation—is sound, doubts can be cast on the solidity of the evidence the Committee relies on. This consists firstly of a report on cases of unsatisfactory implementation of the abortion law drafted in 2013 by the President of "Laiga"—an association of non-objecting gynecologists for the application of the abortion law—, along with "further information based on different

[26] *See*, for example, *Code de la santé publique*, Art. L2212-8(1) and *Doogan*, supra n. 11, at para. 40.

[27] According to the last Report by the Health Ministry on the application of the abortion law in Italy presented on 9 June 2020 to the Parliament (www.salute.gov accessed 1 February 2021) roughly the 69% of the gynaecologists and the 46% of the anaesthetists avail themselves of the conscience clause. The rate, however, significantly varies from one Region to another, overcoming even the threshold of 80% in a few Regions.

[28] *International Planned Parenthood Federation – European Network (IPPF EN) v Italy*, Complaint no 87/2012 (European Committee of Social Rights, 10 March 2014) and *Confederazione Generale Italiana del Lavoro (CGIL) v Italy*, Complaint no 91/2013 (European Committee of Social Rights, 11 April 2016). In the latter decision Italy was also found in breach of Art. 1§2 (right to work) and Art. 26§2 (right to dignity at work) for non-objecting medical personnel being discriminated in terms of workload, distribution of tasks and career development opportunities as well as for the Government's failure to take any preventive action to protect them from moral harassment. By contrast, the Committee rejected the alleged violations of Art. 1§2 under the perspective of forced labour, of Art. 2§1 (just conditions of work) and of Art. 3§3 (right to safe and healthy working conditions), alone and read in conjunction with Art. E.

[29] *IPPF EN*, supra n. 28, at para. 176.

sources, i.e. first hand testimonies, press articles, books, blogs, fora, etc."[30] A convincing dissenting opinion, however, stresses that this evidence is mainly anecdotal and fails to establish a link between conscientious objection and women's difficulties in accessing abortion.[31]

Furthermore, the complainants rely on the annual Reports of the Italian Health Ministry on the application of the abortion law, which undeniably testify that the rate of conscientious objection is extremely high.[32] However, these Reports neither substantiate the claim that women do not have properly access to abortion nor affirm that this is due to conscientious objection, quite the opposite. The Reports drafted in 2014 and 2015, in particular, give an account of the results of a "Technical Panel" convened by the Ministry of Health with the participation of the Regions in order to specifically monitor conscientious objection and its impact on women's access to lawful abortion. In the light of this monitoring's results, the Reports conclude that the number of non-objecting practitioners is adequate for the number of terminations of pregnancy executed.[33] The Committee however held the opposite view, but its rebuttal of the Ministry of Health's Report sounds fairly conjectural.[34] This is not to say that problems in the abortion law's application are mere speculations nor to deny that an extremely high rate of conscientious objection affects the law's correct application but to stress that findings of violation of international obligations should be based on more solid evidence.

Apart from the European Committee of Social Rights' decisions, the extremely high number of medical practitioners that avail themselves of the conscience clause draws attention to two limits of the Italian regulation of conscientious objection. First, Art. 9 of the abortion law does not provide for any mechanism to distinguish sincere objection from opportunistic free-riding. Indeed, conscientious objection is simply more favorable because no other duty is attached to those who avail themselves of the conscience clause. Even those who do not effectively have any sincere

[30] *IPPF EN*, supra n. 28, at para. 110.

[31] Dissenting opinion of Luis Jimena Quesada to *IPPF EN*, supra n. 28. As the dissenting judge notices, the Committee itself acknowledges that "the high number of objecting health personnel in Italy does not per se constitute evidence that the domestic legal provisions at stake are being implemented in an ineffective manner": *IPPF EN*, supra n. 28, at para. 166. The dissenting opinion of Giuseppe Palmisano, joined by Lauri Leppik, Elena Machulskaya, Eliane Chemla and Raul Canoa Usera to *CGIL*, supra n. 28, too considers the evidence put forward by the complainant organization "largely anecdotal and not sufficient to ground a finding of discrimination", as far as the violation of the right to work is concerned. The committee itself acknowledges, to a limited extent, the anecdotal character of the alleged evidence: *see CGIL*, supra n. 28, paras. 278 and 297.

[32] Supra n. 27.

[33] The results of this monitoring are summarized in *CGIL*, supra n. 28, paras. 147 ff. and were confirmed in their substance by the following Reports, including the most recent one, supra n. 27, at p. 52 ff. Curiously enough, however, both the Report of 2014 and that of 2015 do not mention the *IPPF EN* decision of the European Committee of Social Rights. This did not pass unnoticed by the Committee: *see CGIL*, supra n. 28, at para. 138 and 156.

[34] *CGIL*, supra n. 28, at paras. 186 to 188, where the Committee states for example that "the number of non-objecting medical staff *could be overestimated*" (emphasis supplied).

moral opposition to abortion can opt for conscientious objection and, in a vicious circle, may be keen to do so for fear of being burden with all the abortions conscientious objectors do not perform. Second, despite imposing on Regions the duty to supervise and guarantee its implementation notwithstanding conscientious objection, Art. 9 does not specify the means Regions can resort to in order to achieve this goal. It only mentions the possibility to move personnel, which as such is no decisive solution given the high rate of conscientious objections.

As for the first deficiency, it is admittedly not easy to discern sincere from insincere objections without infringing a person's freedom of conscience. Under this perspective, it is frequently claimed that making conscientious objection disadvantageous, for example by precluding objectors' access to higher career positions or securing higher salary to non-objectors, would automatically select sincere objectors. Only those who really cannot accept abortion would accept conscientious objection's disadvantages. In my opinion, however, these solutions should be rejected because they end up in punishing objectors for their conscience's choice. The same result could be reached by requiring conscientious objectors to be involved, apart from their ordinary workload, in activities that are consistent with their conscience's view. With due arrangements, objecting medical practitioners could contribute to abortion's prevention: there would be no contradiction between their conscience and the abortion law, which also aims at reducing the number of abortions.

As for the second deficiency, when the number of non-objecting medical practitioners is objectively inadequate to guarantee women's access to abortion, public-health authorities should not be prohibited from reserving a certain number of vacancies for non-objecting candidates, provided that no other less restrictive means is available and proportionality between the need to grant the service and the restriction to the right to conscientious objection is strictly respected.

4 Conscientious Objection: A Necessary Technique in Pluralistic Societies

In recent years, conscientious objection has been confronted with growing hostility among the public as well as in scholarly debate. The right to conscientious objection has frequently been depicted as an unjust privilege for religious minorities opposing fundamental freedoms' expansion or as part of a broader attack to women's rights and autonomy.[35] In one of the most quoted and influential article on the topic, Savulescu briskly claims that "if people are not prepared to offer legally permitted,

[35] *See* for example Dickens (2014), p. 220 ff.

efficient, and beneficial care to a patient because it conflicts with their values, they should not be doctors."[36]

In my opinion, understandable concerns on conscientious objection's impact on the implementation of abortion laws should be addressed by properly regulating this institution and should not lead to a radical rejection of conscientious objection. As I tried to show in this contribution, if properly understood and regulated, conscientious objection will not necessarily entail administrative malfunctions and arguments and will not jeopardize the laws' correct implementation. With due adjustments, it is not only compatible with the liberal principles western democracies rest on but also of great help in coping with pluralism for it fosters social cohesion, a most valuable asset for contemporary democratic and pluralistic societies. A legal order that, in specific thorny situations of disagreement on fundamental values, does not require an individual to set aside her moral creed to be allowed to serve the public good is certainly more respectful of liberal principles than one that does.[37] Especially in the field of bio-law, cases in which a legal duty clashes with one's most intimate personal beliefs are likely to rise significantly in the future due the growing pluralism of western liberal societies. This will increase the need to take into account and accommodate different value systems, not just on the side of patients but also on the side of public health-care providers. A liberal democratic society that claims to be pluralistic, therefore, should not rashly deprive itself of an instrument that can give an essential contribution in this sense.

References

Böckenförde E-W (1970) Das Grundrecht der Gewissensfreiheit. Veröffentlichungen der Vereinigung der Deutschen Staatsrechtslehrer 28:33–81

Brownlee K (2012) Conscientious objection and civil disobedience. In: Marmor A (ed) The Routledge companion to philosophy of law. Routledge, New York and London, pp 527–539

Capodiferro Cubero D (2015) La objeción de conciencia a la interrupción del embarazo. Centro de Estudios Políticos y Constitucionales, Madrid

de Sousa e Brito J (2002) Minorities and the right to tolerance: the development of a right to conscientious objection in constitutional law. Int Yearb Minor Issues 1:133–170

de Sousa e Brito J (2004) Conscientious objection. In: Lindholm T, Durham WC, Tahzib-Lie B (eds) Facilitating freedom of religion or belief: a deskbook. Springer, Heidelberg, pp 273–289

[36]Savulescu (2006), p. 294. In the course of his article, however, the author expresses a softer position.

[37]From this perspective, the ECtHR decisions *Grimmark v Sweden* App no 43726/17 and *Steen v Sweden* App no 62309/17 (both 12 March 2020) are open to strong criticism. The Court rejected as manifestly ill-founded the applications of two Swedish midwives claiming a right to conscientious objection to abortion under Art. 9 ECHR (conscientious objection to abortion is not allowed in Sweden). As Domenici rightly points out, "the conscience claim brought before the Court by the two Swedish midwives was far from being 'manifestly ill-founded'" and the Court simply "failed to take into consideration the possibility of accommodating conscientious objections within the framework of a pluralist democracy": see Domenici (2021), pp. 46 and 21 respectively.

Del Bò C (2012) Conscientious objection and the morning-after pill. J Appl Philos 29(2):133–145
Dickens BM (2014) The right to conscience. In: Cook RJ, Erdman JN, Dickens BM (eds) Abortion laws in transnational perspective. University of Pennsylvania Press, Philadelphia, pp 210–238
Domenici I (2021) Antigone Betrayed? The European Court of Human Rights' Decisions on Conscientious Objection to Abortion in the Cases of Grimmark v. Sweden and Steen v. Sweden. Eur J Health Law 28:26–47
Galeotti AE (2011) The place of conscientious objection in a liberal democracy. In: Calder G, Ceva E (eds) Diversity in Europe: dilemmas of differential treatment in theory and in practice. Routledge, New York, pp 17–31
Gómez Abeja L (2016) Las objeciones de conciencia. Centro de Estudios Políticos y Constitucionales, Madrid
Paris D (2011) L'obiezione di coscienza: Studio sull'ammissibilità di un'eccezione dal servizio militare alla bioetica. Passigli, Bagno a Ripoli
Savulescu J (2006) Conscientious objection in medicine. Br Med J 332:294–297

Professional Medical Ethics

Elisabetta Pulice

Abstract The paper aims to analyse the role of codes of medical ethics (CME) in the *plurality of pluralisms* affecting the medical profession, patient healthcare and medical liability. CMEs are nowadays gaining growing attention, due to their ability to regulate important aspects of professional conduct, thus complementing the legal framework for various medical issues. The role of CMEs therefore offers a specific perspective from which to study the relationships between individual and collective values, law and medical-scientific evidence, state and professional regulatory systems. After having analysed the legal value of CMEs from a comparative perspective, the present essay sketches some of the most significant and multifaceted interactions between the law and the CME, stressing how professional ethics is at the same time an element of axiological and legal pluralism ("inside" and "outside" the profession) and a tool that (potentially) accommodates pluralism.

1 Between Professional Ethics and Law: Some Preliminary Remarks

The medical sector is characterised by a range of convergences, mutual relationships and antinomies between professional rules, ethical principles and laws governing the various rights and actors involved.

In the *plurality of pluralisms* affecting the medical profession, patient healthcare and medical liability, a crucial role is inevitably played by the source of (soft) law which—by its very nature—is precisely at the intersection between ethics and law, and between state and professional regulation: the code of medical professional ethics.

In this respect, the terminological choices adopted in different European countries (code of medical practice, *code de déontologie médicale*, *ärztliche Berufsordnung*, *codice di deontologia medica*, etc.), although reflecting the different models

E. Pulice (✉)
University of Trento, Trento, Italy
e-mail: elisabetta.pulice@unitn.it

L. Busatta, C. Casonato (eds.), *Axiological Pluralism*, Ius Gentium: Comparative Perspectives on Law and Justice 92, https://doi.org/10.1007/978-3-030-78475-1_7

regulating the relationships between the various sources of law and between state and profession, reveal the specific nature of these instruments, which from both a formal and substantive perspective can be considered at the intersection, at least, between the ethical and legal dimension (by means of the transformation of principles of medical ethics into rules which are binding for professionals).

For the purposes of this paper, the general expression "code of medical ethics" (hereinafter CME) proves to be compatible with the different types of instruments and definitions chosen by EU member states since it refers to a common instrument containing rules of medical ethics, regardless of the specific legal features characterising a given model at national level and having repercussions on the terminology used. From a legal perspective, the adjective 'professional' should nevertheless be added to properly stress the origin of this type of source (namely the professional community), which differentiates it from regulations by the State or by other actors, which may cover the same professional activity.

The wider the scope of rules of professional ethics is, the more intricate their role and their relationships with other sources of law and other jurisdictional bodies are.

As a matter of fact, rules of professional ethics are nowadays gaining growing attention, both at the national and the European level, due to their ability to regulate important aspects of professional conduct. This is particularly true in medicine due to the huge variety of sensitive and controversial rights and issues concerned, and has become even more remarkable due to the tendency of modern CMEs to regulate aspects of medical practice also beyond those directly affecting the "internal" dimension of the professional community.

Moreover, the axiological pluralism within the medical community as well as the technical expertise needed in the decision-making process require the legal dimension to consider and interact with a more flexible source of law, able to integrate the regulation with further and more detailed professional duties, which take into due consideration both the technical and the ethical aspects of medical activities.

Against this background, this paper aims to sketch the role of codes of professional ethics as a specific perspective from which to study the relationships between individual and collective values, law and medical-scientific evidence, state and professional regulatory systems. Although these issues are widespread, the comparative analysis carried out in this essay will be focused on the European context.

2 Codes of Medical Ethics As Sources of Law: Plurality of Actors and Variety of Models

One of the perspectives from which to analyse the role of professional ethics is that of its multifaceted interactions with the plurality of sources of law governing the medical profession and bioethical issues.

In this context, the legal nature of codes of professional ethics affects their concrete function within the legal system. More precisely, the formal relationship between this code and other sources of law is one of the elements shaping the scope of professional medical ethics in biolaw, along with other factors relating to substantial aspects of the interactions between professional ethics and law.[1]

The way in which both formal and substantial factors merge and combine varies from country to country and even from issue to issue within the same state, depending on the specificities of the biomedical field concerned.

The standard feature these interrelations have in common is the plurality of actors and competences involved in shaping the direct or indirect legal nature of the codes of medical ethics. Apart from this common aspect, comparative legal analysis shows the coexistence in Europe of a wide range of models governing the relationships between the law and the CME and a variety of professional ethics regulations.[2]

2.1 Medical Professional Associations As Public-Interest Bodies

Although, as is widely known, medical ethics has a long history, dating back to the so-called Hippocratic Oath, only in more recent times—starting from the nineteenth century and especially after the Second World War—medical associations have published, maintained and generally updated codes of ethics for the profession in the modern sense of the term.[3] The fulfilment of this purpose is linked to (and strengthened by) the renewed role progressively gained by professional associations.

With regard to the abovementioned plurality of actors involved in professional regulations, medical associations are those professional membership bodies representing the collective interests of doctors in the public forum, having the main objective of defending physicians' freedom, independence and ability to practice medicine in the best interest of their patients.

These professional bodies can have different legal status across Europe, varying from private law associations with voluntary membership to public bodies with compulsory membership. Nevertheless, they always combine the interests of practitioners with the protection of public interests, being recognised both by professionals and by the state (although in different ways as to their legal nature).

The latter generally entrusts professional associations with functions that ultimately affect the protection of fundamental rights together with the professional practice itself. It is precisely the protection of fundamental rights and public interests that generally justifies—from both a constitutional and an EU law perspective—the imposition of further requirements on regulated professions, by a variety of sources of law, usually provided for by professional associations or professional regulatory bodies.

[1]For a more detailed comparative analysis see Pulice (forthcoming).

[2]Ibid. and Pulice (2017).

[3]For more information from a historical perspective see, for instance, Patuzzo (2015).

More specifically, the abovementioned functions are particularly significant for regulated professions, namely those professions which, according to the definition given by EU law, require that access to them "is subject to a person holding a specific qualification, such as a diploma from a university".[4] A regulated profession actually implies that professional associations or other bodies may be in charge of assessing the possession of those prerequisites necessary for the pursuit of the given professional activity. Therefore, in many European countries, professional self-regulation and professional associations, including disciplinary responsibility, perform a specific role in the access as well as in the pursuit of a given profession. They constitute at the same time an important guarantee of professional competences and accuracy, also by promoting lifelong education and training, alongside the exercise of disciplinary power.

These functions already give a clear idea of the intersection between profession and state on which the CMEs are based.

The greater the impact of a profession on fundamental rights, the more remarkable and sensitive the role of professional regulations and of the professional bodies entrusted with their enforcement are likely to be. In medicine, these functions and features are undoubtedly crucial and the responsibility for preparing, issuing and enforcing the code of professional ethics proves essential in order to perform them.

At present, European CMEs generally include rules and principles of professional behaviour for physicians, rules governing relationships with colleagues, other professions and society, but above all principles specifically aimed at protecting the rights of patients. A wider protection of patients' rights, along with normative answers to many sensitive and controversial bioethical issues, are the most noteworthy characteristics of the most updated versions of many codes of medical ethics in Europe.

Their increasing importance in the abovementioned plurality of sources of law and actors is based precisely on these factors. At the same time, this plurality leads to different combinations of roles and mutual influences, due both to the importance of the principles embedded in CMEs and to the specific features of each legal system. States have codes of medical ethics, or codes of medical practice or conduct, which traditionally have different legal and ethical origins and different regulatory frameworks.[5]

Although it is generally taken for granted that a coherent and reasonably flexible blend of legal and technical-professional factors is an added value of regulatory interventions in the biomedical field,[6] the ways in which the rules of the CME are

---

[4]Modernisation of the Professional Qualifications Directive - frequently asked questions, paragraph no. 3.3 "Which professions are regulated in the EU?", available at http://europa.eu/rapid/press-release_MEMO-11-923_en.htm?locale=en. The Regulated Professions Database is available at https://ec.europa.eu/growth/tools-databases/regprof/.

[5]For an analysis of the potentialities and limitations of a common European code of medical ethics, starting from these features, see Patuzzo and Pulice (2017).

[6]With regard to the features that may help the law in efficiently coping with scientific challenges see, for instance, Casonato (2017).

recognised as an integral part of the legal system range from a direct and explicit reference to an indirect and controversial legal nature.

It is therefore worth outlining the specific source of law we have to deal with and its related position—if any—in the hierarchy of norms.

2.2 *The Legal Value of Codes of Medical Ethics: A Comparative Overview*

The abovementioned range of models concerning the legal and binding value of codes of medical ethics reflects the authority of medical associations to issue and enforce regulatory acts, the tools through which this task is entrusted to them by the State, their autonomy and levels of interaction with other public state authorities in defining the contents of the codes, as well as in implementing and enforcing them.[7]

The statutory definition of the specific source of law in which the CME is embedded proves also useful for clarifying its position in the hierarchy of norms, even though the related competences and the scope of the authority of CMEs might not always be clear.

To give a few examples, in some countries the law dictates a given form for the CME, thus giving it the legal value of the related source of law, whereas in other countries the CME formally remains an internal regulation of the medical profession, whose legal value must be defined by courts and scholars.

In France, for instance, such a code is defined by the law as a *décret en Conseil d'État*, i.e. a decree of the Prime Minister, whose issue requires an advice on the part of the *Conseil d'État* (Council of State). The medical professional association remains the regulatory authority, but two state bodies are involved in passing the code. As for all other (state) sources of law, the CME is published in the *Journal Officiel.*[8] According to legal scholar,[9] the CME belongs to the so-called "*déontologies étatiques*", which differ from the "*déontologies extra-étatiques*", which do not share the same public regime. Since membership in the local medical council is compulsory, the CME applies to all physicians practising in France. Furthermore, since 2004 the French CME is integrated in the regulatory part of a state code, namely the *Code de la santé publique* (CSP).[10]

In Germany, the legal nature of the CME is affected on the one hand by the federal system and, on the other hand, by the specific framework for self-government and self-regulation of professions.

In accordance with the idea of "regulated self-regulation", the German legal system devolves regulatory powers, which are to be exercised within a policy

[7]For a more detailed comparative analysis see Pulice (2017).

[8]For more information, see, among others, Moret-Bailly and Truchet (2016) and Terrier (2003).

[9]Moret-Bailly (2001).

[10]Cabrol (2005).

framework laid down by a statutory act, to non-governmental and self-regulatory bodies,[11] including the State Chambers of Physicians (*Landesärztekammer—LÄK*), as registered corporations under public law (*Körperschaften des öffentlichen Rechts*[12]).

At federal level, a *(Muster-)Berufsordnung für die in Deutschland tätigen Ärztinnen und Ärzte* (Model Professional Code for Physicians in Germany-hereinafter MBO) is published by the *Bundesärztekammer* (BÄK), i.e. the German Medical Association. The BÄK is the joint association of the 17 LÄK, and therefore the central organisation in the German system of medical self-government, aiming, among other tasks, to achieve "the most uniform possible regulation of professional duties and principles for medical practice in all fields", to ensure good medical care of the population by promoting continuing medical education, constant exchange, coordination and mediation of experience, opinions, goals and activities between the LÄK.[13] In particular, the BÄK oversees the regulation of the *Berufsordnung* (professional code), which is discussed and, if need be, updated through the German Medical Assembly (*Deutscher Ärztetag*). While the BÄK is an unincorporated association, membership of the local LÄK, as self-governing bodies under public law, is compulsory.[14] According to the Act on Medical Professions of each Land, the Chambers of Physicians are entrusted with several regulatory powers to be exercised through the issue of their own specific source of law, the so-called "*Satzung*" (statute). Among these powers, the specification of professional duties and rules is embedded in the *ärztliche Berufsordnung* (professional code for physicians). This regulation is almost completely based on the Federal MBO.[15] Through the transposition into the LÄK statutes—and in conformity with the regulatory choices made therein—the CME published at the federal level thus becomes a specific source of law with legally binding nature, within the scope of the regulatory and disciplinary power of these state professional bodies. Formal approval of the administrative authorities is needed to pass the code.

In other countries, the CME is not a specific source of law, but formally a mere internal regulation of the medical profession, which may however gain relevance within the legal system, especially through case-law and disciplinary responsibility.[16]

Italy is a case in point. Since 2018, no statutory act has provided for the publication of a CME, nor has said CME been mentioned in the laws establishing

---

[11]For a general overview, see for instance OECD (2004).

[12]Literally "corporations of public law", i.e. a specific category of public bodies to which Medical Associations also belong. See, for instance, Sodan and Ziekow (2018), p. 30ff.

[13]See the BÄK website: www.bundesaerztekammer.de/weitere-sprachen/english/german-medical-association/.

[14]Through this compulsory membership, a physician indirectly becomes a member of the BÄK.

[15]For the CME of each Land, see the website of the German Medical Association (www.bundesaerztekammer.de/ueber-uns/landesaerztekammern/). For a more detailed analysis of medical ethics in Germany, for instance, Ratzel et al. (2018); Ries et al. (2012), pp. 87–109.

[16]See, among others, Quadri (2002), p. 925; Quadri (2006), p. 74 ff; Iadecola (2007), p. 551.

and regulating the provincial medical councils and the National Federation (*Federazione Nazionale degli Ordini dei Medici Chirurghi e degli Odontoiatri—FNOMCeO*). In 2018, the Italian Parliament passed a law on the reorganisation of healthcare professional associations, which to some extent clarifies the nature of health professional councils as public authorities with regulatory, disciplinary, administrative and financial autonomy and expressly entrusts them with the task of publishing a CME.[17] Despite this reform, no legal rule defines which kind of source of law the code is, nor its position in the hierarchy of norms, or even its legal nature. The latter remains indeed controversial. As to the plurality of authorities that can play a role in publishing the CME, in the Italian legal system the FNOMCeO is the only body involved. Neither the advice nor the formal approval of state authorities is required. No specific form of coordination between the professional and the legal order is conceived. Despite this entirely "internal" dimension of the CME, in more recent decades rules of professional ethics have been repeatedly amended by the medical category in parallel with the developments in bioethics and the leading cases at the national and the European level.[18]

The path through which the CME gains a legal role is therefore twofold. On the one hand, the CME has its "own" legally binding function linked to disciplinary liability for breaching its rules. Sanctions are provided for by a state statutory act and, since in Italy membership of provincial medical councils is compulsory, these sanctions are likely to affect all physicians. As we will see below, precisely the disciplinary procedure is one of the most considerable examples of interaction between different actors and between jurisdictional and para-jurisdictional bodies, in many European countries.

On the other hand, the abovementioned functions of medical associations in protecting fundamental rights and public interests, as well as the evolution of the Italian CME, led courts to grant legal relevance to its rules. This role concerns both the formal and the substantial nature of the CME. As to the first point, in some cases the Italian Supreme Court (*Corte di Cassazione*) has defined, although not in a uniform way, the rules of codes of professional ethics as legal rules, binding for registered professionals. In a leading case, the Court even considered the codes of professional ethics as sources of law integrating statutory prescriptions and, as such, construable not only by professional authorities but also by the Court itself.[19]

As to the second point, the peculiarities of biolaw and, more generally, of the regulation of medical activities, which require a plurality of sources of law and expertise in addressing sensitive legal, ethical and professional issues, have

---

[17]Law no. 3 of January 11, 2018, on the Delegation of Power to the Government over Clinical Trials of Medicines as well as on Provisions for Reorganizing the Health Professions and on the Health Directorate at the Ministry of Health (so-called "legge Lorenzin").

[18]See, among others, Benciolini (2010).

[19]Cass. civ. Sez. Un., decision no. 26810/2007. Although the decision concerns the code of conduct for Italian lawyers, this principle can be extended to the CME, since they share a similar model of relationships between law and professional ethics.

progressively increased the references made by courts to the rules and principles embedded in the Italian CME. Furthermore, both the courts and legal scholars often stress the role played by the CME in specifying general clauses and legal concepts, especially in assessing both the civil and criminal liability of physicians.[20] In this sense, the CME can also play a role in strengthening the degree of definiteness and clarity required by criminal law.[21]

These are functions shared by many European CMEs, which nevertheless become of crucial importance in the reconstruction of the possible legal role of these codes in those countries where there is no clear legal definition of their nature and of their relationships with the other sources of law.

3 Axiological and Legal Pluralism in Biolaw: The Perspective of the CME

After having analysed the role of CMEs as sources of law from a formal perspective, the aim of this paragraph is to sketch some of the most significant and multifaceted interactions between law and CME, considering their substantial coordination in regulating medical issues.

Further elements which shape the scope of professional medical ethics will therefore be analysed, taking into account the variability of their combinations in each legal system, with regard to both the specific field concerned and the legal nature of the CME.

As a preliminary remark, it is worth stressing the inherent character and proper function of professional medical ethics in addressing the *plurality of pluralisms* which characterises medical activities. As a matter of fact, professional ethics is at the same time an element of axiological and legal pluralism ("inside" and "outside" the profession) and a tool which (potentially) accommodates pluralism.

The process of working out and developing the rules of professional ethics has progressively led the CMEs of European countries to move from an "internal" and "closed" position to a more open attitude towards the protection of fundamental rights and, at the same time, towards the regulation of emerging issues, which are sensitive and challenging from both a professional and a legal perspective. As already stressed, this attitude has boosted the role of CMEs among the plurality of sources of biolaw, and therefore its abovementioned "double nature" (as element of pluralism and instrument for managing it). Besides the legal value of these codes, the other elements having an impact on these roles can be summarised as follows.[22]

First of all, the complexity of the issues to be addressed inevitably affects the ability of professional associations to reach shared decisions to grant the required

---

[20]See, among others, Angioni (2007); Brusco (2013), p. 57 ff.

[21]See, for instance, Caputo (2017), p. 144 ff.

[22]These elements are further analysed in Pulice (forthcoming).

level of certainty while at the same time properly addressing ethical pluralism. This may also increase ethical and normative conflicts, thus requiring adequate democratic arrangements and concrete forms of dialogue within the professional community.

Secondly, the scope of the regulatory autonomy of professional associations is swayed by the choices made by the law-maker in a specific field. The extent of this influence depends on the degree of autonomy given by the state to professional associations and on the legal value, if any, of the CME. There is, in any case, no doubt that declaring a medical act illegal or decriminalising it (abortion, medically assisted reproduction or euthanasia, just to give a few examples) has an impact on the decisions of the professional category, forcing its representative bodies to debate on the related professional rules.

Another element affecting the need for the professional community to pass its own rules is the regulatory model for bioethical and medical issues chosen by national parliaments. The issue of a detailed statutory regulation or rather a lack of proper regulation, as well as a legal framework regulating only the basic tenets (generally under criminal law rules) and devolving regulatory power to other authorities inevitably have an impact on professional regulation.

Furthermore, the concrete role the CME can play in relation to other sources regulating a given medical field is conditioned by the professional category's awareness of the needs and rights at stake and the capacity and willingness of the related regulatory bodies to respond to them, as well as by the degree to which CME rules are able to protect and promote these needs and rights.

Depending on how these elements are combined, the CME shows its strengths as one of the various tools defining the legal framework, limits, duties and conditions under which professionals are allowed or obliged to act in a given field.

3.1 Medical Ethics and Law: Integration Patterns and Conflicting Rules

With regard to the relationships with the legal system deriving from the abovementioned combination of features, comparative analysis shows a variety of situations in which the rules embedded in a CME can complement the law or even predate statutory rules, but also cases of contrast between the related regulatory models.

The collegial medical procedure imposed by French Law 2005-370 (the so-called Leonetti law) for deciding to withdraw or withhold a treatment from patients unable to express their will is an example of integration between professional medical ethics and law, based on the decision of the rule-maker to expressly delegate a key part of the regulation to the CME. The law, in bringing new rights to patients and clarifying medical practices concerning end of life issues, has entrusted the medical ethics regulation with the definition of the collegial procedure. Therefore, starting from

2005, Article 37 of the French CME has been amended several times following (and in accordance with) the legal reforms on end of life issues, thus integrating and complementing the legal framework for the collegial procedure with further conditions, timing, duties and actors involved.[23]

The integration of the French CME in the regulatory part of the CSP serves as another example of integration.

The German framework for assisted medical reproduction is a different way of integrating law and medical ethics without relying on an express act of empowering the CME to complement statutory regulation. The integration is based on the already described system of self-government and self-regulation of the medical profession, as well as on the German legal approach to medical and bioethical issues. In Germany, statutory regulation is mainly based on a criminal law defining basic principles, rights, prohibitions and duties.[24] Against this background, the BÄK passed a detailed regulation in the so-called *(Muster-)Richtlinie zur Durchführung der assistierten Reproduktion*,[25] which since 1998, especially its 2006 version, has performed an essential function in governing medical practice. As the directive has been attached to almost all state CMEs (or expressly mentioned among the related rules), the regulation has progressively gained the same legal value, thus integrating a key part of the legal framework regarding assisted reproduction.[26] More recently, following the legal developments concerning quality and safety of human tissues and cells, especially after the entry into force of the German Tissues and Cells Act (*Gewebegesetz*),[27] the BÄK decided to establish a strategic working group to address the medical-scientific issues of this field in order to distinguish them from the socio-political aspects. In particular, the *Gewebegesetz* has implemented, in the German legal system, the requirements provided for by EU law (EC Tissues and Cells Directive), especially by amending the Medicinal Products Act, the Transplantation Act and the Transfusion Act. For the purposes of this paper, it is worth highlighting that the German Tissues and Cells Act also amended § 16b of the German Transplantation Act (*Transplantationsgesetz—TPG*), which currently entrusts the BÄK with the issue of a *Richtlinie* on issues concerning the removal, transfer and use of human tissue.[28] Accordingly, in 2017 the Executive Board of the German Medical Association decided not to update the previous directive on assisted reproduction, but rather to pass a new directive on the basis of § 16b TPG, namely the *Richtlinie zur Entnahme und Übertragung von menschlichen Keimzellen im*

[23] In 2016, the so-called Claeys-Leonetti law (Loi n. 2016-87) extended the collegial procedure to further decisions, such as those concerning deep and continuous sedation or advance directives.

[24] *Embryonenschutzgesetz* (ESchG).

[25] Bundesärztekammer (2006).

[26] For a general overview of the role of the directive see, among others; Hübner and Pühler (2018), Hepp and Diedrich (2007), Thorn and Wischmann (2008a, b) and Merz and Loewenich (2008).

[27] Gesetz über Qualität und Sicherheit von menschlichen Geweben und Zellen - Gewebegesetz vom 20. Juli 2007 (BGBl. I S. 1574).

[28] Transplantationsgesetz – TPG, § 16b (Richtlinien zum Stand der Erkenntnisse der medizinischen Wissenschaft zur Entnahme von Geweben und deren Übertragung).

Rahmen der assistierten Reproduktion (Directive on removal and transfer of human gametes in the context of assisted reproduction), published in 2018.[29]

The professional rules on medical assisted dying imposed by the Belgian medical association after the entry into force of the act decriminalising euthanasia are another case in point. As we will see below, the duty to refer a patient to another practitioner in the case of refusal of care by a doctor fills what could be perceived as a possible gap in the statutory framework for conscientious objection to euthanasia.[30]

From a more general perspective, medical ethics proves to be useful in each field in which neither the law nor other forms of scientific regulation are able to properly address the variety of needs and issues involved. The physician-patient relationship and the difficulties in balancing professional autonomy and patient self-determination undoubtedly require professional codes to complement the law by specifying further duties and principles of medical ethics.

In addressing medical issues, professional rules can also turn out to be in contrast with legal provisions. From this perspective, it is nevertheless important to stress that in conflicts between the two regulations, medical ethics can act either as a source of law fostering the protection of patients' rights or as a tool undermining it. Different possible roles are due to the variability of each medical field in which law and medical ethics can be combined differently, leading to a mutually advantageous conjunction, or at least compatibility, or, instead, governing medical activities in a contradictory manner. Conflicts can result either from incompatible or opposing needs and drives, or because the law-maker and the professional community fail to collaborate effectively, or even just because one of them fails to properly protect the plurality of rights and values at stake.

The protection of the right to refuse artificial nutrition and hydration granted by the Italian CME was undoubtedly higher if compared to a draft law that has been extensively discussed by the Italian Parliament.[31] The framework for professional autonomy and women's rights of the Italian CME proves to be more suitable to assure decisions taken in a woman's best interest than that of the original version of Law no. 40/2004 on medically assisted reproduction, as confirmed also by the Italian Constitutional Court.[32]

Despite the formal integration of the CME in a state code (CSP), the French Parliament decided not to include the respect of medical ethics rules in the wording of a law concerning patient self-determination, since the professional association failed to change a rule in the CME that was likely to narrow the scope of the related

[29]The current version of the document is available on the BÄK website: https://www.bundesaerztekammer.de/richtlinien/richtlinien/assistierte-reproduktion/. See also, among others, Kentenich (2018) and Kentenich et al. (2018).

[30]Advice of 06/05/2017 on deontological duties in case of refusal to perform euthanasia.

[31]The so-called DDL Calabrò. See, among others, Casonato (2009) and Barni (2009).

[32]Italian Constitutional Court, decision no. 151/2009. On the role of professional autonomy in protecting the right to health in this field, see, for examples, Flick (2010), p. 30. On case-law addressing the relationships between the law and "scientific questions", see, among others, Penasa (2015), Id (2016); Patroni Griffi (2015); Iannuzzi (2018); Casonato (2016).

protection.[33] In 2012, the CME was amended and adapted to the cultural, social and legal developments in the understanding and regulation of the doctor-patient relationship.[34]

The interplay of conflicting rules concerning physician-assisted suicide (PAS) in Germany serves as another example of how criminal law allows, under certain conditions, professionals to perform an activity which is instead sanctioned by professional rules. In cases in which a medical activity can help patients to exercise a right, professional rules may therefore become a limit to the concrete implementation of that right. In the same field, the refusal to amend Article 17 of the Italian CME, which sanctions PAS, expressed by the Italian medical association in view of the statutory reform required by the Italian Constitutional Court[35] to establish the conditions under which a person can be lawfully assisted in suicide, is another example of these conflicts.

From a slightly different perspective, a CME can offer a higher protection of fundamental rights by remedying a lack of proper regulation. Many of the principles now set forth by the Italian law governing informed consent and advance healthcare directives (law n. 219/2017) were already embedded in the Italian CME. In Italy, as a matter of fact, rules of medical ethics have for a long time been the only normative answer to several sensitive issues concerning end-of-life decisions and care.

3.2 *The Conscience Clause Between Professional Autonomy and Fundamental Rights*

A specific CME tool which can complement legal principles, which is at the same time likely to lead to tension between law and medical ethics, is the so-called conscience clause included in the codes of professional ethics. According to said codes, healthcare providers are free to refuse a treatment—except in emergencies and under specific conditions which protect the patient's rights, such as, for instance, the duty to give all information needed to ensure access to care or the duty not to refuse a reasonable request of the patient to consult or to be referred to another professional.

There are many cases in which healthcare providers can cite reasons of conscience as grounds for refusing to provide a given treatment, and these cases are addressed by the law in different ways.

---

[33]Evin et al. (2002).

[34]Laude (2012), p.1694; Debost (2012); Debost et al. (2012); Moret-Bailly (2012); Moret-Bailly (2005).

[35]Italian Constitutional Court, Order no. 207/2018. See, for instance, Casonato (2019). The Court has then decriminalised, under certain well defined conditions, assisted suicide (decision n. 242/2019). The FNOMCeO has simply introduced in a statement attached to the CME the possibility of not sanctioning PAS under the same conditions, while maintaining the ban in the CME.

In some countries, legally recognised forms of conscientious objection differ from clauses of conscience based on the CME. The former concern the right expressly granted—by means of law and in a given field—to practitioners not to perform an act to which they hold a conscientious objection.[36] The latter refer to a more general right to refuse a treatment recognised to healthcare providers by codes of professional ethics and generally based on clinical or ethical beliefs.[37] The scope of these conscience clauses can therefore go beyond the fields covered by those forms of conscientious objection expressly regulated by the law.

Individual conscience and professional autonomy in clinical decision-making are essential rights that must be balanced with the professional duties to accord top priority to patient needs and to adhere to the highest standards of evidence-based care. The impact of conscience-based refusals on other healthcare professionals must also be considered.[38]

If properly balanced with these competing values, conscience clauses are essential tools to reasonably accommodate ethical pluralism in the medical sector and within the professional community. Their inclusion in the CME is therefore needed in order to counterbalance the difficulties in reaching a broad consensus on some intricate and thorny medical issues and to effectively address the impact of the variability of each single case on professional and individual decision-making.

By including a conscience clause, professional associations leave space for both minority values and case-by-case decisions, also in those issues in which a general common position and a reasonable degree of certainty are needed.

Nevertheless, since conscience clauses are based on the CME, i.e. on a peculiar source of (soft) law, their concrete role depends on the abovementioned variety of factors, which differ from one country to another, and from one regulated profession to another. Therefore, sometimes it is difficult to concretely assess the impact of CME-based refusals on patients' access to care, on the protection of rights granted by the legal system, and even on how healthcare is organised. The attitude of a given professional association towards the use of the conscience clause proves crucial in shaping the relationships between medical ethics and law in dealing with these issues, together with the legal value of a given CME and its interrelations with other sources of law.

In this context, considering the state's responsibility for guaranteeing a balance between all the competing values and interests at stake, and bearing in mind the hierarchy of norms, it is important to stress that a CME-based refusal cannot violate the essential core of a constitutional right. Nor can a CME-based clause—if it is not

---

[36]For a more detailed analysis on conscientious objections see the essay by D. Paris in this volume.

[37]For a general overview, see for instance Saporiti (2014), p. 137 ff; Benhida et al. (2011); Casonato and Cembrani (2011), p. 70 ff; Eusebi (2011), p. 182 ff.

[38]On the phenomenon of conscience-based refusal see, for instance, Chavkina et al. (2013). For an interdisciplinary research, through semi-structured and narrative in-depth interviews with professionals, on the reasons behind conflicts of conscience in public hospitals, their impact on the way in which healthcare is structured and organised, as well as on cultural and ethical pluralism, see Ferrero et al. (2021).

based on clinical and scientific reasons—be used by the professional community as a tool to indirectly hinder the basic principles of a given legal framework (for instance, by imposing too many barriers to the concrete implementation of a fundamental right). Otherwise, if not properly counterbalanced, it would ultimately turn into a denial of the ethical, cultural and legal pluralism characterising biolaw.

4 Deontological Liability and Disciplinary Procedure: Jurisdictional and Quasi-Jurisdictional Bodies

Breaches of the CME are another perspective from which to highlight the plurality of actors that might be involved in the relationships between law and medical ethics. The disciplinary procedure is precisely at the intersection between the State and the professional community. The former defines the basic legal framework as to, for instance, the composition of disciplinary commissions, procedural rules, sanctions, appeals and reviews. The latter has the authority and the right to interpret and apply the CME. Therefore, professional associations have autonomy in deciding whether to bring a disciplinary action against a registered professional and in assessing the related CME-based liability, as well as the competence to conduct interviews and collect evidence. Nevertheless, comparative analysis shows different models of how professional and state jurisdictional and/or quasi-jurisdictional bodies are connected.

The differences between legal systems are mainly linked to the composition of disciplinary commissions and to the relationships between them and general jurisdiction.

As to the first point, in some countries disciplinary commissions are exclusively made up of internal members, i.e. registered professionals. Therefore, the CME-based liability of a healthcare professional can be assessed only by members belonging to the same professional community. For the sake of impartiality, some regulations impose at least that members of a given disciplinary commission cannot belong to the same district or local medical council of the professional in question. The first instance of the disciplinary procedure in Italy is a case in point. From this perspective, it must nevertheless be underlined that rules on impartiality have only very recently been passed,[39] while procedural rules still reflect a basic lack of fundamental fair trial principles.[40]

In other European countries, disciplinary commissions also include external members. Within this model, further differences are based on professional

[39]Law no. 3/2018 ("Lorenzin law", see above).

[40]Italian rules governing the disciplinary procedure seem not to be consistent with the ECHR case law, and namely Diennet c. France, of 26 September 1995, req.18160/9; Gautrin et autres c. France, of 20 May 1998, Req. No.21257/93 à 21260/93; Albert and Le Compte v. Belgium, Application no. 7299/75;7496/76 and Le Compte, Van Lauten and De Meyere v. Belgium, Application no. 6878/75; 7238/75. With reference to France, see also Terrier (2003), p. 319 and Bertin (2007).

experience, affiliation and function of external members. In some countries they belong to state authorities, whereas other disciplinary commissions must include a lawyer.

For instance, the role of a lawyer became an integral part of the French "*échevinage*" model introduced in 2007. Prior to this reform, the presence of a lawyer was already compulsory but only with an advisory role, i.e. without voting rights. Instead, in the current French model medical disciplinary commissions are chaired by a judge.[41] Also in some German *Länder* the *Berufsgerichte* (professional courts) are chaired by a judge and another external member, who—depending on the Land—can belong either to the judiciary or to another state authority, is included. In most *Länder,* professional courts of second instance are made up of a higher number of judges.[42] As a matter of fact, in Germany the relationships of these professional jurisdictional bodies with state jurisdictional bodies seem to differ, compared to other countries. Professional courts belong to the "courts for particular fields of law" under Article 101 of the Basic Law, which can be established only by law and which in the case of disciplinary liability of professionals must also include professionals, not only judges, among their members.

In Italy, the CCEPS (*Commissione Centrale per gli Esercenti le Professioni Sanitarie*-Central Commission for healthcare professionals) is a jurisdictional body of second instance (as to its disciplinary tasks), established within the Ministry of Health, made up of members belonging to health professional communities and chaired by a judge.[43]

As to the second point, it is interesting to highlight that in some countries disciplinary courts are part of the general jurisdiction, whereas in others they are non-jurisdictional bodies and the disciplinary procedure only has an administrative nature, without becoming part of the state judicial system. In France, for instance, these commissions belong to the administrative justice system, and are affected, to some extent, by the related procedural rules. Accordingly, appeals are taken to the French Council of State (*Conseil d'État*), which is the highest court for issues and cases involving public administration. Italy has a mixed system, since the disciplinary commissions of first instance are administrative bodies while the CCEPS is a jurisdictional authority, and notably a sort of extraordinary court which nowadays can no longer be established according to the Italian Constitution, although the CCEPS is still considered legitimate as it was established before the entry into force of the Constitution.[44] Appeals are taken to the Italian Supreme Court (*Corte di Cassazione*).

---

[41]Bertin (2007). For a general overview, see Bessis Rudyard (2011) and Laude et al. (2012).

[42]For a general overview, see Ratzel et al. (2018).

[43]Further information is available on the CCEPS website. Before the decision of the Italian Constitutional Court no. 215/2016, the CCEPS was also made up of members belonging to governmental bodies, which has been held unconstitutional.

[44]D.lgs. C.p.S no. 233/1946.

Despite the abovementioned differences, the role of state jurisdictional bodies in appeal hearings provides the opportunity for a dialogue between courts, and ultimately a multilevel application and interpretation of CME rules. Therefore, it is a further example of the abovementioned relationships between law and medical ethics shaped by case-law. In some cases, they are linked to the inclination of the CME to address fundamental rights in medical regulation, thus becoming the object of courts' attention, while in other situations they are based on the enforcement of the CME through professional jurisdiction, thus being affected by the related multi-layered structure.

From this perspective, although in Germany decisions by professional courts of second instance cannot be appealed, the possibility to lodge, under specific and strict conditions, a constitutional complaint (*Verfassungsbewschwerde*, according to Article 93 (1) no. 4a and 4b of the Basic Law) makes it possible for professionals to allege that one of their basic rights has been infringed by a public authority, including professional chambers. Although applicable in exceptional cases only, this possibility gave rise to a leading case by the BVerfG on the relationship between the rule-maker and the regulatory power delegated to professional bodies.[45]

5 Summarising the (Possible) Role of Codes of Medical Ethics: The Case of Physician-Assisted Suicide

The regulation of PAS offers a useful perspective from which to summarise the role of medical ethics in relation to ethical and legal pluralism in biolaw.

Professional associations confronted with the decriminalisation of assisted suicide (and, in some cases, euthanasia) have reacted in different ways throughout Europe. Two opposite directions have been taken by the German and by the Belgian professional communities.

In 2011, the German Medical Assembly decided to amend Paragraph 16 of the MBO by introducing a ban on PAS. At state level, most LÄK (10 out of 17) decided to transpose such a limit into their legally binding CMEs. Since 2015, assisted suicide has not been expressly regulated nor prohibited by criminal law. Although an indirect limit to PAS could be gathered from the Narcotics Law [BtMG], professional rules have constituted the only express limit to medical assistance of this kind. The reform of criminal law in 2015 introduced a new Paragraph 217 which criminalises assisted suicide services ("*geschäftsmäßig*" i.e. business-like assistance, in the sense of a repeated and organised activity). Single cases of assistance appear not to be criminalised. In February 2020 the Federal Constitutional Court held that the prohibition of assisted suicide services set out in the Criminal Code violates the Basic Law.[46] Until May 2021, according to the MBO and to the CME of some

[45]The so-called *Facharztsbeschluss*, BVerfGE. 33, 125.

[46]BVerfG, Urteil des Zweiten Senats vom 26. Februar 2020—2 BvR 2347/15.

Länder, PAS remained prohibited also in those cases which are not criminalised by the law.[47]

Before the reform, the administrative Court of Berlin had already repealed a measure adopted by the local professional chamber against a doctor to prohibit the prescription of narcotics to be used for assisted suicide. Although it accepted the general CME-based ban on assisted suicide, the Court held that its absolute nature and application were unlawful, stressing the need for exceptions to be assessed on a case-by-case basis in particularly sensitive and exceptional situations.[48]

On the contrary, the advice of the Belgian professional association with regard to the law decriminalising euthanasia is clear in stressing a completely different perception of the role of the CME: "*Lorsqu'une législation de ce type est établie dans un état démocratique et respecte la liberté de conscience de chaque médecin, son existence ne peut être ignorée par une institution de droit public comme l'Ordre des médecins. Par conséquent, l'Ordre ne peut préconiser des règles de conduite ou prendre des décisions contraires aux lois adoptées démocratiquement dans notre pays*".[49]

Germany and Belgium do not share the same CME model with regard to the related legal value and system of medical self-government. It is nevertheless interesting to notice that the Belgian professional association, instead of opposing the law, decided to adopt rules and advices to complement the Act on euthanasia with principles of medical ethics considered crucial by the professional community.

With reference to the abovementioned Italian situation regarding PAS, legal comparison can help to highlight some general principles to be applied to each possible conflict between the law and the CME.

Considering, on the one hand, the differences between the German and Italian model concerning the formal role of the CME as a source of law, as well as the granting of self-regulation authority to German LÄK, and, on the other hand, the need for exceptions stressed also by German courts,[50] the following principles can be inferred.

The regulatory power of the professional community should not prevail on the democratic principle in governing issues going beyond its "internal" concerns and

---

[47]On the position taken by the German Medical Association see also the document published by the BÄK on assisted suicide: Bundesärztekammer (2017), p. 336. The MBO has then been amended following the 124th Deutscher Ärztetag (the report is available at https://www.bundesaerztekammer.de/aerztetag/124-deutscher-aerztetag-2021-als-online-veranstaltung/beschlussprotokoll/).

[48]VG Berlin, VG 9 K 63.09—30 March 2012.

[49]Ordre des Médecins (Belgique 2003), Advice of 22/03/2003 on palliative care, euthanasia and other decisions concerning end-of-life care. The medical council underlined that when a law is passed in a democratic state and the freedom of conscience of each physician is respected, the existence of said regulation cannot be ignored by a body of public law such as the medical association. Therefore, the professional association cannot provide for rules or take decisions contrary to democratically adopted laws. See also Ordre des Médecins Belgique (2017) and (2019).

[50]Decision BVerwG 3 C 19.15 of 2 March 2017 by the Federal Administrative Court of Germany. See also the decisions of the Bundesgerichtshof (BGH), 5 StR 123/18 and 5 StR 393/18.

having an impact on fundamental rights. At the same time, the abovementioned role of the CME in opposing a statutory act if a higher protection of rights is needed should also be granted. Nevertheless, the scope of this possible function must be grounded in and limited by respect for constitutional principles and by the level of pluralism that CME rules are able to properly consider, protect and promote.

Moreover, a more coherent model of relationships between the law and the CME is needed to allow for reasonable balancing of the two regulations as mutually complementary sources of biolaw.

References

Angioni F (2007) Il nuovo codice di deontologia medica. Criminalia 2:277–289

Barni M (2009) Dall'atto medico al testamento biologico, la rivincita della deontologia. Riv. it. med. leg 31:825 ff

Benciolini P (2010) La deontologia dai galatei ai codici deontologici. La professione. Medicina scienza etica e società:261 ff

Benhida C, Gaudillère C, Pourquier A-L, Abadou Y, Coutarel E (2011) La clause de conscience. Droit Déontologie & Soin 11:164–166

Bertin L (2007) Réforme de l'Ordre de Médecins. Mise en place de la nouvelle juridiction disciplinaire. Médecine et Droit 89:173–181

Bessis Rudyard P (2011) Les procédures disciplinaires à l'encontre des professionnels de santé et des auxiliaires médicaux. Editions Vision du futur, Paris

Brusco C (2013) Linee guida, protocolli e regole deontologiche. Le modifiche introdotte dal c.d. decreto Balduzzi. Dir. pen. cont.- Riv. trim 4:51–71

Bundesärztekammer (2006) (Muster-)Richtlinie zur Durchführung der assistierten Reproduktion – Novelle 2006. Deutsches Ärzteblatt 103:A1392–A1403

Bundesärztekammer (2017) Verbot der geschäftsmäßigen Förderung der Selbsttötung (§ 217 StGB): Hinweise und Erläuterungen für die ärztliche Praxis. Deutsches Ärzteblatt 17 February

Cabrol V (2005) La codification de la déontologie médicale. Revue générale de droit médical 16:103–123

Caputo M (2017) Colpa penale del medico e sicurezza delle cure. Giappichelli, Torino

Casonato C (2009) Lo schema di testo unificato "Calabrò" su consenso e dichiarazioni anticipate. Forum di Quaderni costituzionali, www.forumcostituzionale.it. Accessed 10 Aug 2019

Casonato C (2016) La scienza come parametro interposto di costituzionalità. Rivista AIC 2:1–11

Casonato C (2017) 1st century biolaw: a proposal. BioLaw J 1:81–95

Casonato C (2019) Assisted suicide in Italy: constitutional right or wishful thinking? BioLaw J 2:147–149

Casonato C, Cembrani F (2011) Il rapporto terapeutico nell'orizzonte del diritto. In: Palermo Fabris E, Zatti P, Lenti L (eds) Trattato di biodiritto, vol: I diritti in medicina. Giuffrè, Milano, p 70 ff

Chavkina W, Leitman L, Polin K (2013) Conscientious objection and refusal to provide reproductive healthcare: A White Paper examining prevalence, health consequences, and policy responses. Int J Gynecol Obstetrics 123:41–56

Debost C (2012) Mise en lumière d'une réforme silencieuse du Code de déontologie médicale. Revue Droit & Santé 48:506–507

Debost C, Giraudeau N, Véron P, Vailla F (2012) La réforme du Code de déontologie médicale. RGDM 44:239–266

Eusebi L (2011) Obiezione di coscienza del professionista sanitario. In: Palermo Fabris E, Zatti P, Lenti L (eds) Trattato di biodiritto, vol: I diritti in medicina. Giuffrè, Milano, pp 173–187

Evin C, Charles B, Denis JJ (2002) Rapport fait au nom de la commission des affaires culturelles, familiales et sociales sur le projet de loi relatif aux droits des malades et à la qualité du système de santé n. 3258

Ferrero L, Pulice E, Vargas AC (2021) Pluralismo etico e conflitti di coscienza nell'attività ospedaliera. I. Scelte riproduttive e dibattiti sulla genitorialità - II. Le scelte di fine vita. Il Mulino, Bologna (English version forthcoming: Ethics pluralism and conflicts of conscience in public hospitals)

Flick GM (2010) La salute nella Costituzione italiana. In: FNOMCeO (ed.), Cento anni di professione al servizio del Paese, Roma, 12–35

German Medical Association: www.bundesaerztekammer.de/weitere-sprachen/english/german-medical-association/. Accessed 10 Aug 2019

German Medical Association. www.bundesaerztekammer.de/ueber-uns/landesaerztekammern/. Accessed 10 Aug 2019

Hepp H, Diedrich K (2007) Richtlinien zur Durchführung der assistierten Reproduktion des Wissenschaftlichen Beirates der Bundesärztekammer – klinische, ethische und rechtliche Aspekte. In: Felberbaum RE, Bühler K, van Der Ven H (eds) Das Deutsche IVF - Register 1996 - 2006: 10 Jahre Reproduktionsmedizin in Deutschland. Springer, Heidelberg, pp 21–32

Hübner M, Pühler W (2018) Systematische Rechtsentwicklung für die Reproduktionsmedizin. Gynäkologe 51:616

Iadecola G (2007) Le norme della deontologia medica: rilevanza giuridica ed autonomia di disciplina. Riv. It. Med. Leg. 2:551

Iannuzzi A (2018) Il diritto capovolto. Regolazione a contenuto tecnico-scientifico e Costituzione. Editoriale Scientifica, Napoli

Kentenich H (2018) Berlin, 17.11.2016 – 239. Stellungnahme der Deutschen Gesellschaft für Gynäkologie und Geburtshilfe (DGGG) zum Richtlinien-Entwurf "Entnahme und Übertragung von menschlichen Keimzellen im Rahmen der assistierten Reproduktion". Geburtshilfe und Frauenheilkunde 78(08):754–755

Kentenich H, Hilland U, Krüssel J-S (2018) 239. Stellungnahme Der Deutschen Gesellschaft Für Gynäkologie Und Geburtshilfe (DGGG) Zur Richtlinie Zur Entnahme Und Übertragung von Menschlichen Keimzellen Im Rahmen Der Assistierten Reproduktion: Berlin, 12.11.2018. Geburtshilfe Und Frauenheilkunde 78(12):1202–1205

Laude A (2012) Le code de déontologie médicale enfin modifié !. Recueil Dalloz, 1694

Laude A, Mathieu B, Tabuteau D (2012) Droit de la santé. PUF, coll.Thémis Droit, Paris

Merz E, Loewenich V (2008) Muster-Richtlinie der Bundesärztekammer zur Durchführung der assistierten Reproduktion, Novelle 2006. Ethik in der Medizin 20:60–61

Modernisation of the Professional Qualifications Directive - frequently asked questions, para no. 3 3. "Which professions are regulated in the EU?" Available at http://europa.eu/rapid/press-release_MEMO-11-923_en.htm?locale=en

Moret-Bailly J (2001) Les déontologies. PUAM, Aix-en-Provence

Moret-Bailly J (2005) Les évolutions récentes des règles d'exercice des professions de santé. RDSS 4:593–602

Moret-Bailly J (2012) La déontologie médicale de la résistance à la contre-offensive (à propos du décret du 7 mai 2012 portant modification du code de déontologie médicale). Revue de droit sanitaire et social:1074–1083

Moret-Bailly J, Truchet D (2016) Droit des déontologies, PUF, coll. Thémis, Paris

OECD (2004) Government Capacity To Assure High Quality Regulation, Regulatory reform in Germany

Ordre des Médecins Belgique (2003) Avis relatif aux soins palliatifs, à l'euthanasie et à d'autres décisions médicales concernant la fin de vie, https://www.ordomedic.be/fr/avis/conseil/avis-relatif-aux-soins-palliatifs-a-l%27euthanasie-et-a-d%27autres-decisions-medicales-concernant-la-fin-de-vie. Accessed 10 Aug 2019

Ordre des Médecins Belgique (2017) Obligation déontologique de renvoi en cas de refus de pratiquer une euthanasie. Avis du Conseil national du 6 mai 2017, https://www.ordomedic.be/fr/avis/conseil/obligation-deontologique-de-renvoi-en-cas-de-refus-de-pratiquer-une-euthanasie-avis-du-conseil-national-du-6-mai-2017. Accessed 10 Aug 2019

Ordre des Médecins Belgique (2019) Code de déontologie médicale commenté. Larcier, Bruxelles

Patroni Griffi A (2015) Il bilanciamento nella fecondazione assistita tra decisioni politiche e controllo di ragionevolezza. Rivista AIC 3, https://www.rivistaaic.it/images/rivista/pdf/3_2015_Patroni%20Griffi.pdf. Accessed 10 Aug 2019

Patuzzo S (2015) Introduction to Percival Thomas, (1803), Medical Ethics, *Etica Medica, ovvero un Codice di Istituzioni e Precetti adattati alla Condotta Professionale dei Medici e dei Chirurghi*, Italian translation by Giada Goracci. Mimesis, Milan

Patuzzo S, Pulice E (2017) Towards a European code of medical ethics. Ethical and legal issues. J Med Ethics 43:41–46

Penasa S (2015) La legge della scienza: nuovi paradigmi di disciplina dell'attività medico-scientifica. Uno studio comparato in materia di procreazione medicalmente assistita. Editoriale Scientifica, Trento

Penasa S (2016) Le "scientific questions" nella dinamica tra discrezionalità giurisdizionale e legislativa. Uno studio comparato sul giudizio delle leggi scientificamente connotate nelle giurisdizioni nazionali, sovranazionale e internazionali. BioLaw J 1:39–79

Pulice E (2017) La deontologia come fonte del diritto. La codificazione dell'etica medica in Francia, Germania e Italia. Diritto Pubblico Comparato ed Europeo 3:745–770

Pulice E (forthcoming) Deontologia e diritto. Modelli comparati, criticità e prospettive in ambito biomedico. Editoriale Scientifica, Napoli

Quadri E (2002) Il codice deontologico medico ed i rapporti tra etica e diritto. Responsabilità civile e previdenza 4-5:925–948

Quadri E (2006) Codice di deontologia medica. In: Alpa G, Zatti P (eds) Codici deontologici e autonomia privata. Giuffré, Milan, pp 69–82

Ratzel R, Lippert H-D, Prütting J (2018) Kommentar zur Musterberufsordnung der deutschen Ärzte (MBO). Springer, Berlin-Heidelberg

Ries H-P et al (2012) In: Ries HP et al (eds). Arztrecht Ärztliches Standesrecht. Springer, Berlin, pp 87–109

Saporiti M (2014) La coscienza disubbidiente. Giuffré, Milano

Sodan H, Ziekow J (2018) Grundkurs Öffentliches Recht. Staats und Verwaltungsrecht. Beck, Munich

Terrier E (2003) Déontologie médicale et droit. LEH, Bordeaux

Thorn P, Wischmann T (2008a) Eine kritische Würdigung der Novellierung der (Muster-) Richtlinie der Bundesärztekammer 2006 aus der Perspektive der psychosozialen Beratung. Journal Für Reproduktionsmedizin Und Endokrinologie 5(1):39–44

Thorn P, Wischmann T (2008b) Eine kritische Würdigung der Novellierung der (Muster-)Richtlinie zur Durchführung der assistierten Reproduktion der Bundesärztekammer 2006. Ethik in der Medizin 20:61–63

Part III
Case Studies

Axiological Pluralism: Conflict in the Hospital, Resolution in the Courts

Roger Brownsword

Abstract Where the ethical differences in a community go deep, to matters of first principle, how are the conflicts implicit in such axiological pluralism to be handled? In particular, how are the risks arising from a perceived legitimacy deficit to be managed? This chapter outlines a number of possible responses to these questions and, then, with the focus on three recent appeals to the UK Supreme Court (namely, the decisions in *Montgomery*, *James*, and *Doogan*), it offers some reflections on the role and responsibilities of the courts when faced with conflicts of this kind.

1 Introduction

New technologies tend to be disruptive, impacting on employment and local economies, transforming social practices, challenging legal concepts, principles and framings, and provoking concerns about risks to health, safety and the environment as well as accentuating ethical divisions.[1] Some technologies are more disruptive than others and the 'hot spots' vary from one technology to another. While some technologies (such as nanotechnologies, synthetic biology, and AI) initially elicit concerns about safety and security, others (such as the technologies associated with human genetics) raise concerns of a more fundamental ethical nature.[2] However, where ethical concerns are raised, we should not assume that all ethical voices are

I am grateful to Deryck Beyleveld for a discussion in Utrecht that helped me clarify some of my thoughts in the first part of this paper. Needless to say, the usual disclaimers apply.

[1]Brownsword et al. (2017), p. 3; Brownsword (2018), Brownsword (2019a), Chs. 8–12; Brownsword (2019b).

[2]Brownsword (2008), Brownsword and Goodwin (2012); and, compare, Fukuyama (2002).

R. Brownsword (✉)
Dickson Poon School of Law, King's College London, London, UK

Bournemouth University, Bournemouth, UK
e-mail: roger.brownsword@kcl.ac.uk

L. Busatta, C. Casonato (eds.), *Axiological Pluralism*, Ius Gentium: Comparative Perspectives on Law and Justice 92, https://doi.org/10.1007/978-3-030-78475-1_8

identical or that they all advocate movement in the same regulatory direction (e.g., to prohibit or to restrict the application of the technology).[3] The fact of the matter is that, in our modern societies, the emergence of new technologies, techniques (such as those for gene-editing),[4] and tests (such as non-invasive prenatal testing)[5] will often provoke a plurality of ethical views. For example, we might find that claimed individual rights (such as the right to reproductive autonomy and the right to know) come into tension with more collectivist or communitarian ethics (emphasising solidarity, inclusion, equality, justice, and so on) while, at the same time, this draws in further tensions between the interests of the present generation and those of future generations, and between medical ethics and public health ethics.

Pluralities can be complex. Nevertheless, at the price of some oversimplification, let me suggest that, where the ethics of modern technologies are debated, we will tend to find three prominent voices in the community.[6] From the scientific and technological sections of the community, utilitarians will argue that the right thing to do is to maximise the promised benefits while minimising (or managing) the risks to health and safety; from the liberal (pro-choice) sections of the community, it will be the need to respect rights that is highlighted; and from more conservative quarters, there will be appeals to professional responsibilities and dignitiarian duties.[7]

The ethical pluralities of our modern societies assume many different forms and complexions. In this chapter, we are concerned with so-called 'axiological pluralism', this being characteristic of a plurality where the ethical differences that are implicated reach back to first principles. Under conditions of axiological pluralism, the protagonists engage rival ethical paradigms (whether rights-based, duty-based, or utility-maximising); it is as if Benthamites are debating with Kantians, or rights-based liberals with duty-based communitarians or Confucians.

Where we find such a fundamental pluralism, the one thing that the protagonists have in common is that they agree upon the importance of moral reason and of humans always trying to do the right thing. However, each paradigm has its own take on the criterion of right action; and each paradigm has its own view on the status of non-human animals, of human embryos and fetuses, of humans who are in a permanent vegetative state, and so on. Exceptionally, it might be agreed in all parts of the plurality that some act should be prohibited (e.g. human reproductive cloning), but as a general rule what axiological pluralism signals is that there will be difference and division—concerning, for example, such deeply contested matters as the use of human embryos for research, the development and use of gene editing

[3]Brownsword (2019c).

[4]Nuffield Council on Bioethics (2018).

[5]Nuffield Council on Bioethics (2017), Brownsword and Wale (2016, 2018).

[6]Let me emphasise, and concede, that this is an over-simplification: compare, for example, Vallor (2016), rejecting both utilitarian and deontological ethics in favour of a virtue ethics that draws on Aristotle, Confucius, and the Buddha. See Brownsword (2003, 2005).

[7]Of course, within each of these ethics, there will be internal divisions, e.g., between act-utilitarians and rule-utilitarians, between theories of negative rights and theories of positive rights, and so on.

technologies, assisted conception, the termination of a pregnancy, assisted suicide, 'mercy' killings, physician euthanasia, and the use of medical interventions, not for 'treatment', but for 'enhancement'.[8] Some of these differences might be resolved, so to speak, 'in-house' by self-regulating groups—for example, by clinical ethics committees in hospitals.[9] However, where 'top-down' intervention is required, how are such profound differences to be resolved? How are legislators to approach such divisions and, in particular, what is the role of the courts?

This chapter responds to these questions in three parts. First, an imaginary conversation is sketched—one that might take place between proponents of rival ethical paradigms who are concerned about the risks presented to their community by conditions of axiological pluralism. These concerns relate to a 'legitimacy deficit' in relation to both legislative and judicial interventions as well as to the impact on effective governance and social order of a lack of respect for such interventions. In this context, depending upon the depth of the concerns, it might be proposed that the community should agree on more 'acceptable' processes—that is to say, processes that will command respect—for the settlement of significant ethical questions. This leads to some short thoughts on six proposed responses to these concerns, each of these responses taking its own approach to the respective roles and responsibilities of the legislature and the courts. Secondly, focusing on the role and responsibilities of the courts, three recent appeals to the UK Supreme Court—respectively, in *Montgomery*,[10] *James*,[11] and *Doogan*[12]—are considered. These are appeals that promise to shed some light on the nature of the plurality in the United Kingdom and how, in that national context, the courts see their role where questions of medical law implicate deep moral divisions. Thirdly, arising from these cases, and returning to the conversation sketched in the first part of the chapter, some further reflections are presented on the role and responsibilities of the courts when faced with axiological pluralism.

Stated shortly, my principal conclusions are as follows. First, whether or not a community feels the need explicitly to address a condition of axiological pluralism—and, if so, how it then responds—depends on the particular local context and culture as well as the complexion of that pluralism. Secondly, the context and culture in the United Kingdom—the political, economic, and social turbulence associated with Brexit notwithstanding—represents a relatively safe and stable environment for axiological pluralism. Thirdly, the decisions in *Montgomery* and *James* (which prioritise patient rights) run with the grain of modern opinion within the plurality and, as such, provoke no serious legitimacy concerns. Fourthly, the decision in *Doogan* might be argued to be illegitimate relative to the legislative background against which the decision was made. However, finally, like *Montgomery* and

[8]Harris (2007), Sandel (2007), Brownsword (2009).

[9]Beyleveld and Brownsword (2002).

[10]*Montgomery v Lanarkshire Health Board* [2015] UKSC 11.

[11]*Aintree University Hospitals NHS Foundation Trust v James* [2013] UKSC 67.

[12]*Greater Glasgow Health Board v Doogan* [2014] UKSC 68.

James, *Doogan* reflects the balance of ethical opinion within the community; and, given the local context and culture, those who judge the decision to be illegitimate, while not being slow to criticise it, will not act in ways that are seriously destabilising.

2 The Risks Presented by Axiological Pluralism: A Possible Conversation

In Europe, when new technologies emerge, it is standard regulatory practice to assess the risks that they might present, to agree upon an acceptable risk management strategy (possibly including a moratorium on further development of the technology),[13] and to devise a communication strategy that will ensure that all users of the technology are properly informed.[14] In some cases, as I have already remarked, new technologies will agitate deep moral differences within the community, provoking debates in both public squares and private quarters, and prompting interventions by both legislators and courts. Yet, although we engage spontaneously in these debates, we rarely pause to consider whether the way in which the community settles its deep moral differences is appropriate.

Let us imagine, therefore, a conversation between parties who represent the principal constituencies of the plurality in which they begin to reflect on just this question. The conversation opens with some thoughts on the kinds of risks that might be presented by axiological pluralism and whether, in the particular community, any of these risks are likely to eventuate. If these are risks to be taken seriously, is some response required? If so, the conversation turns to the question of the kinds of response that might be appropriate.

2.1 *What Kind of Risks?*

Under conditions of axiological pluralism, what kind of risks might there be? The most obvious risk is that of a legitimacy deficit where a decision has to be made on a significant ethical matter that divides the community's members. Those members who contest the decision might claim that it is deficient in one or more of three ways. They might question the *title* (or credentials) of the decision-makers (whether they are legislators, or judges, or supposed ethical experts, or others); they might question

[13]Compare, e.g., the European Group on Ethics in Science and New Technologies to the European Commission (2007), para 4.2.3: 'risk management actions should be aimed at identifying the 'acceptable risk' threshold with regard to the values at stake—and respect for the human body is undoubtedly one of the values deserving the highest legal protection.'

[14]How well, or poorly, Europe has done in this regard is a matter for debate: see, e.g., Lee (2008).

the legitimacy of the *process*; and they will, of course, challenge the legitimacy of the *outcome*. In short, there is the possibility of a triple challenge being mounted against the legitimacy of decisions made on ethical questions that concern the whole community.

If these legitimacy challenges translate into a lack of cooperation, a lack of respect, or organised resistance and rebellion, then there might be various consequential risks. For example, day-to-day governance and administration might be slower and less efficient; or, indeed, government might be unworkable. In the worst-case scenario, social order might break down. Moral differences notwithstanding, we should never forget that there is a common interest (the interest of humanity) in protecting the conditions that enable humans to exist on this planet, to develop a sense of their own interests as well as the legitimate interests of others, and to debate their moral differences. In other words, there are some red lines that set the boundaries for moral plurality and contestation.[15]

2.2 *Is There a Risk?*

It is, of course, a big leap from conditions of axiological pluralism to social disorder. A legitimacy deficit will not necessarily provoke a legitimacy crisis even less a social catastrophe. In some communities, profound moral differences notwithstanding, there might be no real threat of instability. For example, the culture in some communities might be one of tolerance for rival ethical views; protagonists are content to agree to disagree; and, although each part of the plurality will not hold back in arguing for its views, it will accept that its views might not always prevail. Moreover, in some communities the balance of power between the different elements of the plurality—whether as an equilibrium, or a dominant (but not universal) view—might be such that there is little risk of ethical disagreements escalating into serious social disorder. These communities, although fractured by axiological pluralism, are perfectly functional. Accordingly, if this is the context, our imaginary conversation is likely to be quite a short one; for there will be little pressure to change current practices.

On the other hand, the context might be rather different. It might be one in which new technologies have inflamed old ethical antagonisms. It might be one in which the deep differences that exist between key segments of the community are threatening to disable governance and encourage people to take the law into their own hands. Here, the pressure is on to calm the situation and to preserve the conditions in which a community with moral aspirations—albeit a deeply divided moral community—may flourish. In this setting, there will be calls to both prudential and moral considerations to agree upon a more acceptable way of dealing with morally divisive questions.

[15]Brownsword (2017, 2018), Brownsword (2019a), Ch 4; Brownsword (2019b, c).

To be sure, there is no guarantee that such calls will be successful. Within the plurality, there might be elements for whom the only acceptable state of affairs is one in which their view prevails. If so, these elements will not, in any case, accept their invitation to be a party to the conversation: for, they will have no interest in preserving the conditions for an aspirant moral community; the risk that, in a divided moral community, power might fall into the hands of opportunists or amoralists will be regarded as immaterial; and, appeals to moderation and civility will fall on deaf ears. All that matters is that their view, the one and only view to be tolerated, prevails.

Let us suppose, therefore, that while the particular context is free of such fanatical elements, there is nevertheless a sufficient concern about the legitimacy deficit in conditions of axiological pluralism to warrant thinking some more about the way in which the community's ethical differences are resolved. How might the conversation continue? What kind of roles and responsibilities for legislatures and courts might be contemplated?

2.3 Some Proposals for Dealing with the Legitimacy Deficit

No doubt, there might be many proposals for ways in which the risks associated with the legitimacy deficit might be managed. In what follows, a number of possible approaches will be outlined; but it should be emphasised that this is in no sense a comprehensive list and the parties to the hypothetical conversation might come up with quite different ideas.

2.3.1 Deliberative Democracy

First, it might be proposed that the government should seek to embrace, indeed to celebrate, the community's pluralism, ensuring in the spirit of deliberative democracy that all voices are heard, and all reasonable viewpoints understood.[16] Such a public consultation might be led by the government itself, or orchestrated by a commission or a committee of some kind. On analysis, it might turn out that there are significant points of consensus on the basis of which a common position can be developed. The fact that the consensus is not shared all the way down to first principles is accepted; the fact that there is a sufficient consensus is what matters.[17] On the other hand, it might turn out that the protagonists are dug into irreconcilable positions and that there is no prospect of a consensus. In this case, whatever recommendations are made and then acted on, some parties will be deeply unhappy

[16]For application, see, e.g., the Presidential Commission for the Study of Bioethical Issues (2010). See Gutmann and Thompson (2004).

[17]Compare Sunstein (1996) on the idea of an 'incompletely theorised agreement'.

with the outcome. To such discontents, government can make a general appeal to the shared moral aspirations of all members of the plurality. For the time being, a particular moral view has been taken; some think that it is fundamentally wrong; nevertheless, restraint should be exercised lest, in a divided moral community, rule is ceded to interests that are entirely self-serving and amoral.[18] Government might also be able to appeal, more specifically, to the particular moral principles of those who, relative to such principles, judge the outcome to be wrong. If the consequences of resistance are, relative to those principles, more serious than the consequences of acquiescence, then those principles themselves indicate that a degree of acceptance is the lesser of two evils.[19]

2.3.2 Politics as Usual and Conviction Politics

Secondly, there might be a proposal that difficult and divisive ethical questions should be left to 'politics as usual', the legislative assembly debating and then voting on such questions. However, such a proposal is unlikely to be taken seriously—or, at any rate, not so where 'politics as usual' involves, at best, a mix of bargaining, horse trading, and compromising amongst party managers coupled with instructions to individual members to follow the party line and, at worst, capture and corruption. No one can think that this is an appropriate way to engage with profound ethical questions.

However, where ethically contentious issues are presented for debate and decision, what if members of the legislature were to be released from party orders and given a free vote (according to their individual conscience)? On the face of it, this would be a more plausible proposal; but, much would depend upon the political culture and context. For example, if votes could be bought, or if politicians simply lacked the ability to engage in reasoned ethical debate, freeing politicians from their party orders would not be any improvement. Moreover, if the ethical plurality amongst politicians does not broadly correspond with the ethical plurality amongst the general public, there will be a disjunction between the legislative conscience and the collective conscience meaning that the legitimacy deficit will continue to be a concern.

These reservations notwithstanding, in the United Kingdom, when legislative proposals that address highly contentious ethical questions (for example, concerning abortion, or homosexuality, or assisted dying and euthanasia) are debated in Parliament, the custom and practice is to give MPs a free vote. Accordingly, in the 1960s, when David Steel's Private Members' Bill was introduced with a view to creating a framework for lawful abortions—and with 'pro-life' and 'pro-choice' lobbies contesting the right of women to terminate their pregnancies—MPs were given the freedom to vote in accordance with their conscience. The ensuing legislative

[18]Brownsword (2010).

[19]Compare Beyleveld and Brownsword (1986), Ch 2.

framework, in the Abortion Act 1967, was something of a compromise but, in general, the outcome was one that favoured the pro-choice lobby and tilted the balance towards recognising the reproductive rights of women. However, the legislation did not altogether ignore the concerns of pro-life advocates who feared that the enactment was the first step on a slippery slope that would lead to abortion on demand. It did this by entrusting doctors with the responsibility to act as gatekeepers to lawful abortions,[20] a strategy that we might term as one of 'compromise medicalisation'.[21] While compromise medicalisation is more of a response to an ethical impasse than a way of dealing with a legitimacy deficit, it does encourage some movement by protagonists who would not otherwise give ground; and there will be occasion to return to the consequences that flow from this strategy later in the paper when discussing the *Doogan* case in which hospital midwives who opposed abortion wished to exercise their statutory right of conscientious objection.

2.3.3 Special Procedures

Thirdly, if we reject both politics as usual and conviction politics (in the form of a vote in accordance with conscience), it might be proposed that special groundrules be agreed for engaging with divisive ethical issues. For example, in a Rawlsian spirit, it might be proposed that, in such contentious cases, politicians (and other public officers) should set aside their fundamental convictions and, instead, reason in a way that respects certain principles that are agreed to be appropriate and reasonable for public debate and decision.[22] The idea is that, with the legitimacy of the process secured in this way, the outcomes should command respect. But, of course, there are two obvious difficulties with this proposal. First, the principles that now guide public debate and decision are not necessarily principles that govern within each ethical paradigm; so, rather like the criticism of coalition governments, the reasoning and outcomes are not as anyone ideally thinks they should be. In other words, the process (and, possibly, the outcome) is not just second-best for some, it is second-best for everyone. Secondly, if the agreed groundrules are to be presented as acceptable because they are ethically 'neutral' (relative to the different constituencies within the plurality), one wonders whether they will give sufficient direction to the process to enable the parties to resolve their differences; and, if the groundrules are presented as being acceptable, not because they are neutral but because they are 'reasonable', this invites the parties to object where they detect some implicit or indirect bias against their views.

[20] Compare Brazier and Ost (2013, p. 194, 198–199); and Grubb (1990).

[21] Brownsword and Wale (2015).

[22] Compare Rawls (1993).

2.3.4 Shared Responsibility

Fourthly, it might be proposed that the legislature should share responsibility with some independent regulatory body. For example, in relation to a particular field, the legislature might set out a framework of general principles, but then delegate to a regulatory body the responsibility for making particular decisions. In the United Kingdom, this is the way in which assisted conception and the use of human embryos for research have been handled, in both cases by charging the Human Fertilisation and Embryology Authority (HFEA) with the more particular ethical responsibilities. While many admire this approach, the title of the HFEA to undertake this task is weakened if the members of the Authority are all basically in favour of (or, at least, not resolutely opposed to) IVF and the use of human embryos for research—for, even if the HFEA consults with those who take a radically opposed view, the latter will see themselves as outsiders and this will impact on their sense of the legitimacy of the process and the outcome. There is also a problem if the body does not have sufficient resources to run the kind of consultation that government can undertake. Predictably, where the HFEA has licensed activities that arguably go beyond the terms of the authorising legislative framework, pro-life interests have challenged the legality of such decisions by seeking a judicial review.[23]

2.3.5 Embedding a Morality Clause

Fifthly, it might be proposed that government should respond to ethical plurality as a fact of the community's life by embedding an unspecified morality clause (or a contested moral concept) within a legislative framework, and then leaving it to the judicial branch to determine which or whose morality (or whose conception of the concept) is decisive. One particularly striking example of such a strategy is found in European patent law where an invention is not to be treated as patentable if, despite its originality, its commercial exploitation would be contrary to morality.[24] When the European Patent Office (EPO) was first presented with modern biotechnological inventions, objectors argued that patents should not be granted on the relevant processes and products because this would be contrary to morality. For patent examiners who disclaimed any ethical expertise, it might have been tempting to refer the question to an expert ethics committee;[25] however, the examiners did not do this and, instead, they assumed responsibility for interpreting and applying the morality exclusion. Initially, the EPO took a utilitarian approach (giving considerable weight to the promised benefits of the inventions) and then marginalised the exclusion by treating it as applicable only where, in effect, granting a patent would

[23] Brownsword (2008), Ch 6.

[24] See Article 53(a) of the European Patent Convention.

[25] As, in fact, happened in the Norwegian patent office.

be inconceivable from any moral viewpoint.[26] However, when Directive 98/44/EC on the Legal Protection of Biotechnological Inventions was enacted, the general morality clause—in Article 6(1) of the Directive—was supplemented, in Article 6 (2), with some specific examples of exclusion that clearly reflected a particular dignitarian ethic.[27] When the interpretation of the Directive, and specifically the exclusion in Article 6(2)(c) concerning research using human embryos, was tested before the CJEU in *Brüstle*,[28] the underlying problems of axiological pluralism—the conflict between a permissive liberal patenting paradigm and a restrictive conservative patenting paradigm—were brought into the open. Whereas the EPO's marginalisation of the morality exclusion favoured the interests of those states that took a liberal approach, the CJEU's dignitarian interpretation of the Directive not only favoured a conservative approach, it also imposed that approach (as its expression of EU law) on all member states. This provoked claims that the CJEU exceeded its authority as well as more obvious objections to the legitimacy of the dignitarian outcome.[29]

In *Brüstle*, the CJEU found itself caught between a liberal rock and a dignitarian hard place.[30] The European legislative institutions had been unable to find a common position and the Directive that was eventually signed off was a pragmatic compromise, giving the liberals something of what they wanted (the possibility of patenting inventive work around the human genome) while also giving the dignitarians some of the restrictions that they wanted (particularly concerning the protection of human embryos). In effect, in *Brüstle*, the CJEU did little more than uphold the dignitarian side of the compromise rather than 'fudging' the issue or, even more provocatively, defying the Directive and siding with the liberals.

If the courts lack title legitimacy to resolve disputes of an axiological pluralist kind, we might think that they should not be placed in the invidious position of having to engage with such cases. As Aurora Plomer[31] has aptly put it, litigation in a case such as *Brüstle* that ostensibly relates to patents becomes 'a theatre for the re-enactment of moral and religious disputes between secular and religious forces divided on the value of human "life".' Nevertheless, in the common law world, it is the traditional function of the courts to develop significant areas of law that rest on sometimes profound ethical differences—which takes us to the sixth proposed response.

---

[26]Beyleveld and Brownsword (1993).

[27]Beyleveld et al. (2000), Beyleveld and Brownsword (2001).

[28]Case C-34/10, *Oliver Brüstle v Greenpeace e.V.* (Grand Chamber, 18 October 2011).

[29]Plomer (2012).

[30]Brownsword (2014).

[31]Plomer (2015), p. 24.

2.3.6 Leaving it to the Courts

Finally, it might be proposed that the ethical development of the law should be entrusted to the courts. Although, where there is a clear separation of powers, judges are insulated against the more obvious political pressures, this might seem to be an unpromising strategy—for example, because there is little chance that ethical views within the judiciary will map onto the plurality within the community.[32] That said, it is characteristic of common law legal systems that the law is developed case-by-case in the courts; and, even though in modern societies much of the responsibility for law-making has been transferred from the courts to the legislature, there are pockets of law where the judges retain a law-making role. Medical law is one such area and we can now turn to three recent major UK Supreme Court decisions that offer food for thought about how to handle axiological pluralism.

3 Recent Medical Jurisprudence

In the last few years, a number of appeals on difficult points in medical law have been taken to the UK Supreme Court, as some would see it, leading to the creation of a new legal framework for the relationship between doctors and patients. These are not cases where the courts identify ethical pluralism as a problem and debate their own role and responsibility in responding to possible concerns about the legitimacy of their decisions. Nevertheless, these are cases that concretise some of the issues relating to the treatment of ethical plurality in the courts.

3.1 Montgomery[33]

For many years, according to the so-called *Bolam* test,[34] English law has recognised that doctors may respond to a negligence claim by showing that a responsible body of medical opinion (not necessarily the mainstream view) supports their actions (or omissions). However, when doctors discuss with their patients the investigatory and treatment options and risks therein, such a defence seems to have been eliminated by the decision of the UK Supreme Court in *Montgomery v Lanarkshire Health Board*. After *Montgomery*, the law is predicated on a new approach to the doctor/patient relationship.

The principal question in *Montgomery* was whether a pregnant woman who was a diabetic, and whose pregnancy was regarded as high-risk requiring intensive

[32]Griffith (1977).

[33]*Montgomery v Lanarkshire Health Board* [2015] UKSC 11.

[34]*Bolam v Friern Hospital Management Committee* [1957] 2 All ER 118.

monitoring, should have been informed that there was a risk of shoulder dystocia and given the option of delivery by Caesarean Section. Instead, as the court narrated the story,[35] she was not made aware of this particular risk; the risk eventuated during an attempted vaginal delivery that went horribly wrong; and, as a result, the baby was born with severe disabilities. The lower courts, following the *Bolam* principle, held that the acts of the consultant obstetrician and gynaecologist, who was by her own admission reluctant to steer women towards a Caesarean Section, were sufficiently supported by medical practice. However, the UK Supreme Court, resoundingly rejecting the *Bolam* test, held that the relationship between clinicians and patients must be rights-respecting rather than paternalistic and that patients have a right to be informed about their options (together with their relative benefits and risks).

In a few paragraphs, the Supreme Court (in a speech co-authored by Lords Kerr and Reed) rewrote the legal framework governing the relationship between physicians and patients. First, the Court recognised that 'patients are now widely regarded as persons holding rights, rather than as the passive recipients of the care of the medical profession'.[36] Secondly, the Court noted that patients, while not medical experts, are not wholly uninformed. Accordingly, it would be 'a mistake to view patients as uninformed, incapable of understanding medical matters, or wholly dependent upon a flow of information from doctors', from which it followed that it would now be 'manifestly untenable' to make this 'the default assumption on which the law is to be based'.[37] Thirdly, professional guidance to doctors already reflects these changes by encouraging 'an approach based upon the informed involvement of patients in their treatment'.[38] Signalling a distinct movement away from medical paternalism and patient-dependence, the new approach is built on mutual rights and responsibilities, treating patients 'so far as possible as adults who are capable of understanding that medical treatment is uncertain of success and may involve risks, accepting responsibility for the taking of risks affecting their own lives, and living with the consequences of their choices'.[39] That said, *Montgomery* recognises that, in exceptional circumstances, doctors may legitimately withhold information under cover of the so-called 'therapeutic privilege'. However, the Court emphasises that this exception 'is not intended to subvert [the general principle] by enabling the doctor to prevent the patient from making an informed choice where she is liable to make a choice which the doctor considers to be contrary to her best interests'.[40] In short, patients have a right to make their own judgments of what is in their best interests; and it is the responsibility of doctors not to override these judgments but to assist patients by ensuring that their choices are suitably informed.

[35]For some critical comments on this version of the story, see Montgomery and Montgomery (2016).

[36]*Montgomery v Lanarkshire Health Board* [2015] UKSC 11, para 75.

[37]Ibid., para 76.

[38]Ibid., para 78.

[39]Ibid., para 81.

[40]Ibid., para 91.

Without doubt, the headline story in *Montgomery* is that the doctor/patient relationship is now predicated on the rights paradigm rather than ethical paradigms that prioritise professional duties or paternalistic responsibilities or that centre on maximising utility or minimising distress. As Lady Hale, giving a separate but fully concurring judgment, expressed it:

> A patient is entitled to take into account her own values, her own assessment of the comparative merits of giving birth in the 'natural' and traditional way and of giving birth by caesarean section, whatever medical opinion may say, alongside the medical evaluation of the risks to herself and her baby…Gone are the days when it was thought that, on becoming pregnant, a woman lost, not only her capacity, but also her right to act as a genuinely autonomous human being.[41]

Moreover, in addition to noting the growing culture of consumer rights, the court remarked on the increasing influence in judicial thinking of the importance of respecting human rights: 'Under the stimulus of the Human Rights Act 1998, the courts have become increasingly conscious of the extent to which the common law reflects fundamental values'.[42] So, for example, in *Tracey*,[43] the Court of Appeal, anticipating the new approach in *Montgomery*, applied Article 8 of the European Convention on Human Rights to rule that a patient has a right to be consulted by the medical team before a DNACPR (non-resuscitation) order is made.

3.2 *James*[44]

In *James*, which was actually heard a couple of years before *Montgomery*, it was agreed that the patient, a 68 year old man who had been admitted because of a problem with a stoma, but who then suffered severe complications and whose neurological state deterioriated, lacked the capacity to make decisions about his medical treatment. It was also agreed that the prognosis was poor and, in fact, the patient suffered a cardiac arrest and died within days of the Court of Appeal hearing the case. The general question raised by the proceedings was whether a number of treatment options would be in the patient's best interests. While the clinical team took the view that the treatments would not be in the patient's best interest (because there would be little or no net benefit and a considerable burden), the patient's family took the view that there was still some quality in his life and that he would want to be treated. Peter Jackson J, hearing the hospital trust's application in the Court of Protection, ruled against the clinicians' view holding that it undervalued the non-medical aspects of the patient's situation, particularly the pleasure that he got

[41] Ibid., paras 115–116.

[42] Ibid., para 80.

[43] *R (Tracey) v Cambridge University Hospitals NHS Foundation Trust and others* [2014] EWCA Civ 822.

[44] *Aintree University Hospitals NHS Foundation Trust v James* [2013] UKSC 67.

from seeing his family and friends. The Court of Appeal took a different view of the patient's best interests, emphasising that the treatments were futile in the sense that there was no prospect of the patient recovering and going home as well as the burdensome nature of the treatments. On further appeal, the Supreme Court unanimously preferred the reasoning of Peter Jackson J but held that, in the light of the patient's dramatically reduced circumstances by the time of the appeal hearing, the Court of Appeal had reached the right result albeit for the wrong reasons.

While it is agreed that, where a patient lacks mental capacity, decision-makers (whether clinicians or courts) should strive to act in accordance with that patient's 'best interests', how should that test be interpreted? Guided by the provisions of the Mental Capacity Act 2005, by the thinking of the Law Commission (1995), by the Explanatory Notes to the Bill, by the *Code of Practice* (2007) published pursuant to the Act, and by the case-law, Lady Hale summed up the legal position as follows:

> The most that can be said, therefore, is that in considering the best interests of this particular patient at this particular time, decision-makers must look at his welfare in the widest sense, not just medical but social and psychological; they must consider the nature of the medical treatment in question, what it involves and its prospects of success; they must consider what the outcome of that treatment for the patient is likely to be; they must try and put themselves in the place of the individual patient and ask what his attitude to the treatment is or would be likely to be; and they must consult others who are looking after him or interested in his welfare, in particular for their view of what his attitude would be.[45]

It followed that, within this holistic approach, the question of whether a treatment is 'futile' is not whether (as the Court of Appeal implied) it has a real prospect of curing or at least palliating the illness (even if in practice the term 'futility' is applied to treatments that have no such prospects); and, to the extent that the Court of Appeal took the reference point for a patient's best interests to be that of an objectively reasonable person, this was fundamentally mistaken—rather, the 'purpose of the best interests test is to consider matters from the patient's point of view'.[46] Of course, in a case of mental incapacity, it might not always be possible to ascertain the patient's wishes, beliefs, and values; but, insofar as it is possible to do so, 'it is those which should be taken into account because they are a component in making the choice which is right for him as an individual human being'.[47]

Although *James*, where, at the relevant time, the patient no longer had mental capacity, might seem to be a very different kind of case to *Montgomery*, there is a strong connecting thread. That thread is recognition of the patient's right to self-determination which, so far as possible, should be respected and promoted by doctors. In Lady Hale's judgment in *James* we see a clear signal of this line of reasoning early on when she cautions against thinking that the basic question is whether it would be in the patient's best interests to *withhold* the treatments at

[45] *Aintree* (n 27), para 39.

[46] Ibid., para 45.

[47] Ibid., para 45.

issue.[48] Rather, if the treatments are not absolutely useless or pointless, the question is whether it is in the patient's best interests for the treatments to be *given*; and that hinges on whether the particular patient would have consented to the administration of the treatments.[49]

Accordingly, in *James*, as in *Montgomery*, the most striking feature of the case is that the rights paradigm is applied as against physician paternalism (although, unlike *Montgomery*, there was no suggestion in *James* that the clinical view involved elements of moral paternalism) and, once again, the courts decline to defer to what would be considered reasonable in clinical practice.[50]

3.3 *Doogan*[51]

Unlike *Montgomery* and *James*, *Doogan* really is a different kind of case. It concerns the interpretation and application of section 4, the conscience clause, of the Abortion Act 1967. Effectively, the clause provides that no person shall be under a duty 'to participate in any treatment authorised by this Act to which he has a conscientious objection.' In an earlier case, *R v Salford Health Authority, ex parte Janaway*,[52] it was held that the conscience clause did not extend to a secretary and receptionist in a health centre who objected to typing a letter from a GP that referred a patient to a hospital consultant with a view to a possible termination. 'Treatment' within the conscience clause, the House of Lords held, referred to the process undertaken in hospital to terminate a pregnancy and 'participation' meant actually taking part in that process. However, the petitioners in *Doogan* were midwives who worked at the South General Hospital in Glasgow. Their concern was that, following the closure of one of the three hospitals in Glasgow that provided maternity services, and the consequent reorganisation of such services, they might find themselves being expected to perform functions to which they had a conscientious objection. The question narrowed to whether 'delegating, supervising and/or supporting staff to participate in and provide care to patients throughout the termination process' would qualify as activities from which the midwives might exempt themselves on the grounds of conscience. The midwives' application was unsuccessful at first instance

[48]Ibid., para 17.

[49]Ibid., para 22.

[50]Although this is not the place to open a discussion about the Charlie Gard case, which, in 2017, attracted worldwide attention, the dispute between the hospital and the parents/family clearly has echoes of the issues in *James*. While there is the question of *what* is in the best interests of a young child, if anything, the more important question seems to be that of *who* should decide—should it be the hospital, or the child's parents, or a judge? See, further, Cave and Nottingham (2018), Montgomery (2019).

[51]*Greater Glasgow Health Board v Doogan* [2014] UKSC 68.

[52][1989] AC 537.

but then succeeded on appeal. On final appeal, the Supreme Court ruled against the applicants.

The conscience clause in the Abortion Act is open to broad or narrow readings depending upon how we interpret 'treatment' and 'participate in'. Assuming that treatment means the process of terminating the pregnancy (whether the procedure is surgical or medical), the critical question is the meaning of 'participate in'. Lady Hale posed the issue in the following terms:

> The employers accept that it [the phrase 'to participate in'] could have a broad or a narrow meaning. On any view, it would not cover things done before the course of treatment began, such as making the booking before the first drug is administered. But a broad meaning might cover things done in connection with that treatment after it had begun, such as assigning staff to work with the patient, supervising and supporting such staff, and keeping a managerial eye on all the patients in the ward, including any undergoing a termination. A narrow meaning would restrict it to 'actually taking part', that is actually performing the tasks involved in the course of the treatment.[53]

Without more ado, Lady Hale declared that she believed that the narrow meaning was more likely to accord with Parliament's intention. After all, the conscience clause related to acts made lawful by the legislation, acts to which the opponents of the legislation objected, from which it followed that it was unlikely that Parliament was contemplating an exemption from 'the host of ancillary, administrative and managerial tasks that might be associated with those [now lawful] acts'.[54]

The Supreme Court's ruling is not necessarily the final word. As the court emphasised, there is still the possibility of the midwives arguing before an employment tribunal that, even if they are not protected by the conscience clause (as now interpreted), their employers are required by the Human Rights Act 1998 (incorporating Article 9 of the ECHR) and by the Equality Act 2010 to make 'reasonable adjustments to the requirements of the job in order to cater for their religious beliefs'.[55]

At this stage, it suffices to make three short points about *Doogan*. First, although the Abortion Act was legislated in a context of conspicuous axiological pluralism, it is not clear that the decision in *Doogan* takes sides on the questions that divided the politicians. Arguably, rather like the CJEU in *Brüstle*, the Supreme Court was in an invidious position and, no matter which way it decided the case, it would provoke one ethical (and, in this case, strongly religious) constituency. Secondly, reliance on what Parliament contemplated as a basis for either the broad or the narrow interpretation of the conscience clause is vulnerable to the objection that parliamentarians were seriously divided. Whether the narrow reading favoured by the court aligns with the historic legislative intention probably depends on whether one is guided by the views of the pro-life or the pro-choice MPs of that time. Thirdly, having left it to the employment tribunal to decide whether it is necessary to adjust the hospital's

[53]*Greater Glasgow Health Board v Doogan* [2014] UKSC 68, para 37.

[54]Ibid., para 38.

[55]Ibid., para 24.

requirements if they are to be compatible with the midwives' human rights, there is a suspicion that the Supreme Court adopted a utilitarian approach and simply balanced the distress to the midwives if they were required to perform ancillary tasks against the inconvenience and disruption to the hospital if the midwives' objections to doing such work had to be accommodated.

Having skimmed the surface of these three cases, we can now revisit them—recalling our earlier imaginary conversation concerning the risks associated with, and the possible responses to, axiological pluralism—in an attempt to bring the responsibilities of the courts more sharply into focus.

4 The Institutional Role and Responsibilities of the Courts

To return to my earlier remarks, let us suppose that axiological pluralism is a feature of the community's moral life; and let us suppose that the pluralism is constituted by a three-way conflict between rights-based, duty-based and utilitarian ethics. In such a community, the trajectory of medical law in the three cases discussed above will seem to be very much towards rights-thinking and away from duty-based perspectives (although, in *Doogan*, the midwives' dignitarian views arguably were defeated by utilitarian rather than rights-based considerations). However, to form a view about the responsibilities of the courts, we need to distinguish between those cases, such as *Montgomery*, that are decided on common law principles and those, such as *James* and *Doogan*, that come into the courts against the backcloth of a governing legislative framework. We also need to distinguish between axiological pluralism and intra-ethical pluralism (or, plurality within a particular ethic).

Let us suppose that a community treats the legislature as having the principal responsibility for law-making (ethically contentious or not). Under conditions of axiological pluralism, a legislative body might settle on a compromise (as was the case with both the Abortion Act 1967 and the biotech patent Directive), or it might come down firmly on one side (as when, in 2015, the rights-driven arguments for relaxation of the UK law on assisted suicide were decisively rejected by parliamentarians).[56] If the courts are called upon to interpret such a legislative response, their responsibility is to interpret it faithfully, whether the response is a compromise or a clear choice. Unless the courts have been clearly mandated to adjust the legislative position, their responsibility is to uphold the legislative position not to rewrite it and engage with axiological pluralism in their own way.[57]

In a common law jurisdiction, however, there is also the possibility that the legislature will not have responded but will have left it to the courts to manage the

[56]Gallagher and Roxby (2015).

[57]Even where human rights are perceived to be at issue, the courts might exercise restraint in intervening in legislative processes, see *R (on the application of Nicklinson and another) v Ministry of Justice; R (on the application of AM) (AP) v The DPP* [2014] UKSC 38.

plurality. In a case such as *Montgomery*, there might be axiological pluralism in both the community at large and amongst the members of the medical profession. Here, the courts have three principal options, namely: (i) deferring to the practice of the medical profession (as per the *Bolam* principle); (ii) trying to reflect the dominant view of the community; or (iii) making a choice between conflicting paradigms and using it to set the standard. The virtue of the first option is that it, so to speak, lets sleeping dogs lie. However, it means that patients can shop around to find a doctor whose ethics align with their own needs; and it means that the mainstream of medical practice might be out of touch with general community ethics. The virtue of the second option is that it tries to get a better alignment between community ethics and professional medical ethics, although it obviously invites resistance from the latter. And, the third option is bold but it invites legitimacy questions unless it is accepted that courts have title to set standards rather than simply to reflect them.

Although everyone can agree that in *Montgomery* there is a paradigm shift, from duty-based paternalism to patient rights, it is not clear how the court viewed its responsibilities for engaging with axiological pluralism. On the face of it, the court acted as a mini-legislature, setting new standards for the doctor/patient relationship, and clearly siding with those who argue for a rights-based ethic. Alternatively, the court assumed legislative responsibility but, rather than setting its own standards, it endeavoured to reflect what it took to be general community standards; and, it then tried to achieve a better alignment between those standards and the values that inform medical practice. One thing that the court did not do was to defer to paternalistic medical practice, or indeed to any aspect of medical practice—at any rate, not so unless we read the court as trying to crystallise an approach that was implicit in much of the professional guidance but not necessarily in hospital practice.

These different readings suggest that, in dealing with axiological pluralism through the common law, there are two levels of decision for the courts. First, they must decide whether their institutional role is to *set* ethical standards or to *reflect* such standards. Secondly, if they are to set standards, they must decide which standards they will impose (e.g. rights or some other ethic); and, if they are to reflect standards, they must decide whose standards they will endeavour to reflect (e.g., the ethics of medical practitioners or of patient groups or of the public, and so on).

Technically, the court in *James* is charged with interpreting the best interests test in the Mental Capacity Act 2005. Given that the Act is underpinned by rights-based thinking, the court's approach is consistent with a faithful interpretation.[58] To be

[58]Section 1 of the Act declares its 'rights' basis by specifying the following five guiding principles: (i) a person must be assumed to have capacity unless it is established that he lacks capacity; (ii) a person is not to be treated as unable to make a decision unless all practicable steps to help him to do so have been taken without success; (iii) a person is not to be treated as unable to make a decision merely because he makes an unwise decision; (iv) an act done, or decision made...for or on behalf of a person who lacks capacity must be done, or made, in his best interests; and (v) before the act is done, or the decision is made, regard must be had to whether the purpose for which it is needed can be as effectively achieved in a way that is less restrictive of the person's rights and freedom of action.

sure, within a community committed to rights, there might well be different views about how best interests should be judged when the right-holder no longer has mental capacity. Lady Hale emphasises the importance of trying to track a person's critical interests but others might revert to a calculation of net welfare or minimisation of distress. If we allow that these are all defensible views that might be articulated in a rights ethic, what we have at this point is not a case of axiological pluralism so much as reasonable plurality within the shared rights paradigm (i.e., intra-ethical plurality).[59]

This brings us back to *Doogan* which definitely is a case that is decided against the backcloth of a legislative compromise. Was the narrow interpretation of the conscience clause faithful to that compromise? If compromise medicalisation is to work as a strategy for dealing with persistent ethical conflict, it is imperative that both the courts and the medical profession hold the line; it is not their job to make running adjustments to the compromise as the community's views evolve.[60] In the case of the Abortion Act, it is clear that the terms of the compromise have not been adhered to. Whereas the compromise was intended to prevent any possible slide from termination as a special case exception to abortion on demand, in all but name, the latter is now what we have. Those pro-life politicians who accepted the compromise would be shocked (although some, no doubt, would declare 'We told you so!'). At the same time, though, community opinion has changed and termination at will is now accepted by many as a woman's right. So, if the compromise had been adhered to, the midwives in *Doogan* would have been objecting to participating in special exception terminations rather than everyday routine procedures; from their ethical perspective, having anything to do with these special cases would have been distressing and objectionable; and, having to work round these objections, would not have been any great inconvenience for the hospital. With such a change in both context and culture, it is hard to be confident that the Supreme Court got it right in adopting the narrow interpretation. Indeed, critics might fairly complain that the courts, having failed to prevent the slide towards abortion on demand, then failed to recognise, let alone respond to, the strain on conscience that this abdication of judicial responsibility has generated.

If we are to justify the court's interpretation in *Doogan*, we probably need to change the premiss that the 1967 Act is an instance of compromise medicalisation. If, instead, we assume that the legislative expectation was that the medical profession would align its practice with (what were expected to be) more liberal social attitudes and that the courts would then fall into line with this, the narrow interpretation in *Doogan* would fit with the more evolutionary role assigned to the judiciary. For, although the rhetoric of *Doogan* is to give effect to what the legislature of 1967 contemplated and intended, the underlying reality is that the interpretation fits much more smoothly into a twenty-first century context in which (as per *Montgomery*) a

[59]Compare the use of the notion of the 'margin of appreciation' in the jurisprudence of the European Court of Human Rights, McGoldrick (2016); and for a more critical view, see Scott (2018).

[60]Brownsword and Wale (2015).

woman's reproductive autonomy is respected, terminations are accepted as routine, the finances and resources of the NHS are overstretched, and there is limited room to accommodate minority (in the UK) beliefs.

4.1 Taking Stock

When we set the specific features of the three cases that we have discussed alongside our more general reflections about the risks associated with axiological pluralism and the role and responsibilities of the courts, how should we pull together the threads? Perhaps, three points should be highlighted.

First, it is clear that the local context and culture is extremely important. If our imaginary conversation were to take place in the United Kingdom, the parties would probably agree that the legitimacy deficit presents no great risks. Of course, given axiological pluralism, where particular legislative or judicial decisions favour rights rather than duties (or vice versa), or utility rather than rights or duties, and so on, these decisions will have their critics; inevitably, some will question the legitimacy of the outcome. However, few will question the legitimacy of the title of either the legislature or the courts to make such decisions and nor will they question the legitimacy of the process. Where highly contentious ethical questions are debated in Parliament, these debates are usually part of a much larger public debate (with extensive media coverage) that displays many of the elements of deliberative democracy; and, because the courts have traditionally developed the common law, no one thinks that in a case such as *Montgomery* they are exceeding their remit. Moreover, the British public tend to be fairly pragmatic about their ethical differences, accepting that life goes on and that there will be opportunities in future to renew debates and review decisions. Accordingly, while the parties to our imaginary conversation would not be complacent,[61] they might well conclude that, as things stand, no action is required.

Secondly, each of the three cases reminds us that the balance of opinion under conditions of axiological pluralism can change. The complexion of ethical pluralism in Victorian England would not correspond with that in the 'permissive' 1960s any more than it would correspond with ethical pluralism in the United Kingdom today. In today's plurality—at any rate, in relation to medical care—rights-based views have the upper hand in debates with utilitarian views and both rights and utility tend to dominate duty-based ethics. In support of the Supreme Court, we can argue that, in each of the cases, it kept the law connected to the changing complexion of the plurality; and, moreover, we can argue that it did so without provoking serious doubts about the legitimacy of its decisions. To this, the one reservation is the decision in *Doogan*. If the intention behind the legislative compromise in the

[61] Nb, the apparently growing gulf between Britain's 2.7 million Muslims and other sections of the community: see, Dean (2016), p. 2.

Abortion Act was to give those who opposed any relaxation in the law an assurance that this was not a 'slippery slope', then the Court should have supported a broader reading of the conscience clause and left it to Parliament to redraw the terms of the compromise.

Thirdly, unlike *Montgomery* and *Doogan*, where axiological pluralism is engaged, it is not clear that *James* is actually such a case. Arguably, *James* is a case where the protagonists are operating within the same (rights-based) ethical paradigm but interpreting some aspect of the paradigm (the best interests test) in different ways. We should not think that plurality within a shared ethical paradigm is not a possible cause for concern. For example, there might be fierce disputes between rights theorists as to, say, the scope of the privacy right or the priority between privacy and free expression, and so on. However, in general, and certainly in the UK context, ethical pluralism of this kind is less challenging than axiological pluralism.

5 Conclusion

Broadly speaking, my conclusion is that it is difficult to draw general (or universal) lessons with regard to the relationship between axiological pluralism and the role of the courts. So much hinges on local context and culture, together with the complexion of the pluralism.

Hence, where we find axiological pluralism in a group, it is not necessarily a problem: members of the group might be able to live with one another their deep moral differences notwithstanding; and good governance and administration might be perfectly workable. So, even if axiological pluralism threatens a legitimacy deficit, it is not necessarily a recipe for violence, disorder, and social breakdown. Indeed, it would be very helpful to understand more about the conditions in which axiological pluralism really is a problem. However, in the absence of such an historical and sociological appreciation of this matter, the discussion in this chapter has proceeded on the assumption that there might be some circumstances in which members of the community feel the need to reflect on whether there might be more acceptable ways of resolving their ethical differences.

Where the legislature is given the primary responsibility for settling questions that are morally divisive, there are a number of ways in which it might proceed—adopting special procedures for ethically contentious questions, delegating some responsibility to arms-length bodies, and so on. Unless the legislature simply transfers the responsibility to the courts, the role of the latter is to stay faithful to the legislative intent. Where the legislative response has been one of compromise medicalisation, the role of the courts (like the role of the medical profession) is one of maintaining the integrity of the compromise—even if, as in *Doogan*, the terms of the compromise no longer reflect the shifting balance of views in the community.

In all cases, where judges are convinced that the legislature has failed to support the right ethical paradigm, there is a strain on their conscience and a temptation to back their own moral judgments. However, where the strategy is to give the legislature the first and the last word, there is an obvious concern that, if judges *openly* back their own ethical convictions against the position taken by the legislature, then this could precipitate a legitimacy crisis that really could be destabilising. Whether or not judges, who find themselves faced with legislation that offends their conscience, would do better to back their own ethical convictions more discreetly, by employing some suitable doctrinal device, is a complex question. Arguably, for each particular judge, it is a matter of assessing one's own confidence in making the ethical judgment, determining the seriousness of the legislative error, and assessing the risk of one's 'noble lies' being exposed for what they are.[62]

That said, in common law jurisdictions, the development of the law through the cases leaves the courts with a choice of approaches towards axiological pluralism. Whilst there is an expectation that judges will keep faith with the precedents—indeed, many would see the development in *Montgomery*, radical though it was, as one that was foreshadowed in earlier decisions[63]—there is usually so much flexibility within the law that the appeal courts can shift the ethical paradigm if they wish. Given this doctrinal flexibility, the prior question is whether a court sees its role as one of setting standards or of reflecting them. So long as the court, whether as a standard setter or as a standard reflector, is broadly in line with mainstream community ethical views, its decisions should enjoy outcome legitimacy and it should not be destabilising.

For those who believe that judges should back their ethical convictions, this might seem too cautious an approach. Certainly, if the context is one of intra-ethical pluralism, as arguably was the case in *James*, we might think that judges should act on what they take to be their best interpretation of the community's shared moral commitments.[64] However, where the context is one of axiological pluralism, we need to know whether the ice on which judges are skating is thick or thin. Where there is a serious legitimacy deficit and possibly a risk of destabilisation, communities with moral aspirations need to be aware that the ice is thin. In such a context, the institutional role and responsibility of judges is more complex; and, arguably, the default position for the courts should be to respect the groundrules that have been agreed by the community for the handling of its ethical differences (at any rate, provided that those groundrules are not arbitrary or wholly unreasonable).

---

[62] Dworkin (1986).

[63] In particular, see *Bolitho v City and Hackney Health Authority* [1996] 4 All ER 771; and *Pearce v United Bristol Healthcare NHS Trust* [1998] EWCA Civ 865.

[64] Dworkin (1978, 1993), Beyleveld and Brownsword (1986), Ch 9.

References

Beyleveld D, Brownsword R (1986) Law as a moral judgment. Sweet and Maxwell, London

Beyleveld D, Brownsword R (1993) Mice, morality and patents. Common Law Institute of Intellectual Property, London

Beyleveld D, Brownsword R (2001) Human dignity in bioethics and biolaw. Oxford University Press, Oxford

Beyleveld D, Brownsword R (2002) Ethics committees: public interest, private interest, and the ethics of partnership. In: Lebeer G (ed) Ethical function in hospital ethics committees. IOS Press, Amsterdam, pp 135–149

Beyleveld D, Brownsword R, Llewelyn M (2000) The morality clauses of the directive on the legal protection of biotechnological inventions: conflict, compromise, and the patent community. In: Goldberg R, Lonbay J (eds) Pharmaceutical medicine, biotechnology and European law. Cambridge University Press, Cambridge, pp 157–181

Brazier M, Ost S (2013) Medicine and the criminal law volume III: medicine and bioethics in the theatre of the criminal process. Cambridge University Press, Cambridge

Brownsword R (2003) Bioethics today, bioethics tomorrow: stem cell research and the 'Dignitarian Alliance'. Univ Notre Dame J Law Ethics Public Policy 17:15–51

Brownsword R (2005) Stem cells and cloning: where the regulatory consensus fails. N Engl Law Rev 39:535–571

Brownsword R (2008) Rights, regulation and the technological revolution. Oxford University Press, Oxford

Brownsword R (2009) Regulating human enhancement: things can only get better? Law Innov Technol 1:125–152

Brownsword R (2010) Regulating the life sciences, pluralism, and the limits of deliberative democracy. Singapore Acad Law J 22:801–832

Brownsword R (2014) Regulatory coherence—a European challenge. In: Purnhagen K, Rott P (eds) Varieties of European economic law and regulation: essays in honour of Hans Micklitz. Springer, Heidelberg, pp 235–258

Brownsword R (2017) From Erewhon to alpha go: for the sake of human dignity should we destroy the machines? Law Innov Technol 9:117–153

Brownsword R (2018) Law and technology: two modes of disruption, three legal mind-sets, and the big picture of regulatory responsibilities. Indian J Law Technol 14:1–40

Brownsword R (2019a) Law, technology and society: re-imagining the regulatory environment. Routledge, Abingdon

Brownsword R (2019b) Law disrupted, law re-imagined, law re-invented. Technol Regul 1:10–30

Brownsword R (2019c) Law, regulation, and technology: supporting innovation, managing risk and respecting values. In: Pittinsky T (ed) Handbook of science, technology and society. Cambridge University Press, New York, pp 109–137

Brownsword R, Goodwin M (2012) Law and the technologies of the twenty-first century. Cambridge University Press, Cambridge

Brownsword R, Wale J (2015) Compromise medicalisation. In: Stanton C, Devaney S, Farrell A-M, Mullock A (eds) Pioneering health care law: essays in honour of Margaret Brazier. Routledge, Abingdon, pp 292–303

Brownsword R, Wale J (2016) The development of non-invasive prenatal testing: some legal and ethical questions. Jahrbuch für Recht und Ethik 24:31–48

Brownsword R, Wale J (2018) Testing times ahead: non-invasive prenatal testing and the kind of community that we want to be. Mod Law Rev 81:646–672

Brownsword R, Scotford E, Yeung K (eds) (2017) Oxford handbook on law, regulation and technology. Oxford University Press, Oxford

Cave E, Nottingham E (2018) Who knows best (interests)? The case of Charlie Gard. Med Law Rev 26:500–513

Dean J (2016) Two thirds of Muslims would not give police terror tip-offs. The Times, London

Dworkin R (1978) Taking rights seriously, rev edn. Duckworth, London
Dworkin R (1986) Law's empire. Harvard University Press, Cambridge
Dworkin R (1993) Life's dominion. Knopf, New York
European Group on Ethics in Science and New Technologies to the European Commission (2007) Opinion on the ethical aspects of nanomedicine. Opinion No 21
Fukuyama F (2002) Our Posthuman future. Profile Books, London
Gallagher J, Roxby P (2015) Assisted Dying Bill: MPs reject 'right to die' law. BBC News. Available at http://www.bbc.co.uk/news/health-34208624
Griffith JAG (1977) The politics of the judiciary. Fontana, London
Grubb A (1990) Abortion law in England: the medicalization of a crime. JLME 18:146–161
Gutmann A, Thompson D (2004) Why deliberative democracy? Princeton University Press, Princeton
Harris J (2007) Enhancing evolution. Princeton University Press, Princeton
Law Commission (1995) Report on Mental Incapacity. Law Com No 231, London
Lee M (2008) EU regulation of GMOs: law and decision making for a new technology. Edward Elgar, Cheltenham
McGoldrick D (2016) A defence of the margin of appreciation and an argument for its application by the human rights committee. ICLQ 65:21–60
Montgomery J (2019) The 'tragedy' of Charlie Gard: a case study for regulation of innovation? Law Innov Technol 11:155–174
Montgomery J, Montgomery E (2016) *Montgomery* on informed consent: an inexpert decision? J Med Ethics 42:89–94
Nuffield Council on Bioethics (2017) Non-invasive prenatal testing: ethical issues. London
Nuffield Council on Bioethics (2018) Genome editing and human reproduction: social and ethical issues. London
Plomer A (2012) After *Brüstle*: EU accession to the ECHR and the future of European patent law. Queen Mary J Intellect Prop 2:110–135
Plomer A (2015) Patents, human rights and access to science. Edward Elgar, Cheltenham
Presidential Commission for the Study of Bioethics (2010) New directions: the ethics of synthetic biology and emerging technologies. Washington
Rawls J (1993) Political liberalism. Columbia University Press, New York
Sandel M (2007) The case against perfection. Harvard University Press, Cambridge
Scott R (2018) Reproductive health: morals, margins and rights. Mod Law Rev 81:422–451
Sunstein CR (1996) Legal reasoning and political conflict. Oxford University Press, Oxford
Vallor S (2016) Technology and the virtues. Oxford University Press, New York

Axiological Pluralism and Health Claims as a Challenge to the Democratic Principle. The Cases of Non-Validated Therapies and Vaccinations

Marta Tomasi

Abstract The paper aims at investigating how much room legal orders leave for individual positions on health unsupported by scientific evidence. This analysis requires to properly balance individual rights and freedoms with the need to set general public health rules. To this aim, the paper focuses on two paradigmatic issues, fiercely discussed during recent years both in Europe (in particular in Italy) and in the U.S.: non-validated therapies and vaccines. A critical reading of these two topics allows concluding that axiological pluralism—entailing different visions of health and mainly derived from misinformation, emotional involvement or distrust—is sustainable only to a certain extent. Beyond that threshold, scientific rigorousness, the need to protect vulnerable subjects, and considerations about justice (equality and resource allocation) require selecting individual claims, transposing only some of them from the realm of human needs to the terrain of actionable legal rights.

1 Introduction: The Sustainability of Axiological Value Pluralism in Health

How much room is there for individual positions on health and treatments unsupported by scientific evidence? To what extent does a legal order have the possibility to give recognition and protection to such instances? Which criteria are suitable for solving the tensions between individual rights and governmental public health measures and choices?[1] The answer to these pressing questions can be reached by beginning with an analysis of two paradigmatic issues, fiercely discussed during recent years both in Europe (in particular in Italy) and in the U.S. The first one is related to access by severely ill patients to non-validated therapies. In Italy, the

[1] King (1999), pp. 1448–1449.

M. Tomasi (✉)
University of Trento, Trento, Italy
e-mail: marta.tomasi@unitn.it

L. Busatta, C. Casonato (eds.), *Axiological Pluralism*, Ius Gentium: Comparative Perspectives on Law and Justice 92, https://doi.org/10.1007/978-3-030-78475-1_9

matter was addressed in a case known as the "Stamina case", concerning a supposed experimental stem cell treatment, which was authorized by public health authorities but then stopped after it was administered to a rather wide range of patients affected by neurodegenerative diseases. In the U.S., similar issues were debated with regard to right-to-try laws, allowing terminally-ill patients access to very early stage developmental drugs. Moving on to treatment refusal, the second example discusses the evolution of vaccination policies both in the U.S. and in Italy.

In these cases, individual conceptions of health give rise to requests for treatments of dubious or null efficacy or, on the contrary, to skeptical attitudes or even open aversion towards well-established medical practices; the sustainability of such positions (in particular when involving children) needs to be carefully scrutinized.

This thorny task often falls on the judiciary, which is in charge of translating health requests—deeply affected by individual moral conceptions of life, wellbeing and illness—into protected rights. Judges, in fact, are frequently required to play a fundamental role in selecting individual positions to be granted protection and balancing them with the need to defend public health. Increasingly, courts have exerted substantial control over public health policies by determining the boundaries of governmental power and by creating zones of autonomy, privacy, and liberty to be afforded to individuals.[2]

The space given to individual positions concerning health determines the broadness of pluralism within a given society. As the following analysis shows, the recognition of a multiplicity of individual instances, often unrelated to scientific evidence, is barely sustainable, and reasonable selection criteria have to be found.

2 Individual Health Claims and Pressing Emotional Needs: The Stamina Case in Italy

Since the summer of 2012, across Italy, the parents of some severely ill children have filed several petitions before different courts, seeking authorization to have access to or to continue with supposed stem cell treatments offered by the Stamina Foundation. These treatments, administered in a public hospital (Spedali Civili di Brescia), had been blocked by the Italian Medicines Agency (AIFA), due to security and transparency reasons, following an inspection of the laboratories of the hospital where the infusions were performed.[3]

In the very first phase, the legal basis for those treatments was found in a decree by the Italian Ministry of Health concerning the use of gene therapy and human somatic cell therapy.[4] According to that decree, those treatments could lawfully be

[2]Gostin (2008), pp. 84–85.

[3]The story was repeatedly and critically addressed also by scientific international journals such as Nature. See Abbot (2013), Bianco et al. (2014) and, more recently, Abbott (2016).

[4]Ministry Decree 5 December 2006, Official Journal of the Italian Republic, no.57, 9 March 2007.

administered, outside of clinical trials, only where no alternative therapy was possible and where patients were in health- or life-threatening situations. Further requirements concerned a favorable opinion expressed by an ethics committee, the acquisition of patients' consent, the existence of scientific publications in international reviews and journals and the respect of safety procedures during the infusions.

The interpretation of those requirements, and the following diverging judicial adjudications, produced ambiguities and a situation of uncertainty. To cope with that, the Italian government decided to modify the normative framework and to address the specific issue with a dedicated law-decree.[5] The new discipline allowed for (i) the initiation of a formal clinical trial, and (ii) the administration of the treatments proposed by the Stamina Foundation only to those people who have already received authorization from the judiciary or have already had one or more infusions. All of this happened despite the fact that the scientific community has tended, since the very beginning of the matter, to deny the efficacy of the treatments and to warn against possible harm stemming from them. In a letter to the Ministry, many Italian stem cell scientists described the decision to permit use of an untested treatment as providing "a dangerous short circuit between patients' hopes and lucrative commercial practices" of organizations operating outside the "scientific and moral foundations" of medicine.[6]

The judicial decisions, ruling both under the former and the latter normative framework in favour of access to the treatments offered by the Stamina Foundation, show the downsides of judicial interventions in health policies: many judges proved to be strictly influenced by the tragic features of some cases, often directed by expert opinions that were unrepresentative of mainstream thought on public health, and intently focused on individual interests at the expense of communal claims to public health protection.[7]

Besides many other problematic aspects raised by this event, the main concern relates to the notion of health to be protected which ended up, in some cases, being much wider than is acceptable and rational. Due to the pressing nature of health claims, the Italian legal order, like many others, is used to allowing treatment strategies which can get around the time-consuming procedures of clinical trials. A case which took place in the 1990s, for example, brought the Italian Constitutional Court to state that when faced with extreme therapeutic needs, where no alternative cure is available, the right to health can be extended to cover expectations stemming

[5]Law decree 25th March 2013, n. 24, converted into law 23rd May 2013, n. 57 (Official Journal of the Italian Republic 25th May 2013, no. 121).

[6]According to Italian scientists "The decision seems to be dictated by emotions raised by public opinion rather than by scientifically based reasons. (...) "The freedom of any citizen to adopt any personal health decision, including the wish to refuse any cure, does not imply that the Government is obliged to authorize all medical procedures that anyone may suggest as appropriate. (...) It is not the Government's role to respond to pressure from patients to translate an individual choice into a therapeutic option for ready use in any health structure" (translation provided by EuroStemCell).

[7]Gostin (2008), pp. 84–85.

from ongoing clinical trials.[8] In this sense, compassionate use of experimental therapies is allowed under specific circumstances.[9] The aforementioned ministerial decree of 2006 further extended this approach, making it possible to access non-validated treatments, even outside of clinical trials.

In the Stamina case, however, the borders of the concept of health were stretched even beyond the coverage of "expectations" deriving from continuous scientific development in medicine.

The borders of the concept of health were expanded beyond acceptable, rational limits.

Reading the many decisions delivered by several judges,[10] different interpretations of the concept of health can be found, and only some of them can be deemed to be compatible with the whole constitutional framework. For example, quite understandably, the Court of Pordenone,[11] following a misleading expert witness, argues that the proposed treatment, even if unable to heal the patient, could nonetheless contribute to slowing the progression of the disease and allowing the patient to communicate with his family. More problematic is the approach chosen by the Court of Marsala, which sacrifices the individual dimension of health in favour of the public and collective one:[12] according to the Court, the rejection of the claim for access to the new treatment would imply an unreasonable compression of the right to improve public life and health. Interruption of the treatment would thus impede the appreciation of the features, limits and perspectives of a possible future use of mesenchymal stem cell treatments. Even greater concerns arise from those arguments that detach the concept of health from even the most basic scientific rationale: in this sense, the Court of Asti clearly states that the legal requirement of a minimum degree of scientificity of new developmental treatments and the requisite of approval by an ethics committee are to be considered unconstitutional.[13]

This trend appeared to some Authors to be confirmed by the intervention of the legislator who, in a moment in which scientific truths were being constructed,[14] endorsed the treatments offered by the Stamina Foundation, paving the way for extremely abstract claims. The government, driven by emotional considerations, enacted Law Decree no. 24/2013. According to Article 77 of the Italian Constitution, the Government has the power to adopt law decrees, under its own responsibility, in

[8]See Constitutional Court judgment no. 185/1999 concerning the so-called Di Bella therapy, a presumed revolutionary alternative cure for cancer. Parts of the story can be found in Benelli (2003), pp. 179–186 and Fattore (1999), pp. 123–142.

[9]See also art. 83 of Regulation (EC) No. 726/2004 concerning compassionate use programs.

[10]Original texts of several judgments have been collected on the website www.biodiritto.org.

[11]Pordenone Tribunal, judgment 5th August 2013.

[12]Marsala Tribunal, judgment 11th April 2014.

[13]Asti Tribunal, judgment 12th November 2013.

[14]Two different *ad-hoc* scientific committees were created to give an opinion about the safety and efficacy of the Stamina treatments. Both committees concluded expressing an openly negative judgment suggesting not even beginning clinical trials for lack of scientific preconditions (September 2013 and October 2014).

extraordinary cases of necessity and emergency; these acts need to be converted into laws by the Parliament. The documents accompanying the law-decree state that the need to continue or to begin treatments previously authorized by judges allows for dealing with the state of profound distress of people hoping to obtain from Stamina's stem cell treatments benefits which can't be achieved by alternative means. Moreover, the first version of the decree approved by the Government (subsequently properly adjusted by the Parliament) permitted the continuation of already started therapies even if these had been prepared in laboratories which do not comply with European pharmaceutical good manufacturing standards.[15]

The recognition of such claims, removed from basic scientific standards, defined in Italy as "right to hope", and in the USA as "right to try",[16] determined a constitutional challenge of the Italian Law Decree no. 24/2013 which allowed only some individuals to access new unapproved treatments, excluding others. Furthermore, these people were identified on the basis of the sole chronological datum of having obtained an authorization by the judiciary (which, as said before, was anything but consistent) or a previous infusion within the date of entry into force of the decree: this would have discriminated seriously ill patients just by reason of the moment in which they had asked to access the therapies.[17]

In its judgement,[18] the Constitutional Court discussed the issue of the capability of the Italian legal order to include individual visions of health and to give satisfaction to the related claims. With its ruling, the Court upheld the decree which, intervening within an "abnormal context", privileged principles of therapeutic continuity and the need not to interfere with the authority of the judiciary. It would therefore be unreasonable to extend such a time-limited derogation to other patients, to whom the peculiar and exceptional circumstances which motivated the legislator do not apply.[19] For these patients, the more general principle of caution in the validation and administering of drugs should prevail.

The "abnormal context" in which the legislator's intervention is rooted is determined, according to the Court, by the fact that the treatments proposed by the Stamina Foundation were activated within the national health service circuit (outside of clinical trials, despite their developmental nature) and by the fact that some infusions were authorized by judges as a matter of urgency. The Court excludes

[15]See Article 2.2 of law decree 24/2013, stating, in the Italian wording, that treatments should not be discontinued: "anche se preparati presso laboratori non conformi ai principi delle norme europee di buona fabbricazione dei medicinali e in difformità delle disposizioni del decreto del Ministro della salute 5 dicembre 2006".

[16]See *infra*.

[17]The constitutional challenge was raised by the Taranto Tribunal, judgment n. 4960, 24th September 2013.

[18]Constitutional Court, judgment no. 274, 1st December 2014, Italian Official Gazette n. 51, 10th December 2014.

[19]It might be relevant to note that the Court was not asked (and was consequently not allowed to take a position) about the constitutionality of the choice to allow scientifically-ill treatments for some patients, but only about the constitutionality of the choice to select some requests.

that the equality principle should require the normative derogation to be extended to patients who presented their claims for having access to the treatments after the decree entered into force. In fact, patients allowed to have access to the treatments and patients excluded found themselves in different factual situations, the different normative regime being consequently justified. Underlying this conclusion is the critical aspect of the identification of the right to be protected. If the normative intervention, derogating from the general rules governing administration of new drugs, was aimed at directly protecting patients' right to health, it would be unreasonable to exclude from the normative extension patients who find themselves in analogous conditions, only on the basis of a difference in the timing of the presentation of a request. The Constitutional Court, excluding that the rationale of the legislative provision can be found in the direct protection of the fundamental right to health, recalls a recent decision by the European Court of Human Rights, concerning the treatments offered by the Stamina Foundation.[20] In its judgment, the ECtHR stated that, in view of the still-developing state of knowledge in the field of stem cell treatments, the decision of a judge to restrict patients from access to the Stamina treatments lawfully pursues the aim of protecting their health, being proportionate to said aim. The Italian regulation, similarly, is directed at protecting the expectations encouraged in some people by the first infusions or by the judicial authorizations.

The decision of the Constitutional Court marks the limit of those individual positions the legal order can take charge of, determining the capacity of the pluralist principle to confer protection to individual health-related claims. The decision restates that not even the broadest idea of health, inclusive not only of physical but of psychological and relational aspects as well, can disregard, in its realization, the temporary, progressive and incomplete acquisitions of science.

3 Right-to-Try Laws in the U.S. and the Need to Ground the Right to Health in a Rational Basis

Very similar issues, in a different setting, come along with the widely debated topic of the so-called "right to try" in the U.S. The core question underlying the discussion is whether to grant access to experimental drugs, well before their final approval by the FDA. The issue dates back to the 1970s when some phase I studies shone a light

[20]The reference is to the European Court of Human Rights' decision in the case of *Durisotto v. Italy* (application no. 62804/13). The Court, by a majority, declared inadmissible the application of a father alleging that there had been a violation of his daughter's right to life and health on account of the fact that it was impossible for her to obtain the compassionate therapy known as "Stamina" under Law decree no. 24/2013 due to a refusal given by Italian courts. The ECtHR held that the prohibition to access to this therapy, imposed by the Italian court in application of law decree no. 24/2013, pursued the legitimate aim of protecting health and was proportionate to that aim. The national court's decision had not been arbitrary, since the therapeutic value of the "Stamina" method had, to date, not yet been proven scientifically. See Rial-Sebbag and Blasimme (2014), pp. 39–43.

upon the compound Laetrile, purported to prevent the spread of cancer. Due to the lack of authorization for the use of the drug in the U.S., some patients travelled to Mexico to obtain the cure, while some others challenged in courts the federal rules impeding them access to the treatment.[21]

The issue reached the Supreme Court which, with the landmark decision United States v. Rutherford,[22] reversed the decision of the Court of Appeals and excluded the existence in the Federal Food, Drug, and Cosmetic Act (1938, FDCA) of any exception allowing terminally-ill patients to access non-validated treatments. Vulnerable people deserve a heightened standard of protection, especially in cases in which the proposal of new promising treatments delays or hampers traditional therapies of proven efficacy.[23]

According to the Court of Appeals, notions such as safety and effectiveness cannot find application in relation to terminally-ill patients. On the contrary, the Supreme Court recalls the importance for a treatment not only to cure, but also to "produce [...] the results claimed for it under prescribed conditions", including life-prolonging or pain-reducing effects. At the same time, it is a federal interest to grant safety to vulnerable patients, even more than to others.[24]

The specific debate about a right to try originates from the dramatic case of Abigail Burroughs, who died of cancer in 2001. The physicians informed the young patient about the existence of two experimental drugs, Genfitinib and Cetuximab, which could have helped to improve her condition and, perhaps, save her life. Despite many attempts and the interest of the media, the girl was not able to access the experimental treatments.[25] On these grounds, the Abigail Alliance for Better Access to Developmental Drugs, founded by the girl's father after her death, sued the FDA for violating a terminally ill patient's fundamental right to access life-saving developmental treatments.[26] According to the claimants, this right is protected under the Due Process Clause of the V and XIV Amendments, which restrict State interference with fundamental rights to what is "narrowly tailored to serve a compelling state interest" (strict scrutiny analysis). The judges of first instance identified, in the denial by the FDA, the pursuit of a general state interest in the protection of

---

[21]Chin (2008), p. 1982.

[22]*United States v. Rutherford*, 442 U.S. 544 (1979).

[23]The general rule is set by Section 505: "Necessity of effective approval of application - No person shall introduce or deliver for introduction into interstate commerce any new drug, unless an approval of an application filed [...] is effective with respect to such drug" (U.S.C. § 355(2012).

[24]*United States v. Rutherford*, 442 U.S. 544, 545, 555 (1979).

[25]Okie (2006), pp. 437–440.

[26]The FDA refused an agreement stating that the requests advanced "would upset the appropriate balance [...] by giving almost total weight to the goal of early availability and giving little recognition to the importance of marketing drugs with reasonable knowledge for patients and physicians of their likely clinical benefit and their toxicity" (*Abigail Alliance*, 700 (D.C. Cir. 2007)). At that time a bill was drafted to modify drugs approval procedures: ACCESS Act, S. 1956, 109th Congress (2005).

public health.[27] On the contrary, the District Court of the District of Columbia recognized the fundamental nature of the contested right, concluding "where there are no alternative government-approved treatment options, a terminally ill, mentally competent adult patient's informed access to potentially life-saving investigational new drugs determined by the FDA after Phase I trials to be sufficiently safe for expanded human trials warrants protection under the Due Process Clause".[28] Recalling the Glucksberg doctrine,[29] the Court recognizes the claimed right to be sufficiently determined and finds its basis in the history and the traditions of the nation: the federal regulation on drugs, in fact, dates back to less than a century ago and the requirements of safety and efficacy were introduced in 1962.[30] Moreover, referring to the jurisprudence on the right to refuse a life-sustaining treatment,[31] the Court states that every patient should be "free to decide for herself whether to assume any known or unknown risks taking a medication that might prolong her life",[32] somehow forgetting the specifications made in Rutherford.

The opinion of the majority is opposed by a dissenting one according to which a balance has to be found "between the uncertain risks and benefits of medical technology".[33] The majority opinion would be mistaken in maintaining that drugs that have passed phase I "probably have a medical benefit with sufficiently minimal risks".[34]

The decision was reversed by the United States Court of Appeals, District of Columbia Circuit,[35] which found that the asserted right satisfies Glucksberg's "careful description" requirement but is not deeply rooted in the Nation's history and tradition. According to the Court "creating constitutional rights to be free from regulation based solely upon a prior lack of regulation would undermine much of the modern administrative state, which, like drug regulation, has increased in scope

[27]*Abigail Alliance for Better Access to Developmental Drugs v. McClellan*, 2004 WL 3777340 (D.D.Cr 2004).

[28]*Abigail Alliance for Better Access to Developmental Drugs v. von Eschenbach*, 445 F.3d 470, 486 (D.C.Cir.2006).

[29]*Washington v. Glucksberg*, 521 U.S. 702 (1997).

[30]The first federal act concerning public health was the Federal Food and Drugs Act of 1906 which prohibited the production and marketing in States of altered or irregular drugs. With the FDCA of 1938, wide surveillance powers were attributed to the FDA, in particular in reference to the duty to ensure "safety, effectiveness, and reliability of drugs" (Drug Amendments of 1962, Pub. L. No. 87-781).

[31]*Cruzan v. Director, Missouri Department of Health*, 497 U.S. 261, 110 S. Ct. 2841, 111 L. Ed. 2d 224, 1990 U.S.

[32]*Abigail Alliance*, 484 (D.C.Cir.2006).

[33]*Abigail Alliance*, 499 (D.C.Cir.2006). The judge refers to the decision of the Supreme Court against the marketing of Laetrile and the prohibition by the federal Congress against medical marijuana.

[34]*Abigail Alliance*, 487 (D.C.Cir.2006).

[35]*Abigail Alliance for Better Access to Developmental Drugs v. von Eschenbach*, 495 F.3d 695 (D.C. Cir. 2007), cert. denied, 128 S. Ct. 1069 (2008).

as changing conditions have warranted".[36] The non-existence of a fundamental right allowed the Court not to apply a strict scrutiny but to identify the existence of a rational basis for ensuring that there is a scientifically and medically acceptable level of knowledge about the risks and benefits of the drug.[37]

Being the completion of phase I studies just the first step of a long and burdensome procedure leading to the commercialization of a drug, a precautionary approach aimed at security sounds more than reasonable at this stage.[38]

Nevertheless, the Court, dealing with public health issues, showed signs of reluctance as regards interfering with "unknown questions of science and medicine"[39] and recalls, with deference, the fundamental role of the democratic bodies in deciding the proper balance between the uncertain risks and benefits of medical technology.

An opposite decision, namely allowing access to phase I drugs, favouring a deregulation process and opening to the logics of free market, would have undermined a minimum standard of individual and collective security and delegitimized the FDA and its actions. Where to draw the line of admissible and legitimate health claims is a matter to be dealt with by the legislators.

The judicial call found an answer in more recent times: since the very first months of 2014, many States adopted specific statutes aimed at allowing terminally-ill patients to access developmental drugs, treatments and devices. Until 2018, 41 States had adopted this kind of regulation and on May 30, 2018, President Donald Trump signed S.204, the federal Right to Try Act.[40] All of the legislations are based on the

[36]Abigail Alliance, 707 (D.C. Cir. 2007).

[37]"(...) the Government has a rational basis for ensuring that there is a scientifically and medically acceptable level of knowledge about the risks and benefits of such a drug" (Abigail Alliance, 713 (D.C. Cir. 2007).

[38]Chin (2008), pp. 1989–1990.

[39]*Abigail Alliance*, 708 (D.C. Cir. 2007).

[40]Colorado was the first State to approve in 2014 a right to try law titled *Access to Treatments to Terminally Ill Patients. Right to try* (Colorado House Bill 14-1281). Similar laws were approved in Alabama, Alaska, Arizona, Arkansas, California, Colorado, Connecticut, Florida, Georgia, Idaho, Illinois, Indiana, Iowa, Kentucky, Louisiana, Maine, Maryland, Michigan, Minnesota, Mississippi, Missouri, Montana, Nebraska, Nevada, New Hampshire, North Carolina, North Dakota, Ohio, Oklahoma, Oregon, Pennsylvania, South Carolina, South Dakota, Tennessee, Texas, Utah, Virginia, Washington, West Virginia, Wisconsin, and Wyoming. The list is reported at http://righttotry.org/. Some general information can be found in Martin C (2016), 177, footnote 115.

In California, the governor refused at first to sign the law which was then approved one year later on 27 September, 2016. On the Californian case see Tong (2016), pp. 551–575. In 2017 the Texas legislature passed HB 810, which allows clinics offering unapproved stem cell treatments to treat patients. A recent study, published in the journal Stem Cells and Development, looks at the impact of the law and concludes that, despite some recent amendments, there are still concerns about the law including the fact that: (i) it allows treatment only if the patient has a "severe, chronic" illness but does not define what that means; (ii) it does not define procedures on tracking and reporting; (iii) there is no Food and Drug Administration (FDA) oversight of the patients being treated; (iv) there are fears that this will "open up the state to unsavory and predatory practices by individuals preying on vulnerable patients". The researchers conclude that ""While HB 810 opens up access to patients,

federal law about compassionate use of drugs, but they introduce noticeable novelties.[41] The discussion was started by the 2014 Report by the Goldwater Institute titled "Everyone deserves the Right to Try: Empowering the Terminally Ill to Take Control of their Treatment".[42] The document suggests the idea of a fundamental right to access post phase I drugs and proposes a model of a Right to Try Act, which has been used as a template for many of the cited state laws.[43]

The core idea is that the subjects better entitled to decide about those treatments to be adopted are patients and physicians, rather than the government. According to this model, the legal order "recognizes that patients who have a terminal disease have a fundamental right to attempt to pursue the preservation of their own life by accessing available investigational drugs, biological products, and devices".[44] The requirements for accessing non-approved treatments, beyond the respect of a minimum standard of safety (often not better identified), concern the documentation to be prepared by physicians for prescribing the developmental treatment and proof of the informed consent of terminally-ill patients.[45]

Despite small differences between state laws, all of the acts aim at hindering the strictness and slowness of FDA procedures for drugs approval. These tools, in their attempt to stretch the concept of health to the point of including claims unconnected

it also increases significant risks for their safety and financial cost for something that might have no positive impact on their disease" (Matthews et al. (2018), pp. 1463–1465.

[41]Tsakopoulos et al. (2015), p. 631. Differences between State laws are considered by Kearns and Bateman-House (2017), pp. 170–176.

[42]Corieri (2014).

[43]More recently, two bills were presented at the federal level to prevent the government from hampering the production and distribution of developmental drugs and devices authorized by state legislations: H.R.3012 (Right to Try Act 2015), and S.2912 (known as Trickett Wendler Right to Try Act). The former "[b]ars the federal government from prohibiting or restricting the production, manufacture, distribution, prescribing, dispensing, possession, or use of an experimental drug, biological product, or device that is: (1) intended to treat a patient who has been diagnosed with a terminal illness; and (2) authorized by, and in accordance with, state law" and "[d]efines an "experimental drug, biological product, or device" as one that: (1) has successfully completed a phase 1 clinical investigation; (2) remains under investigation in a clinical trial approved by the Food and Drug Administration; and (3) is not approved, licensed, or cleared for commercial distribution under the Federal Food, Drug, or Cosmetic Act or the Public Health Service Act". The latter "[b]ars the federal government from prohibiting or restricting the production, manufacture, distribution, prescribing, dispensing, possession, or use of an experimental drug, biological product, or device that is: (1) intended to treat a patient who has been diagnosed with a terminal illness; and (2) authorized by, and in accordance with, state law" and "[d]efines an "experimental drug, biological product, or device" as one that: (1) has successfully completed a phase 1 clinical investigation; (2) remains under investigation in a clinical trial approved by the Food and Drug Administration; and (3) is not approved, licensed, or cleared for commercial distribution under the Federal Food, Drug, or Cosmetic Act or the Public Health Service Act".

[44]*Ibidem.*

[45]Normally this is defined as "an advanced stage of a disease with an unfavourable prognosis and no known cure". As noted, the definitions of "terminal disease" vary from legislation to legislation and a third of these laws is applicable also to persons in "permanent state of unconsciousness" and to PVS patients. See Bateman-House et al. (2015), pp. 796–797.

to basic safety and efficacy standards, are questionable both in their theoretical construction and practical applicability.

First of all, being phase I studies performed on restricted populations, often composed of healthy people, safety information which can be obtained is partial and not definitive.[46]

Similarly, as to efficacy, indications coming from phase I studies are minimal, considering the low dosages used, aimed at evaluating the toxicity of the drug. Moreover, in the first two phases of a clinical trial no interaction with other drugs is verified and no patients with serious comorbidities are involved.[47]

Another aspect deeply impacting the efficacy of the new laws concerns the costs of the developmental treatments, which fully fall on the patients. In this sense, neither a duty for insurance companies to cover similar costs, nor a duty for manufacturers to provide non-validated therapies for free, were introduced.[48]

These features of the asserted right to try create inequities and subordinate the right to health to financial means.

A wider issue pertains to the whole system of clinical trials, which could be eroded because of a misleading of patients who might prefer a quick and direct request for drugs from manufacturers to the long and burdensome procedures of a clinical trial.[49] This possibility would turn into a huge waste of fundamental information, considering that no law requires monitoring activities or communication duties about benefits or side effects produced by new developmental treatments.[50]

The imbalance of positions created by these laws, which clearly disadvantages patients, is even more evident when considering those provisions which discourage licensing boards from adopting disciplinary sanctions against health care providers recommending access to or treatment with an investigational drug, or limiting civil liability of physicians or manufacturers for damages derived from developmental treatments.[51]

This approach, attempting to answer pressing and desperate conditions, legitimized claims based on individual visions of health, unrelated to basic standards of safety and efficacy and unsupported by scientific data, producing rights which are empty and difficult to enact. In this case, the judicial call to the legislator to better balance individual needs and general interests found a quite unsatisfactory answer.

The questionable state interventions, now framed by the federal Right to Try Act, contributed to draw attention to these issues, in accordance with the theory which has

---

[46]Tsakopoulos et al. (2015), p. 636 ss.

[47]Hogan (2016), p. 187.

[48]An exception can be found in the Texan law which requires developmental treatments to be offered for free and in Utah where a Foundation to help patients was created. See Bateman-House (2016), p. 4.

[49]The main incentive for taking part in clinical trials is related to the possibility of access to state-of-the-art therapies (Chin 2008, p. 1991).

[50]On the contrary federal rules concerning compassionate use require physicians to comply with strict monitoring and reporting duties (Chin 2008, p. 1991).

[51]Dresser (2015), p. 1641 and Martin (2016), p. 176.

States acting as laboratories of democracy,[52] leading the FDA to partially modify its rules for accessing developmental treatments. With the aim of rebalancing the positions and interests involved, in 2015 the FDA modified the rules for accessing the Compassionate Use program, introducing a new form which can be filled in in 45 min (Form FDA 3926[53]) and is answered in 30 days at the most. Moreover, a new procedure has been introduced for "emergency applications" which can be answered and obtain authorization to access, in the first phase, via telephone.[54]

Only time will tell whether right-to-try laws will have any concrete impact. So far, it is evident that breadth in the legislative attitude towards different health claims is not in itself sufficient to guarantee the effectiveness of the remedies offered.

4 The Debate About Vaccination Mandates as a Test for Pluralism

One of the topics which have been vehemently debated recently around the world concerns compulsory vaccinations and, in particular, the ever-growing phenomenon of people rejecting treatments which are defined by the majority as "one of the greatest medical achievements of modern civilization".[55]

The so-called anti-vaxxers and the broader category of vaccine-hesitants[56] defend their positions either making reference to general arguments, such as a strong understanding of self-determination in health matters, or contesting more specific features of the treatments, such as the use of vaccine adjuvants, the aggressive nature of the vaccine schedule, the combinations of different vaccines, and the like.

All these claims, based on moral, philosophical, cultural or (supposedly) scientific arguments, need to be filtered by judges and regulators in order to ensure the protection of all of the positions and interests involved and to ensure a proper functioning of the whole system. A too wide acceptance of these individual conceptions would undermine—and, in fact, in some countries already undermined—the so-called "community immunity", a specific threshold (set by the WHO at about 95% of the whole population) ensuring most members of the community to be protected against a contagious disease because there is little opportunity for an outbreak. This threshold is considered to be sufficient also to protect people who

[52]Justice Louis Brandeis in New State Ice Co. v. Liebmann, 285 U.S. 262, 311 (1932) describes how a "state may, if its citizens choose, serve as a laboratory; and try novel social and economic experiments without risk to the rest of the country."

[53]U.S. Department Of Health And Human Services (2015).

[54]Yang et al. (2015), p. 2597.

[55]Malone and Hinman (2007), pp. 338–360.

[56]The World Health Organization has called "vaccine hesitancy" one of the 10 most serious health threats of 2019 (WHO, Ten threats to global health in 2019, https://www.who.int/emergencies/ten-threats-to-global-health-in-2019).

are not eligible for certain vaccines (because of age or personal conditions, such a pregnancy or immunodeficiencies, or due to choice).[57]

4.1 *The Rule-Plus-Exemption Model of the U.S.: How Broad Can Exemptions Be?*

In the U.S. the role of selecting interests is played by a system of state legislations aimed at introducing specific duties regarding vaccines; these acts generally require a vaccine certificate in order to access the school system.

Aware of the importance of balancing public health needs with individual claims, and thus offering an example of integrative pluralism,[58] most of the laws introduced at the state level provide for specific "medical exemptions", aimed at protecting the health of those who are not eligible for some vaccines, and other "religious/belief or philosophical exemptions" allowing parents to exempt children from vaccinations due to personal reasons.[59]

The selection of individual positions to be protected is thus made *ab origine* by the lawmaker, but it is often the judiciary who is in charge of concretely applying the norms and, therefore, of defining the broadness of the moral pluralism accepted in a certain legal order.

To trigger the exemptions recognized by State laws, three conditions have to be realized: (i) a good reason for the existence of the general rule; (ii) a good reason for providing for an exception; (iii) a limited applicability of the exemption.[60] The grounds for introducing a general duty to vaccinate children can easily be found in the need to protect public health.[61] More problematic, with regard to nonmedical exemptions, are the second and third points, which represent the keys to define the extension of accepted axiological pluralism.

Personal exemptions, in general, find their justification both in considerations of liberal justice, stressing individual freedom, and, more practically, in the functioning of community immunity, exercising its protection with less than 100% of people immunized: some exemptions are therefore acceptable. Nevertheless, recent episodes, such as measles outbreaks, have called the mechanism based on exemptions into question and led state legislators to revoke non-medical exemptions.[62]

---

[57]On the weakness of the concept of "herd immunity", see Buttenheim and Asch (2013), pp. 2674–2675.

[58]See Busatta L, in this volume.

[59]For the general framework see Orenstein and Hinman (1999), pp. S19–S24; Salmon et al. (2006), pp. 436–442, and Omer (2006), pp. 1757–1763.

[60]Barry (2002), p. 62.

[61]Freed (2005), p. 755.

[62]In 2019, three bills were enacted: Washington House Bill 1638 removes the personal belief exemption for the measles, mumps and rubella vaccine requirement for public schools, private

A good example of this evolution is provided by California. With SB 277, passed in June 2015, California requires all children enrolled in public or private daycare, preschool, elementary school, junior high, or high school to have had all doses of 10 vaccines, refusing religious and philosophical (personal belief) exemptions to any dose of any vaccination for any child throughout the State. Predictably, the anti-vaccine movement reacted to this and repeatedly challenged SB 277 on constitutional grounds. For instance, the bill was contested[63] in front of the District Court of the Southern District of California for violation of free exercise, equal protection, due process and right to education.[64] In particular, according to the Plaintiffs, SB 277 would violate their constitutional guarantee of the free exercise of religion under the First Amendment, in addition to other fundamental rights, without a compelling governmental interest. Additionally, they claim that even if the government shows a compelling interest, SB 277 is not narrowly tailored nor does this solution represent the least restrictive means of satisfying that interest. Plaintiffs therefore sought a preliminary injunction barring the enforcement of SB 277.

In general, the District Court notes that all courts, state and federal, for over a century, have held that there is no question that society has a compelling interest in fighting the spread of contagious diseases through mandatory vaccination of school-aged children.

With regard to the first claim, the District Court recalls the US Supreme Court jurisprudence according to which fundamental rights under the First Amendment to the United States Constitution do not overcome the State's interest in protecting a child's health. Specifically, in *Prince v. Massachusetts*, 321 U.S. 158 (1944), the Court stated: "The right to practice religion freely does not include liberty to expose the community or the child to communicable disease or the latter to ill health or death."

With regard to equal protection, Plaintiffs allege that SB 277 (i) treats children with personal belief exemptions differently from other children in denying the former an education, (ii) treats children with personal belief exemptions who have reached "checkpoints"[65] differently from children with PBEs who are not at "checkpoints" in excluding the former from school; (iii) treats children with individualized education programs (IEPs) differently in providing for them an exemption from the vaccination mandate. According to the District Court, in all the disputed classifications, the children are not similarly situated, which dooms the Plaintiffs' equal protection claim.

---

schools and daycare centers; Maine House Bill 586 removes personal and religious belief exemptions for public school immunization requirements; the New York Senate Bill 2994 removes the religious exemption for public school immunization requirements.

[63] *Whitlow v. Cal. Dept. of Education* (S.D.Cal. 2016) 203 F.Supp.3d 1079.

[64] *Whitlow v. California*, US District Court Southern District of California, Case no. 16-cv-1715 DMS (BGS) (S.D. Cal. Jul. 5, 2016).

[65] The law refers to children who are first-time enrollees in daycare or kindergarten or who are enrolling in the seventh grade. Cal. Health & Safety Code § 120335(g).

First, there is a rational basis, related to the State's interest in protecting public health and safety, for treating children with PBEs differently from other children. Moreover, the reason for treating children with PBEs at "checkpoints" differently from children with PBEs outside of "checkpoints" is that of providing parents with an orderly opportunity to comply with the law and of ensuring a graduated application of SB 277. The exemption for students with IEPs ensures the right of access to education and furthers the State's legitimate interest in providing special education and related services to those students.

Lastly, the right to education, relevant as it may be, is no more sacred than any of the other fundamental rights that have readily given way to a State's interest in protecting the health and safety of its citizens, particularly schoolchildren. While removing the PBE is an aggressive step, it is deemed to be necessary and narrowly tailored to address the identified interest of providing a means for the eventual achievement of total immunization.

To date, five lawsuits have been filed against the law and five trial courts (two state, three federal) have so far rejected these suits. Two of these cases were appealed, and have recently been decided upon.

In *Brown v. Smith*,[66] six plaintiffs challenged the law claiming that it was invalid because the state could not constitutionally mandate "unavoidably unsafe" products, such as vaccines. This violated their religious freedom as protected by the First Amendment and the Constitution of California, and their children's right to education because it violated equal protection.[67]

The Court rejected the plaintiffs' First Amendment claims, because, according to existing jurisprudence, the right to practice religion freely does not include the liberty to expose the community or the child to communicable disease or the latter to ill health or death.

On the same basis as the Whitlow[68] precedent, the Court found the right to education according to the Constitution of California did not prevent the state from imposing an immunization mandate and noted that "removal of the [personal beliefs exemption] is necessary or narrowly drawn to serve the compelling objective of SB 277."

Furthermore, SB277 survives strict scrutiny: preventing communicable diseases is a compelling interest, compulsory immunization has long been recognized as the gold standard for preventing the spread of contagious diseases, and the plaintiffs did not specify an alternative means.

Extensively drawing on *Whitlow v. California* and *Brown v. Smith*, on 20 November 2018, the California court of appeal for the third appellate district, defining plaintiffs' arguments "strong on hyperbole and scant on authority", rejected a challenge by the anti-vaccine organization A Voice for Choice and three individual

[66] *Brown v. Smith* (2018) 24 Cal.App.5th 1135.

[67] Plaintiffs also claimed that the law violates a legal prohibition of medical experiments, but the court rejected that argument swiftly.

[68] *Whitlow v. California*, 203 F.Supp.3d 1079 (2016).

plaintiffs to SB277.[69] Consolidated jurisprudence thus recognizes discretion to state legislatures in defining rules and exemptions, highlighting the balanceable nature of individual freedoms and drawing attention to solidarity duties aimed at the realization of a general interest.[70]

The individual rights enshrined in personal belief exemptions have a special nature, their protection being under the availability of the legislators, according to an evaluation of their degree of dissemination. In the light of changing conditions, the scope of individual rights can be tailored, and exemptions stand as long as they are firmly rooted in verifiable technical elements (e.g. medical exemptions) and cease when linked to forms of uncontrolled subjectivism.

4.2 *The Italian Case: The Chance for Spontaneous Adhesion and the Need for Legal Mandates*

The issue of vaccination mandates is widely debated in Italy as well. The Italian model could, until some years ago, have been considered as a hybrid model, both for the coexistence of legally mandated vaccinations together with recommended ones and for the bizarre stratification of different sources of law which had taken place during the years. This framework was radically changed with the entry into force of Law Decree no. 73/2017, approved by the Italian government in June 2017 and converted into law by the Parliament.

Besides very recent interventions, the itinerary of vaccination mandates in Italy is of the utmost relevance when the possibility of integrating individual health-related instances into the general system of rights and duties is discussed.

Originally, the norms imposing vaccinations against diphtheria, tetanus, poliomyelitis and hepatitis B[71] were accompanied by the provision of criminal sanctions (then turned into administrative fines). A further, albeit indirect, incentive for

[69]*Torrey Love v. State of California Department of Education.*

[70]As already stated in *Henning Jacobson v. Commonwealth of Massachusetts* (197 U.S. 11, 25 S. Ct. 358, the landmark decision with which the Supreme Court upheld vaccination mandates back in 1908): "the liberty secured by the Constitution (. . .) does not import an absolute right in each person to be, at all times and in all circumstances, wholly freed from restraint. There are manifold restraints to which every person is necessarily subject for the common good. On any other basis organized society could not exist with safety to its members. Society based on the rule that each one is a law unto himself would soon be confronted with disorder and anarchy. Real liberty for all could not exist under the operation of a principle which recognizes the right of each individual person to use his own, whether in respect of his person or his property, regardless of the injury that may be done to others".

[71]These were the compulsory vaccinations existing in Italy up to 2017, imposed respectively by law no. 891, 6th June 1939 and law no. 166, 27th April 1981 (diphtheria); laws no. 292, 5th March 1963 and law no. 419, 20th March 1968 (tetanus); law no. 51, 4th February 1966 (poliomyelitis) and law no. 165, 27th May 1991 (hepatitis B). Many other vaccinations were very strongly recommended by Italian health institutions and provided for free.

respecting the vaccination mandate derived from the rule requiring vaccinations for admission to all levels of compulsory education. This requirement was removed in 1999[72] and the possibility of actually enforcing the legal mandate was excluded by law in 1994.[73]

The statutory vaccination mandate, formally unchanged, yielded to a more flexible and tolerant path oriented towards forms of voluntary acceptance.

At the same time, the vaccination mandate was repeatedly upheld by the highest jurisdictions of the country: the Constitutional Court and the Court of Cassation. Both Courts analyzed in-depth the grounds on which individual objections are rooted and granted them full legitimization only when linked to solid scientific bases. In this sense, the Court of Cassation states that the duty to protect children, which can represent a justification for being exempted from the vaccination mandate, cannot be grounded in general fears, but has to refer to the specific reasons of danger created in the specific case by the vaccine.[74] In other words, the interest that parents want to defend has to be scientifically qualified and based on empirical evidence.

Similarly, the Constitutional Court upheld the vaccination mandates, highlighting the need to distinguish a general conviction about their incompatibility with the Constitution from a concrete danger for the child, deriving from the immunization procedure. This danger could derive either from the child's medical condition or from the composition of the vaccine. In both cases, evidence has to be produced.[75]

In Italy, the creation of medical exemption, which in the U.S. is provided for by state laws, was left to the judiciary;[76] in doing so, judges found in the scientific element a proper filter to select individual claims and to tailor pluralism to a sustainable measure.

Despite confirmation coming from the Courts about the constitutionality of the vaccination mandate, its standing was called into question from a substantial viewpoint starting from the introduction of the national Vaccinations Plan 2005–2007. In this document, the Ministry of Health, stressing the importance of policies of information, advocated the possibility for Regions to embark on an experimental path towards the suspension of national mandatory vaccinations. This recognition of

[72]Decree of the President of the Italian Republic no. 355, 26th January 1999.

[73]Law decree no. 273, 6th May 1994.

[74]Court of Cassation, I sez. civ., judgment no. 14384, 8th July 2005 and, analogously, Court of Cassation, I sez. civ., judgment no. 11226, 18th July 2003. In Italian: "[i]l dovere di tutelare la salute del minore da parte del genitore che costituisce causa di giustificazione della infrazione non può risolversi [...] nel timore generico di un pregiudizio per il minore, ma deve concretarsi nella prospettazione di specifiche ragioni che nel singolo caso rendono la vaccinazione pericolosa e nella dimostrazione di particolari controindicazioni, desunte dalla salute del soggetto da vaccinare, o quanto meno di fatti concreti che siano comunque tali da giustificare l'erronea persuasione di un pericolo per il minore".

[75]Constitutional Court, judgment no. 262, 8th -22nd July 2004.

[76]Medical exemption is now explicitly recognized by Article 1.3. of law decree 73/2017, according to which compulsory vaccinations can be omitted or delayed in case of proven danger for health in relation to specific clinical conditions documented by a general physician or by a pediatrician.

regional autonomy allowed some Regions to suspend administrative fines for not complying with the vaccination mandate.[77] Moreover, the Veneto Region was allowed to experience, with the introduction of Law 7/2007, the suspension of all mandatory childhood vaccinations. The legal mandate was replaced by an active and free offer of all vaccines recognized as safe and effective and the experiment was carefully monitored to avoid loss of compliance and a reduction in immunized children.

This national strategy, promoting forms of spontaneous adhesion to vaccinations, proved not to be functional:[78] regardless of specific reasons, immunization rates in Italy were worryingly decreasing, immunization rates for legally mandatory vaccinations being below the safety threshold of 95%.[79]

This situation determined an immediate reaction from both national and regional institutions. On the one hand, the new National Vaccinations Plan 2017–2019 highlights the importance of promoting vaccinations and the need to offer scientifically sound information based on evidence. On the other hand, some Regions and local institutions adopted normative decisions stating that children could not enter daycare centres, nursery schools and kindergartens without having received, at least, the four legally compulsory vaccinations.[80] These decisions, which had the virtue of reaffirming the relevance of vaccination for public health, reignited the debate.

In particular, the decision adopted by the Trieste municipality,[81] introducing the vaccination mandate for enrollment in kindergartens, was challenged in front of the Tribunale Amministrativo Regionale (administrative regional tribunal) of the Friuli Venezia Giulia Region.[82] In rejecting the plaintiffs' claims, the Tribunal reasons on the balance between individual and collective rights and interests in this field: the risks related to a lack of immunization are perceived as lower than those coming from vaccinations just as long as the majority of people choose to opt for vaccinations. Claims about the safety of the condition of non-immunized people rely on the respect of duties of solidarity by other people.

According to the Tribunal, the existence itself—and not only the broadness—of the individual right to decide not to vaccinate children (nb: not of the right of the child) depends on the opposite decision being made by other parents. For these reasons, the decision of the public authority must be in favor of vaccination, the sole

[77]See, for example, the decision of the regional authorities of Piedmont (no. 63/2598, 10th April 2006).

[78]It has to be acknowledged that, in relation to the past, there is no proof of a direct link between the vaccination mandate and an increase of immunization rates or vice-versa.

[79]Data are presented by the OECD at https://data.oecd.org/healthcare/child-vaccination-rates.htm.

[80]This happened in the Emilia-Romagna Region (Regional law no. 19, 25th November 2016), in the Trieste municipality and a similar decision was discussed in the Region of Tuscany.

[81]Decision of the Trieste Municipality no. 72, 28th November 2016.

[82]Administrative Regional Tribunal Friuli Venezia Giulia, sez. I, judgment no. 20, 16th January 2017.

tool able to protect public health which, by its own nature, must prevail over individual health.[83]

The arguments made in this judgment highlight the inextricable link existing between individual health claims and duties of solidarity: individual claims come to be recognized as rights, and thus protected, if the majority of people decide not to exercise those rights and, on the contrary, to act in compliance with duties of solidarity. Consequently, the democratic principle, entailing also forms of moral pluralism, is sustainable insofar as it is scientifically reasonable.

At the national level, the first vigorous reaction by the government can be found in the enactment of the aforementioned decree (No. 73/2017) which determines that children who are not compliant with the mandatory vaccinations cannot be enrolled in childcare and kindergarten (0-6 years). Minors up to age 16 must comply with the vaccinations according to a schedule which depends upon their year of birth. The original version of the decree required vaccinations against 12 diseases, three times as many as were previously compulsory, and introduced fines up to 30 times as much as those previously existing (as seen, suspended in some Regions) for non-compliant parents (new fines from €500 up to €7500). The parent or the parental authority of the child who violates the obligation to vaccinate was to be reported to the local health authority and to the Juvenile Court for the possible suspension of parental authority (Article 1.4). Some of these provisions were tempered by the intervention of Parliament: the latest version of the law,[84] which converts the decree, confirms the mandates, but only for ten vaccines (against diphtheria, Haemophilus influenzae Type B, hepatitis B, measles, mumps, pertussis, polio, rubella, tetanus, and varicella) and reduces the sanctions (for children aged 6–16, the only sanction is a fine up to €500; children under 6 are also not allowed to attend school). As stated above, according to the new legislation, vaccinations can only be omitted or deferred in the event of an established health condition in relation to specific, documented proof issued by a general practitioner or pediatrician (medical exemption).

Epidemiological data[85] seem to support and make this shift inevitable; nonetheless, any form of "duty to health" or "duty to stay healthy" impacts the most deeply rooted foundations of liberal societies and the limits of parental responsibility are called into question. The recent introduction of indirect sanctions for non-compliant parents in Italy requires the resolution of the possible contrast between the need to protect children from dramatically serious diseases, their right to education[86] and parents' right to make decisions concerning how to raise them. Scientific data concerning vaccines' safety and efficacy and the decreasing rate of immunization

[83]This decision was appealed and then upheld by the Consiglio di Stato (decision 14th February 2018, n. 962).

[84]Law no. 119, 31 July 2017, Official Journal of the Italian Republic, no. 182, 5 August 2017.

[85]According to recent data reported by the Italian National Institute of Health, cases of measles had risen more than fivefold across Italy in April since the same month of 2016. Data recently published by the Ministry of Health are available at http://www.salute.gov.it.

[86]Homeschooling is not a widespread reality in Italy.

across the nation pushed the Italian government to strictly reduce the possibility of affirming individual visions of health and, consequently, of refusing medical treatments. It might be interesting to note that until the dimension of the problem became alarming, individual claims against vaccinations were somewhat tolerated and found their place within the system (either via regional exemptions or via the praxis of not proceeding in front of juvenile courts), even though they were scientifically ill-founded. The protection of the health of every *single* child, thus, does not seem to be the primary concern underlying this kind of legislation. Moral conceptions, expressed through skeptical attitudes towards traditional medicine and the opinions of the majority of the scientific community, come to be ruled out as soon as their dimension jeopardizes the survival of public health.

The new legislation was challenged before the Constitutional Court, which upheld it on the basis of several arguments. First of all, the Court deemed necessary the intervention of national authorities to restore a situation of equality in health, which had been jeopardized by the different attitudes shown at the regional level. Secondly, according to the Court, the choice of the legislator is reasonable because it aims at protecting individual and collective health and finds its foundations in the duties of solidarity enshrined in Article 2 of the Italian Constitution. As a third argument, to support the legitimacy of the new mandatory framework, the Court recalls the critical epidemiological context, marked by a serious decrease of the coverage level, as an element to be considered in support of the introduction of new mandates. Furthermore, the Court positively welcomes two elements, which have tempered the rigorous approach of Decree no. 73/2017: the reduction of the sanctions and the provisions concerning the procedural steps to be followed before the application of said sanctions, such as informative meetings between non-compliant families and health authorities.

Lastly, the Court highlights the importance of reasonably balancing the two fundamental rights of health and education, making the latter prevail, where it becomes a duty (children over 6).

In this decision, the Constitutional Court duly followed its prior jurisprudence by confirming the legitimacy of mandates as instruments to protect collective health, but it also carved out the main features the mandate must show to be constitutionally oriented: it should be framed in terms of proportionality, reasonableness, and scientific consistency.

While the scientific validity of vaccines as a means to ensure a wide and necessary immunization is not contested by the majority of the scientific community, the opportunity for the law to intervene with strict mandates, in order to push for creating social consent, can be discussed. The vaccine mandate, to avoid being transformed into a counterproductive measure of exclusion, needs to go together with information and communication procedures capable of building trust. In pluralistic societies, characterized by ever growing zones of self-determination, the call for respect of duties of solidarity and the importance of building institutional trust require much more than mere coercion.

5 Axiological Pluralism and the Democracy of Science

One of the most intriguing debates in contemporary medicine tries to answer the following fundamental question: is science democratic? Most scientists easily answer no, and it is not supposed to be. Tough, but fair. Nonetheless, in order to agree with this statement, a sharp and clear distinction has to be made between social access to science and the theoretical assertions made by science. On the one hand, science has to be made accessible, comprehensible, and usable by everybody (especially when its findings are related to human health) and it can be inclusive and participatory in its process of production;[87] on the other hand, with regard to content, personal opinions and views have to give way to theories based on facts and data.

This statement does not lead to stillness and stagnancy, nor to a tyranny of the majority in science, but it ensures that progress and knowledge revolutions happen according to a rigorous scientific method.

Even if the public cannot be expected to be composed of experts on scientific issues, the trend of distrust of the scientific community or of passive ignorance of its findings is becoming worrisome. Poor information, together with a misinterpretation of the concept of autonomy in the medical field, may give rise to legal claims based on minority theories, unsupported by data and facts. This ill system of "moral value-pluralism" —which is better described as "plurality"— may lead to a deference to patients' reasons for asking for or refusing a specific treatment. The need to translate health requests—deeply affected by individual moral conceptions of life, wellbeing and illness—into protected rights, represents today a serious challenge that judges and lawmakers must assess.

The cases presented in this paper, albeit different in their specific features, represent well this tension between the recognition of a principle of self-determination in health (and the consequent need to respect individual conceptions of health and illness) and the pursuit of public health as a global goal.

Axiological pluralism entailing different visions of health, derived from misinformation, emotional involvement or distrust, is sustainable only to a certain extent, linked for example to a minimum of scientific reasonableness or to the need not to impact the health of others. Beyond that threshold, scientific rigorousness, the need to protect vulnerable subjects, and considerations about justice (equality and resource allocation) impose a selection of individual claims, with the consequence that only some of them can be transposed from the realm of human needs to the terrain of actionable legal rights.

---

[87] In particular, the effort to involve laypeople in decision making on sociotechnical controversies is pivotal. On this aspect see Bucchi (2009) and Kleinman (2000). More generally, on the multifaceted issue of the participatory efforts to "democratize" science, see Jasanoff (2003), pp. 223–244.

References

Abbot A (2013) Italian stem-cell trial based on flawed data. Scientists raise serious concerns about a patent that forms the basis of a controversial stem-cell therapy. Nature. News 2 July 2013. https://www.nature.com/news/italian-stem-cell-trial-based-on-flawed-data-1.13329. Accessed 30 July 2019

Abbott A (2016) Stem-cell scandal gets fresh scrutiny. Nature 539:340

Barry B (2002) Culture and equality. Polity Press, Cambridge

Bateman-House A (2016) Findings on "Right to Try" Laws and PreApproval/Compassionate/Expanded Access to Investigational Medical Products. Executive Summary Findings on "Right to Try" Laws and Pre-Approval/Compassionate/Expanded Access to Investigational Medical Products. http://www.med.nyu.edu/pophealth/sites/default/files/pophealth/FindingsRTTexecutivesummary.pdf. Accessed 30 July 2019

Bateman-House A, Kimberly L, Redman B, Dubler N, Caplan A (2015) Right-to-try laws: hope, hype, and unintended consequences. Ann Intern Med 163(10):796–797

Benelli E (2003) The role of the media in steering public opinion on healthcare issues. Health Policy 63(2):179–186

Bianco P, Cattaneo E, De Luca M, Pani L (2014) Stamina therapies: let the record stand. Nature 506 (7489):434

Bucchi M (2009) Beyond technocracy: science, politics and citizens (trans: Belton A). Springer, Dordrecht

Buttenheim AM, Asch DA (2013) Making vaccine refusal less of a free ride. Human Vaccin Immunother 9:2674–2675

Chin BR (2008) One last chance: Abigail Alliance v. von Eschenbach and the right to access experimental drugs. University of California. Davies Law Rev 41:1969–2000

Corieri C (2014) Everyone deserves the right to try: empowering the terminally ill to take control of their treatment. Policy Report 266(2014):1–30. https://goldwatermedia.s3.amazonaws.com/cms_page_media/2015/1/29/Right%20To%20Try.pdf. Accessed 30 July 2019

Dresser R (2015) Symposium: science challenges for law and policy: the "right to try" investigational drugs: science and stories in the access debate. Tex Law Rev 93(7):1631–1657

Fattore G (1999) Clarifying the scope of Italian NHS coverage. Is it feasible? Is it desirable? Health Policy 50(1–2):123–142

Freed GL (2005) Vaccine policies across the pond: looking at the U.K. and U.S. systems. Health Aff 24(3):755–757

Gostin LO (2008) Public health law. Power, duty, restraint. University of California Press, Berkeley

Hogan E (2016) "Right to Try" legislation and its implications for the FDA drug approval process. Wash Univ J Law Policy 50:171–194

Jasanoff S (2003) Technologies of humility: citizen participation in governing science. Minerva 41 (3):223–244

Kearns L, Bateman-House A (2017) Who stands to benefit? Right to try law provisions and implications. Ther Innov Regulat Sci 51(2):170–176

King S (1999) Vaccination policies: individual rights v. community health. Br Med J 319 (7223):1448–1449

Kleinman DL (2000) Science, technology, and democracy. State University of New York Press, Albany

Malone KM, Hinman AR (2007) Vaccination mandates: the public health imperative and individual rights. In: Goodman RA, Hoffman RE, Lopez W, Matthews GW, Rothstein M, Foster K (eds) Law in public health practice, 2nd edn. Oxford University Press, Oxford, pp 338–360

Martin C (2016) Questioning the "right" in state right to try laws: assessing the legality and effectiveness of these laws. Ohio State Law J 77:159–194

Matthews K, Kunisetty B, Sprung K (2018) Texas H.B. 810: increased access to stem cell interventions or an increase in unproven treatments? Stem Cells Dev 27(21):1463–1465

Okie S (2006) Access before approval - a right to take experimental drugs? New England J Med 355:437–440
Omer SB (2006) Nonmedical exemptions to school immunization requirements. Secular trends and association of state policies with pertussis incidence. JAMA 296:1757–1763
Orenstein WA, Hinman AR (1999) The immunization system in the United States. The role of school immunization laws. Vaccine 17(Supp. 3):S19–S24
Rial-Sebbag E, Blasimme A (2014) The European Court of Human Rights' ruling on unproven stem cell therapies: a missed opportunity? Stem Cells Dev 23(S1):39–43
Salmon DA et al (2006) Compulsory vaccination and conscientious or philosophical exemptions: past, present, and future. Lancet 367(9508):436–442
Tong RW (2016) AB 159: can it really hurt "to try"? Univ Pac Law Rev 47:551–575
Tsakopoulos A, Han J, Nodler H, Russo V (2015) The right to try: an overview of efforts to obtain expedited access to unapproved treatment for the terminally ill. Food Drug Law J 70:617–641
U.S. Department Of Health And Human Services (2015) Individual Patient Expanded Access Applications: Form FDA 3926; Draft Guidance for Industry. http://www.fda.gov/downloads/Drugs/GuidanceComplianceRegulatoryInformation/Guidances/UCM432717.pdf. Accessed 30 July 2019
Yang YT, Chen B, Bennet C (2015) "Right-to-try" legislation: progress or peril? J Clin Oncol 33 (24):2597–2599

Reliance on Scientific Claims in Social and Legal Contexts: An 'HIV and AIDS' Case Study

Andrea Perin

Abstract This chapter deals with the issue of reliance on scientific claims in contexts other than scientific ones. Both social and natural sciences are supposed to be able to provide decision-making processes with objective and neutral points of view on the natural order. Nevertheless, several factors—such as the constant evolution of scientific research, scientific uncertainty, and social implications of scientific debates—make increasingly difficult to access clearly reliable scientific knowledge. The thirty-year scientific-public dispute between the official hypothesis on HIV/AIDS and the so-called 'AIDS denialism' allows us to corroborate this general observation. Taking this example as a starting point and common thread, the author discusses the importance of improving experts' communication towards society and the need to provide lay-persons with reasonable explanations. Indeed, paradigmatic comparative case-law confirm that also judges have to independently decide whether to admit scientific evidence in court, determining which claims are (more) reliable (than others). In his conclusions, the author points out that better scientific communication requires accepting complexity and constant variability characterising scientific matters. Instead, over-reliance on science might induce a lack of trust in scientific institutions, inevitably increasing relativism, confusion, and manipulation.

1 Putting Science Out of Place

The title of this paragraph evokes on purpose the book entitled *Putting science in its place*, where David N. Livingstone raises and discusses an epistemological question which is specifically geographical, 'Can the location of scientific endeavor make any difference to the conduct of science? And even more important, can it affect the

A. Perin (✉)
Facultad de Derecho, Universidad Andrés Bello, Santiago, Providencia, Chile
e-mail: andrea.perin@unab.cl

L. Busatta, C. Casonato (eds.), *Axiological Pluralism*, Ius Gentium: Comparative Perspectives on Law and Justice 92, https://doi.org/10.1007/978-3-030-78475-1_10

content of science?'.[1] Here, we shall address a somehow different, although similar and complementary epistemological issue: the reliance on scientific claims in contexts (places) *other than scientific ones.* So, as 'the often-problematic relationship between 'expert knowledge' and the 'public' typically emerges in every-day life as part of particular issues',[2] let us consider few paradigmatic examples.

Dealing with the public debate on same-sex marriages in Italy, some lawyers took position against extending the application of the so-called stepchild adoption to gay couples, arguing that (more) scientific evidence was required on possible adverse effects in children living with same-sex parents.[3] In fact, although some have sustained that 'decades of research has failed to reveal important differences in the adjustment or development of children or adolescents reared by same-sex couples compared to those reared by other-sex couples',[4] others hold that 'such conclusions appear premature in the light of more recent data in which some different outcomes have been observed'.[5] So, could this uncertainty justify legal limitations to same-sex parenthood?

Since 2009, some Italian civil courts decided to entitle compensation to plaintiffs,[6] in light of claims indicating some vaccines may cause autism, a hypothesis widely disregarded by the mainstream scientific community.[7] Hence, are those rulings scientifically legitimate?

In 2018 the National Toxicology Program (NTP) released partial results from a long-term study of the effects of cellphone radiofrequency radiation (RFR) on mice and rats, expressing 'confidence in the association between RFR exposure and the neoplastic lesions' observed.[8] In 2011 the International Agency for Research on Cancer (IARC) had already classified radiofrequency electromagnetic fields as 'possibly carcinogenic to humans'. Now Falcioni et al.[9] suggest it is time for IARC to 'consider changing the RF radiation designation to a "probable" human carcinogen'. So, should governments provide precautionary measures in order to protect public health?

---

[1]Livingstone (2003), p. 1.

[2]Irwin and Wynne (1996), p. 1. This chapter was written before the outbreak of the COVID-19 pandemic. This experience confirms the topicality of the following reflection on the relationships between Policy, Law and Science, and the importance of science communication for society.

[3]E.g. Miotto (2015).

[4]Patterson (2006).

[5]Schumm (2016), p. 641.

[6]Tomasi (2016).

[7]British doctor Andrew Wakefield first sustained this thesis in a work published in *The Lancet* in 1998. Nevertheless, this work has been retracted by the publishing review in 2010, as according to the judgment of the UK General Medical Council's Fitness to Practise Panel of January 28, 2010, 'several elements of the 1998 paper by Wakefield *et al* are incorrect, contrary to the findings of an earlier investigation. In particular, the claims in the original paper that children were "consecutively referred" and investigations were "approved" by the local ethics committee have been proven to be false'. The Editors of The Lancet (2010), p. 445.

[8]Wyde et al. (2018), p. 19.

[9]Falcioni et al. (2018).

There is an assumption that empirical—both social and natural—sciences are able to provide decision-making processes with objective and neutral points of view on the natural order. For example, empirical evidence is required to prove suggested causal links in tort litigation and criminal trials (we shall focus on it in paragraph 4); also, it may enable lawmakers or courts to assess certain risks as unacceptable and thereby take or justify precautionary decisions.[10] Nevertheless, the constant evolution of scientific research and resulting scientific uncertainty are making increasingly difficult to access clearly reliable scientific knowledge; therefore, the way we turn to experts claims becomes itself increasingly questionable even on the proper scientific field.[11]

A post-positivistic way to deal with uncertainty in science-based decision-making could be to accept that uncertainty itself is not pathological, but rather physiological in scientific matters.[12] It means to assume, first of all, that natural sciences—such as biology or physics—can explain what is neither ontological nor objectively true: their goal is not to say how nature *is*, rather how it *could work*, that is, which 'natural laws' appears to regulate the natural order. Also, scientific theories about those natural laws should be considered as mere hypothesis that need research and discussion to be tested, corroborated, improved, or otherwise rejected.[13]

In this regard, it has been argued also that empirical hypothesis and scientific claims are often conditioned by subjective observation, certain socio-political factors as well as external—i.e. non-scientific—interests.[14] Nevertheless, challenging the scientistic dogmas of objectivity and neutrality of evidence-based science, as well as encouraging new sources of likely-scientific information, the 'epistemology of uncertainty'[15] takes a big risk, that is: to legitimate 'lay perspectives'.

Although the crisis of public confidence in science is not a new phenomenon,[16] it explains why scientific debates have increasingly gained a public dimension.[17] The number of social sites where scientific knowledge is discussed increases. Likely scientific opinions are provided not only by traditional institutions—such as universities, research institutions, laboratories, clinics, expert articles, etc.—but also by social movements and alternative (nonmainstream) organisations.[18] For this reason, it becomes increasingly difficult to determine boundaries between scientific,

[10]Esteve Pardo (2009), pp. 141–150.

[11]Esteve Pardo (2009).

[12]E.g. Villa (1984).

[13]Popper (2002). We specifically refer to the 'demarcation problem' as addressed by Karl Popper, because the criterion of 'falsifiability' has been assumed by important judicial sentences in order to establish whether scientific evidence is sufficiently reliable and therefore admissible in court. See below, paragraph 4.

[14]E.g. Kuhn (1970), Ravetz (2004), p. 350; Kearns et al. (2016).

[15]E.g. Tallacchini (2005).

[16]Irwin and Wynne (1996), p. 7.

[17]E.g. McCormick (2007).

[18]Preda (2005), p. 4.

pseudo-scientific or political discourses; and the opposing of *science* with *culture* (values, aims, interests, etc.) becomes even more problematic, making scientific debate increasingly difficult to understand and easier to manipulate.[19]

In sum: as a paradoxical result, or unintended consequence, the increasing need to make science-based decision-making processes more democratic might make society less democratic.[20]

2 Mainstream Science, Alternative Narratives, and (Mis)Communication

Among many other recent examples,[21] the thirty-year scientific-public dispute between the mainstream hypothesis on HIV/AIDS and the so-called ‘AIDS denialism’ allows us to deal with the issue of ‘public understanding of science in action’.[22]

According to the generally accepted scientific hypothesis, as reported by the Centers for Disease Control and Prevention (CDC), HIV infection is a dynamic process and has a variable rate of progression in infected people. The ‘Acquired immunodeficiency syndrome’ (AIDS) is the third and most severe stage of the typical HIV progression. And people are diagnosed with AIDS when their CD4 cell count drops below 200 cells/mm and when they develop certain—predetermined—opportunistic illnesses.[23]

Therefore, the causal link between HIV infection, certain CD4 count and opportunistic illnesses (the three main elements of the notion) must be proven. In fact, one can be infected with HIV and (still) not develop AIDS, depending on several possible factors—e.g. genetic factors[24]—or due to medical prescriptions of antiretroviral therapy (ART). Furthermore, human immunodeficiency may have multiple explanations (i.e. causes, or ‘sets of conditions’), being sometimes unrelated to HIV. One HIV+ can develop immunodeficiency disorders and/or suffer AIDS-related opportunistic illnesses, although this does not automatically mean that the HIV infection provoked them. Multiple etiological factors and different possible sets of conditions (other infections, chemotherapy, genetic predisposition, antibiotic

[19]E.g. Goertzel (2010).

[20]Indeed, a ‘democratic society depends on the ability of its members to make rational choices. But rational choices must be based on rational beliefs. If we can’t tell the difference between reasonable and unreasonable claims, we become susceptible to the claims of charlatans, scoundrels, and mountebanks’: Theodor Schick and Lewis Vaughn, cited by Sidky (2018), p. 38.

[21]Think about the public debate on the climate change and its possible causes, the controversial safety of certain technologies (Mobile phones, Wi-Fi Technologies, Genetically Modified Organisms, especially with regard to their use in producing food, etc.).

[22]Irwin and Wynne (1996), p. 3.

[23]For more information: https://www.cdc.gov/hiv/basics/index.html. Accessed 8 August 2019.

[24]Poropatich and Sullivan (2011).

treatment, etc.) can provoke and therefore explain immunosuppression, jointly or separately.[25]

Although this definition seems to be clear and easily accessible, 'HIV' and 'AIDS' are still generally thought to be practically synonymous.[26] Even legal scholars (academics), when dealing with criminal liability for HIV non-disclosure, exposure, and/or transmission, occasionally use ambiguous expressions like 'AIDS-carrier'[27], instead of 'HIV-carrier', or 'AIDS infection'[28], instead of 'HIV-infection'.

This might generate confusion.

However, things are even more complicated. In fact, a closer look at the history of AIDS reveals that several alternative narratives regarding its etiological explanation have been sustained, mostly during the 90s.[29]

One of the most famous examples of the so-called 'AIDS denialism'[30] is the 1996 book entitled *Inventing the AIDS Virus*, which is important to consider here as it was intended for lay-persons and newcomers to the issue. Its author, Peter Duesberg, essentially defended the following: (a) the retrovirus called HIV does not exist—in any case, if it does, there is no proof that HIV causes AIDS; (b) various illnesses included under the 'AIDS umbrella' are actually brought on by long-term recreational drug use, as well as other unhealthy living conditions, so AIDS is not infectious; (c) the long-term consumption of Retrovir (AZT, also known as Zidovudine)—an antiretroviral medication prescribed to HIV+ people in order to treat or prevent AIDS—is the real main causal factor that provokes their immunodeficiency; (d) hence, any definition of AIDS which considers HIV as the main, or sole, etiologic agent is unacceptable.[31]

Peter Duesberg tried to challenge the virus-official hypothesis on AIDS publishing his studies also on scientific journals.[32] Moreover, other scientists, as well as some academic researchers and physicians, maintained similar hypothesis.[33] Hence, we are not referring to mere 'junk' or 'fake' information uploaded and found on Facebook, YouTube or any other web source,[34] but to hypothesis maintained by experts and supported by certain—although minimum—consensus within the scientific community.

25 See Vineis (1990), p. 11.

26 Mangosing (2015).

27 E.g. Summerer (2001).

28 E.g. Masera (2008).

29 Preda (2005), pp. 113–187.

30 See e.g., Kalichman (2009), pp. 1–23; Goertzel (2010).

31 Duesberg (1996).

32 E.g. Duesberg et al. (2003, 2011).

33 E.g. Ruggiero et al. (2009).

34 On the critical role that new information and communication technologies play on this field, see e.g. Svalastog et al. (2015).

So why should we—lay-persons—blindly trust in the official HIV/AIDS explanation? In other words: 'why should we believe something just because it claims to be scientific?'.[35]

This question sounds provocative, but it is based on the simple observation that the 'majority criterion' is definitely unsatisfactory.[36] After all, 'Science is far too complex an object to be characterizable by a single trait—and the same holds for pseudoscience'.[37] Hence, in order to reconsider the relational principle of 'trust',[38] the only way seems to be induce 'science' to a better communication—it should explain why certain explanations are (more) reliable (than others)—and provide lay-persons with rational, understandable, and convincing reasons to believe that.

However, communication in scientific matters represents a very problematic challenge due not only to the difficulties that scientific explanations imply *per se*, but also to the aforementioned side effects of the 'democratisation'. Although this is not the sole relevant assumption,[39] as a matter of fact, people generally do not possess sufficient expertise to judge by themselves imminent related matters. They often do not have even elementary information.[40]

Our example about HIV and AIDS show us how a scientific-academic debate might become very quickly a controversial matter in social and cultural debates. Both health and research institutions constantly operate with notions of 'risk' associated with the construction of *social groups*. Scientific research has been constantly oriented according to social criteria like 'risk persons' (gay men and drug users, mostly) and 'risky behaviours', due to the statistical impact that HIV and AIDS have in their 'risk groups'.[41] Accordingly, health institutions challenge the AIDS risk trying to increase the knowledge of those groups and their members, turning to the same concepts and criteria. So, when service providers are asked about the risk of HIV transmission from an exposure to HIV through sex, each patient is generally put into a specific category, depending on his/her sexual orientation and the kind of sex practised, which correspond to a certain statistical risk of HIV transmission.

Several studies have tried to estimate the average risk of HIV transmission from a specific type of unprotected sex. For example, a meta-analysis of ten studies published in 2009 estimates the risk of HIV transmission through receptive vaginal sex to be 0.08% (i.e., 1 transmission per 1250 exposures)[42]; instead, a single study[43]

[35]Irwin and Wynne (1996), p. 9.

[36]As we will see below, while considering the shift from the so-called *Fry test* to *Daubert*'s criterion.

[37]Bunge (1984), p. 36.

[38]Irwin and Wynne (1996); Camporesi et al. (2017).

[39]Irwin and Wynne (1996), p. 6.

[40]Sidky (2018), pp. 38–39.

[41]Preda (2005), pp. 2–4.

[42]Boily et al. (2009).

[43]Jin et al. (2010).

estimates the risk for insertive anal sex to be 0.11% for circumcised men and 0.62% for uncircumcised men.[44] More recently, other studies and meta-analyses providing similar or comparable data have been discussed, and new studies will be certainly published in the future.

But here is the problem. Estimates of the per-act risk of HIV transmission can be certainly useful for individuals and public care programs,[45] as they allow to assess strategies of prevention and communication. Nonetheless, statistics might raise problems because very often people cannot understand what practitioners are telling them, and this might affect patients' consent to medical treatments.

Imagine, for instance, that one had unprotected sex and, taken by anxiety, turns to the healthcare services for post-exposure prophylaxis (PEP).[46] In such a case, advice provided to patients is of critical importance. Indeed, the assumption of antiretroviral medications might provoke serious side effects, and sometimes, if taken improperly, they might increase the risk of HIV drug resistance.[47] That is why all risks should be assessed carefully, so that it requires the information provided to be not only complete and updated, but also understandable and clear.

Nevertheless, being merely statistical, the 'per-act risk' only refers to small and not necessarily representative groups of HIV-negative individuals. This should be explained clearly. Persons enrolled in those studies might be requested to report information like the following: how many times they have had sex in a given period of time, what type of sex they had, how often they used condoms, and the HIV status of their partners.[48] So, obviously, results might be inaccurate and therefore not entirely reliable. For example, one cannot always know the HIV status of the partner.[49] Moreover, statistics do not explicitly tell patients that a variety of factors can make a major difference to the risk of HIV exposure in each individual case. That is why it is impossible to provide an individual with his/her exact risk of HIV transmission from a single concrete exposure. Those numbers should be considered only as 'rough estimates' of the risk of transmission in the absence of other biological (such as other sexually transmitted infections and a high viral load) or circumstantial factors, which can increase the concrete risks of transmission.[50]

But do physicians always provide complete and understandable information in order to receive patients' consent before start drug therapies?

---

[44] Nonetheless, this does not automatically imply that circumcision does effectively reduce the risk of HIV infections; moreover, the issue is polemic and still widely discussed: see e.g. Earp and Darby (2015).

[45] Patel et al. (2014).

[46] See on PEP, Siedner et al. (2018).

[47] E.g. Singh et al. (2018), pp. 5–7.

[48] Patel et al. (2014).

[49] Wilton (2012).

[50] Patel et al. (2014).

3 Accepting Pluralism: Moving from Mystification to Argumentation

Let us change a little bit our previous example and imagine now that the patient wants to be tested to know if he/she is HIV+ or not. As screening tests should be taken few days or weeks after the dubious exposure, in the meantime, during the so-called 'window period', this person might search for information in order to overcome fear and anxiety, and eventually find alternative hypothesis, like those defended by Peter Duesberg, and related information.[51]

Many reasons can make this kind of information more convincing than official versions.[52] Narratives enable people to meet specific needs[53] and become persuasive when they can give false hopes, confirming prejudices or ideological positions.

Now, the majority of the scientific community says Duesberg was completely wrong.[54] Nevertheless, one might observe that also other experts expressed serious concerns about the toxicity of antiretroviral therapies—although this controversy appears to have to do more with the trial of AZT and its dosages, than with the AZT itself.[55] Moreover, it must be recognised that, for a simple question of logic, HIV as a causal sole-factor cannot explain all concerning AIDS progression (or non-progression), due to the possible influence of many—positive or negative, known or even unknown—factors; indeed, 'human pathologies cannot be explained nor predicted on the basis of linear or deterministic causal models, but according to probabilistic correlations and "web of causation"'.[56] Finally, Duesberg efficaciously highlighted a serious problem affecting scientific-academic research (yet in 1996, and still today), that is: the possible lack of independence and increasing of conformism, due (also) to the deep conditioning of private and public research funding programs as well as commercialization,[57] that inevitably influence scientific activities in determining the goals to achieve.

These considerations show how an 'alternative hypothesis', even though it is considered unfounded by the most part of the scientific community, might include persuasive arguments, thereby reaching people's needs. And that is why the way scientists occasionally criticise similar alternative hypothesis, i.e. just refusing and

---

[51]For example, this website: http://www.virusmyth.com/aids/. Accessed 30 Nov 2018.

[52]Kalichman (2009), p. XIII.

[53]Foster (1998), p. 158.

[54]Kalichman (2009), pp. 25–90. According to some studies—e.g., O'Briena and Goedert (1996); Chigwedere and Essex (2010)—he erroneously criticised the official explanation turning to the Koch's postulates—see Duesberg (1996), pp. 30, 174, 188, 199–, that is, four criteria formulated to describe the etiology of tuberculosis, and then generalised to other diseases: e.g., Vineis (1990), Harde (1992).

[55]E.g. Richman et al. (1987); Kalichman (2009), p. 78.

[56]Vineis (1990), p. 11.

[57]Duesberg (1996), pp. 67–68, 454–456.

banning them, might make their narratives even more credible, arousing suspects and nurturing false hopes.

Mystification or personal attacks are never good strategies, being even more unfortunate when your rival can turn also to good arguments. Indeed, those convincing statements can easily meet approval, hiding the bad and unfounded side of their narrative.

But we can validate our observation also on an epistemological level. Indeed, despite positivistic monism conceived natural science as a model for legal science, Social Sciences and Humanities like Law—its 'operating modes', 'procedures' and 'decision-making practices'—can represent a methodological as well as heuristic model for natural science.[58] This essentially means to recognize that knowledge grows dialectically[59]; that every 'theory choice' requires arguing the greater plausibility or reliability of one theory or the other.[60]

Therefore, instead of rejecting alternative theories labelling them 'deniers' and the like,[61] scientists should provide people (including courts and institutions of law enforcement, as we shall see below) with reasonable explications, accepting debates as useful and avoiding misunderstandings, ambiguity, and counterproductive simplifications that might encourage people trust just what they need to.

4 Reliance on Scientific Evidence in Tort Litigation and Criminal Trials. Can Judges Establish How to Distinguish 'Science' from 'Non-Science'?

The problem of reliance on scientific claims in contexts other than scientific ones typically arises when Courts are required to prove causal links between defendants' conducts and adverse events.

Legally speaking, the concept of 'cause' refers to each antecedent condition that cannot be assumed hypothetically absent without failure of certain effect (*conditio sine qua non*).[62] Hence, a defendant's conduct can be considered as 'cause' of an offence if it belongs to the set of necessary and jointly sufficient conditions that effectively provoked the alleged event.

---

[58]Villa (2005), pp. 36, 37.

[59]Villa (2005), p. 31.

[60]See Villa (2005), p. 38, 41. Although it does not imply a sort of post-positivistic 'monism'. Rather, this means a recognition of a methodological pluralism which allows the 'unity of science' to recover on an epistemological level: Villa (2005), pp. 34, 37. In this sense, consider e.g., the pluralistic conception of the 'unity of science' defended by Breitenbach and Choi (2017); and Gijsbers (2016), according to which a certain amount of isolation between the different sciences is both present and unavoidable.

[61]See on that also Bunge (1984), p. 46.

[62]E.g. Ryu (1958), Di Giovine (2002).

According to the 'abductive reasoning',[63] as it has been assumed, for instance, by the Italian Court of Cassation (2002), the proof of causality requires judges to follow two fundamental steps.[64] First, provided by experts, they have to consider all possible law-covered explanations of the offence, i.e., all possible sets of necessary and jointly sufficient conditions of the alleged event ('general causality'). Secondly, in the light of all available evidence and the proved circumstances of fact, judges should determine whether the defendant effectively caused the event—being his/her conduct a condition which cannot be assumed absent without failure of the effect—according to the most reliable and relevant law-covered explanation found (among all the others he/she found).

So, causality as a question of evidence involves both logical and epistemological issues. The evaluation of alternative explanations according to the proper inferential reasoning entails the consideration of empirical claims in terms of validity, credibility, and reliability. And we need methods for assessing evidence.[65] Indeed, in order to prove the 'individual causality', it is necessary to exclude all possible alternative explanations, beyond any reasonable doubt.

On this regard, until 1993 the leading reference was *Frye vs. United States* (Federal Circuit Court of Appeals for the District of Columbia 1923). Dealing with the question of the scientific validity of an early version of a lie detector test, the court of appeal in *Frye* formulated an admissibility standard based on whether the evidence was 'generally accepted in the scientific community' (Federal Circuit Court of Appeals for the District of Columbia 1923: 1014). According to this criterion, some authors have sustained that unreliable scientific evidence would not have met the general acceptance standard.[66] Nonetheless, as many judges were actually ignoring *Frye* and evaluating only whether the evidence was *relevant* (i.e., related to the topic that was before the court) but not if it were *reliable*,[67] courts have been admitting scientific evidence that actually lacked scientific credibility.[68]

Then, in 1993, the Supreme Court of United States addressed again the admissibility issue in the famous *Daubert case*. *Daubert* was one of many cases involving the question of the causal association between Bendectin, a prescription drug for preventing morning sickness during pregnancy, and some malformations in babies of women who had been taking this drug. The Supreme Court hold that 'general acceptance' could not be the sole determinant criterion of whether the scientific evidence was admissible in Court and set up a list of factors to provide the courts with guidance to take decisions about the admissibility of scientific evidence. These criteria are the following: (a) whether the theory that is proposed had been tested or

[63]Peirce (1935), Burks (1946), Tuzet (2006), Pardo and Allen (2008), Ilari and Russo (2014), p. 20; Jones (2018).

[64]E.g. Di Giovine (2002); Viganò (2013).

[65]E.g. Ilari and Russo (2014), p. 46, 56.

[66]Rabin (2004), p. 127.

[67]Rabin (2004), p. 127.

[68]Huber (1991); Jasanoff (1995).

not (testability); (b) whether there is publication of works related to the theory in peer-reviewed journals; (c) what the error rate and standards for controlling the technique's operation have been in the field in which the theory has been tested (rate of error); (d) the Frye-test (Supreme Court 1993).

Similarly, in 2010 the Italian Court of Cassation stated that judges should carry out an independent evaluation to decide whether experts' opinions are sufficiently reliable (or more reliable than others). Therefore, the Supreme Court proposed the following criteria: (a) the identity, the qualification, the scientific prestige, and the independence of expert(s); (b) the quality and objectivity of their research; (c) its empirical basis; (d) the related scientific discussion in the scientific community; (e) the explicative capability of the theory/technique; (f) the consensus, or degree of acceptance, in the scientific community (the Frye-test); (g) the reliability of methodology (Court of Cassation 2010).

All these standards are merely 'suggestive' considerations that judges should have in mind when deciding cases of scientific admissibility at trial.[69] So, we cannot get an exhaustive list or set of standards for estimating the credibility of certain scientific findings from it.[70] However, those decisions send a clear message to courts, that is: although the reliability of scientific hypothesis is still uncertain and debated (i.e., not yet 'generally accepted' in the scientific community), judges have to independently decide whether to admit scientific evidence in court, determining which scientific claims are (more) reliable (than others).[71]

Therefore, the question is: can judges establish themselves on how to distinguish 'science' from 'pseudoscience', or 'junk science', as well as strictly scientific from metaphysical speculations and mere common experience? And if the answer to the first is yes, the second question is: how can judges decide which scientific claims and evidence are sufficiently reliable within those complying with certain epistemological standards?[72]

Let us go back to the HIV-AIDS discourse and focus on the following example.

---

[69]Rabin (2004), p. 129. See also Risinger (2007).

[70]On the contrary, see the one proposed by LeBel et al. (2018).

[71]On the limits of this 'reliable approach' (that is also our approach here), and for more references on expert admissibility and judicial gatekeeping, O'Brien (2018).

[72]Perin (2014), pp. 1381–1382.

5 The Use of Phylogenetic Analysis in Prosecutions for Sexual Transmission

Depending on the legal system, HIV-related offences can substantially change. Indeed, while some legal systems punish mere exposures (for HIV non-disclosure),[73] others require negligent, reckless, or intentional transmission (that is, the adverse event).[74]

In criminal trials involving the alleged transmission of HIV, the proof of causation represents a key challenge for prosecutors. What judges need to be proved, in fact, is that the defendant infected the victim, and this requires being able to exclude any alternative source of transmission (i.e., alternative explanations of the alleged event: e.g. the complainant could have been infected by someone else, through drug use or via medical procedures), beyond any reasonable doubt.

In some cases, prosecutors have been able to introduce into evidence phylogenetic analyses of virus samples to hold that the defendant did infect the complainant.

Phylogenetic analysis essentially allows examining and comparing small differences in HIV's genes. In fact, HIV's RNA changes rapidly, and this is what permits to scientists to create hypothetical diagrams (known as 'phylogenetic trees') to estimate how closely related the samples of HIV taken from two or more individuals are likely to be in comparison to others.[75] However, scientists do not agree on what this technique allows to prove. In particular, some experts have maintained that even with appropriate controls, phylogenetic analysis cannot directly prove transmission, so that the only safe use of the technique in criminal HIV transmission cases would be to exonerate the accused or to (merely) support the alleged hypothesis of transmission excluding some possible alternative sources.[76]

Phylogenetic analysis has been used for the first time for forensic purposes in 1990, in order to investigate the possible transmission of HIV from a dentist to his patients during the course of invasive dental surgery.[77] In this case, while some experts claimed that the analysis clearly showed that the defendant did infect six of his patients,[78] others maintained the impossibility of determining whether, when, and how the transmissions occurred.[79]

Then, phylogenetic analysis was introduced as scientific evidence in a criminal trial in 1992, in Sweden. An HIV+ male was convicted of rape and transmission of HIV in the Stockholm district court. In preparation for his appeal, the prosecution

---

[73]See, also for more references, Mykhalovskiy and Betteridge (2012).

[74]On legal, policy and public health issues surrounding sexual transmission of HIV and its criminalisation, see e.g., Bennett (2000); Weait (2005); Adam et al. (2008); Dodds et al. (2009); Lazzarini et al. (2013); Boyd et al. (2016); Mehta et al. (2019); Miyashita Ochoa et al. (2019).

[75]Bernard et al. (2007), p. 4.

[76]Pillay et al. (2007), p. 460.

[77]Bernard et al. (2007), p. 4.

[78]Ciesielski et al. (1994), p. 886.

[79]Bernard et al. (2007), p. 3.

asked a group of experts to determine 'the degree of relatedness between the strain of HIV in the suspect and the alleged victim'.[80] Their subsequent study provides suggestions on how the analysis could be used in courtrooms. In particular, the authors stressed that even though 'the analysis revealed that the sequences from the male and the female were very closely related', they 'could not determine the direction of transmission', nor could they 'formally rule out the possibility that both the male and the female were infected by a third party'.[81]

Another important leading case was *State of Louisiana vs. Richard J. Schmidt* in 1997.[82] Again, the group of virologists who performed the phylogenetic analysis published a study to discuss the method used and their conclusions. They underlined that 'although the inferred sister relationship between patient and victim viruses is consistent with the alleged transmission event, this finding by itself does not establish the direction of the transmission nor does it prove that additional individuals could not have been involved in a series of intermediate transmissions'. However, 'if the sequences are sampled close enough in time to the transmission event, the direction between a suspected pair can often be established'.[83]

More recently, other jurisdictions have ruled phylogenetic analysis reliable as forensic evidence in criminal prosecutions for HIV as well as for HCV transmission.[84] In Spain, for example, this technique has been used in the *Maeso case,*[85] in order to demonstrate that the accused, a Valencian physician, had recklessly infected with the hepatitis C virus (HCV) 275 patients in the four hospitals where he had been working as anesthetist.[86] Nevertheless, its admission in court still raises problems for both scientists, who provide expert testimony in court, and judges, who should assess the validity, credibility, and significance of the analysis and its results.

The scientific forensic debate, in particular, deals with the possibility of proving that a direct infection occurred between two individuals by inferring (whether possible) route, direction, and timing of transmission. In fact, although some studies hold that the sequencing of a large number of virus genomes from the individuals involved can allow establishing the direction and therefore the source of transmission,[87] other scholars highlight that this is not identical to demonstrate direct transmission from one to another.[88] Therefore, although phylogenetic evidence can provide support for linkage between individuals, especially if correctly integrated with epidemiological and serological data,[89] it would not provide beyond

[80]Bernard et al. (2007), p. 4.

[81]Albert et al. (1994), p. 5918, 5921, 5923.

[82]Bernard et al. (2007), p. 5.

[83]Metzker et al. (2002).

[84]E.g. Bhandari et al. (2013), pp. 17–19.

[85]Barreda (2007).

[86]The conclusions of the analysis have been discussed in González-Candelas et al. (2013).

[87]Scaduto et al. (2010); Chen et al. (2015).

[88]Vandamme and Pybus (2013).

[89]Chen et al. (2015); Li et al. (2020).

reasonable doubt the proof of transmission by itself. In fact, other explanations cannot be excluded, for example: the accused has been infected by the complainant; both the two subjects were infected by one or more third parties with similar viral strains; a third party mediated HIV transmission from one subject to the other; the complainant was already HIV+ and was re-infected.[90]

The use of viral phylogenetics in court requires experts not only to present their results but also to provide judges and/or jurors with their opinion on what those results (might) mean. In particular, they could be asked to take position on whether the evidence should be used only conservatively (to exclude a proposed source or direction of transmission) or to establish that one person did infect another person. So, they can hold that phylogenetic evidence is sufficiently persuasive to prove the suggested causal link or only to support the charge.

In sum, experts might differ in their view on how the technique should be used, giving different interpretations to results. Especially, they can differ in the way they communicate those results to judges, inevitably influencing the 'translation' of technical opinions in judicial decisions turning to legal categories (e.g. the 'reasonable doubt' legal standard).

All this shows the importance of evidence other than phylogenetic analysis (whether admitted in court) when building a case for direct transmission. In order to exclude alternative explanations of the alleged event it might be useful, or even necessary, turn to a combination of strictly scientific and other evidence, such as the documented sexual health histories of both accused and complainant and testimony.[91] More in general, however, all this shows the need for Judges to be always conscious of the limitations that specifically characterise each type of evidence,[92] even though certain conduct might be characterised per se by strong social disapproval.

6 Improving Scientific Communication and Public Understanding of Science (Concluding Remarks)

This paper consists of a mere overview of issues that are of critical importance for the society as a whole,[93] as they concern the relationships between Policy, Law and Science, that is, the way scientists, jurists, and policy-makers interact defining the 'laws' (scientific hypothesis and legal norms, respectively) that make both our lives and social coexistence possible.[94]

---

[90]Boyd et al. (2016), p. 411; Li et al. (2020).

[91]Vandamme and Pybus (2013), pp. 83, 84.

[92]Kidd (2016), p. 21.

[93]Irwin and Wynne (1996).

[94]Beck (2011), p. 55.

Regarding the use, or misuse, of scientific evidence in court, the establishment of mixed-composition tribunals, putting together jurists and non-legal experts, could be a reasonable solution. However, issues arising from each judiciary case should be addressed with caution and dialectically, without impeding the entrance of scientific issues in trials.[95] Indeed, there is a deep, inevitably epistemological relationship between legal categories (e.g. causality, abduction, reasonable doubt, etc.) and scientific knowledge, and this would require judges and legal scholars to more adequately understand scientific culture and its language.[96]

On the other hand, scientists and experts themselves should improve their communication towards society.[97] Scientific communication should be clear and effective. Above all, a good start could be to no longer address the questions of validity and reliability of scientific claims turning to the simplistic 'true/false' pair.[98] This old-fashioned—we may say positivistic—way to take position still characterises scientific disputes and their transmission to society. Nevertheless, it does not allow lay-persons to understand. Understanding requires accept complexity and constant variability characterising scientific matters. Also, such (mis)communication might induce the same lack of trust in scientific institutions that, on the other side, certain epistemology of uncertainty has fomented during decades increasing relativism, confusion, fanatism, and manipulation.

Acknowledgments The author would like to thank Giacomo Beggio, MD, for his helpful comments and suggestions.

References

Adam BD, Elliott R, Husbands W et al (2008) Effects of the criminalization of HIV transmission in Cuerrier on men reporting unprotected sex with men. Can J Law Soc 23(1–2):137–153. https://scholar.uwindsor.ca/socanthpub/17. Accessed 24 Aug 2019

Albert J, Wahlberg J, Leitner T et al (1994) Analysis of a rape case by direct sequencing of the HIV-1 pol and gag genes. J Virol 68(9):5918–5924. http://jvi.asm.org/cgi/reprint/68/9/5918.pdf. Accessed 24 Aug 2019

Barreda I (2007) Caso Maeso: entre la verdad genética y la certidumbre jurídica. Actualidad del derecho sanitario 138:367–368

Beck U (2011) Conditio humana. Il rischio nell'età globale. Laterza, Bari

Bennett R (2000) Ignorance is bliss? HIV and moral duties and legal duties to forewarn. J Med Ethics 26(1):9–15

Bernard EJ, Azad Y, Vandamme AM et al (2007) HIV forensics: the use of phylogenetic analysis as evidence in criminal investigation of HIV transmission. National AIDS Manual Briefing Papers:1–11. http://ssrn.com/abstract=967915. Accessed 24 Aug 2019

---

[95]See also Locke (2002).

[96]Pulitanò (2007), p. 876; see also Penasa (2016).

[97]See Kramer (2012).

[98]See again Camporesi et al. (2017), p. 23.

Bhandari D, Saxena R, Lemos R et al (2013) HIV: a weapon of crime and its phylogenetic analysis. Int J Curr Res Rev 5(24):16–22. http://www.ijcrr.com/abstract.php?article_id=988. Accessed 24 Aug 2019

Boily MC, Baggaley RF, Wang L et al (2009) Heterosexual risk of HIV-1 infection per sexual act: systematic review and meta-analysis of observational studies. Lancet Infect Dis 9(2):118–129. https://doi.org/10.1016/S1473-3099(09)70021-0

Boyd M, Cooper D, Crock EA et al (2016) Sexual transmission of HIV and the law: an Australian medical consensus statement. Med J Aust 205(9):409–412. https://doi.org/10.5694/mja16.00934

Breitenbach A, Choi Y (2017) Pluralism and the unity of science. Monist 100(3):391–405. https://doi.org/10.1093/monist/onx017

Bunge M (1984) What is pseudoscience? Skept Inq 9:36–46

Burks AW (1946) Peirce's theory of abduction. Philos Sci 13(4):301–306

Camporesi S, Vaccarella M, Davis M (2017) Investigating public trust in expert knowledge: narrative, ethics, and engagement. J Bioeth Inq 14(1):23–30. https://doi.org/10.1007/s11673-016-9767-4

Chen M, Ma Y, Yang C et al (2015) The combination of phylogenetic analysis with epidemiological and serological data to track HIV-1 transmission in a sexual transmission case. PLoS ONE 10(3). https://doi.org/10.1371/journal.pone.0119989

Chigwedere P, Essex M (2010) AIDS denialism and public health practice. AIDS Behav 14 (2):237–247. https://link.springer.com/article/10.1007/s10461-009-9654-7. Accessed 24 Aug 2019

Ciesielski CA, Marianos DW, Schochetman G et al (1994) The 1990 Florida dental investigation: the press and the science. Ann Int Med 121(11):886–888. https://doi.org/10.7326/0003-4819-121-11-199412010-00011

Di Giovine O (2002) Lo statuto epistemologico della causalità penale tra cause sufficienti e condizioni necessarie. Riv It Dir Proc Pen 45(2):634–688

Dodds C, Bourne A, Weait M (2009) Responses to criminal prosecutions for HIV transmission among gay men with HIV in England and Wales. Sex Reprod Health Matt 17(34):135–145. https://doi.org/10.1016/S0968-8080(09)34475-4

Duesberg P (1996) Inventing the AIDS virus. Regnery Publishing, Washington, DC

Duesberg P, Koehnlein C, Rasnick D (2003) The chemical bases of the various AIDS epidemics: recreational drugs, anti-viral chemotherapy and malnutrition. J Biosci 28(4):383–412. https://link.springer.com/article/10.1007/BF02705115. Accessed 24 Aug 2019

Duesberg P, Mandrioli D, McCormack A et al (2011) AIDS since 1984: no evidence for a new, viral epidemic-not even in Africa. Ital J Anat Embryol 116(2):73–92. http://www.ncbi.nlm.nih.gov/pubmed/22303636. Accessed 24 Aug 2019

Earp BD, Darby R (2015) Does science support infant circumcision? Skeptic 25(3):23–30

Esteve Pardo J (2009) El Desconcierto del Leviatán. Política y Derecho ante las Incertidumbres de la Ciencia: Marcial Pons, Barcelona

Falcioni L, Bua L, Tibaldi E et al (2018) Report of final results regarding brain and heart tumors in Sprague-Dawley rats exposed from prenatal life until natural death to mobile phone radiofrequency field representative of a 1.8 GHz GSM base station environmental emission. Environ Res 165:496–503. https://doi.org/10.1016/j.envres.2018.01.037

Federal Circuit Court of Appeals for the District of Columbia, 293 F. 1013 (D.C.Cir. 1923), Frye

Foster C (1998) Of tales, myth, metaphor and metonym. In: Barbour RS, Huby G (eds) Meddling with mythology. AIDS and social construction of knowledge. Routledge, London, pp 144–159

Gijsbers V (2016) Explanatory pluralism and the (dis)Unity of science: the argument from incompatible counterfactual consequences. Front Psych 7(32):1–10. https://doi.org/10.3389/fpsyt.2016.00032

Goertzel T (2010) Conspiracy theories in science. EMBO Rep 11(7):493–499. https://doi.org/10.1038/embor.2010.84
González-Candelas F, Bracho MA, Wróbel B et al (2013) Molecular evolution in court: analysis of a large hepatitis C virus outbreak from an evolving source. BMC Biol 11(76):1–13. http://www.biomedcentral.com/1741-7007/11/76. Accessed 24 Aug 2019
Harde VA (1992) Koch's postulates and the etiology of AIDS: an historical perspective. Hist Philosophy Life Sci 14(2):249–269. https://www.jstor.org/stable/23331663. Accessed 24 Aug 2019
Huber P (1991) Galileo's revenge: junk science in the courtroom. Basic Books, New York
Ilari P, Russo F (2014) Causality. Philosophical theory meets scientific practice. Oxford University Press, Oxford
Irwin A, Wynne B (eds) (1996) Misunderstanding science? The public reconstruction of science and technology. Cambridge University Press, Cambridge
Jasanoff S (1995) Science at the bar law. Science, and technology in America. Harvard University Press, Cambridge
Jin F, Prestage GP, Imrie J et al (2010) Anal sexually transmitted infections and risk of HIV infection in homosexual men. J Acquir Immune Defic Syndr 53(1):144–149. https://doi.org/10.1097/QAI.0b013e3181b48f33
Jones N (2018) Inference to the more robust explanation. Br J Philosophy Sci 69:75–102
Kalichman SC (2009) Denying AIDS: conspiracy theories, pseudoscience, and human tragedy. Springer, New York. https://link.springer.com/book/10.1007/978-0-387-79476 1. Accessed 24 Aug 2019
Kearns CE, Schmidt LA, Glantz SA (2016) Sugar industry and coronary heart disease research. A historical analysis of internal industry documents. JAMA Int Med 176(11):1680–1685. http://archinte.jamanetwork.com/article.aspx?articleid=2548255. Accessed 24 Aug 2019
Kidd P (2016) Phylogenetic analysis as expert evidence in HIV transmission prosecutions. HIV Aust 14(1):21-24. https://bit.ly/2MDFVAc. Accessed 24 Aug 2019
Kramer D (2012) Scientists share blame for public's ignorance of science. Phys Today 65(7):23–24. https://doi.org/10.1063/PT.3.1635
Kuhn TS (1970) The structure of scientific revolutions. The University of Chicago Press, Chicago
Lazzarini Z, Galletly CL, Mykhalovskiy E et al (2013) Criminalization of HIV transmission and exposure: research and policy Agenda. Am J Public Health 103(8):1350–1353. https://doi.org/10.2105/AJPH.2013.301267
LeBel EP, McCarthy RJ, Earp BD et al (2018) A unified framework to quantify the credibility of scientific findings. Adv Methods Pract Psychol Sci 1(3):389–402. https://doi.org/10.1177/2515245918787489
Li W-Y, Huang S-W, Wang SF et al (2020) Source identification of HIV-1 transmission in three lawsuits using ultra-deep pyrosequencing and phylogenetic analysis. J Microbiol Immunol Infect. https://doi.org/10.1016/j.jmii.2019.12.002
Livingstone DN (2003) Putting science in its place. Geographies of scientific knowledge. The University of Chicago Press, Chicago
Locke S (2002) The public understanding of science: a rhetorical invention. Sci Technol Human Values 27(1):87–111. https://doi.org/10.1177/016224390202700104. Accessed 24 Aug 2019
Mangosing DA (2015) HIV-positive: exploring the communicative messages of HIV in a Post-AIDS Era. Paper presented at the International Association for Media and Communication Research (IAMCR) 2015 conference at Montreal, Canada. https://bit.ly/33XegQm. Accessed 24 Aug 2019
Masera L (2008) Contagio da Aids e diritto penale: alcuni spunti di riflessione. Dir Pen Proc 9:1174–1183
McCormick S (2007) Democratizing science movements. A new framework for mobilization and contestation. Soc Stud Sci 37(4):609–623. https://doi.org/10.1177/0306312707076598
Mehta SR, Schairer C, Little S et al (2019) Ethical issues in HIV phylogenetics and molecular epidemiology. Curr Opin HIV AIDS 14(3):221–226. https://doi.org/10.1097/COH.0000000000000538

Metzker ML, Mindell DP, Liu XM et al (2002) Molecular evidence of HIV-1 transmission in a criminal case. PNAS 99(22):14292–14297. https://doi.org/10.1073/pnas.222522599

Miotto G (2015) Stepchild adoption omoparentale ed interesse del minore. Dir Civ Cont 2(2)

Miyashita Ochoa A, Cordero L, Pulsipher C et al (2019) California HIV Laws. https://www.californiaaidsresearch.org/topic-areas/hiv-laws_final.pdf

Mykhalovskiy E, Betteridge G (2012) Who? What? Where? When? And with what consequences? An analysis of criminal cases of HIV non-disclosure in Canada. Can J Law Soc 27(1):31–53. https://doi.org/10.3138/cjls.27.1.031

O'Brien TL (2018) Beyond reliable: challenging and deciding expert admissibility in U.S. civil courts. Law Probab Risk 17(1):29–44. https://doi.org/10.1093/lpr/mgx010

O'Briena SJ, Goedert JJ (1996) HIV causes AIDS: Koch's postulates fulfilled. Curr Opin Immunol 8(5):613–618. https://doi.org/10.1016/S0952-7915(96)80075-6

Pardo MS, Allen RJ (2008) Juridical proof and the best explanation. Law Philos 27(3):223–268. https://doi.org/10.1007/s10982-007-9016-4

Patel P, Borkowf CB, Brooks JT et al (2014) Estimating per-act HIV transmission risk: a systematic review. AIDS 28(10):1509–1519. https://doi.org/10.1097/QAD.0000000000000298

Patterson CJ (2006) Children of Lesbian and Gay parents. Curr Dir Psychol Sci 15(5):241–244. https://doi.org/10.1111/j.1467-8721.2006.00444.x

Peirce CS (1935) Collected papers of Charles Sanders Peirce, vol 6. Belknap Press, Cambridge

Penasa S (2016) The "scientific questions" in the dynamic between judiciary and legislative discretion. A comparative study on the case-law of national, international and supranational courts. BioLaw J (1):39–79. https://bit.ly/2NqmTgu. Accessed 24 Aug 2019

Perin A (2014) The crisis of the "nomological model" between explanation and foreseeability in criminal Law. Introductory notes and preliminary issues on criminal negligence. Riv It Dir Proc Pen 57(3):1371–1409

Pillay D, Rambaut A, Geretti AM et al (2007) HIV phylogenetics: criminal convictions relying solely on this to establish transmission are unsafe. Br Med J 335(7618):460. https://doi.org/10.1136/bmj.39315.398843.BE

Popper K (2002) The logic of scientific discovery. Routledge, London

Poropatich K, Sullivan DJ (2011) Human immunodeficiency virus type 1 long-term non-progressors: the viral, genetic and immunological basis for disease non-progression. J Gen Virol 92(2):247–268. https://doi.org/10.1099/vir.0.027102-0

Preda A (2005) AIDS, rhetoric, and medical knowledge. Cambridge University Press, Cambridge

Pulitanò D (2007) Il diritto penale fra vincoli di realtà e sapere scientifico. In: Scritti per Federico Stella. Jovene, Napoli, pp 851–890

Rabin RL (2004) Reliance on scientific evidence in tort litigation: the U.S. experience. In: Comandé G, Ponzanelli G (eds) Scienza e diritto nel prisma del diritto comparato. Giappichelli, Torino, pp 125–138

Ravetz J (2004) The post-normal science of precaution. Futures 36(3):347–357. https://doi.org/10.1016/S0016-3287(03)00160-5

Richman DD, Fischl MA, Grieco MH et al (1987) The toxicity of Azidothymidine (AZT) in the treatment of patients with AIDS and AIDS-related complex. N Engl J Med 317:192–197. https://doi.org/10.1056/NEJM198707233170402

Risinger M (2007) The irrelevance, and central relevance, of the boundary between science and non-science in the evaluation of expert witness reliability. Villanova Law Rev 52(4):679–722

Ruggiero M, Galletti MP, Pacini S (2009) On the risk of contracting AIDS at the dissection table. Ital J Anat Embryol 114(2-3):97–108. http://www.ncbi.nlm.nih.gov/pubmed/20198822. Accessed 24 Aug 2019

Ryu PK (1958) Causation in criminal law. Univ Pa Law Rev 106(6):773–805. http://www.jstor.org/stable/3310397

Scaduto DI, Brown JM, Haaland WC et al (2010) Source identification in two criminal cases using phylogenetic analysis of HIV-1 DNA sequences. PNAS 107(50):21242–21247. https://doi.org/10.1073/pnas.1015673107

Schumm WR (2016) A review and critique of research on same-sex parenting and adoption. Psychol Rep 119(3):641–760. https://doi.org/10.1177/0033294116665594

Sidky H (2018) The war on science, anti-intellectualism, and 'alternative ways of knowing' in 21st-century America. Skept Inq 42(2):38–43. https://bit.ly/2PczIxq. Accessed 24 Aug 2019

Siedner MJ, Tumarkin E, Bogoch II (2018) HIV post-exposure prophylaxis (PEP). BMJ:363. https://doi.org/10.1136/bmj.k4928

Singh AE, Tan D, Hull M (2018) Canadian guidelines on HIV pre-exposure prophylaxis (PrEP) and non-occupational post-exposure prophylaxis (PEP): discussion beyond the guidelines and commentary on the role of infectious diseases specialists. Jammi 3(4). https://doi.org/10.3138/jammi.2018-0024

Summerer K (2001) Contagio sessuale da virus HIV e responsabilità penale dell'Aids-carrier. Riv It Dir Proc Pen 44(1):299–330

Supreme Court, 509 U.S. 579, 1993, Daubert v. Merrel Dow Pharmaceuticals, Inc

Supreme Court of Cassation, united sections, 11.09.2002, No. 30328, Franzese

Supreme Court of Cassation, section IV, 17.09.2010 – 13.12.2010, No. 43786, Cozzini et al

Svalastog AL, Allgaier J, Gajović S (2015) Navigating knowledge landscapes: on health, science, communication, media, and society. Croat Med J 56(4):321–323. https://doi.org/10.3325/cmj.2015.56.321

Tallacchini MC (2005) Before and beyond the precautionary principle: epistemology of uncertainty in science and law. Toxicol Appl Pharmacol 207(2 suppl):645–651. https://doi.org/10.1016/j.taap.2004.12.029

The Editors of The Lancet (2010) Retraction—Ileal-lymphoid-nodular hyperplasia, non-specific colitis, and pervasive developmental disorder in children. Lancet 375(9713):445. https://doi.org/10.1016/S0140-6736(10)60175-4

Tomasi M (2016) Jurisdictional and scientific uniformity: how to make pluralism sustainable. BioLaw J 1:81–103. https://bit.ly/33XBAgF. Accessed 24 Aug 2019

Tuzet G (2006) La prima inferenza. L'abduzione di C. S. Peirce fra scienza e diritto. Giappichelli, Torino

Vandamme AM, Pybus OG (2013) Viral phylogeny in court: the unusual case of the Valencian anesthetist. BMC Biol 11(83). https://doi.org/10.1186/1741-7007-11-83

Viganò F (2013) Il rapporto di causalità nella giurisprudenza penale a dieci anni dalla sentenza Franzese. Dir Pen Cont - Riv Trim 3:380–398. https://dpc-rivistatrimestrale.criminaljusticenetwork.eu/pdf/DPC_Trim_3_2013-386-404.pdf. Accessed 28 Jun 2021

Villa V (1984) Teorie della scienza giuridica e teorie delle scienze naturali. Modelli e analogie. Giuffrè, Milano

Villa V (2005) Il diritto come modello per le scienze naturali. Dir & Quest Pubbl 5:31–41. http://www.dirittoequestionipubbliche.org/page/2005_n5/mono_V_Villa.pdf. Accessed 24 Aug 2019

Vineis P (1990) Modelli di rischio. Epidemiologia e causalità. Einaudi, Torino

Weait M (2005) Knowledge, Autonomy and Consent: R. v Konzani. Crim Law Rev:763–772

Wilton J (2012) Putting a number on it: The risk from an exposure to HIV. Prevention in Focus. https://www.catie.ca/en/pif/summer-2012/putting-number-it-risk-exposure-hiv. Accessed 24 Aug 2019

Wyde M, Cesta M, Blystone C et al (2018) Report of Partial findings from the National Toxicology Program Carcinogenesis Studies of Cell Phone Radiofrequency Radiation in Hsd: Sprague Dawley® SD rats (Whole Body Exposure). https://doi.org/10.1101/055699

Reproductive Rights in Italy

Elena Falletti

Abstract The intervention of medicine in human reproduction (contraception, abortion, artificial procreation) has blurred the boundaries between nature and culture regarding the beginning of human life. This change has led to an unprecedented possibility to increase self-determination, and, therefore, individual responsibility with respect to the choice of giving birth, no longer a gift of God, but a realistic chance to accomplish a wish. This circumstance has opened a debate as to whether or not the right to parenthood and procreation is absolute, and if the person has the right to choose whether or not to conceive. Indeed, the Italian debate is related to two specular aspects of the same issue concerning the alleged absolute inviolability of the embryo: on the one hand, the request of infertile couples to be able to conceive a child through assisted reproduction, including through the use of biological materials external to the couple, subject to rulings of the Constitutional Court, and on the other hand, on the still controversial access to abortion, governed by a law that came into force in 1978, over 40 years ago.

In light of these considerations, the relationship between pluralism, religion, culture and jurisdiction on contraception, abortion, assisted reproduction, and childbirth will be analysed, with particular attention placed on the influence of conscientious objection, which is allowed under certain conditions by Italian law, and how it is used as a boycotting tool by certain professional categories in relation to individual choices.

E. Falletti (✉)
University Carlo Cattaneo-LIUC, Castellanza, Italy
e-mail: efalletti@liuc.it

L. Busatta, C. Casonato (eds.), *Axiological Pluralism*, Ius Gentium: Comparative Perspectives on Law and Justice 92, https://doi.org/10.1007/978-3-030-78475-1_11

1 Self-determination in Reproductive Rights: Contraception and Sterilisation

1.1 Contraception

Human fertility control is one of the most debated topics in legal pluralism under the cultural and social influence concerning parenting choices.[1] In this perspective, recognising the right to have access to contraception was the first step towards the liberalisation of female bodies from male domination, and, thus, to recognising the equality of women.[2] In Italy, this step was accomplished by Law No. 194 of 1978 "on social protection of motherhood and voluntary interruption of pregnancy", which represented a compromise between political, religious and moral values. At the same time, this law repealed some specific crimes against contraception as "procured impediment to procreation"[3] while "incitement to practices against procreation"[4] and "abortion of a consenting woman"[5] were declared unconstitutional by the Constitutional Court.[6] Indeed, parenting choices regard both sexes, and both prospective parents may decide whether to become parents or not, even before sexual intercourse, through the use of contraceptives and sterilisation.

Religious influence is very strong,[7] not only because of the well-known biblical words "*And you, be ye fruitful, and multiply*",[8] but also because it is particularly persistent in a country with a steady Catholic culture,[9] which at the time expressed a significant political majority linked to the "Christian Democrats", the Catholic-inspired party.

Regarding female contraception, monotheistic religions, especially Christianity, affirm that sexual abstinence is the only reliable form of contraception.[10] On the other hand, there has been a very intense juridical debate on the "morning-after pill".[11] In fact, Catholic believers consider that human life begins from conception,

---

[1]Ferrando (1994), p. 12; Malinowski (2006), p. 550; Prasad (2012), p. 230; Balistreri (2016), p. 25; Zaret (2016), p. 1833.

[2]Coontz and Henderson (1986), p. 35; Reeves Sanday (1991), p. 5; Heritier (2002).

[3]Former Article No. 552, Criminal Code, "Procurata impotenza alla procreazione". It was declared unconstitutional by Constitutional Court, 16 March 1971, No. 47. Betta (2012), p. 131.

[4]Former Article No. 553 Criminal Code, "Incitamento di pratiche contro la procreazione".

[5]Former Article No 546, "Aborto di donna consenziente". Nuvolone and Lanzi (1992), p. 33.

[6]Constitutional Court, 18 February 1975, No. 27.

[7]Foucault (1984), p. 19.

[8]King James Bible, KJV, Genesis 9:7.

[9]Zizola (1991), p. 240.

[10]Thornton (1985), p. 383 ss; Srikanthan and Reid (2008), p. 130; Maternini and Scopel (2012), p. 28.

[11]Decree No. 510 of 26 September 2000 of the Health Ministry authorizing commercialization of Norlevo (well-known as "Morning after pill"). TAR Lazio, 21 November 2011. See in this volume Paris, Reckoning with Growing Pluralism. Potentials and Limits of Conscientious Objection:

with the union of the egg and spermatozoid,[12] an act which is impeded by emergency contraception. According to this opinion, preventing the implantation of the fertilised egg constitutes termination of pregnancy, and, therefore, could give rise to conscientious objection by the pharmacist who must sell the "morning-after" pill.[13]

Conscientious objection is a case provided for in Article 9 of Law 194/1978 on abortion. It gives the faculty to gynaecologists, but not of pharmacists, who have a purely executive role in medical services. However, legal scholars of Catholic inspiration have much discussed this issue and some bills have been submitted to Parliament[14] so far unsucessfully.[15] On this issue, a relevant administrative court[16] affirmed that the "morning-after" pill merely acts with contraceptive effects at an earlier stage of ovum implanting in the womb, so it has to be excluded from the field of application of the law on abortion and, therefore, from conscientious objection.[17]

1.2 Sterilisation

Sterilisation pertains to a very sensitive juridical area. Indeed, historical experience has shown terrible cases of planned eugenic sterilisation;[18] although in this case, I refer only to individual choice in this matter, made by persons able to make a decision, because those unable to do so are subject to Law 9 January 2004, No. 6, which requires a court decision.[19]

For persons who are able to give legal consent, sterilisation has shifted between the self-determination principle and the prohibition of acts of disposition of his or her own body that could involve a permanent reduction of physical integrity or, if contrary to law, public order or morality according to Article No. 5 of the Civil Code.[20] The Italian Supreme Court of Cassation affirmed that voluntary sterilisation is legally allowed under both criminal and civil perspectives,[21] and both for male

Conscience Clauses in Abortion Laws in Europe, section 2; Boni (2001), p. 677 ss; Pellecchia (2010), p. 31 ss.; Benciolini (2015), p. II, 3 ss.

[12]Wojtyla (1995), p. I, 11.

[13]Comitato Nazionale per la Bioetica (2011), p. 10.

[14]Lalli (2011), p. 118; Benciolini (2015), p. 2003.

[15]XVI Parliament (2008–2013), Bill No. 1212; XVII Parliament (2013–2018), Bill No. 1087; XVIII Parliament (2018-2023) Bill No. 22, Bill No. 183; Bill No. 1066; Bill No. 1664.

[16]T.A.R. Lazio, II sez., 12 October 2001, No. 8465.

[17]Cassano (2002), p. 20751.

[18]Casonato (2004), p. 841.

[19]Aprile and Benciolini (2011), p. 795.

[20]Facci (2004), p. 155.

[21]Cass. Pen., 18 June 1987, No. 7425 in [1998] Foro it., II, 447.

vasectomy[22] and female tubal sterilisation.[23] This surgery, even though invasive, does not conflict with Article No. 32 of the Italian Constitution protecting the fundamental right to health. Rather it is the correct interpretation key of Article No. 5 c.c. In fact, physical integrity and protection of health do not always coincide, since the state of good mental and physical health may require interventions on physical integrity,[24] including sterilisation, as, for example, in the case of those who suffer gender dysphoria.[25] The lawfulness of so-called voluntary, or "hedonistic", sterilisation[26] is more dubious but a court of first instance[27] affirmed that it represents an expression of the principle of self-determination as a fundamental right, according to Articles No. 2 (protection of dignity) and No. 13 (protection of freedom) of the Italian Constitution.[28]

In other cases, after a series of pregnancies, a woman may decide to undergo tubal sterilisation surgery.[29] The operation could fail and consequently the woman could claim compensation for pecuniary damages for undergoing an unwanted pregnancy and for the cost of child support (this situation is different from wrongful life, which will be discussed in the section concerning abortion). Associated to this, there is a non-patrimonial right, protected by Articles No. 2, 13 and 32 of the Constitution, to not have personal choices unlawfully interfered with, i.e. those expressing the most intimate personal and individual freedoms, such as choices pertaining to parenting and motherhood. In this case, this choice involves not only the woman as a mother, but also the man (her partner or husband) as a father. The damage comes from the fact that the couple has been deprived of their right, in accordance with the provisions of Law no. 194/1978 (Article No. 1), to affect the fate of the pregnancy as a right to family planning.[30]

Elements of pluralism are welfare policies,[31] such as the presence of family counselling[32] and nurseries. The former is important for managing the reproductive health of minors with medical counselling[33] and the prescription of contraceptives. The latter could support child education and management for working mothers. Both

---

[22]App. Roma Sez. III, 14 November 2006.

[23]Cass. sez. III 24.10.2013 No. 24109.

[24]Cass. Pen. 18 June 1987, cit.

[25]The Italian Constitutional Court affirmed that a gender reassignment surgery is no longer mandatory for the purposes of sex change on the birth certificate. This is consistent with constitutional values that allow the person involved to choose the way to achieve his/her transition path with the assistance of specialists, in order to compose properly his/her gender identity (Constitutional Court, 5 November 2015, No. 221). See Mauceri (2018), p. 1475.

[26]Comitato Nazionale per la Bioetica (1998), p. 18.

[27]Trib. Venezia, 10 September 2002.

[28]Aprile and Benciolini (2011), p. 795.

[29]Trib. Reggio Emilia, 7 October 2015.

[30]Sardella (2015), p. 617.

[31]Spallarossa (2011), p. 1388.

[32]Law 29 July 1975, No. 405.

[33]T.A.R. Emilia-Romagna, 29 January 1981, No. 30.

are subject to a strong spending review policy that is already having negative effects on family planning.

2 Abortion

Until 1975 abortion was a crime in Italy under Article No. 546 of the Penal Code (Abortion by a consenting woman). The Constitutional Court established its unconstitutionality since it did not allow pregnancy interruption in the case of harm or serious risk to the health of the mother.[34] The Constitutional Court affirmed that the protection of the unborn child could not be placed among the fundamental rights protected by Article No. 2 of the Constitution, although the foetus deserves a specific protection with special features.[35] However, there is no equivalence between the right to life and health of existing people, like the mother, and right to life of a prospective person that is not yet born, i.e. the embryo. Balancing law and morality and giving a sort of monition to Parliament in order to protect women's right to health, the Constitutional Court opened the doors to the promulgation of Law 22nd May 1978, No. 194, which allowed abortion. Article No. 1 of the law implemented the guideline suggested by the Constitutional Court itself, and represents a sort of bridge between the directions of the Court and the intentions of Parliament. It states that the right to conscientious and responsible procreation is guaranteed. On the other hand, this law recognises the social value of motherhood and the protection of human life from its beginning.

Under a comparative perspective, the Italian Parliament discarded the long-standing American model,[36] related to a significant preference given to privacy protection understood as a prospective mother's absolute freedom to self-determination.[37] Instead, it arranged a solution inspired in part by the German model,[38] which protects women's health, and in part by the French one,[39] oriented towards protecting women from a distressing situation.[40] Indeed, Article No. 4 of the Law 194/1978 states that voluntary pregnancy interruption should be performed within 90 days from conception in "*circumstances for which the continuation of pregnancy, childbirth or motherhood would entail a serious risk to [the mother's] physical or*

[34]Constitutional Court 18 February 1975, No. 27.

[35]Pellecchia (2010), p. 31 ss.

[36]Bognetti (1991), p. 1 ss.; Rizzieri (2001), p. II, 228 ss.

[37]Pellecchia (2010), p. 31 ss.; Reingold and Gostin (2019), p. 21. However, the heritage of the American Supreme Court historical decision Roe v. Wade (410 U.S. 113 (1973)) seems to be under discussion by conservative laws approved in Georgia, Ohio, Kentucky, Mississippi and Louisiana, and the conservative orientation showed by the Supreme Court Justices nominated by President Trump in 2017 (Justice Gorsuch), 2018 (Justice Kavanaugh), and 2020 (Justice Coney Barrett).

[38]Pellecchia (2010), p. 31 ss.

[39]Sliger (2004), p. 229.

[40]Pellecchia (2010), p. 31 ss.

mental health, or in relation to her state of health, or her economic or social or family condition, or the circumstances in which conception occurred, or predictions of anomalies or malformations of the unborn child".[41]

Law No. 194/1978 stresses that voluntary termination of pregnancy is not a means of birth control. It also indicates the necessary measures to prevent abortion with serious investigation into risks for the mother's physical and psychological health if she carries through with her pregnancy. Under this view, the legitimacy of abortion must be connected to the prior assessment of the reasons that drive the woman to this choice.[42] Indeed, the Italian legal system as a whole recognises that the unborn has the possibility of becoming a rights holder (Article No.1 c.c., par. 2). In fact, some of the Civil Code provisions are dictated for the conceived child's inheritance (Article No. 462, par.1 of the Civil Code) and donation (Article No. 784, par. 1 of the Civil Code) rights. Forms of legal protection of the unborn child are also provided for in other laws, such as the law on medically assisted reproduction, No. 40/2004, section 3 of which contains "*provisions relating to the protection of the unborn child*"; Law No. 405/1975 establishes medical counselling services which refer to the right to health of unborn children recognised by Article No. 32 of the Constitution; and finally the abovementioned Law No 194/1978 attests that human life is protected from its beginning. Similar protection for the unborn child is recognised by the Supreme Court, which, in addressing the projected compensatory damages, has repeatedly considered a person not yet born at the time of the tort commission worthy of receiving damage restoration.[43]

From the legislative point of view, especially from the perspective of Article 4 of Law No. 194/1978, access to abortion is not an absolute right, as the Italian legal system allows for the possibility of abortion only in specific cases. However, this possibility is still controversial, as shown by a constitutional controversy[44] raised by a court of merit after the "Brüstle"[45] decision of the European Court of Justice on embryo stem cell patentability. It was applied in a case concerning an underage girl who wanted to interrupt her pregnancy without her parents' consent. The court of first instance justified its claim to the Constitutional Court affirming that forbidding human embryo destruction is equivalent to establishing, under the fundamental principles of European Union law, the absolute disvalue of the human embryo loss due to a conscious human act, even if carried out by invoking requirements of scientific progress. Thus, this represents the not very implicit affirmation of the legal existence of a subject, the "*human embryo which, in any case, must find protection in an absolute form*".[46] However, the Court of first instance's reference to the CJEU decision in Brüstle is inappropriate. First of all, because abortion is a matter of

---

[41] Article No. 4, Law No.194/1978. Translation by the author.

[42] Constitutional Court, 18 February 1975, No. 27.

[43] Court of Cassation, 8 August 2014, No. 17811.

[44] Constitutional Court, 19 July 2012, No. 196. See Scalera (2012), p. 977.

[45] Case C-34/10 Oliver Brüstle v. Greenpeace eV. [2011] ECR 2011 I-09821.

[46] Trib. Spoleto, 3 January 2012.

national law, and secondly because the judge extended a principle pertaining to patentability to the balance of interest between the rights of the mother and the rights of the embryo. In fact, the embryo is considered by the referring court as having an "*independent legal subjectivity for which the legal system must take responsibility*". This is an element that goes beyond what is stated, albeit symbolically, by Article No. 1 of the law 19 February 2004 No. 40, concerning the "*Rules on medically assisted procreation*", which "*ensure the rights of all parties involved, including those of the unborn child*". Conversely, the court of first instance did not consider the constitutional rights of the mother, her self-determination nor her privacy. In this specific case, she is a person already holding legal capacity, though not yet provided with the legal capacity to act. The Constitutional Court declared the claim manifestly inadmissible under the counter-limits theory.[47] The Constitutional court did not even take into consideration the legal arguments relating to absolute protection of the embryo. Indeed, it reiterated that the power of the magistrate in cases such as these is not qualified as a co-decision-making power, since such decision is only under the responsibility of women. The magistrate must only ensure that the conditions of the woman who takes such a decision are of full moral freedom.[48]

Latterly, the Italian debate on abortion has intensified because of the introduction of the RU468 pill. To be effective, the pill must be administered within 49 days of conception. However, the use of this drug has caused a new wave of objections and criticisms that it would make abortion "easy and hasty". These arguments reflect a prejudice about women's choices.[49] The abortion pill is to be administered in strict compliance with the provisions of the law No 194/1978; otherwise, the crime of procured abortion may apply according to Articles No. 5 and 8 of Law No 194/1978.[50]

3 The Debate on Abortion and Wrongful Life

The problem regarding the protection of the unborn child also gives rise to a much debated issue in comparative law in terms of the admissibility of legal action for wrongful life. This issue concerns the situation of a severely disabled child who may sue the physician or the healthcare structure (through a legal guardian, generally his or her parents) for failing to prevent the child's birth. It assumes that if the parents had had appropriate information about his or her health condition, they—especially the mother—would have interrupted the pregnancy.[51]

[47]Caponi (2011), p. 915 ss.

[48]Constitutional Court 19 July 2012, No. 196, cit.

[49]Pellecchia (2010), p. 31 ss.

[50]Court of Cassation, 30 September 2011, No. 44107, Dir. Pen. e Processo [2012] 2 153.

[51]Court of Cassation, 6 July 2020, No.13881. See Poiatti (2021), p. 89 ss.

Omitted information could refer both to a pre-existing disease, even genetic, and not diagnosed in time, and as a result of medical malpractice. The Italian legal system imported suggestions from both common law and civil law. Indeed, it is not possible to find a common trend in judicial decisions concerning wrongful life at a comparative level, and the compensation line seems to follow the division between common law (where it seems to be prevalent) and civil law (in which it is generally denied).[52] Italian scholars are divided,[53] while the prevailing case law has often agreed to compensate the tort of wrongful life to disabled children for both pecuniary and non-pecuniary damages.[54] On this point, some scholars stressed that the restoration of a liability related to the "right not to be born" of the foetus is inconceivable, since the Italian legal system is oriented to protect, directly or indirectly, the right of both mother and child for the best childbirth possible. Affirming wrongful life as a tort would be in contrast with the principle of solidarity stated by Article No.2 of the Italian Constitution and the principle of unavailability of one's body according to Article No. 5 of the Italian Civil Code.

This legal approach was confirmed by the most pertinent decision of the Supreme Court of Cassation in 2015. The Court of Cassation affirmed that in the case of genetic malformation the wrongful life damage to the child attributable to medical negligence is not compensable. Indeed, the difficulties of life that genetic illnesses could cause to disabled children must be faced through social care assistance. The Court of Cassation explained that attributing a wrongful life compensation to civil liability would lead to a distortion of the tort system itself, since this compensation would replace the care that is the resposibility of social services.[55] However, courts recognise pecuniary and non-pecuniary loss to both parents for the expenses and stress due to raising a disabled child from his or her birth.[56]

Embryos and foetuses are "objects" protected by Italian laws as fundamental values pertaining to human life,[57] around which the Constitution is entirely focused. However, some clarification is due. As a relevant scholarly opinion observed,[58] embryos and foetuses are "living matter", they are human life, but not yet human beings. "*Just treating intrauterine life as a body part, as a complex of living human cells, could help to detach from the misunderstanding that has to do with the personification of a human archetype*".[59] Embryos and foetuses are both living entities that "physically" receive life from another body, and this process demands

[52]Baudouin (2005), p. 1175; Mastrorilli (2013), p. 343; Piraino (2016), p. 450.

[53]Gorgoni (2009), p. 2075; Gerbi and Sardella (2013), p. 1221; Mussi (2014), p. 293.

[54]Court of Cassation, 27 November 2015, No. 24220.

[55]Court of Cassation, 22 December 2015, No. 25767.

[56]Court of Cassation, 5 February 2018, No 2675; Court of Cassation, 29 January 2018, No. 2070; Court of Cassation, 11 April 2017, No. 9251; Trib. Perugia, 9 June 2017. See Carbone (2018), p. 923.

[57]Mazzoni (2016), p. 461 ss.

[58]Mazzoni (2016), cit.

[59]Mazzoni (2016), cit.

protection, which is ensured by the constitutional system as their own proper and original interest.[60] In this perspective, the Supreme Court of Cassation's decision is fair and correct: the disabled child cannot sue for tort liability, not even for his or her interest to have a family properly prepared to willingly care for him or her, since the legal system does not contemplate a tort related to "wrongful life", nor could the child's life represent a "consequent liability" of the physician's omission.[61]

4 The Law on Medically Assisted Reproduction: A Judicial Reshaping

After a perennial social and political debate on medically assisted reproduction (hereinafter "MAR"), the Italian Parliament approved the law of 19 February 2004 No. 40 (hereinafter "law 40/2004") "Rules on medically assisted procreation". Its wording is characterised by a strong influence of a religious and prohibitionist approach and allows for only sterile and infertile heterosexual married or cohabiting couples to access medical support in conception. The original text of law 40/2004 established strict limitations to parenting choices and medical discretion, fully adhering to the Catholic Church Magisterium, although it does not represent the moral conscience of the Italian population as a whole. However, this law oriented the whole regulatory framework; indeed, it constitutes one of the strong breaches of state secularism.[62] Even though respect and consideration are due to individual conscience, imposing a public ethic not shared by all members of a community constitutes an unacceptable abuse. Following its entry into force, Law No 40/2004 has been subjected both to an abrogative referendum and to several challenges in courts. The abrogative referendum was invalid because of its failure to reach the quorum,[63] whereas the judicial path has been longer and more difficult, including the intervention of both the Italian Constitutional Court and the European Court of Human Rights. In fact, law No 40/2004 has been reshaped by several focused interventions of case law decisions, supported also by lay and human rights associations. The three main controversial issues of law No 40/2004 that have been subjected to judicial review by European and Constitutional courts on different occasions are: 1. the implanting of three embryos into the uterus of the prospective mother in a single, mandatory and simultaneous surgical procedure, while forbidding the physician to make any evaluation on the impact of this intervention on the would-be mother's health; 2. the prohibition of genetic preimplantation diagnosis for fertile prospective parents that are healthy carriers of a genetic disease; 3. gamete donation.

[60]Mazzoni (2016), cit.

[61]Court of Cassation, 22 December 2015, No. 25767.

[62]Pugliese (2011), p. 32.

[63]Veronesi (2005), p. 14.

Regarding the first point, on the one hand, law 40/2004 breached women's self-determination regarding health protection and regarding the decision to become a mother, imposing the implantation of three embryos to develop in pregnancy. On the other hand, it does not allow physicians to properly evaluate each case of artificial procreation according to the health condition of each mother-to-be in the light of the physician's experience and the latest scientific knowledge on the matter. The Constitutional Court declared Article 14 of the law 40/2004 unconstitutional, relating to the words "one single and simultaneous implantation, and in any case not more than three" under Article No. 3 of the Constitution, because it breached both principles of equality and reasonableness, as law 40/2004 reserved the same treatment to dissimilar situations. At the same time, the Constitutional Court affirmed that this mandatory embryo implantation could potentially harm the mother-to-be and embryos under Article 32 of the Constitution.[64] Scholars were divided in their reactions: some of them affirmed that this judgment re-established the protection of the mother-to-be, while others declared that it would allow embryos to be murdered, forgetting that an embryo is human matter although not a fully-formed human person, as the Constitutional Court itself explained in its constant case law[65] on limiting the legislative discretion in the field of scientific research and medicine.

The second point is related to Preimplantation Genetic Diagnosis (hereinafter PGD), which is a diagnostic technique based on the isolation of embryos, allowing for the identification of defects that can cause genetic diseases in the blastomere cell structure.[66] It is strongly contested by the followers of the doctrine of the inviolability of the embryo because of doubts about the morality of medical intervention on human embryonic material, even if it is oriented towards caring for the embryo itself. In fact, according to that vision, the embryo can be defined as a project of person[67] that has the potential to become a human being from the time of formation of the zygote. Therefore, the embryo should be entitled to the same level of full protection reserved for persons themselves. Even though Article No. 1 of the Law ensures the "conceived", as a formed person, has the same rights as all parties involved in the medically assisted procreation process,[68] scholars and courts argued that this provision has a "purely declaratory value".[69] The challenged prohibition concerns access of fertile couples who are healthy carriers of serious genetic disorders to this diagnostic tool. After much restrictive case law, the turning point came from the European Court of Human Rights, regarding the Costa and Pavan case.[70] The

---

[64]Constitutional Court, 8 May 2009, No. 151. See the English Translation available on http://www.cortecostituzionale.it/documenti/download/doc/recent_judgments/CC_SS_151_2009_EN.pdf.

[65]Constitutional Court, 14 November 2003, No. 338; Id., 19 June 2002, No. 282; Id., 26 May 1998, No.185; Id., 20 March 1978, No. 20.

[66]Pavone (2011), p. 99; Santosuosso (2011), p. 179.

[67]Wojtyla (1995), p. I,11.

[68]Santosuosso (2011), p. 179.

[69]Costitutional Court 28 January 2005, No. 48.

[70]Costa and Pavan v. Italy, app no 54270/2010 (ECHR, 28 August 2012).

applicants were a heterosexual married couple who were healthy carriers of cystic fibrosis. They had already generated a daughter suffering from the disease and the woman had had an abortion of a foetus suffering from the same disease, which had been diagnosed in the foetus in early pregnancy.[71] In front of the ECtHR, the Italian Government apodictically assumed that PGD assures the protection of the unborn child and maternal health, the guarantees of ethics and freedom of conscience of involved medical practitioners, and it represents a strong limit against eugenics-type practices. The ECtHR refused this argument, countering that according to Article No. 8, par. 2 of the European Convention of Human Rights, equating an embryo grown in vitro and a born child is not sustainable.[72] Additionally, the Strasbourg judges, who unanimously signed the decision, emphasised that this issue was not about being entitled to having healthy children whose strong genetic traits are contained in pre-selected embryos, or requested by the applicants, since the risk of disease would persist unchanged, there remaining unknown elements during pregnancy due to the presence of other pathologies.[73] Subsequently, the Italian Constitutional Court followed the ECtHR decision, indeed stressing that the abolished regulation did not allow the woman to have proper information about the embryo's health before implanting it in her womb. Allowing PGD should prevent an *ex post* decision more damaging for the prospective mother's health, while the diseased embryo remains exposed to the risk of abortion.[74] Following the Constitutional Court decision, however, there were very few cases in which courts allowed PGD.[75]

As regards the division between biological and legal truth, a deep attachment to tradition is challenged by technology. Under this perspective, heterologous fertilisation through both male and female gamete donations to sterile and infertile prospective parents formed by heterosexual couples was prohibited according to the former Article No. 4 Paragraph No. 3 of the Law 40/2004.[76] The Constitutional Court banned this prohibition, arguing that it damaged the parents' freedom of self-determination both from the physical perspective, for couples where one was absolutely sterile or infertile, and from the economic perspective, because it constituted a different treatment according to the economic capacity, to the advantage of couples who can have access to such techniques abroad.

The Court held that such interest would be prevalent within the constitutional balance of interests involved, compared with the right to genetic identity of the child. However, the Constitutional Court explicitly underlined the distinction between heterologous fertilisation and surrogacy, which is expressly prohibited by Article No. 12, paragraph 6, Law no. 40/2004, and remained uncensored and in no way and

[71] Costa and Pavan v. Italy, app no 54270/2010 (ECHR, 28 August 2012).

[72] Costa and Pavan v. Italy, app no. 54270/2010 (ECHR, 28 August 2012).

[73] Venturi (2012), p. 10.

[74] Constitutional Court, 5 June-2015, No. 96.

[75] Trib. Milano, 18 April 2017; Trib. Milano, 21 July 2017, Trib. Vercelli, 15 October 2018; Trib. Rovigo, 19 March 2019. See Iannicelli (2018), p. 44.

[76] Constitutional Court, 10 June 2014 No. 162.

at no point touched on by the ruling 162/2014, thus maintaining validity and effectiveness.[77] The effect of this strict conceptual distinction appears paradoxical: a discrepancy seems permissible between the birthing mother and the genetic mother, while a similar distinction is absolutely unacceptable between a surrogate mother and the intended mother. Indeed, the Constitutional Court recently confirmed that surrogacy is prohibited in the Italian legal system, but it stated that transcription of the birth certificate of a child born abroad through a surrogacy contract could be allowed "case by case" under the principle of protection of the best interest of the child.[78] However, this perspective has been overturned by the Supreme Court of Cassation,[79] which affirmed that public order is a place for the protection of fundamental values, such as the human dignity of the pregnant woman and the institution of adoption. The protection of these values is not unreasonably considered prevalent over the interests of the child, especially in the context of a balancing carried out directly by the Parliament, to which the judge cannot substitute his or her own evaluation. This issue does not exclude the possibility of conferring importance on the parental relationship, through the use of other legal instruments, such as step-child adoption, provided for by article No 44, first paragraph, pt. d), of the law No. 184/1983.[80]

These scientific and technological innovations led legally and factually to the overturning of the centre of interest: from the transmissibility of the paternal name and family heritage to male offspring as absolute rights to the centrality of the children's rights and their overriding interest in the relationship between parents and children. In this regard, a Court[81] established that in the case of children born outside of wedlock and in consequence of a heterologous fertilisation, third parties cannot challenge the child's status through an action of disavowal, according to a combined interpretation between Article No. 9 of Law 40/2004, as a result of the constitutional ruling No. 162 of 2014 and Article 263 of the Civil Code, related to the disavowal action itself. In the current regulatory environment, legitimising "any interested party" to an action that has its unique premise in the discrepancy between the truth resulting from the statement of recognition and substantive and objective truth of filiation could represent a difference that is the very essence of the practice of heterologous fertilisation. It would result in the denial of the legitimacy of the practice and the exposure of the child born of heterologous fertilisation to the inexorable unconstitutionality of his or her status. A different interpretation, moreover, which recognised the active legitimacy in favour of "any interested party" to appeal for the veracity of recognition, would give rise to suspicion of unconstitutionality and to unjustified disparities in treatment of the child born out of wedlock

[77]Constitutional Court, 10 June 2014, No 162, cit. See Querci (2015), p. 1142.

[78]Constitutional Court, 9 March 2021, No. 33; Constitutional Court, 18 December 2017, No. 272. See Gorgoni (2018), p. 541.

[79]Court of Cassation, 8 May 2019, n. 12193. *Contra,* Court of Cassation, 29 April 2020, No. 8325.

[80]Ferrando (2019), p. 677; Dogliotti (2019), p. 667; Lecis Cocco Ortu (2019), p. 68.

[81]App. Milano, 10 August 2015.

by medically assisted procreation with heterologous technique. This birth could be exposed to the appeal of the truth of that recognition proposed by "any interested person" with respect to a child born in wedlock, as well as medically assisted procreation with use of the same technique.

The Court of Cassation authorised the recognition of the status of filiation to a child born from the embryo formed with homologous post-mortem fertilisation through the father's cryopreserved sperm. This decision allowed the attribution of the deceased father's surname to the child even if the child's birth exceeds the limits established by the paternal legal presumption, that is 300 days from the death of the father.[82] This has been legally justified under Law 40/2004, since the father did not withdraw his consent to MAR before dying. Indeed, according Article No. 6 of Law 40/2004 consent could be withdrawn up until the embryo formation, so the embryo artificially formed could be implanted in the prospective mother's womb, even if the prospective parents ended their relationship (for separation or divorce), and also in the case where the divorced husband no longer agreed to have a child.[83]

What remains of law 40/2004 as a result of several abrogative court interventions? In addition to the ban on surrogacy, the ban on access to medically assisted procreation techniques for same-sex couples[84] and the prohibition of scientific research on embryos continue.

5 Reproductive Rights and Conscientious Objection

Conscientious objection recalls the noble figure of Antigone who does not breach "the unwritten laws of the gods" and disobeys Creon's order to leave her subversive brother's body without the tribute of funeral honours.

When military service was compulsory, conscientious objection concerned the exception paid at high costs in terms of trials and criminal convictions of young pacifists who refused to fulfil the duty of military service. Since the approval of the law 22 May 1978 No. 194, specifically with Article No. 9 concerning conscientious objection to performing an interruption of pregnancy, this issue came into the bioethics debate because it allows health personnel and ancillary activity operators

[82]Court of Cassation, 16 May 2019, No. 13000. See Giunchedi (2020), p. 27; Faccioli (2019), p. 1282.

[83]Trib. Santa Maria Capua Vetere, 25 February 2021.

[84]The Constitutional Court ruled that mandatory gender diversity of the couple accessing MAR is a clear condition in the family legal framework. Under this perspective the Italian legislator has also taken into account the social acceptance of "homosexual parenthood", since there was not a sufficient agreed consent on this point at the time of Law 40/2004 enforcement (Constitutional Court, 23 October 2019, No. 221). This interpretation has been reaffirmed by two subsequent decisions of the Constitutional Court. Both affirmed that accessing MAR techniques by would-be same-sex parents could only be established through a law (Constitutional Court, 20 October 2020, No. 230; Constitutional Court, 9 March 2021, No. 32).

to decline to take part in the procedures laid down in Articles 5 and 7, and the measures for the interruption of pregnancy. In the case of conscientious objection, the medical personnel involved have to sign a prior declaration about their conscientious objection choice. According to the opinion of the Italian National Bioethics Committee (NBC)[85] conscientious objection has to be considered as the "*claim of the individual to be exonerated from a legal obligation because his or her belief that the requirement is contrary to a command from their own conscience and is also detrimental to an important fundamental right in the field of bioethics and bio-law*". Faced with a position where the individual cannot remain silent, a health care worker, such as a doctor, nurse, or pharmacist, may claim to exercise a right that is as equally important as the law assigned to him or her. In fact, the criticality of the recognition of conscientious objection stems from the fact that there are so many objectors who refuse to provide a service that there is a risk of nullifying the recognition of the exercise of rights by the person who holds them.[86] Also, the arbitrary choice to exercise the objection may lead to stress and the professional isolation of health care professionals who guarantee the service.[87] There is, therefore, an irreconcilable conflict of rights, and the solution that the case law experience has taken over the years addresses the balance between fundamental rights. There are several examples, starting with voluntary interruption of pregnancy, where the right to the exemption of health workers to contribute to the abortion procedure is contrary to the right of the mother to protect her health.[88] Similarly, in relation to MAR procedures regulated by Law No. 40/2004 which, albeit symbolically, grants protection to the conceived child, in this case, the objection of health workers to participation in extracorporeal fertilisation contrasts with the right to self-determination of parenthood recognised by the same law to the couple of childbearing age, as long as they are of opposite sex, married or cohabiting. Even the administration of epidural anaesthesia may be the subject of conscientious objection by health officials concerning the rights to protect a mother's health.

Regarding this specific issue, after a claim by the CGIL, the main Italian Labour Union, the European Committee of Social Rights of the Council of Europe[89] condemned Italy for numerous violations of the European Social Charter, as it prevents women from exercising their right to an abortion under the conditions laid down by law No. 194/1978. Although according to the law every hospital and every region must always ensure access to termination of pregnancy, it is effectively

[85]Comitato Nazionale per la Bioetica (2012), p. 13.

[86]See in this volume Paris, Reckoning with Growing Pluralism. Potentials and Limits of Conscientious Objection: Conscience Clauses in Abortion Laws in Europe, section 2.

[87]Lalli (2011), p. 59; Farace (2018), p. 798.

[88]Lalli (2011), cit.

[89]European Committee of Social Rights of the Council of Europe, a decision published on 11 April 2016, the Italian General Confederation of Labour (CGIL) against Italy, complaint. 91/2013. This decision followed that one of the European Committee of Social Rights of the Council of Europe, 10 March 2014, International Planned Parenthood Federation European Network v. Italy, No. 87/2012.

denied by a growing number of objecting doctors, since many facilities do not have an adequate number of physicians on their staff to ensure the correct and effective application of the law No. 194/1978. These circumstances create dual disparities. On the one hand, it concerns the possibility of actual access to an abortion: if a woman cannot obtain the service at her local hospital, she is forced to travel to another region to search for an available hospital or sanitary structure. On the other hand, it regards discrimination between women seeking access to abortion as a health service, which abortion is, and those intending to access other health services, not concerning abortion, for their health. Additionally, the Italian State has been sentenced for employment discrimination, as doctors who do perform abortions are more penalised in terms of work organisation and career opportunities than those who object.

References

Aprile A, Benciolini P (2011) La sterilizzazione: aspetti clinici e casistica medico legale. In: Rodotà S, Zatti P (eds) Governo del corpo. Trattato di Biodiritto. Giuffrè, Milano, pp 795–804
Balistreri M (2016) Il futuro della riproduzione umana. Fandango, Rome
Baudouin JL (2005) Wrongful life: un aperçu de droit comparé. Familia:1175–1181
Benciolini P (2015) Obiezione di coscienza? Nuova Giur. Civ. 1(II):3–8
Betta E (2012) Note sulla storia dell'articolo 553 del codice penale italiano. In: Betta E, Caglioti DL, Papadia E (eds) Forme del politico tra Ottocento e Novecento. Studi di storia per Raffaele Romanelli, Viella Roma, pp 131–152
Bognetti G (1991) Aborto, III, Diritto comparato e straniero. In: Enc. giur. Treccani, I. Ed. Enc., Roma
Boni G (2001) Il dibattito sull'immissione in commercio della c.d. pillola del giorno dopo: annotazioni su alcuni profili giuridici della questione, in particolare sull'obiezione di coscienza. Dir. fam. e pers:677–717
Caponi R (2011) La tutela della identità nazionale degli stati membri dell'U.E. nella cooperazione tra le corti: addio ai 'controlimiti'? Il diritto dell'Unione Europea:915–926
Carbone V (2018) Nascita indesiderata: anche il padre ha diritto al risarcimento dei danni. Corriere Giur:921–927
Casonato C (2004) Diritto, diritti ed eugenetica: prime considerazioni su un discorso giuridico altamente problematico. Humanitas 4:841–856
Cassano G (2002) Concepimento versus «pillola del giorno dopo» (T.A.R. Lazio, II Sez., 12.10.2001, N. 8465). Nuova Giur. Civ. 5(II):571
Comitato Nazionale per la Bioetica (1998) Il problema bioetico della sterilizzazione non volontaria. Presidenza del Consiglio dei Ministri, Roma
Comitato Nazionale per la Bioetica (2011) Nota in merito alla obiezione di coscienza del farmacista alla vendita dei prodotti contraccettivi di emergenza. Presidenza del Consiglio dei Ministri, Roma
Comitato Nazionale per la Bioetica (2012) Obiezione di coscienza e bioetica. Presidenza del Consiglio dei Ministri, Roma
Coontz S, Henderson P (1986) "Explanations" of male dominance. In: Coontz S, Henderson P (eds) Women's work, men's property. The origin of gender & class. Verso, London, pp 1–42
Dogliotti M (2019) Le Sezioni Unite condannano i due padri e assolvono le due madri. Famiglia e Dir. 7:653–676
Facci G (2004) Il danno da sterilizzazione non riuscita. Resp. Civ.:155

Faccioli M (2019) La condizione giuridica del soggetto nato da procreazione assistita *post mortem*. Nuova Giur. Civ. 6:1282–1287
Farace D (2018) Interruzione volontaria della gravidanza e situazioni giuridiche soggettive. Riv. Dir. Civ.:798–828
Ferrando G (1994) Il «caso Cremona»: autonomia e responsabilità nella procreazione. Giur It I (2):995
Ferrando G (2019) Maternità per sostituzione all'estero: le sezioni unite dichiarano inammissibile la trascrizione dell'atto di nascita. un primo commento. Famiglia e Dir. 7:677–686
Foucault M (1984) Histoire de la sexualité, vol. 2: L'usage des plaisirs. Gallimard, Paris. Italian translation: Foucault M (2015) L'uso dei piaceri. Storia della sessualità 2 (trans: Guarino L). Feltrinelli, Milano
Gerbi M, Sardella I (2013) Il danno alla persona derivante da attività sanitarie. Danno e Resp 12:1221–1245
Giunchedi D (2020) La procreazione assistita post mortem tra responsabilità procreativa e *favor stabilitatis*. Fam e Dir.:39–47
Gorgoni M (2009) Nascituro e responsabilità sanitaria. Resp. civ. e prev.:2075
Gorgoni A (2018) Art. 263 cod. civ.: tra verità e conservazione dello status filiationis. Nuova Giur. Civ.:540–546
Heritier F (2002) Masculin-Féminin II. Dissoudre la hiérarchie. Odile Jacob Paris. Italian edition: Heritier F (2004) Dissolvere la gerarchia, Maschile/Femminile II, (trans: Panaro A). Raffaello Cortina, Milano
Iannicelli MA (2018) Diagnosi genetica preimpianto e coppie fertili portatrici di malattie genetiche trasmissibili: il giudice di merito applica la sentenza della Corte Cost. n. 96/2015. Corriere Giur:52–63
Lalli C (2011) C'è chi dice no. Dalla leva all'aborto. Come cambia l'obiezione di coscienza. Il Saggiatore, Milano
Lecis Cocco Ortu AM (2019) L'obbligo di riconoscimento della genitorialità intenzionale tra diritto interno e CEDU: Riflessioni a partire dal primo parere consultivo della Corte Edu su GPA e trascrizioni. Genius 1:68–80
Malinowski MJ (2006) Creating life? Examining the legal, ethical, and medical issues of assisted reproductive technologies: a law-policy proposal to know where babies come from during the reproduction revolution. J Gender Race Just 9:549
Mastrorilli (2013) To be or not to be: comparare l'incomparabile. Danno e Resp 5:492–497
Maternini MF, Scopel L (2012) La bioetica e le confessioni religiose. Edizioni Università, Trieste
Mauceri T (2018) Identità di genere e differenziazione sessuale. Problemi interpretativi eprospettive normative. Nuove Leggi Civ. Comm. 6:1475–1507
Mazzoni CM (2016) Vita e non vita in cassazione a proposito di cass. n. 25767/2015. Nuova Giur. Civ. 3:461–462
Mussi CA (2014) Nascita indesiderata per omessa diagnosi di malformazioni del feto e risarcimento del danno iure proprio del nascituro. I Contratti 3:293–308
Nuvolone P, Lanzi A (1992) Gravidanza (interruzione della), Digesto - IV edizione, Discipline Penalistiche VI. UTET, Torino
Pavone IR (2011) La Convenzione europea sulla biomedicina. Giuffrè, Milano
Pellecchia E (2010) Aborto farmacologico e disciplina dell'interruzione volontaria della gravidanza. Nuova Giur. Civ. 1:31–38
Piraino F (2016) I confini della responsabilità civile e la controversia sulle malformazioni genetiche del nascituro: il rifiuto del c.d. danno da vita indesiderata. Nuova Giur. Civ. 3:450–460
Poiatti F (2021) La critica al danno da nascita indesiderata e la complessità del danno permanente futuro. Danno e Resp.:89
Prasad A (2012) Like a virgin. How science is redesigning the rule of sex. Oneworld, Oxford
Pugliese V (2011) Il diritto a diventare genitori. Procreazione medicalmente assistita e caduta dei divieti. Edizioni Laterza, Roma-Bari

Querci A (2015) La maternità "per sostituzione" fra diritto interno e carte internazionali. Fam. Dir.:1142–1157
Reeves Sanday F (1991) Female power and male dominance. Cambridge University Press, Cambridge
Reingold RB, Gostin LO (2019) Women's access to reproductive health services. JAMA 322 (1):21–22. https://doi.org/10.1001/jama.2019.8437
Rizzieri A (2001) L'aborto nella giurisprudenza della Corte Suprema degli Stati Uniti. Nuova Giur. Civ. 3:228–270
Santosuosso A (2011) Diritto, scienza, nuove tecnologie. Cedam, Padova
Sardella I (2015) Quali danni risarcibili se nasce un figlio non desiderato. Danno e Resp.:617–624
Scalera A (2012) La legge 194 ancora una volta al vaglio della Consulta. Fam e Dir 11:979–983
Sliger F (2004) Since Roe: access to abortion in the United States and policy lessons from Western Europe. New Eng J Int Comp Law 10:229
Spallarossa MR (2011) La procreazione responsabile. In: Rodotà S, Zatti P (eds) Governo del corpo. Trattato di Biodiritto. Giuffrè, Milano
Srikanthan A, Reid R (2008) Religious and cultural influences on contraception. J Obstet Gynaecol Can 30(2):129–137
Thornton A (1985) Reciprocal influences of family and religion in a changing World. J Marriage Family 47(2):381–394
Venturi P (2012) Sulla legittimità della legge n. 40/2004 sulla procreazione assistita in relazione alla Cedu. Giur. It.:1993–1998
Veronesi P (2005) Diagnosi preimpianto: i nodi al pettine. Dopo il referendum tocca alla Consulta. D&G 33:14
Wojtyla K (Johannes Paulus II) (1995) Evangelium Vitae I, 11
Zaret A (2016) Editing embryos: considering restrictions on genetically engineering humans. Hastings Law J 67:1805
Zizola G (1991) Il modello cattolico in Italia. In: Ariès P, Duby G (eds) La vita privata. Il Novecento. Laterza, Roma, pp 239–299

End of Life Issues

Ricardo Chueca

For Nieves

Abstract The end of life is an event that exceeds the law. But all societies need to set the terms on which scientific knowledge about life and its end strikes new balances with its identifying values and shapes them into legally articulated compromises.

It is a process that always reveals an axiological pluralism and induces a variety of responses to the legal treatment of the end of life. Different ways of understanding the capacity of disposition over one's own life and the position and function of the health system.

In this context, we are witnessing the emergence of "fragments" of European standards, sometimes stimulated by changes in the jurisprudence of certain supra-state courts (ECtHR and CJEU).

The text proposes grouping state responses into three models or patterns: inactive, preclusive, and promotional. Accordingly, it describes the adaptation of the pattern of end-of-life treatment.

Finally, it describes the foreseeable patterns of evolution of national legal systems, supranational rules and the courts that interpret them.

Adaptation and translation by Gonzalo Arruego. Linguistic revision by Oscar Urrutia.

This research is part of the Research's Project FRONTIUSFUND (Cod. DER2014-52817-P), financed by the Spanish Ministry of Economy, Industry and Competitiveness, and DERFUNDAT (PGC2018-093737-B-I00), financed by the Spanish Ministry of Science and Innovation.

R. Chueca (✉)
Universidad de la Rioja, La Rioja, Spain
e-mail: ricardo.chueca@unirioja.es

L. Busatta, C. Casonato (eds.), *Axiological Pluralism*, Ius Gentium: Comparative Perspectives on Law and Justice 92, https://doi.org/10.1007/978-3-030-78475-1_12

1 Introduction

"End of life" is a confusing expression; it is a no man's land where points of view and problems pile up.

"End of life" refers to an imprecise process, the beginning and end of which are unknown.[1] Not even the definitions of either life or human life are clear.[2] This is not a mere juridical problem, as life and death are a matter of study and reflection from the perspective of different scientific disciplines.[3] The result is that the juridical approach to such a vague expression lacks any solid and undisputed basis.

Life and death are difficult to formalize as juridical terms and legal orders usually evade the issue of their definition even though they regulate many matters that depend on it.

We have to reckon with this difficulty. Death, on the one hand, is a cultural event the sense and meaning of which are hard to define as it is a "no-act".[4] Its only sense and meaning are those experienced by the deceased throughout the life that he or she lived. Death, as the epilogue of a specific life, may have an array of different meanings. But to the deceased, death is always the freest, unavoidable, and necessary among the acts of man.[5]

On the other hand, death is a natural fact; which means that the beginning of life and its end are biological phenomena alien to the individual's will. From this point of view the expression "end of life" is vague as every life begins to end since birth. This excludes any pathological approach to death; death is just the natural end of what is truly exceptional: life.[6]

To summarize the above mentioned, we approach the problems associated to what we call "end of life" from uncertainty.

Every legal order is a formal system of rules according to a certain conception of the world; a set of rules and techniques the aim of which is to intervene in social processes and which therefore needs to formalize them first. Without this earlier step, no juridical regulation is possible and it is precisely at this point that trouble starts.

Law and Life Sciences comply with different scientific paradigms. Furthermore, the velocity at which technology evolves and generates knowledge does not keep pace with the ability of society to process that knowledge. The issue at stake here is not whether societies should keep pace with progress, or when and how they should do it; for our present discussion, this is simply a fact that we should take into consideration.

Nowadays, we know that biological life is a system in a never-ending rearrangement process due to its chaotic nature. This might not be so in the future, but for the time being, lawyers cannot deny this evidence.

[1]Brosset (2011), p. I 88.

[2]Foley (2011), p. 3.

[3]DeGrazia (2005) (1980) 9(2), pp. 105–133; McMahan (2006). In Shoemaker (2010), pp. 481, 489.

[4]Commission de réflexion sur la fin de la vie en France (2012), p. 83.

[5]Comité Directeur pour la Bioéthique (CDBI) (2008), p. 13.

[6]Commission de réflexion sur la fin de la vie en France (2012), p. 13.

Formal rules govern living systems. Chaos, continuous change, randomness, and diversity are inherent features to interaction processes which are still unknown and incomprehensible to a great extent. In other words, while life challenges us with the complexity of its own chaos, the mission assigned to the legal order is to respond to this challenge, at least partly, by using a complex set of its own specialized means: regulatory techniques, contradictory Case Law, Committees, soft-law...

Under such circumstances, some juridical malfunctions are simply unavoidable when studying end of life issues. Let us point out some of them.

When we neglect all those elements that are difficult to formalize, we are really imposing juridical formalisation on living processes. This happens, for example, when we resort to the classical juridical distinction between person and thing regarding the regulation of the use and availability of human tissues.

We change our paradigms by introducing elements from Life Sciences aiming to formalize a reality that does not fit into theoretical systems. For instance, we do this when we develop a purely juridical argument with the aid of biomedical criteria: such would be the case of the concept of parenthood in private law because of the existing level of development in fertilization and reproduction techniques.

The Law faces strong limitations and conditions when regulating new biomedical techniques: it must do so without neglecting its primary function: the institutionalization of a complex set of social representations, the survival of which depends upon it. The problem is that we lack the resources to close the gap between Life Sciences and such social representations.[7] This explains the inability of the Law, for example, to draw the line separating life and death: such a task is simply beyond the ability of the Law.

To summarize the above, Legal Science has to face the ongoing and formidable challenge of "a new complexity in reality".[8]

All these circumstances might explain the excessive use of the Bioethical debate particularly when Bioethics attempts to make decisions "beyond the Law".

However, among the relevant issues associated with the end of life, there are two which are especially worrying.

On the one hand, there is the problem of the media. The *media tsunamis* associated to cases with great social impact are replacing public debate; a problem worsened in the internet era, and the outcome of which is a harmful mess of terms, concepts, and meanings. *Pretty*, *Sampedro*, *Englaro*, *Lambert* become just the names of media shocks associated not only to what we usually call *hard cases* but especially to bad quality information.[9] This is yet another hurdle before the necessary public debate prior to the adoption of any legal measure.[10]

---

[7]Concluding on Carter v Canada (Attorney General), [2015] SCC 5, [2015] 1 SCR 331, 'Rather than implementing an incremental change, their legalizing physician-assisted suicide and euthanasia represents a *seismic shift in our fundamental societal values*, not just another step on a path we have already taken'. Chan and Somerville (2016), p. 175. (Emphasis added).

[8]On the limitations of legal science described here, Pedrot (2007), pp. 77–82.

[9]Lantero (2016), p. 310.

[10]Issues that have a connection but not only in the media. For example, in a Spanish Sociological Research Centre's (CIS) survey, one item questioned simultaneously about euthanasia, suicide, abortion and IVF. Estudios 2752 and 2759 (2008). About recent surveys in Spain see Serrano del Rosal and Heredia (2018), pp. 103–120; Bernal (2020), pp. 112–115.

On the other hand, there is an issue that is rarely mentioned: end of life issues has a crucial economic background. In developed societies, the standard of living relates not only to an excellent quality of living but to an excellent quality of dying too. In other words, economically speaking, we die following the way we lived.[11] In addition to the above, the intense medicalisation of the final stages of life implies increasing economic costs linked to hospitals or similar facilities.[12] We then fall into a spiral: the expression "end of life" links to that of palliative care and, in short, with death.[13] This combination of elements can sometimes be extremely enlightening.

To finish this section, let us not forget a false paradox: although statistically speaking these issues only affect a few people, it is a major problem since it concerns the essence of the link between the individual and the State.

2 The Emergence of Legal Issues Concerning the End of Life

Some of the difficulties that legal orders face when regulating end of life decisions result from the circumstances in which these decisions are made. Although we cannot examine this feature in depth here, it is necessary to draw attention to a few aspects.

The "end of life" is a recurring topic. Since the death of Socrates, if not before, history is full of examples of different perspectives on the end of a human life. But it was in the second half of the twentieth century when developed societies witnessed the ubiquitous occurrence of new and powerful symptoms of the problem. The spectacular technological progress and its application in medicine, along with the idea of the human being as the *dominus* of life in a wide sense –his life included-, have persuaded society into wrongly regarding technological progress as boundless.

Secondly, life expectancy has spectacularly increased in those same developed societies and so has the occurrence of new pathologies or the worsening of those associated with longevity.[14] It should be underlined that in most cases those pathologies have a negative nature or are incurable and irreversible.

There is a third factor linked to the welfare State: public medical assistance is universal to the extent that, in Europe, a universal public health system lies at the

[11]Commission de réflexion sur la fin de la vie en France (2012), p. 25.

[12]Foley (2011), p. 256.

[13]As Dworkin acutely said: "...the Court has assumed that dying patients have a constitutional right to end life support even when this means that they will die immediately; and there is as much danger that such patients will be coaxed into a request to die in that way as by requesting lethal pills, particularly since life-support techniques are typically very expensive". Dworkin (1997).

[14]In the twenty most developed European countries life expectancy has increased by 6% in the last 25 years. *INEBASE* Accessed 7 Aug 2019.

very heart of the notion of State.[15] This fact has led to a situation where the elderly and the terminally ill are the exclusive competence of the public powers. This situation has irreversibly resulted in the existence of a link between the State and the ill person in the final stages of her life. In developed societies death has been medicalized within hospitals or similar facilities where the elderly, even though not suffering from a terminal pathology, unhurriedly reach the final stages of their lives.

To sum it all up, the process of dying has more than ever become a matter which concerns the State.

Clinical and medical elements become crucial components of the concept of dying, and death increasingly evolves into a technical matter under the exclusive responsibility of the public powers.[16] And this new concept of death poses new demands to jurists.

To begin with, we should acquire the necessary technical knowledge to set up the scope of the decisions concerning the end of one's own life. This is a consequence of the fact that technological progress makes *de facto* possible new capacities that widen the potential juridical space of decision. In this context, the rule of law struggles to impose legally the notion of the dying person as holder of fundamental rights the exercise of which is crucial in such a defining moment.

Therefore, end of life decisions undoubtedly has a technical side which has generated a new space where the individual is able to exercise *personal* rights in their deepest sense. A truly difficult compromise.

Under these new circumstances, the traditional idea of death has been altered. End of life decisions not only have become a technical matter, they also have a more sophisticated nature. Limitation of the therapeutic effort, withholding or withdrawing medical treatment, assisted suicide or euthanasia are expressions which described personal options created to a greater or lesser extent by technical progress.[17] In other words, more technical progress implies more decisions. The future has only begun.[18]

Despite the novelties in this scenario, it is already possible to expect two especially difficult problems, which are linked to the coexistence of increasingly complex and differentiated systems of values in our societies. These, in turn, interact with technological progress, scientists and, especially, medical staff. Thus, axiological pluralism permeates legal systems.

The first problem arises from the conflict between this new medical context and a system of fundamental rights, both national and supranational, according to which a space of self-determination concerning the end of one's own life is progressively acknowledged. Obviously, the conflicts and imbalances between end of life decisions and fundamental rights are constant. It is true that both the legal doctrine and the Courts are progressively showing a catalogue of situations deriving from specific

---

[15]Daly (2015), pp. 197–213.

[16]Commission de réflexion sur la fin de la vie en France (2012), pp. 10, 13, 20.

[17]Feuillet (2015), p. 176.

[18]Riccioni et al. (2016), pp. 126–127.

cases and that medical treatments are increasingly defined starting from the priority given to the terminally ill. However, there still is a long way ahead where legal certainty cannot be given up under any circumstances.

The second one is more problematic. Death has become more technical; a fact that poses a new challenge to the role of the medical profession. Doctors find themselves increasingly involved in processes which have no therapeutic nature or that exceed palliative care. And their intervention is usually needed by those legal orders allowing assisted suicide and euthanasia to guarantee certainty and compliance with the established legal requirements. Obviously, this has nothing to do with their traditional therapeutic or palliative activity. This is not a problem of conscientious objection, it is a matter of the public health systems lacking the necessary specialised personnel involved in the exercise of those rights concerning the end of one's own life.[19]

3 The European Standard of *Minima*, Between Silence and Integration

The ratification of the *European Convention on Human Rights* by the ex-communist countries has widened and strengthened its fundamental rights system.[20] This process has been amplified by the increasing performance of the *Charter of fundamental rights of the European Union* which is reinforcing the European standard of protection of fundamental rights.[21]

Furthermore, the *Convention for the protection of Human Rights and Dignity of the Human Being with regard to the Application of Biology and Medicine: Convention on Human Rights and Biomedicine* (Oviedo Convention),[22] plays a homogenizing role in the field of biomedicine; an especially intense role in regard to the legislative and executive bodies of its signatory States.[23]

---

[19] Lehmann and Prokopetz (2012), pp. 97–99; Chan and Somerville (2016), pp. 143–175.

[20] Roma, 4 November 1950; the Convention came into force in 1953 and up today it has been ratified by 47 European. It has been amended by the Protocols 11 and 14 and supplemented by the Additional Protocol and Protocols. 4, 6, 7, 12 and 13.

[21] 2012/C 326/02. Arts. 1, 4, 7, 8 and 35.

[22] Oviedo, 4 April 1997. Up to date 35 European states have subscribed it and 28 have ratified it.

[23] But, problematically, not only: "(. . .) the applicant could allege instead breach of article 8 of the ECtHR (1950) which protects the individual's right to respect for his private and family life and rely on the provisions on consent contained in the CHRB as a guide to the scope of application of Art 8 in a biomedical context. The ECtHR followed precisely this approach in *Glass v UK*, where the ECtHR for the first time relied on the Council of Europe's CHRB in its Reading of Art. 8 (. . .) There might therefore come a point when the UK, and any other member States of the Council of Europe which have not signed or ratified the Convention, could nevertheless in theory find itself indirectly in breach of the provisions contained in the CHRB (. . .) On this basis, it seems that the potential legal impact of the CHRB on the jurisprudence of the ECtHR could be considerably greater than anticipated. In the UK, the Human Rights Act 1998 directs UK courts to determine cases in the light

Nevertheless, beyond this *acquis,* it is the European Court of Human Rights' Case Law which has fragmentarily shaped a European standard on end of life decisions, especially in the last 25 years. However, due to the servitudes of its international nature and to the widening of the States' margin of appreciation, it is the lowest possible standard.[24] Even if this is true, everything shows that a consistent and universal standard is being adopted.

Its origin lies in articles 2 and 8 of the ECtHR even though both have divergent functions within the logic of the Convention and have undergone transformations in the last 15 years. The majority of the legal doctrine claims that this process can be understood in terms of a shift in the current social values; but this might be a partial explanation.

The right to life is enshrined in article 2 of the Convention in the post-WWII context. Its main goal was the prohibition of the intentional taking of human life, especially by public powers. Inferring from that prohibition that disposing of one's own life is unlawful exceeds its meaning and scope, as the ECtHR has finally accepted despite its first decisions.[25]

The restrictions that article 2.1 of the Convention is subject to, are a consequence of its being a rule and not a principle, as the exception contained in its second paragraph shows and the Court has explained in *Pretty*.[26]

When defending that article 2 of the Convention prohibits the taking of one's own life, the Court ignored a distinction without which it becomes partially inconsistent. A distinction still presents in *McCann* but which was abandoned in *Pretty*:[27] the difference between the fundamental right to life itself and life as the subject-matter of that fundamental right. Some distinctions make possible the exception contained in paragraph two despite the universal assertion of paragraph one. But in *Pretty*, and not for the first time, the Court disregarded that distinction resulting in an argument which exceeds the scope and meaning of article 2 ECtHR.

If the fundamental right has a negative content meaning that the only faculty that its holder is entitled to is of a reactive nature, the Convention legitimises the State to deprive the fundamental right holder of his life, though not of his right to life. This contradiction is increasingly hard to bear by the Convention as the scope of the decisions concerning the end of one's own life in its final stages becomes wider.[28]

This inconsistency is present in *Pretty* when the Court replies to the plaintiff's comparison with the freedom of association, which encompasses not only the

---

of the jurisprudence of the ECtHR. The CHRB might thus gradually reshape domestic law both in the UK and in other member States which have not ratified the CHRB", Plomer (2005), pp. 18, 21.

[24]Protocol 15, 23 May 2013.

[25](ECtHR) art. 2.1 "Everyone's right to life shall be protected by law. No one shall be deprived of his life intentionally save in the execution of a sentence of a court following his conviction of a crime for which this penalty is provided by law".

[26]Pretty *v.* UK.

[27]McCann and others *v.* UK, 147.

[28]On these features of the right to life see Arruego (2011), Arruego (2019a, b), p. 111 and (2019/2) 247-286.

positive freedom to be part of an association, but also the negative liberty of not belonging to any.[29] The Court simply rejects the argument based on the different nature of both rights and therefore disregards the different nature of the subject-matters of both fundamental rights: a biological process which is alien to the individual's will, and a social activity dependent on the person's will.[30] The difference remains unexplained by the Court; maybe because it is legally unexplainable.

The ECtHR seems to have finally accepted that the role of article 2 of the Covenant about end of life decisions is very restricted, especially after Protocols 6 and 13.[31]

This is the reason why the Court has explored the possibilities opened by article 8 of the Convention, even if not at its full potential, leaving aside its eventual role as a kind of "last frontier" to face future challenges.[32] The Court is still unclear about the relationship among rights. In this sense, and despite having asserted that there is no hierarchy of rights within the Convention, the right to life seems to enjoy a prominent position.[33]

The physical and psychological self-determination guaranteed by article 8 ECtHR and the quality of life considerations arising from it, must coexist with the principle of "Sanctity of life".[34] It is true, however, that since *Pretty* there are no express mentions to the principle of "Sanctity of life" in the argumentation of the Court.[35] This absence is the expression of a shift in the doctrine of the Court. The ECtHR has therefore started to set up the basics of end of life decisions to face the new scenarios that the national legal orders are now dealing with. At the same time, the Court has widened the "national margin of appreciation" in this field.

---

[29]Youngand Webster *v.* UK, (Article 50) (Application no. 7601/76; 7806/77) 18 October 1982. Merkouris (2012), p. 111. Opinions not shared by De Schutter (2003), pp. 76–79.

[30]A clear distinction, however, in the reasoning of the Court: "It safeguards the right to life, without which enjoyment of any of the other rights and freedoms in the Convention is rendered nugatory" Pretty *v* DPP 37.

[31]Protocol n.6 28 April 1983 and Protocol n.13 3 May 2002.

[32]On the evolution of the ECtHR's doctrine on art. 8 of the Convention, recently Elvira (2015), pp. 203–213.

[33]A pioneering position already in 2002, though complying with the Court's doctrine, in the Report of the Belgian Council of State on the legislative projects on euthanasia and palliative care. Sénat de Belgique, Sess 2000-2001, 2 July 2001, Avis du Conseil d'État, 31.441/AV-AG et 31.442/AV-AG.

[34]With remarkable support in Rodriguez v. the Attorney General of Canada [1994] 2 Law Reports of Canada 136.

> Without in any way negating the principle of sanctity of life protected under the Convention, the Court considers that it is under Article 8 that notions of the quality of life take on significance. In an era of growing medical sophistication combined with longer life expectancies, many people are concerned that they should not be forced to linger on in old age or in states of advanced physical or mental decrepitude which conflict with strongly held ideas of self and personal identity. (Emphasis added). Pretty 65.

[35]Very significant because the Court continues to use the terms *sanctity of home* and *sanctity of human rights*. Only one exception in *Lambert* but in a reference to *Pretty*.

This is possible due to the nature of the subject-matter of the rights proclaimed in article 8 of the Convention. Article 8 guarantees a space of *agere licere*; a space which *prima facie* excludes the interference of any public power, which is therefore subject to scrutiny to verify its legitimacy. Of course, this boosts the margin of appreciation of the Court to adapt to the changes experienced by biomedicine and social values. This aspect is under stress due to the diverse ways (when not simply opposing one another), in which the societies of the signatory countries have regulated end of life issues. In this context, article 8 of the Convention provides a certain degree of flexibility. But it should be borne in mind that it obviously has its limitations; limitations that accumulate as the Case Law of the Court grows.

The way in which the Court weighs the rights proclaimed in article 8 against the duty of the State to preserve life (again, not the right to life) has to be highlighted: the Court is not actually balancing them but just making an unbalanced weighing based on the statistical fact that only five of the signatory countries have recognised a right to dispose of one's own life.[36] Based on that quantitative assertion, the Court simply fails to reach a true balance between the rights involved; the balance is excluded by the margin of appreciation. A remarkable description of this subtle shift can be found in Haas v. Switzerland.[37]

The Court restrains itself so as to circumvent the fact that it believes both rights not to weigh the same in the logic of the Convention.[38] This leads to the conclusion that article 8 has limits; limits, it is true, that the Court discovers there and then.[39]

The Court reaches a subtle and fragile balance as follows: "I can cause my own death but I do not have a right to do so" . . .Or just depending on the specific legal order.[40]

We could summarize the ECtHR's doctrine this way.

Especially since *Haas* and *Koch* and following the Oviedo Convention, the Court undoubtedly acknowledges that the individual has a wide legal capacity of self-determination concerning his or her own life; with regard, both to medical treatment refusal and to the moment to end one's own life, it is literally the person's right. But, as said in *Pretty*, it can collide with the States' obligation to protect life.

However, if a State has recognised the legal capacity to dispose of one's own life, a capacity that includes the right to oppose to the duty of the State to protect life, article 8 ECtHR prevails. Under these circumstances, the State should support the

[36]Haas 55, Koch *v.* Germany, (Application no. 497/09) 19 July 2012 70, Lambert and others v. France (Application no. 46043/14) 5 June 2015. In both cases there is a subtle allusion to the different scales of social values and opinions about the end of life in different European societies, Merkouris (2012), p. 123.

[37]"Lastly, certain other countries accept only acts of «passive» aid. Note that the clear majority of member States seem to attach more weight to the protection of the individual's life than to his or her right to end it. It follows that the States enjoy a considerable margin of appreciation in this area." Haas *v.* Switzerland, (Application no. 31322/07) 20 January 2011 55.

[38]Willems (2016), p. 325.

[39]Samanta (2016), p. 16.

[40]Brosset (2011), p. 83.

correct exercise of that legal capacity and guarantee the free and undoubted will of the person who decides to end his or her own life.[41] In addition to it, if a legal order accepts assisted suicide, its regulation should be utterly unambiguous throughout.[42]

To summarize the above, the Convention progressively enshrines a sort of *hybrid right* which combines legal capacities protected both by articles 2 and 8. Life still retains a *special* nature under article 2 ECtHR, but under certain circumstances, the individual can dispose of his or her own life; a right which guarantees a partial, conditional, and limited *agere licere* the scope of which depends on each specific legal order. In other words, one's own life is not fully dependent upon one's will yet, but the person has the autonomy to govern the final stages of his or her own life. Death is part of life; death is part of the object of the right to life. Each legal order manages this fact within its own wide margin of appreciation.[43]

The conclusion is that the European Court of Human Rights is discretely and slowly transforming the meaning of life as the object of the right proclaimed in article 2 of the Convention.[44]

The (unstable) standard of the ECtHR, attached to the margin of appreciation, allows for a range of various positions of the States in relation to how to deal with this issue. A range of positions including rejection of regulation, silence, or their integration in the legal system that corresponds to the following three ideal types or models.

Preclusive Model A pattern which tends to deny/refuse pluralism: the legal framework is particularly rigid; therefore, the jurisdiction acknowledges and guarantees the balance among the different components of pluralism (scientific, cultural, religious, moral individual and collective…)

Inactive Model A pattern which tends not to regulate these situations: the law-maker is silent. The jurisdiction is called to give an answer to arising needs and issues at a scientific and social level in the absence of a specific regulation.

Promotional Model A pattern which tends to acknowledge and support the various levels of pluralisms.

Let us examine all this in next section.

---

[41]Haas 57-58.

[42]Gross *v.* Switzerland 69.

[43]A recent decision, exemplary in terms of legal rigor, in Carter *v.* Canada [2015] 1 R.C.S. 331 overruling *Rodriguez v. British Columbia* (Attorney General), [1993] 3 S.C.R. 519. It is expected a profound influence on European regulations now under review.

[44]On the origins and foundations of this emerging process is very useful Willems (2016).

4 Diversity of National Options: Denial *v.* Integration

The dilemmas posed by end-of-life issues are common to developed democracies because their health services and biomedical technologies are at a similar stage of development and they share a similar standard of protection of fundamental rights. However, other circumstances, which are complex and diverse in nature, explain the existing different legal responses.

The regulation of end of life issues forces the State to remove all doubts, avoid hypocrisy and face the widening of the responsibilities of the health system concerning the management of the final stages of life. However, the real deterrent factor is that end of life issues concern the most personal and intimate aspects of the human being.

Nonetheless, the quest for real equality in the final stages of life, regardless of personal circumstances, and the goal of bearing with dignity the anguish usually experienced by those who are dying, must coexist with different cultural traditions and conceptions of life and death, if not simply prevail in extreme cases.

There is a common challenge, but not a common pattern to face it. Actually, the responses from each society are very diverse and this could be the reason why only a few States have a direct legal regulation of these issues.[45]

4.1 Belgium

Due to its technical quality, the Belgian regulation is going to serve as model to other legal orders.[46]

After the 1999 elections and the formation of a non-confessional Government, the passing of a Law governing euthanasia began. The Law was finally passed in 2002 along with other two laws regulating palliative care and the rights of the patient.[47] To

---

[45]Recent statistic data on the limitation of treatments, assisted suicide and euthanasia in Riccioni et al. (2016), p. 133.

[46]McMorrow (2019). This is the case of the *Loi concernant les soins de vie end* of Quebec, 5 Juin 2014 (http://legisquebec.gouv.qc.ca/en/ShowDoc/cs/S-32.0001, updated 31 october 2020. And, by extension, of Canada, which is now undertaking the reform of the criminal law forced by Carter *v* Canada, in February 2015, the SCC rendered a unanimous (9-0) judgement in favour of the plaintiffs in the Carter case, declaring the challenged provisions of the Criminal Code. Act to amend the Criminal Code (medical assistance in dying), Bill C-7, December 10, 2020.

While the High Court will have to rule on the constitutionality of the *Quebecois* law. Quebec argues that “la mort n’est pas federal”.

[47]*Loi du 28 du mai 2002, relative à l’euthanasie*, extending it to childrens matures by *Loi du 28 février 2014 modifiant la loi du 28 mai 2002 relative à l'euthanasie, en vue d'étendre l'euthanasie aux mineurs. Loi du 22 août 2002 relative aux droits du patient. Loi du 14 juin 2002 relative aux soins palliatifs. Technical reform of relevance of arts. 4 and 14 by 2020.*

reflect its different nature, euthanasia was legalized while not changing criminal regulation.

The Commission plays a key role *de contrôle et d'évaluation*, which not only makes thorough reports for the Parliament, but also controls the compliance of every euthanasia procedure with the law.[48] The main criticism focuses on the fact that the intervention of the Commission takes place after the practise of euthanasia. This being true, it is also difficult to find how an earlier control could be implemented. The point of this argument is to underline the obvious fact that the causation of death is irreversible.

Belgium would be the best-defined example of a *promotional model* of regulation.

4.2 England and Wales

Even though suicide is punished under the *Suicide Act* (1961),[49] prosecution will be carried out only according to the criteria established by the *Director of Public Prosecution (DPP)*; criteria proved after Purdy *v.* DPP[50] but the origins of which can be traced back to *Pretty v. The UK*. These criteria are many and precise, those describing the circumstances under which no prosecution be carried out being even more clearly defined.

This is obviously not a solution but a way to skip the problem which is incorrect from a juridical point of view and extremely blurry: *depending on the decision taken by the DPP the alternatives are no prosecution or the possibility of facing imprisonment up to 14 years*.[51]

This is the reason why both the House of Lords and the DPP have called for an urgent legislative reform which, despite different attempts, has not taken place yet. As Lewis has pointed out "We are now in uncharted territory, with a reluctant legislature, little guidance from the courts and an opaque process of informal legal change by prosecutor".[52]

---

[48]CFCEE Rapport Euthanasie 2020 (latest published).

[49]"Criminal liability for complicity in another's suicide

(1) A person ("D") commits an offence if

(a) D does an act capable of encouraging or assisting the suicide or attempted suicide of another person, and (b) D's act was intended to encourage or assist suicide or an attempt at suicide."

[50]'Policy for prosecutors in respect of cases of encouraging or assisting suicide', issued by the Director of Public Prosecutions (2010, updated 2014) https://www.cps.gov.uk/legal-guidance/suicide-policy-prosecutors-respect-cases-encouraging-or-assisting-suicide Accessed 19 March 2021.

[51]Coroners and Justice Act 2009, 59 1 (1C).

[52]Lewis (2011), p. 247.

The "reluctance [of the House of Commons] to establish, at least, the circumstances under which assisted suicide would be lawful, is giving way to proposals which increase the existing legal uncertainty".[53]

We could not conceive of a more complete preclusive model.

4.3 France

Because of an almost permanent public debate which encompasses an ongoing public reflection and regular minor legislative adjustments, the situation in France could be termed as "fluid". It is true, however, that such a "soft law feeling" is subject to review precisely due to the impression that legal regulation is a permanent consequence of the last *hard case* or the last decision of the ECtHR or the *Conséil d'État*.

In France, there is a social majority in favour of euthanasia and aided suicide[54] and a shared republican culture on the core aspects of end-of-life issues.[55]

In the twenty-first century, the *Code de la Santé Publique* (CSP) has changed on three occasions.[56] The last reform, Loi n° 2016-87 du 2 février 2016 *créant de nouveaux droits en faveur des malades et des personnes en fin de vie*, introduced deep and continuous palliative sedation as an innovation while keeping its strict

---

[53]Last draft Bill rejected by the Commons -free vote- on May 24, 2015. A current and correct description of the situation in England and Wales, but without sharing the final proposal, in Samanta (2016), pp. 1–23.

A subsequent draft Bill "Homelessness (End of Life Care)" has not advanced, after its first reading on February 2, 2018 in the House of Commons. https://publications.parliament.uk/pa/bills/cbill/2017-2019/0163/18163.pdf, Accessed 18-3-2021. The Bill failed to complete its passage through Parliament before the end of the session. This means the Bill will make no further progress, https://bills.parliament.uk/bills/2209/news. Accessed 18-3-2021.

[54]Between 80 and more than 90% in favour of assisted suicide and euthanasia. Latest data in Le regard des Français sur la Loi Leonetti et la fin de vie, IFOP pour l'ADMD, April 2015. https://www.ifop.com/wp-content/uploads/2018/03/3010-1-study_file.pdf Accessed 7 Aug 2019. For a recent evaluation of the performance of the law, Barret et al. (2018), *Évaluation de l'application de la loi du 2 février 2016 sur la fin de vie*. http://www.igas.gouv.fr/spip.php?article709. Very recently, BVA, Fin de vie: le regard des Français sur la loi du 2 Février 2016, 5 ans après, February 2021. https://www.bva-group.com/sondages/fin-de-vie-le-regard-des-francais-sur-la-loi-du-2-fevrier-2016-5-ans-apres/. Accesed 18-3-2021.

[55]Commission de réflexion sur la fin de la vie en France (2012) 15, 16, *passim*...

[56]Loi n° 2002-303 du 4 mars 2002 relative aux droits des malades et à la qualité du système de santé (Loi Kouchner). Later Loi n° 2005-370 du 22 avril 2005 relative aux droits des malades et à la fin de vie (Loi Leonetti).

distinction with euthanasia;[57] The improvement experienced by the regulation of advanced directives (art. 1111-11 CSP) is also very remarkable.[58]

Additionally, there is a singularity that we must point out: the regulation of assisted suicide (*Code Pénal*, art. 223-13)—*provocation au suicide*—was initially designed to cover situations of assisted suicide that are diverse in nature. Under these circumstances, the Courts resort to mercy to deal with the problems posed by a regulation conceived for a different kind of action...but the concept of mercy is open to various different "sensitivities".[59]

To sum it all up, slowly but surely, France faces the reality of a vast social majority in favour of the regulation of these issues. On the one hand, this could be a consequence of the perception that the effectiveness of legal regulation is relative and, on the other, of the avoidance of the Courts to fully punish participation in assisted suicide. But there is no doubt that France is on the road towards the legal regulation of assisted dying within the framework of her legal system and the doctrine of the ECtHR.[60]

The French Republic would now be slowly evolving *from a preclusive model to a slightly promotional one.*[61]

Perhaps the "Lambert affair" has highlighted some aspects of the current regulation in France and the need to continue with regulatory changes.[62]

4.4 Spain

In the last decade of the twentieth century Spanish society has been transforming its position on the end-of-life aspects in terms similar to those described in general. Particularly since the Sampedro case, which was the catalyst for a change of heart in Spanish society.

In the final review of this paper, the *Ley Orgánica 3/2021*"Organic Law 3/2021, *de regulación de la eutanasia* has been published. Despite its title, the law regulates the "Provision of Aid to Die" as an individual right that includes its benefit nature,

---

[57]'Art. L. 1110-5-2.-*A la demande du patient d'éviter toute souffrance et de ne pas subir d'obstination déraisonnable, une sédation profonde et continue provoquant une altération de la conscience maintenue jusqu'au décès, associée à une analgésie et à l'arrêt de l'ensemble des traitements de maintien en vie, est mise en œuvre dans les cas suivants...' CSP.*

[58]A precise description of the legislative change in Bourdaire-Mignot and Gründler (2016), pp. 1–16.

[59]*Ibidem*, 62, with a disturbing description of the delicate situations criminal courts face.

[60]Latest *Etats Généraux de la bioéthique : Rapport de synthèse du Comité consultatif national d'éthique*, (2018), pp. 129–147.

[61]Horn (2017), pp. 1–2.

[62]Hennette Vauchez (2015). Ordonnance n° 2020-232 du 11 mars 2020 relative au régime des décisions prises en matière de santé, de prise en charge ou d'accompagnement social ou médico-social à l'égard des personnes majeures faisant l'objet d'une mesure de protection juridique.

under the National Health System and with public funding, and can also be provided on a private basis.[63]

The right consists of having the necessary means at one's disposal in favor of the person who expresses a wish to die. There are two ways: direct administration of a substance to the patient by the competent healthcare professional or the prescription or supply to the patient by the healthcare professional of a substance, for self-administration.

The law ensures the right to conscientious objection of health personnel and establishes a set of system controls under the responsibility of a Guarantee and Evaluation Commission under the scope and competence of each Autonomous Community. In addition to the jurisdictional controls inherent to a State governed by the rule of law.

As a right, the legislator bases it on a set of fundamental rights enshrined in the Constitution, such as the right to life, the physical and moral integrity of the person (art. 15 EC), ideological freedom and freedom of conscience (art. 16 EC), the right to privacy (art. 18.1 EC); but also on basic constitutional values and statements such as human dignity (art. 10 EC) and the superior value of freedom (art. 1.1 EC).[64]

4.5 Switzerland

According to articles 114 and 115 of the 1937 Swiss Criminal Code, both euthanasia and assisted suicide are unlawful but only when performed "from selfish motives", which means that when they are performed unselfishly, they are not punishable.[65]

Within this legal framework, different private organisations and associations help those willing to end their lives. As health care is an exclusive competence of the Cantons, and the federal authorities held in 2011 that they had no competence on the matter and that the existing regulation was enough to avoid abuse, at present, only

[63] *Boletín Oficial del Estado (BOE)*, n 72, 25 march, Sec. I. p 34037-34049- Entry into force will take place 3 months after this publication. https://www.boe.es/boe/dias/2021/03/25/pdfs/BOE-A-2021-4628.pdf Accesed 25 March 2021.

Parliamentary documentation, https://www.congreso.es/web/guest/busqueda-de-iniciativas?p_p_id=iniciativas&p_p_lifecycle=0&p_p_state=normal&p_p_mode=view&_iniciativas_mode=mostrarDetalle&_iniciativas_legislatura=XIV&_iniciativas_id=122%2F000020. Accesed 18-3-2021.

[64] The Constitutional Court Portuguese is knowing the constitutionality of the *Decreto da Assembleia da República n 109/XIV, Regula as condições em que a morte medicamente assistida não é punível e altera o Código Penal,* because *requerimiento* of President of Republic to Constitutional Court for *a fiscalização preventiva da constitucionalidade de diversas «normas constantes do Decreto n.° 109/XIV...*". The regulation is similar to Spanish promotional model.

[65] «Celui qui, poussé par un mobile égoïste, aura incité une personne au suicide, ou lui aura prêté assistance en vue du suicide...»

the Cantons of Vaud, Neuchâtel, Genève and Valais allow this kind of activities under strict conditions; any commercial aim is prohibited.[66]

Assisted suicide is not a medical act, but a doctor, as well as any other citizen, can take part in it. The Courts used to rule difficult cases using the current rules, made by a private organisation, the *Swiss Academy of Medical Sciences* (*SAMW-ASSM*), the protocols and criteria of which are stringent both scientifically and professionally.

The criteria to bear in mind in order to consider that assisted suicide is lawful, and that have to be checked out by a third party which does not necessarily have to be a doctor, are the following: suffering an illness which is going to cause imminent death; the application of the treatments accepted by the patient; fully aware patient; a firm, free and pondered will to die.[67] The decision has to be documented and every death has to be reported to the authorities as "not natural";[68] if assistance was provided by a doctor, he or she will not be able to certify the death.

Of all imaginable prototypes of *inactive model,* Switzerland probably is the closest to perfection.[69]

4.6 The Netherlands

The Dutch model has a peculiar origin and is likely to have been imitated. It stemmed from a 1973 *hard case*: "The Postma case".[70] According to articles 293 and 294 of the Criminal Code, both euthanasia and aided suicide were, and still are, criminal offences.[71] But due to the circumstances in the case, the merciful killing of her mother by a family doctor, the Court resorted to the concept of *vis major* supported by article 40 of the Criminal Code. This meant the impossibility to punish the committed criminal offence. Since then, the Netherlands' legal order has progressively described the detailed circumstances under which euthanasia is not punishable, with the participation of the medical profession. After 30 years, this now

[66]The last *avis* of *Conseil Federal* about a physician prosecuted for euthanasia reiterates the existence of sufficient federal regulation on the matter. https://www.parlament.ch/fr/ratsbetrieb/suche-curia-vista/geschaeft?AffairId=20104163 Accessed 8 Aug 2016.

[67]SAMW-ASSM (2018) Attitude face à la fin de vie et à la mort. https://www.samw.ch/dam/jcr:c336fd1b-1751-40e1-a1b0-36a80cf487ed/directives_assm_fin_de_vie_et_mort.pdf. Accessed 19-3-2021.

[68]Autorités cantonales compétentes pour la réception des notifications (2018) https://www.samw.ch/dam/jcr:4f10260c-fe3d-4546-8c61-2d96efc071d9/directives_assm_fin_de_vie_et_mort_annexe_liste_autorites_cantonales.pdf. Accessed 19-3-2021.

[69]Recently, 18 September 2020, the Conseil Fédéral has published an important Rapport, «Améliorer la prise en charge et le traitement des personnes en fin de vie» http://www.nfp67.ch/SiteCollectionDocuments/nfp67-bessere-betreuung-und-behandlung-von-menschen-am-lebensende-fr.pdf, A. 18-3-2021.

[70]An overview of the Netherlands' case in Rietjens et al. (2009). Recently Kouwenhoven et al. (2018).

[71]*Wetboek van Strafrecht.*

rooted practice enjoys an overwhelming social and medical support and shapes into *The Termination of Life on Request and Assisted Suicide (Review Procedures) Act.*[72]

The core of the Dutch regulation lies in the guarantee that euthanasia and assisted suicide will be performed by a doctor in any case, while at the same time recognizing the right to conscientious objection by the medical professionals.

The circumstances under which euthanasia and assisted suicide are lawful systematize the well-established criteria traditionally followed by doctors (art. 2) and, among other measures, secure control by a declaration procedure with the intervention of the forensic scientist (*coroner*) and five territorial Commissions.[73] The Netherlands are the first country to deal with the issue of euthanasia in newborns (Groningen Protocol).[74]

The Netherlands are a clear case of promotional model.[75]

5 The Right to One's Own Death

As described above, death is a natural fact that societies deal with according to their social and cultural values. It is a unique, unrepeatable, and unavoidable experience; a clinical, cultural, and personal event undergoing deep transformations over the last decades.

From a constitutional point of view, merging those three changing perspectives of death is transforming the position of the individual as holder of fundamental rights. This is a consequence of new possible decisions coming up concerning the end of one's own life in which the objects of already existing fundamental rights can be perfectly identified. In other words, it is not a *new* arising right to die, but the materialization of new possibilities to exercise *old* rights because of technological progress. What is new is the increasing possibility of expressing wishes concerning the length of one's own life formally. A new scenario which takes personal decisions to a new dimension.

Up to now, in most cases, the problems concerning the length of life related to how to manage the final stages of life. But this is just the beginning, as decisions over the extension of one's own life are going to be increasingly possible. Under these

[72] *Wet toetsing levensbeëindiging op verzoek en hulp bij zelfdoding*, 12 April 2001.

[73] Doomen (2018), pp. 225–230.

[74] Verhagen and Sauer (2005), pp. 959–962. See also Casonato et al. (2016).

[75] Last report of Regionale Toetsingscommissies Euthanasie (RTE) (2019) https://english.euthanasiecommissie.nl/binaries/euthanasiecommissie-en/documents/publications/annual-reports/2002/annual-reports/annual-reports/RTE_annual+report+2017.pdf. Accessed 18-3-2021. Last Euthanasia Code (2018) https://english.euthanasiecommissie.nl/binaries/euthanasiecommissie-en/documents/publications/euthanasia-code/euthanasia-code-2018/euthanasia-code-2018/euthanasia-code-2018/EuthanasieCode_2018_ENGELS_def.pdf. A. 18 March 2021.

About a recent controversial see, Miller et al. (2019).

circumstances, death will no longer be unexpected but planned. And this is not science fiction, but a new reality waiting for us, jurists, just around the corner.[76]

The end of life increasingly is a process over which the individual decides. And the decision is not about his or her death but about his or her life; a reality that has sparked the debate about the quality of life.[77]

However, this personal perspective of death coexists with the other two. Death is the object of a personal decision according to one's personal values, it is a cultural and social event, and it is a medical fact, although setting the exact moment in which death occurs and life ends is an unresolved issue.[78]

These *three deaths* have never coincided, but it has not been until now that it has become clear that they are different, and the problem is that we are asking the Law to regulate the three of them consistently and simultaneously. The different national regulations briefly described above can be understood as different answers to an unsolvable problem.[79]

Nevertheless, let us suppose that a certain legal order, for instance that of Belgium, adopts a legal regulation which proves to be satisfactory from a technical point of view. The problem is that this would not guarantee the stability of this regulation because the Law lacks a true definition of the end of life. To put it bluntly, we simply do not know when life ends, and we are not referring to a merely clinical and technical issue subject to the sometimes unsettling advance of neurology (brain death).[80]

The biggest problem of the Law is its inability to provide itself with a concept of death. Just with one concept. The recent debate between Duncan Purves and David Shoemaker reminds us of the inconsistencies of every legal regulation and invites judges to a sensible self-restraint.[81] The problem had already been pointed out by David DeGrazia. In the legal realm, different definitions of death coexist; and in some cases, those diverse concepts are subject to the continuous scientific, biomedical, and technical progress which affects the concept of personal identity. To summarize all these ideas that we have just mentioned: When does death occur? When does the personal identity vanish? When does the human organism stop functioning as such? For example, technical advances made in transplantation is already posing important problems concerning the definition of the end of life.

---

[76]Davis (2016), pp. 165–172.

[77]On the idea of *sacredness* in Dworkin, Willems 2016.

[78]Daly (2015), p. 210.

[79]On the limited scope of personal autonomy in the right to die, Gandsman (2017).

[80]A view of the problem, associated with organ donation for transplantation, Eichinger (2015), pp. 9–17. Do not share some author's views.

[81]Shoemaker (2010), p. 486; Purves (2015), pp. 681–682. doi:10.1111/bioe.12175. DeGrazia (2005), pp. 115–158.

A recent proposal on the difference between brain death and death of the organism in Moschella (2016), p. 6.

6 The Right to One's Own Death As a Constitutional and a Public Authorities' Matter

The State was created to guarantee existence, just existence; and, therefore, the State defined the circumstances under which it was possible to take a human life. That is to say, the relationship between the State and its subjects was obviously simple: the State could kill only in certain previously defined cases. From this point of view, the history of the State can be regarded as the progressive extension of the circumstances under which the State cannot end a subject's life i.e. cannot kill one of its subjects. Even today, every State decides with the utmost certainty the circumstances under which it does not guarantee the life of its subjects, e.g. in times of war, because of death penalty, etc.

However, the situations described above are a new scenario which asks the State for a kind of intervention that is alien to its nature and to the purposes it was created for. This could explain the problems arising from resorting to Criminal Law categories when trying to understand end of life issues.[82] The only help we can expect from this perspective is the one provided by the enforcement of the prohibition of all those actions expressly rejected by society.

Death, as the end of life, is now a constitutional matter. This is true even though the constitutional order lacks the ability to regulate it. The reason to understand this clear paradox is very simple: it is the Constitution that enshrines the rules set to guarantee individual freedom; it defines the framework within which the end of life should be regulated.

Every legal order, whether constitutional or not, has always been the expression of values. The problem of the current legal order lies, precisely, in the conversion of those values into *legal* values. In other words, this is about the conversion of those values into legal norms that must be complied with and enforced especially by the Courts and, more specifically, by Constitutional Courts, leaving aside their peculiar normative nature within their respective legal order.[83]

We should however bear in mind that legal principles are not legal rules, a distinction that prevents the Courts from creating *ex novo* complex legal norms. Legal principles are optimization commands, assertions of the utmost importance about fundamental rights. Likewise, not every court has the power to derive a legal mandate from a constitutional principle; and when possible, it should be done complying with the rules governing such a procedure.[84]

Courts are specially exposed to the risk of confusing legal rules, legal principles, and legal values. It is true that the law-maker's silence should be partly blamed for this risk; although it is also true that it is a logical and rational silence. We should

[82]An example in the case of Italy, Palmaro (2012).

[83]We will ignore the eternal problem concerning the limits of constitutional interpretation and its difference with the patent alteration of the precise legal wording. On constitutional interpretation about end of life scenarios, Agosta (2012), pp. 202–213.

[84]*Sensu contrario*, Merkel (2016), pp. 353–360.

acknowledge that end of life issues has a transverse nature, which means that any decision poses a risk in political terms, and therefore explain the reluctance of any governing majority to get to grips with this problem. Very often, the Courts have protested the legislative's idleness e.g. Lord Browne-Wilkinson in *Airedale*:

> Those are questions of law. But behind the questions of law lie moral, ethical, medical and practical issues of fundamental importance to society. [...] regulating the termination of artificial life support being given to patients must, to be acceptable, reflect a moral attitude which society accepts. This has led judges into the consideration of the ethical and other non-legal problems raised by the ability to sustain life artificially which new medical technology has recently made possible. But in my judgment in giving the legal answer to these questions judges are faced with a dilemma. The ability to sustain life artificially is of relatively recent origin. Existing law may not provide an acceptable answer to the new legal questions which it raises. Should judges seek to develop new law to meet a wholly new situation? Or is this a matter which lies outside the area of legitimate development of the law by judges and requires society, through the democratic expression of its views in Parliament, to reach its decisions on the underlying moral and practical problems and then reflect those decisions in legislation?[85]

The result has been the conversion of death into a jurisdictional issue and into a paradigm of the risks and pathologies associated with the application and interpretation of values and principles by the Courts, as the legal doctrine has repeatedly remarked. Firstly, because the judicial decision is often an answer just to the specific case, but not to the general problem; and an answer which in the *hard cases* is provided in the worst possible conditions.[86] Secondly, because the sole recourse to values and principles biases legal argumentation ethically and undermines legal certainty.[87] And lastly, because the courts suffer from *functional stress* when facing death related issues, such as whichever death penalty, medical treatment refusal or life support treatment withdrawal.

Asking the courts to answer whether the Constitution guarantees a right to die or a right to die *with dignity,* or to prove when and how the plaintiff should die is asking too much.

7 And the Future...

Nowadays, the constitutional analysis of end-of-life issues derives/results from the existence of *a right to be helped to die which, at least in Europe, has a constitutional and supranational basis and is nationally implemented.* The biggest difficulty when tackling these issues from a juridical perspective is to discern among medical, bioethical and criminal law scenarios. It is true that they are partly coincident, but

[85]Lord Browne-Wilkinson, Airedale N.H.S. *v.* Bland, pp. 877–878.

[86]Samanta (2016), p. 2.

[87]So, they warn, on *Carter v Canada,* Chan and Somerville (2016), pp. 161–162.

their respective natures are very different. Moreover, the right to be helped to die is different to those three scenarios.

This is so, on the one hand, because it is not the role of Ethics to replace the law. On the other hand, and from the point of view of Constitutional Law, we need to find the scope and the limits of constitutional values and principles on new scenarios, particularly when they concern the most personal and intimate aspects of human life.[88] It should be noted that even the Constitutional order has its boundaries. And, finally, we must free ourselves from classic Criminal Law categories, as they belong to a currently meaningless repressive reasoning. Those concepts, though still valid in their own field, only create confusion when applied to the debate on the help to die. This is the case, for instance, when a Court finds that a given action *constitutes* passive euthanasia.[89] Such an inconsistency shows that the distinction between actions and omissions lacks in this context its traditional relevance and leads to the "resuscitation" of moral criteria.[90]

It is a methodological must to clarify our argument. Killing a patient or letting a patient die are obviously not equivalent either from an ethical, juridical, medical or philosophical point of view. But transferring the consequences of the distinction from one discipline to another is a gross mistake. A medical or ethical misconduct is not necessarily unlawful and vice versa.[91] If the right to be helped to die is dealt with using hybrid arguments the door is open to practices that each one of those perspectives rejects.[92]

As described above, death is highly medicalised nowadays, but this reality does not transform death or the assistance to die into a medical act. On the contrary, doctors' compromise is with the preservation of life and with the quality of life; a new problem that the current legal frameworks have satisfactorily solved.

Nevertheless, the situation is very different in those legal orders where the assistance to die does not exist yet. *Under such circumstances the position of the medical profession is extremely difficult.*

Of course, there is an ongoing social debate…

Our immediate future is an ever-changing scenario due to an extremely fluid technological horizon and the reality of an irreversibly medicalized death.

[88]Mancuso (2011), p. 413; Bin (2007), pp. 11–52.

[89]*Bundesgerichtshof–BGH, BGH,* 20 June 2010, n.2 StR 454/09. In Lantero (2016), p. 312; Schlegel (2014).

[90]Chan and Somerville (2016), p. 158.

[91]Maybe Gillon would make this mistake, Gillon (2016).

[92]A proposed ruse to circumvent the Israeli law in Glickm (2015), p. 680; Ravitsky (2005), p. 415.

References

Agosta S (2012) Bioetica e costituzione, I/II. Giuffré, Milano
Airedale NHS Trust v Bland: HL 4 Feb 1993
Arruego G (2011) Vida, integridad personal y nuevos escenarios de la biomedicina. Granada, Comares
Arruego G (2019a) Los confines del derecho fundamental a la vida. Revista Española de Derecho Constitucional 115:111–137. https://doi.org/10.18042/cepc/redc.115.04
Arruego G (2019b) La inelasticidad del derecho fundamental a la vida y su relación con la muerte asistida. In: Chueca R (ed) Las fronteras de los derechos fundamentales en la Constitución normativa. Centro de Estudios Políticos y Constitucionales, Madrid, pp 247–286
Barret L, Fillion S, Viossat LC (2018) Évaluation de l'application de la loi du 2 février 2016 sur la fin de vie. Inspection Générale des Affaires Sociales, http://www.igas.gouv.fr/spip.php?article709. Accessed 10 Aug 2019
Bernal I (2020) Euthanasia: trends and opinions in Spain. Rev Esp Sanid Penit 22(3):112–115. https://doi.org/10.18176/resp.00020
Bin R (2007) Ché cosa é la costituzione? Quaderni costituzionali 1:11–52
Bourdaire-Mignot C, Gründler T (2016) La nouvelle loi française sur la fin de vie. Premiers regards sur la loi du 2 février 2016 créant de nouveaux droits en faveur des malades et des personnes en fin de vie. BioLaw Journal–Rivista di BioDiritto (1/2016). https://doi.org/10.15168/2284-4503-134
Brosset E (2011) La fin de la vie et le droit européen. In: Negri S (ed) Self-determination, dignity and end-of-life-care. regulating advance directives in international and comparative perspective. Martinus NIJHOFF, Leiden, pp 87–105
BVA, Fin de vie: le regard des Français sur la loi du 2 Février 2016, 5 ans après, February 2021. BVA Group. https://www.bva-group.com/sondages/fin-de-vie-le-regard-des-francais-sur-la-loi-du-2-fevrier-2016-5-ans-apres/. Accesed 18 Mar 2021
Carter v. Canada (Attorney General) 2015 SCC 5
Casonato C et al (2016) Forum: Eutanasia e minori. Biolaw-Rivista di BioDiritto 3:5–79. https://doi.org/10.15168/blj.v0i3
Centro de Investigaciones Sociológicas. Estudio 2752. http://www.cis.es/cis/opencm/ES/1_encuestas/estudios/ver.jsp?estudio=9200. *Estudio* 2759 http://www.cis.es/cis/opencm/ES/1_encuestas/estudios/ver.jsp?estudio=9360. Accessed 6 Aug 2019
CFCEE Rapport Euthanasie 2020. Commission fédérale de Contrôle et d'Évaluation de l'Euthanasie https://organesdeconcertation.sante.belgique.be/sites/default/files/documents/8_rapport-euthanasie_2016-2017-fr.pdf. Accessed 18 Mar 2021
Chan B, Somerville M (2016) Converting the "right to life" to the "right to physician-assisted suicide" and euthanasia. Med Law Rev 24(2):143–175. https://doi.org/10.1093/medlaw/fww005
Comité Directeur pour la Bioéthique (CDBI) (2008) Les décisions médicales dans les situations de fin de vie et les implications éthiques des choix possible. Rapp. Lucie Hacpille. Conseil de l'Europe, Strasbourg
Commission de réflexion sur la fin de vie en France. Rapport à François Hollande Président de la République Française (2012) Penser solidairement la fin de vie. Paris. https://solidarites-sante.gouv.fr/IMG/pdf/Rapport-de-la-commission-de-reflexion-sur-la-fin-de-vie-en-France.pdf. Accesed 20 Nov 2016
Daly P (2015) Palliative sedation, foregoing life-sustaining treatment, and aid-in-dying: what is the difference? Theor Med Bioeth 36:197–213. https://doi.org/10.1007/s11017-015-9329-5
Davis JK (2016) Four ways life extension will change our relationship with death. Bioethics 30 (3):165–172. https://doi.org/10.1111/bioe.12161
De Schutter O (2003) L'aide au suicide devant la Cour européenne des droits de l'homme. Rev trim dr h 53:76–79
DeGrazia D (2005) Human identity and bioethics. Cambridge University Press, Cambridge

Doomen J (2018) The struggle unto death. BioLaw J Rivista di BioDiritto (2):225–230. https://doi.org/10.15168/2284-4503-315
Dworkin R (1997) Assisted suicide: what the court really said. New York Review of Books 44 (14) sept. Accessed 6 Aug 2019
Eichinger T (2015) Brain death, justified killing and the zombification of humans – does the transplantation dilemma require new ways of conceptualizing life and death? In: Jox RJ et al (eds) Organ transplantation in times of donor shortage. Springer, Heildelberg. https://doi.org/10.1007/978-3-319-16441-0_2n
Elvira A (2015) La dignidad humana en el Tribunal Europeo de Derechos Humanos. In: Chueca R (ed) Dignidad humana y derecho fundamental. CEPC, Madrid, pp 203–213
Etats Généraux de la bioéthique: Rapport de synthèse du Comité consultatif national d'éthique (2018). https://www.ccne-ethique.fr/sites/default/files/rapport_de_synthese_ccne_bat.pdf. Accessed 10 Aug 2019
Feuillet B (2015) Fin(s) de la vie: quelles perspectives? Rapport de synthèse. In: Bévière-Boyer B, Belrhomari N (eds) Les enjeux de la fin de vie dans le domaine de la santé. Regards partagés entre politique, médecine, droit et éthique. LEH, Paris, pp 176–183
Foley EP (2011) The law of life and death. Harvard University Press, Cambridge
Gandsman A (2017) The paradox of choice and the illusion of autonomy: the construction of ethical subjects in right to die activism. Death Stud. https://doi.org/10.1080/07481187.2017.1396646
Gillon R (2016) Why wrote my advance decision to refuse life-prolonging treatment: and why the law on sanctity of life remains problematic. J Med Ethics:5. https://doi.org/10.1136/medethics-2016-103538
Glickm S (2015) Withdrawing or withholding life-sustaining therapy. Bioethics 29(9). https://doi.org/10.1111/bioe.12172
Gross v. Switzerland (Application n° 67810/10) ECtHR
Haas v. Switzerland (Application no. 31322/07) ECtHR
Hennette Vauchez S (2015) Pourquoi l'affaire Lambert n'en finit pas. BioLaw J Rivista di BioDiritto (3/2015). https://doi.org/10.15168/2284-4503-105
Horn R (2017) The 'French exception': the right to continuous deep sedation at the end of life. J Med Ethics:1–2. https://doi.org/10.1136/medethics-2017-104484
Koch v. Germany (Application no. 497/09) ECtHR
Kouwenhoven PSC, van Thiel GJMW, van der Heide A, Rietjens JAC, van Delden JJM (2018) Developments in euthanasia practice in the Netherlands: Balancing professional responsibility and the patient's autonomy. Eur J General Practice. https://doi.org/10.1080/13814788.2018.1517154
Lantero C (2016) Euthanasie et suicide assisté. In: Byk C, Marliac C (eds) 20 ans de lois de bioéthique. MA ed, Paris, pp 301–326
Lehmann LS, Prokopetz JJZ (2012) Redefining physician's role in assisted dying. N Engl J Med 367(2):97–99. https://doi.org/10.1056/NEJMp1205283
Lewis P (2011) Law at the end of life in England and Wales. In: Negri S (ed) Self-determination, dignity and end-of-life-care. regulating advance directives in international and comparative perspective. Martinus Nijhoff Publishers, Leiden, pp 221–248
Mancuso F (2011) Non-negotiability of ethical values and constitutional democracy. In: Negri S (ed) Self-determination, dignity and end-of-life care, pp 411–418
McCann and others *v.* UK (Application no. 18984/91) ECtHR
McMahan J (2006) An alternative to brain death. J Law Med Ethics 34(1):44–48. https://doi.org/10.1111/j.1748-720X.2006.00007.x
McMorrow T (2019) Voluntary euthanasia, assisted suicide & law reform: a sketch of the Canadian experience. BioLaw J Rivista di BioDiritto (1/2019):267–282. https://doi.org/10.15168/2284-4503-364
Merkel R (2016) Killing or letting die? Proposal of a (somewhat) new answer to a perennial question. J Med Ethics 42:353–360. https://doi.org/10.1136/medethics—103495

Merkouris P (2012) Assisted suicide in the jurisprudence of the ECtHR. In: Negri S (ed) Self-determination, dignity and end-of-life care. Brill, Leiden, pp 107–126
Miller DG, Dresser R, Kim SYH (2019) Advance euthanasia directives: a controversial case and its ethical implications. J Med Ethics 45:84–89
Moschella M (2016) Integrated but not whole? Applying an ontological account of human organismal unity to the brain death debate. Bioethics 30(8):550–556. https://doi.org/10.1111/bioe.12258
Palmaro M (2012) Eutanasia: diritto o delitto? Il conflitto tra i principi di autonomia e di indisponibilità della vita umana. Giappichelli, Milano
Pedrot P (2007) Vie et mort: la frontière brouillée. In: Doat M, Le Goff J, Pedrot P (eds) Droit el complexité. Pour une nouvelle intelligence du droit vivant. PU Rennes, Rennes, pp 77–82
Plomer A (2005) The law and ethics of medical research. Cavendish Publishing, London
Pretty v. UK (Application no. 2346/02) ECtHR
Purves D (2015) The significance of personal identity for death. Bioethics 29(9):681–682. https://doi.org/10.1111/bioe.12175
R (on the application of Purdy) *v.* Director of Public Prosecutions House of Lords, Sess. 2008-09, [2009] UKHL 45
Rapport du Conseil Fédéral, Suisse, "Améliorer la prise en charge et le traitement des personnes en fin de vie" http://www.nfp67.ch/SiteCollectionDocuments/nfp67-bessere-betreuung-und-behandlung-von-menschen-am-lebensende-fr.pdf, Accesed 18 Mar 2021
Ravitsky V (2005) Times on ventilators. BMJ 330:415. https://doi.org/10.1136/bmj.330.7488.415
Riccioni L, Busca MT, Busatta L, Orsi L, Gristina GR (2016) La limitazione dei trattamenti: una forma di eutanasia? Un approccio scientifico al dibattito sulle decisioni alla fine della vita. Recenti Prog Med 107(3):127–139. https://doi.org/10.1701/2182.23602
Rietjens JAC, van Tol DG, Schermer M, van der Heide A (2009) Judgement of suffering in the case of a euthanasia request in The Netherlands. J Med Ethics 35(8). https://doi.org/10.1136/jme.2008.028779
Samanta J (2016) Enforcing human rights at end of life: is there a better approach? In: Diver A, Miller J (eds) Justiciability of human rights law in domestic jurisdictions. Springer, Cham, pp 1–23. https://doi.org/10.1007/978-3-319-24016-9
Schlegel E (2014) La libéralisation de l'euthanasie passive en Allemagne–Aspects comparatifs au regard de l'affaire Lambert. RGD 7:65–71. https://www.revuegeneraledudroit.eu/blog/2014/07/06/dossier-special-sur-laffaire-lambert-vi-la-liberalisation-de-leuthanasie-passive-en-allemagne/. Accessed 8 Aug 2019
Serrano del Rosal R, Heredia A (2018) Spanish attitudes towards euthanasia and physician-assisted suicide. REIS 161:103–120. https://doi.org/10.5477/cis/reis.161.103
Shoemaker D (2010) The insignificance of personal identity for bioethics. Bioethics 24(9):481–489. https://doi.org/10.1111/j.1467-8519.2009.01719.x
Verhagen E, Sauer PJJ (2005) The Groningen protocol—Euthanasia in severely ill newborns. N Engl J Med 352:959–962. https://doi.org/10.1056/NEJMp058026
Willems G (2016) The ECtHR "end of life" case law in the light of the concept of "intrinsic value of life" theorized by Ronald Dworkin. In: Hoc A, Wattier S, Willems G (eds) Human rights as a basis for reevaluating and reconstructing the law. Bruylant, Bruxelles, pp 313–333

Patients' Rights at the End of Life in Chilean Juridical System. Legal and Jurisprudential Analysis from Biolaw's Perspective

Erick Valdés and Juan Alberto Lecaros

Abstract In this chapter, we will show that the legislative framework to protect patients' rights in Chile is inherently reductionist and points to a limited conception of autonomy, which dwindles patients' abilities of self-determination. Given such legal context, biolaw can play a key role in designing and establishing effective biojuridical models to solve conflicts between different moral values and visions, arisen in jurisdictional and para-jurisdictional bodies, especially when the laws are inconsistent or ambiguous. We will conclude that Chilean legal frameworks are quite unable to support the rapid evolution of new healthcare quandaries and define a legal way to regulate healthcare practices at the end of life, as well as to delimit normative impact of them in our society, within so sensitive axiological contexts such as individual autonomy and the right to self-determine the vital project.

1 Introduction

As biolaw is aimed at understanding legal implications of new quandaries arisen in bioscientific settings, it also seeks to: (1) Resolve difficult dilemmas emerged by virtue of rapid advances of health technologies and new possibilities for treatment, and (2) Peruse how these new possibilities impact societies' legal frameworks.

These tasks have not been carried out by Chilean legal system thus far. Jurists and legal theorists have been immune to the need of giving the fields of medicine and clinical practices an effective regulation. In this fashion, the above mentioned has prevented legal certainty and security from colonizing medical field. It is true that the problem of creating a legislative framework for patients right has already been addressed in Chile through the Law No. 20.584 (2012), which rules rights and duties persons have in healthcare's atmospheres. However, such regulation is outdated and

E. Valdés (✉)
International Network of Biolaw, Washington, DC, USA

J. A. Lecaros
Observatory of Bioethics and Law, Universidad del Desarrollo, Santiago, Chile
e-mail: jlecaros@udd.cl

L. Busatta, C. Casonato (eds.), *Axiological Pluralism*, Ius Gentium: Comparative Perspectives on Law and Justice 92, https://doi.org/10.1007/978-3-030-78475-1_13

counterintuitive, since, far from being grounded on a new biojuridical hermeneutics, it is based upon traditional law's categories. As a matter of fact, let us see one of its various controversial points. In its article 16, Law No. 20.584 states:

The person informed that his health condition is terminal has the right to give or withhold his willingness to undergo any treatment having the effect of artificially prolonging his life, insofar as ordinary care is held. In no case, refusal will aim the artificial acceleration of death.

In other words, the article points out that the patient has the right to refuse any treatment, which artificially prolong the process of imminent death insofar as his goal is to not anticipate death. However, it happens that, whatever the patient's purpose is, rejecting an artificial life support treatment will always mean speeding up the process of death regarding the clinical means applied to delay that process. In other words, what the law states is that the patient is allowed to do A as long as he does not intend it occurs B. However, the legislator seems not to notice two very important things: (1) In situations of terminally ill patients, it is expected that when A is made, B always occurs, and (2) The law does not determine who judges the patient's intention (if such a thing is possible). At this point, it might well be that any refusal of treatment of a terminally ill patient was understood as a positive intention to die as soon as possible. Therefore, the law authorises the patient to do something impossible, which, strictly speaking, means that it allows him to do nothing.[1]

Consequently, we will prove that the Law No. 20.584 is inherently reductionist and points to a limited conception of autonomy, which dwindles patients' abilities of self-determination. Given such legal context, biolaw can play a key role in designing and establishing effective biojuridical models to solve conflicts between different moral values and visions, arisen in jurisdictional and para-jurisdictional bodies, especially when the laws are inconsistent or ambiguous.

Therefore, in Chile, juridical criteria to rule medical practices and physicians-patients' relationship are still insufficient as we will see in the jurisprudential analysis of a paradigmatic case of Chilean jurisprudence we will carry out upon later. However, before doing that, we need to identify, define and justify some biojuridical categories related to and, in some way, grounded on axiological pluralism, which are useful to configure our analysis.

2 Biolaw and Axiological Pluralism

Biolaw has historically had an eclectic epistemology.[2] Since its first relevant theorical articulation,[3] various conceptions have arisen and been fossilised in the international academic context. These epistemologies differ very significantly from

[1]Valdés (2015), p. 1204.

[2]Valdés and Lecaros (2019).

[3]Rendtorff and Kemp (2000).

one another, and justify the meaning and nature of biolaw from divergent arguments, criteria and ideologies.[4] Therefore, there is neither clarity nor consensus on what biolaw is about, and what its boundaries regarding bioethics should be.

Understanding biolaw as intrinsically depending on bioethics is a mistake. The conceptual lightness of biolaw's traditional conceptions that their theoretical basis is ethical instead of juridical. This does not mean that ethics is trivial or insubstantial, or there is no any relationship between bioethics and biolaw. However, affirming that biolaw cannot be understood without bioethics is, on the one hand, going too far and, on the other, saying too little about this new field. Asserting that "biolaw is only understood if one takes into account its necessary and intimate link with bioethics",[5] or that "biolaw became a concept that covers all legal judgments about bioethical questions, independent of the type of legal system in which these legal decisions are made",[6] or that "legal arguments presuppose moral arguments in all cases,"[7] or that "biolaw became a philosophy of law that researches legal issues in bioethics",[8] or that "in the United States, legal norms have emerged as central to discussions of bioethics",[9] and accept that "the legal framework for bioethics issues has intentionally or self-consciously adopted ethical norms and ethical modes of reasoning",[10] represent very reductionist statements that have understood, almost by inertia, that biolaw is parasitical upon bioethics and does not represent an independent epistemological field.[11]

This wrong intellection has been strengthened from seven different relationships that diverse biolaw's conceptions have built over the years between this new field and bioethics. These relationships have been called: juridification, complementation, subjection, overlap, substitution, colonization, and intersection.[12]

The first epistemology has been called European conception of biolaw[13] and it is characterised by an alleged jurdification of bioethical principles and a diffuse complementation between bioethics and biolaw. In fact, this theory understands biolaw as a juridified bioethics,[14] meaning common morality norms originally systematised by American bioethics[15] and lacking binding legal force, are also considered as legal canons to govern bioscientific and biomedical practices that entail important risks for human beings. The idea of biolaw developed by Rendtorff

[4]Valdés (2019, 2021).

[5]Gros Espiell (2011), pp. 177–178.

[6]Kemp (2019), p. 20.

[7]Beyleveld and Brownsword (2000), p. 179.

[8]Kemp (2019), p. 20.

[9]Johnson et al. (2008), p. 1.

[10]Johnson et al. (2008), p. 1.

[11]Singer (2019), p. viii; Valdés (2019), p. 43.

[12]Valdés (2021).

[13]Valdés (2019, 2021).

[14]Rendtorff and Kemp (2000).

[15]Beauchamp and Childress (2019).

and Kemp was accepted, deepened and disseminated in most of the countries of central and northern Europe, including England. For this reason, it was called it European conception.

While this school accepts American principlism as a deliberative and also normative framework, it does not work with the same principles. Rendtorff and Kemp[16] identify the principles of European biolaw as autonomy, dignity, integrity and vulnerability, which they certainly call, "principles of European bioethics and biolaw." These general norms are considered as an expression of the European humanist tradition, which emphasizes the ontological value of the human being, as well as its self-realization and development in society. In this sense, these principles would be binding guidelines to deliberate and rule legal and ethical controversies arising in biomedical environs.

This conception defines the principles of biolaw as common morality standards with no legally binding force. In this sense, European biolaw is simply a soft law. Moreover, the alleged legal nature of European biolaw is arbitrary since its principles are general ethical norms that, from a naturalistic perspective, should be positivized like any natural law. In this fashion, the principles of European biolaw are also bioethical principles, which is not compellingly justified. In addition, as the principles are sometimes ethical norms and sometimes legal norms, confusion comes into play, and even worse, an overlap of normative dimensions emerges.

Therefore, European biolaw lacks epistemological density since it is based on vague, general and content-thin norms. In addition, as this conception does not specify these principles into rules of narrower scope and greater content it has no regulatory accuracy.

The second epistemology is called Mediterranean conception.[17] This conception is clearly anthropocentric, since it takes several epistemological bases of human rights, and considers the human being as the first and only target of any regulation. Most of the Spanish, French and Italian jurists have developed this idea of biolaw, which is why, despite being, strictly speaking, a theory born and distilled in the old continent, it was called Mediterranean conception, since it was necessary to specify it and distinguish it, methodologically and epistemologically, from the European conception.

There are authors who highlight some novel aspects of bioethics' methodology, such as its interdisciplinary discourse, namely, its approach to conflicts provoked by bioscientific practices from different but complementary perspectives converging inside bioethics.[18] Nevertheless, while these authors assume biolaw's disciplinary emancipation from bioethics, they fail to discern the epistemological and normative gaps take biolaw apart from bioethics. In fact, Romeo Casabona and Romeo

[16]Rendtorff and Kemp (2000), pp. 25–56.

[17]Valdés (2019, 2021).

[18]Romeo Casabona and Romeo Malanda (2019), p. 67.

Malanda affirm that from a broad sense, and taking into account bioethics' empirical scopes, law should also be integrated into it.[19]

According to French biojurists, biolaw is a constellation of bioethical laws[20] or bionorms,[21] which provide more content to bioethics in order for it to infers, understands and discerns what the best regulation for bioscientific practices should be.

On the other hand, the French school affirms a consubstantial relationship between the so-called bioethical laws and fundamental values of European society.[22] Namely, the legally binding status of a bioethical law must be in full harmony with and be based on a *prima facie* non-binding moral standard. This connects Mediterranean conception of biolaw with the human rights' doctrine, which makes evident some features this school shares with the European and International conceptions of biolaw.

According to the above, biolaw implies a consubstantial relationship between bioethics and human rights, since Mediterranean biolaw works with universal moral principles, pointing to the recognition of new fundamental rights such as to freely dispose of one's body (as long as it does not violate personal dignity), and the right to a bodily integrity.[23]

Also, this conception understands biolaw as an open, updated and attentive law.[24] It is an open law because it is building laws for decision-making at the intersection of science and ethics. In other words, biolaw, apart from being an open law, would also be an instrument of bioethics.

Therefore, the Mediterranean conception, overall considers biolaw to be a field tributary upon bioethics, since its theoretical and practical justification, as well as its legitimization to address juridical quandaries arisen from biomedical practices, depends on bioethical evolution. Having said that, it is possible to affirm that this conception encompasses subjection of biolaw upon bioethics, and an overlap of two different normative dimensions.

The third theory was called American conception,[25] which utters a consubstantial relationship between bioethics and biolaw. This relation is determined by a bioethical colonization of American courts as well as a complementation between bioethics and traditional law. In fact, American biolaw would be a law supported by bioethics' epistemology, aimed at addressing legal issues emerged from new genetic techniques. In other words, biolaw would simply be law applied to new problems of bioethical interest, which means substitution and colonization between those two fields.

---

[19]Romeo Casabona and Romeo Malanda (2019), p. 67.

[20]Lenoir (2000), p. 221.

[21]Fagot-Largeault (2000), p. 27.

[22]Lenoir (2000), pp. 222–223.

[23]Lenoir (2000), p. 224.

[24]Casonato (2019), pp. 77–91.

[25]Valdés (2019, 2021).

This conception is also principlist, but, unlike what European biolaw proposes,[26] it rejects the idea of using a special framework of principles for Europe.[27] Indeed, the European conception considers that Europe has a moral and human rights tradition different from that of the United States, which is why it supposed to need a framework different from the American principlist model. In this fashion, it has been stated that Georgetown bioethics principles are only effective within a common American moral framework, widely divergent from European morality and tradition.[28] However, this claim seems to be weak, as misunderstands American principlism.[29] Indeed, Beauchamp and Childress configure bioethical principles as common (universal) morality norms able to work in Europe or any other place in the world.[30] Otherwise, principlism should be based on tradition, culture, beliefs, identity and, at the end of the day, prejudices of American morality.

On the other hand, the American legal system has played a very important role in how public opinion perceives the field of bioethics.[31] However, it is not only the public mass that recognizes the intrinsic connection between law and bioethical issues, but also leading scholars in the field, paradigmatic books, and bioethical organizations in general. All of them agree on the relevance that law has had in achieving a deeper and more mature understanding of bioethics.

An obvious point of convergence between biolaw and bioethics would be the methodology used in both fields as the common law system rests on a methodology that has been preponderant in the bioethical discourse.[32] Indeed, as the essential method of common law model is law evolving from court's' rulings, facts and circumstances examined case by case create priors for subsequent judicial decisions. In this way, common law principles emerge from the analysis of convergences and divergences of different concrete situations. This casuistry, which, together with principlism, is a key deliberative model in the history and development of bioethics, is also remarkable in the evolution of biomedical law or biolaw.

However, American biolaw's advance depends on jurisprudence's evolution, which implies an unsystematic deployment of it as well as an important epistemological fragility in its configuration.

Moreover, by obeying a realistic model of law, American biolaw is excessively reactive and, therefore, seems unable to create normative universes of relevant conceptual and hermeneutical density.

The fourth theory is called International conception of biolaw,[33] which understands this field as a collection of international instruments mostly created by

[26]Rendtorff and Kemp (2019).

[27]Beauchamp (2019), p. 8.

[28]Holm (1994), p. 333.

[29]Beauchamp (2019), p. 9.

[30]Beauchamp and Childress (2019).

[31]Mekinoff (2001), pp. 1–3.

[32]Johnson et al. (2008), p. 2.

[33]Valdés (2021).

UNESCO and the EU, containing an extensive cast of non-legally binding provisions and recommendations to be adopted in the European regulation of biomedicine. The entire catalogue of recommendations, namely all non-binding provisions, come from the intersection between American bioethics and human rights. In this sense, all the provisions are an expression of *prima facie* moral principles lacking relevant epistemological muscle.

Some instruments of International biolaw are:

- Universal Declaration on the Human Genome and Human Rights, UNESCO, 1997.
- Declaration on the Responsibilities of the Present Generations Towards Future Generations, UNESCO, 1997.
- Convention for the Protection of Human Rights and Dignity of the Human Being with Regard to the Application of Biology and Medicine, EUROPEAN UNION (Oviedo Convention), 1997.
- Charter of Fundamental Rights of the European Union, European Union, 2000.
- International Declaration on Human Genetic Data, UNESCO 2003.
- 25 Recommendations on the Ethical, Legal and Social Implications of Genetic Testing, European Communities, 2004.
- Universal Declaration on Bioethics and Human Rights, UNESCO, 2005.
- United Nations Declaration on Human Cloning, United Nations, 2005.
- The Precautionary Principle, UNESCO 2005.

All of them share three features: i) the principles underlying the recommendations, ii) principles' meaning and content, and iii) dignity as the overriding principle of each instrument.

This seems to be a tautological conception of biolaw. Indeed, being a constellation of instruments and principles working as non-binding provisions of international biolaw, being replicated in most conventions and declarations is practically inevitable. International biolaw's principles are found several times repeated themselves in different instruments. This means the prescriptive configuration of the principles is also similar and, in many cases, identical in almost all instruments.

Finally, by pointing to an intersection between bioethics and human rights, international biolaw represents only a cast of non-binding recommendations turning into a soft law, which is clashing to the binding regulatory outcome that biolaw must achieve as a new branch of law.

Regarding all the above mentioned, we can recognise some specific features of biolaw that none of the traditional conceptions have been able to identify. By now, we can highlight that biolaw:[34] i) opens new regulatory frameworks, through the identification and redefinition of traditional legal categories; ii) identifies and defines new individual subjective rights (biorights); iii) identifies and defines new obligations for individuals and for the State; iv) provides greater legal certainty and security to rule and legislate on healthcare practices; v) identifies and defines

[34] Valdés (2021).

principles and rules of deliberative purpose and public policy implications; vi) is a new branch of law able to enhance other traditional branches; and vii) has a horizontal and multilateral legal perspective, namely, it influences and irradiates other areas of law, providing a comprehensive approach to healthcare issues of legal scope.

In addition, the social relevance of the consequences and legal implications of healthcare is indisputable, since such importance is rooted in complex multifactorial relationships that involve not only science and bioethics, but also, law and culture in general. On the other hand, there is a close connection between biojuridical affairs, constitutional law, and human rights within the framework of axiological pluralism: How should patients' autonomy be read in countries with constitutions characterised by an axiological content? What is more important: the right to make healthcare decisions or the unconditional protection of human life? These questions point out key juridical categories that claim for more pluralistic hermeneutics, such as dignity, self-determination, integrity, justice, and equality, among others.

The preceding diagnosis indicates the need to identify and define a more flexible and pluralistic binding legal framework to legislate and regulate controversial cases in healthcare field. This urgency becomes even more evident if we consider some objective facts that show the ineffectiveness of Chilean positive law to address certain healthcare issues:

i) There exist legal polarized positions on these issues, which preclude a fruitful dialogue that moves forward towards a consensus, as well as paralyzes the law-making process.
ii) Current legal categories are insufficient to address complex cases, insofar as the interpretation of the facts and their implications and consequences is subjective (contingent to inclinations, beliefs, values and preferences), and judges often declare ignorance on those matters.
iii) There are regulatory gaps and loopholes, as legislation and regulation regarding healthcare issues is incomplete or non-existent.

These facts reveal inadequacies of Chilean legal system to regulate different aspects of healthcare practices. In this sense, as we shall see, it is essential to: i) redefine and extend the epistemological scope of traditional legal concepts to ensure a better understanding of possible impacts and legal implications of healthcare advances, and ii) identify new categories or legal instruments that imbue the field of healthcare legislation and regulation of greater legal certainty and security.

Learning from the European experience is essential to promote the integration of biorights into Chilean legal system, giving them constitutional status and recognizing their category of fundamental rights.[35] Also, following the successful French experience, we think that the constitutional block can open fruitful paths for such integration. In fact, the improvement of the constitutional protection of fundamental

[35]Rendtorff and Kemp (2000), p. 143.

rights requires a pluralistic reception of international standards on individual subjective rights.

We emphasize here that what we call biorights are not only the result of dogmatic development occurred by virtue of healthcare issues addressed by international law in the European Union and the Council of Europe. Nevertheless, they rather emerge from an epistemological and methodological deepening into the general principles of biolaw—autonomy, dignity, integrity and vulnerability—where a European legal framework aimed at protecting human beings has derived from.[36] Biorights' origin, then, is inherently linked to fundamental rights, and demands Chilean legal system to enhance traditional legal categories in order to extend biorights protection as an essential dimension of constitutional democracy.

In this fashion, the constitutionalization of biorights must be supported according to the way their effective protection is carried out. As they are related to personality rights, they play an important role in how the states will allocate their resources to deal with these new problematic scenarios. Therefore, biorights immediately become a matter of public order, which must be addressed from a pluralistic perspective. This does not mean an overstated dispersion of new categories of constitutional norms, but rather the extension of fundamental rights, tuned with the new possibilities of damage opened in healthcare systems.

Considering all the above, we shall carry out a jurisprudential analysis of the following case, by demonstrating that Chilean Law No. 20.584 is unable to effectively recognise and develop workable and useful juridical standards to observe and respect patients' rights at the end of life.

3 Analysis of the Law No. 20.584 Applied to the Case

Before analysing the case study, and considering the merits of judges' arguments as well as the judicial function in a legal model that, as we shall see, strongly restricts axiological pluralism, we must address some dimensions of the law applied to the case in order to assess the jurisdictional response.

Taking into consideration the functions of biolaw that we discussed in the previous section, we can identify three dimensions in which biolaw can contribute by generating legal norms to regulate plural and complex values issues in open and democratic societies, such as healthcare decisions at the end of life. These dimensions work as an evaluative framework for any biojuridical legislation regarding its adequacy or flexible adaptation to rule clinical practice in those complex and axiologically diverse contexts. In other words, this evaluative framework contributes to the construction of a "new model of sustainable pluralism" for biolaw.[37]

[36] Valdés (2015, 2021).

[37] Busatta (2016), p. 36.

The three dimensions in which biolaw can contribute to engender an adequate normative suitable to axiologically plural contexts such as biomedical and clinical practice are: i) the legislative design (coherence of rules system); ii) the legislative technique (internal consistency of norms); iii) the para-jurisdictional institutional pluralism. These are the dimensions we analyse in the law applied to the case study.

With the evaluation of the law applied to the case, we seek to demonstrate that the imbalance between these dimensions leads to an unsustainable biolaw model. Indeed, we will argue that the law applied to the case reflects a protectionist biolaw model that fails in fully guaranteeing the rights that it should enshrine the right to accept or refuse treatment. This model represents an extreme in biolaw, characterised by stiffening certain *a priori* values by preventing their balancing from being carried out in relation to other legally protected interests. At the other end we have a model that we call divergent or legally anomic. In this model, the legislator opts for not regulating morally controversial situations in societies where debate on clinical decisions about life and death of human beings is strongly polarised.[38]

The middle way between the two models would be a third one that we call "reflective equilibrium model", borrowing the concept developed by Rawls, mainly in his *Theory of Justice*. With this concept, we suggest a biolaw model that enables dynamically adjusting legal principles and considered judgments applied to the rapid advances in life sciences and their technological applications, which constantly challenge our beliefs schemes, lifestyles and social practices. This concept can be explored to be applied into biolaw, understood as a constructive model to dynamically balance principles and considered judgments, so that we can justify them when facing ever-changing social situations.[39]

A biojuridical legislation that tends towards a model of "reflective equilibrium" should be able to balance a plurality of axiological contexts (personal, social, cultural, religious, scientific and medical) in order to maximise the protection of legally relevant interests and, especially, enhance people self-determination according to their own beliefs, values and life projects.

In the draft law No. 20.584, the legislator established that one of its inspiring principles, together with the principle of dignity and autonomy in clinical decisions, is respect for terminally ill persons:

Enshrining the possibility of "limiting therapeutic effort" in order to avoid what has been called therapeutic obstinacy or stubbornness, is today, in our view, a general bioethical consensus. Theoretical and practical difficulties of the necessary distinction of this situation, in which extraordinary and unnecessary actions are avoided, regarding those in which death process is artificially accelerated, either through positive acts whose purpose is to seek death or through deliberate omission

[38]Lecaros (2019).

[39]Rawls (1971), p. 18.

of reasonable, necessary or ordinary actions, is the crucial challenge of the proposed legal formulation.[40]

The legislator justified this principle adopting a protectionist approach to decisions at the end of life. According to this approach human life is understood as an absolute good, reflecting a lack of consistency or rationality in various rules governing patient autonomy.[41]

While the legislator recognizes the patient's right to accept or refuse any procedure or treatment related to his healthcare, in a free, voluntary, intentional and informed way, he restricts a full exercise of this right, even denied that same right already recognised. This glaring contradiction of the legislator appear in the three dimensions that we have mentioned before.

3.1 *Legislative Design Problems: A Protectionist Model*

The set of rules that guarantees patients' autonomy in the law No. 20.584 (Paragraph 6°. On persons' autonomy in their healthcare, Articles 14 to 20) is designed in such a way that results in a merely declaratory recognition of self-determination of persons in clinical practice. In our view, this affects the essence of fundamental rights recognised and protected in Chilean Constitution, such as right to life, and to physical and mental integrity, (Article 19 No. 1) and freedom of conscience (article 19 No 6). These rules configure a protectionist model of patient's autonomy.

First, the right to accept or refuse treatment is limited by a restrictive clause that goes beyond the limits that comparative law establishes for this kind of right (for instance, public health risk and people in emergency situations). Indeed, in two rules of this law (the general rule of patient autonomy and the special rule of terminally ill patient autonomy, respectively, Articles 14 and 16), the legislator reiterates the same restrictive clause of autonomy: "In no case, refusal will aim the artificial acceleration of death."

As we shall see, this logical contradiction (since an omission can never cause an effect) points out a legislator's confusion between letting die a patient by the natural course of a disease and killing him. In comparative jurisprudence, there is consensus that the right to refuse medical treatment does not include the right to receive a lethal drug, which requires special and different regulations.[42] However, the patient is entitled to receive palliative care as in the context of legal interventions justified by this kind of care is relieving suffering through drugs which can speed up the process of dying, always as a side-effect that is not sought either as a means or as an end.

---

[40]Biblioteca del Congreso Nacional (https://www.bcn.cl/historiadelaley/nc/historia-de-la-ley/4579/), p. 9.

[41]Casonato (2012), pp. 199–201.

[42]Bascuñán (2016).

Secondly, this restrictive clause on patient's autonomy produces a new level of contradiction, as it can limit the exercise of patients' rights to receive palliative care. This right is recognised in the same article where the legislator incurs in contradiction: "Persons who are in this terminally ill state will have the right to live with dignity until the moment of death. Consequently, they are entitled to palliative care to make disease's effects more bearable." (Art. 16.4).

Third, restrictions on the refusal of treatment as well as on the right to receive palliative care are intensified with the procedural rules that the legislator established to resolve complex clinical decisions. The legislator designed the same rule of procedure for two different scenarios: i) when the physician doubts about the competence of a patient to decide on his care, and ii) when the professional does not agree with a competent patient's or with his representatives' decision in insisting on a treatment not medically indicated. In this fashion, the procedure is applicable both for patient's refusal cases and patient's insistence on a not indicated treatment, and consist in consulting the institutional ethics committee, whose opinion is not binding, and if "the patient or representatives do not agree with committee", as expressed by the legislator, they may file a special protective action before the Court.

As we see, the procedure involves a flagrant violation of a basic principle recognised in comparative law, which is to respect the autonomy of the competent patient. Now, when there are doubts about the patient's competence, they should be resolved by a physician and not by a committee. Finally, in cases where the patient is incompetent, a surrogate decision should be carried out to respect his will (if known) or to seek his best interest. Therefore, all above mentioned rules not only point out an evident contradiction in a law that recognises patient's autonomy, but also introduces distrust in the physician-patient relationship, by opening room enough to judicialize clinical decisions through classical law's devices, when the norm should precisely be aimed at avoiding so.

Fourth, we can recognise some mistakes in these design problems, which shows a legislator's distrust of axiological plurality in clinical decision making, especially at the end of life. Indeed, the Chilean legislator wrongly kept the expression related to advanced directives, which was eliminated from the law for the same reasons that justified autonomy's restrictive clauses, namely the fear to open a space to what the legislator calls "euthanasia practices." The argument put forward during the law's discussion was that patients would be able to request euthanasia at any time through such procedure. However, the legislator never noticed that decisions on advance medical directives could never contradict the laws, because an expression of will contrary to the law is void.

3.2 Problems of Legislative Technique: A Model of Protected Self-determination

The legislator wanted to reinforce his contradictory conception of the right to life, as a total and absolute unavailable good, restricting the patient's right to autonomy in several ways. This conception is contradictory because it confuses self-determination regarding the rejection or interruption of treatments able to cause death with the self-determination to request euthanasia or assisted suicide:

i) Persons who are in a terminally ill state, by virtue of Article 16 of the law, are free to refuse or withdraw treatment, under two restrictions. The first is incoherent from a formal logical point of view ("In no case, refusal will aim the artificial acceleration of death") and even though a prohibitive rule is nt totally binding because of its murky ambiguity, it does engender a legal confusion for the practice of palliative medicine whose interventions can indirectly produce the anticipation of death. The second restriction is also inconsistent from a logical point of view, but at a semantic level. The law states: "The person informed that his health condition is terminal has the right to give or withhold his willingness to undergo any treatment having the effect of artificially prolonging his life, insofar as ordinary care is held." (Article 16 inc. 1). The semantic inconsistency is that if ordinary care measures (artificial nutrition and hydration) are treatments that can artificially prolong life, which is contradictory with the patient's right to autonomy.
ii) The general rule of patient autonomy (article 14) echoes the restriction of article 16, adding new expressions that increase confusion: "in any case refusal may be aimed at accelerating death, and performing practices of euthanasia or assisted suicide" (article 14.3). In addition to this logical inconsistency (any omission may result into an action), the vagueness of the term "euthanasia practices" reaffirms the legislator confusion between "letting die" and "killing".

3.3 Problems of Non-jurisdictional Institutional Pluralism

One of the mechanisms that biolaw has used to promote and ensure axiological pluralism in decision-making on clinical interventions is giving recognition to the qualified opinion of advisory body as institutional ethics committees, which play a key role to help resolve conflicts in this context. A historical milestone in the recognition of para-jurisdictional bodies was the sentence *In re Quinlan* (70 NJ 10, 1976), in which The New Jersey Supreme Court pointed out that the resolution of moral problems that occur in clinical practice should be resolved by a committee without courts' intervention.

Contrary to the aforementioned, the Chilean legislator established a jurisdictional mechanism for conflict resolution in clinical contexts (a special legal action to be processed according to the rules established by the Chilean Constitution in Article

20 for the protection of constitutional guarantees to an upper court) in detriment of the para-jurisdictional body (the Committee). Procedural rules, as we discussed above, are confusing and reveal legislator's distrust about conflicts between doctors and patients can be resolved in a clinical scenario as well as a glaring confusion between active and passive euthanasia.

Considering the legislator's distrust that people can freely decide to end their lives by refusing or interrupting treatments, it is not strange that he established a public action that could oppose their interests. In effect, the physician or any other person on behalf of the patient can bring this action to prevent a free decision. For example, a civil association that promotes their religious beliefs may oppose the withdrawal of ordinary care measures by virtue of considering it counterproductive regarding to the right to life. Undoubtedly, this decision of the legislator goes in the opposite direction to the jurisprudential evolution of courts in cases related to refusal of treatments at the end of life.[43]

4 The Case

In 2013, Patricio Figueroa Rozas, representing Clinical Services, in accordance with the provisions of Article 17 of Law No. 20.584, filed a protective action in favour of Mrs. Laura Parodi Bustos, and against Clinica Las Condes and Marcelo Miranda Cabezas, Physician, by alleging the threat on the constitutional guarantee of the right to life, covered by Article 19 of Chilean Constitution.

He also noted that Laura Parodi, widow, 87 years old, is home at the care of the appellant from September 17, 2009, by medical prescription and at the request of her spouse, Gerald Gibbons Mac-Kay, now deceased. Mrs. Parodi is connected to invasive mechanical ventilation, and undergoes a tracheostomy and gastrostomy by virtue of an advanced progressive supranuclear palsy, as well as a severe spasticity and severe dysphagia.

The appellant also indicated that on Saturday May 25, 2013, the nurse Macarena Martinez, by doing her daily visit to the patient, noted that an electroencephalogram had been recently made to Ms. Parodi at home, by indication of her current treating physician, Dr. Marcelo Miranda Cabezas. On May 29, the patient had severe vomiting, so the nurse phoned Dr. Miranda, who told her that no action would be taken in this regard as family had referred the willingness to withdraw all life support, a situation that would have been consulted to the Institutional Ethics Committees of Clinica Las Condes, which would favour thereof. The above information was communicated to the Technical Manager of Clinical Service, Ms. Viviana Jechan, who in turn contacted Dr. Miranda, and he told her that the disconnection would take place on May 31 at 9 am.

[43]Vivanco (2014), pp. 395–403.

However, in order to ensure an alleged interest and protect Mrs. Parodi's right to life, in accordance with the final paragraph of Article 16 of the Law No. 20.584, the plaintiff requested to withhold the artificial ordinary means of support until the patient's death.

As we will see, the Court of Appeal decided and declared that Mrs. Parodi should continue to maintain the artificial care she was receiving to sustain her life. The Court clearly disavowed in its verdict several fundamental constitutional principles, especially if we consider that, in the case analysed we are in front of a terminally ill person, in a permanent and irreversible vegetative state, with no any chance to live on her own means, and whose life extension implies intangible costs of suffering and agony. Therefore, withdrawing the artificial means of support that maintain the patient alive seems to be entirely reasonable and tuned with articles 16 and following of the Law No. 20.584, as well as to the recommendations of the Institutional Ethics Committees of Clinica Las Condes, and to the Chilean constitution,

5 Jurisprudential Analysis from a Biolaw's Perspective

What follows is an analysis of the Court's arguments and the jurisprudential function from a biolaw's perspective.

5.1 A Restricted Judicial Discretion

Judges' arguments to decide largely reflects the legislator's contradiction to guarantee the right to patients' autonomy at the end of life. The legislator's contradiction consists in recognising, on the one hand, the right to withdraw or refuse treatment and, on the other hand, limiting this right to the point of affecting the core of it. Judges avoided ruling on the merits and decided from formal aspects by maintaining legislator's contradiction and ambiguity. Certainly, in this case, judges assumed a behaviour of self-restraint against legislator's discretion.[44]

The protective action was filed by the appellants by virtue of the threat to the constitutional guarantee of the patient's right to life. The Court argued that this right is not threatened by an illegal or arbitrary act or omission because "when a person is in a terminally ill state or permanent vegetative state and has no chance to live on his own means with intangible costs of suffering and agony, a protective action is entirely reasonable and in line with articles 16 and following of Law No.20.584".

However, the Court also argued that the appeal is a special protective action that is not itself an appeal for protection of constitutional guarantees and thereby must be strictly interpreted in the light of what the law states. Therefore, it is a resource

---

[44]Penasa (2016).

intrinsically related to the rights of autonomy enshrined in the law (Articles 14 and 16). In tune with this argument, the Court concludes that the action must be upheld due to the lack of adequate representation of the patient. Indeed, there is no certainty that the relative who assumes the representation (nephew of the patient's husband) is one of the authorised persons in Article 16 of the law 20.584, namely relatives according to the preferential and exclusive order established by Article 42 of the Chilean Civil Code.

5.2 Judicial Proceedings Against a Protectionist Model of Autonomy

The Court in its formalistic argument comes to legitimize the legislator's contradictions and his fear of making decisions at the end of life. If the case would have been handled by a constitutional protective action, the same court, probably following the national jurisprudence on treatments' refusal, would not have upheld the request to maintain life. While we agree that judicial intervention cannot take care of the complexity of clinical conflicts without a legislation that guarantees minimum rights and mechanisms to resolve such conflicts, under a model that tends to reflective equilibrium, we also have to assert that judges have the function to overcome the legislator's discretion, even more when the regulatory framework restricts basic constitutional principles such as dignity and bodily integrity.

6 Conclusions

Biolaw acquires special value in Chilean legal system to ensure an effective mechanism for the protection of those fundamental rights which, in this context, concern to every member of society, and to point out the State obligation to protect those rights, and foster their implementation and respect instead of their detriment.

In addition, biolaw could enhance Chilean constitutional law by providing a new and more complete conception of fundamental rights that allow the state to fulfil its international obligations in this field and give such rights efficacy in the internal jurisdictional context.

Therefore, our conception of biolaw in the framework of an axiologically pluralistic understanding is very applicable in Chile, in light of its constitution. However, this assertion requires a very important condition of possibility: to understand that Chilean Constitution is a normative body and not simply a programmatic one. This crucial point highlights the importance of recognising biorights insofar as they are a platform to place fundamental rights in their deserved valuation range, and means to the state a demanding proficiency test to validate its task as guarantor of those rights.

Therefore, the importance of biolaw lies not only on its procedural or doctrinal contribution to traditional law, but involves a consequence of greater scope: biolaw can be the starting point for a new individual subjective rights' constitutionalitation.

In this way, we promote a better understanding of the incompatibilities between existing Chilean legal system and new problems arisen in healthcare settings. We have conclusively sought to establish the inability of current Chilean legal frameworks to support the rapid evolution of new healthcare quandaries and define a legal way to regulate healthcare practices at the end of life, as well as to delimit normative impact of them in our society, within so sensitive axiological contexts such as individual autonomy and the right to self-determine the vital project.

References

Bascuñán A (2016) Recent case law about the right to die. Rev Med Chile 144:483–487

Beauchamp TL (2019) A defense of universal principles in biomedical ethics. In: Valdés E, Lecaros JA (eds) Biolaw and policy in the twenty-first century. Springer, Cham, pp 3–18

Beauchamp TL, Childress JF (2019) Principles of biomedical ethics, 8th edn. Oxford University Press, Cambridge

Beyleveld D, Brownsword R (2000) Legal argumentation in biolaw. In: Kemp P, Rendtorff JD, Johansen NM (eds) Bioethics and biolaw, Vol I: Judgement of life. Rhodos International Science and Art Publishers & Center for Ethics and Law, Copenhagen, pp 179–218

Biblioteca del Congreso Nacional. Historia de la Ley N° 20.584. Santiago de Chile. https://www.bcn.cl/historiadelaley/nc/historia-de-la-ley/4579/. Last entry: March 3, 2021

Busatta L (2016) Per la costruzione di un pluralismo sostenibile nel rapporto tra diritto e scienze de la vita. BioLaw J Rivista di BioDiritto 1:9–38

Casonato C (2012) Introduzione al Biodiritto, 3rd edn. Giappichelli, Torino

Casonato C (2019) The essential features of 21st century biolaw. In: Valdés E, Lecaros JA (eds) Biolaw and policy in the twenty-first century. Springer, Cham, pp 77–92

Fagot-Largeault A (2000) Evaluating and judging: Bionorms vs. human judgment. In: Kemp P, Rendtorff JD, Johansen NM (eds) Bioethics and biolaw, vol I: judgement of life. Rhodos International Science and Art Publishers & Center for Ethics and Law, Copenhagen, pp 27–39

Gros Espiell H (2011) Bioderecho internacional. In: Casabona CR (ed) Enciclopedia de Bioderecho y Bioética. Comares, Granada, pp 177–187

Holm S (1994) Not just autonomy – the principles of American biomedical ethics. J Med Ethics 21:332–338

Johnson SH, Iltis AS, Hinze BA (2008) Law and bioethics. In: Johnson SH, Iltis AS, Hinze BA (eds) Legal perspectives in bioethics. Routledge, New York, pp 1–9

Kemp P (2019) The idea of European biolaw: basic principles. In: Valdés E, Lecaros JA (eds) Biolaw and policy in the twenty-first century. Springer, Cham, pp 19–32

Lecaros JA (2019) Biolaw and bioethics: convergences and divergences. In: Valdés E, Lecaros JA (eds) Biolaw and policy in the twenty-first century. Springer, Cham, pp 93–118

Lenoir N (2000) Legal argumentation in biolaw. In: Kemp P, Rendtorff JD, Johansen NM (eds) Bioethics and biolaw, Vol I: judgement of life. Rhodos International Science and Art Publishers & Center for Ethics and Law, Copenhagen, pp 219–242

Mekinoff J (2001) Law and bioethics. An introduction. Georgetown University Press, Washington, DC

Penasa S (2016) Le "scientific question" nella dinamica tra discrezionalità giurisdizionale e legislativa. Uno studio comparato sul giudizio delle leggi scientifcamente connotate nelle giurisdizioni nazionali, sovranazionale e internazionali. BioLaw J Rivista di BioDiritto 1:39–79

Rawls J (1971) A theory of justice. The Belknap, Cambridge
Rendtorff JD, Kemp P (2000) Basic ethical principles in European bioethics and biolaw, vol I. Institut Borjà di Bioètica & Centre for Ethics and Law, Barcelona and Copenhagen
Rendtorff JD, Kemp P (2019) Four ethical principles in European bioethic and biolaw: autonomy, dignity, integrity and vulnerability. In: Valdés E, Lecaros JA (eds) Biolaw and policy in the twenty-first century. Springer, Cham, pp 33–40
Romeo Casabona CM, Romeo Malanda S (2019) Approach to biolaw as an autonomous juridical discipline. In: Valdés E, Lecaros JA (eds) Biolaw and policy in the twenty-first century. Springer, Cham, pp 59–76
Singer P (2019) Foreword. In: Valdés E, Lecaros JA (eds) Biolaw and policy in the twenty-first century. Springer, Cham, pp vii–ix
Valdés E (2015) Bioderecho, daño genético y derechos humanos de cuarta generación. Boletín Mexicano de Derecho Comparado 58(144):1197–1228
Valdés E (2019) Towards a new conception of biolaw. In: Valdés E, Lecaros JA (eds) Biolaw and policy in the twenty-first century. Springer, Cham, pp 41–58
Valdés E (2021) Biolaw: origins, doctrine and juridical applications on the biosciences. Springer, Cham
Valdés E, Lecaros JA (2019) Biolaw and policy in the twenty-first century : building answers for new questions. Springer, Cham
Vivanco A (2014) Disposición sobre la vida humana y principios constitucionales: análisis del caso chileno. Ediciones Universidad Santo Tomás, Santiago

The manufacturer's authorised representative in the EU is Springer Nature Customer Service Centre GmbH, Europaplatz 3, 69115 Heidelberg, Germany. If you have any concerns regarding our products, please contact ProductSafety@springernature.com

Printed and bound by CPI Group (UK) Ltd, Croydon, CR0 4YY
30/09/2026
02225296-0006